# Warrior Mountains Folklore

# WARRIOR MOUNTAINS FOLKLORE

Rickey Butch Walker

Warrior Mountains Folklore

2nd edition

Copyright 2022 © Bluewater Publications

BWPublications.com

Bluewater Publications

Florence, Alabama

Library of Congress Control Number: 2022937466

ISBN: 978-1-958273-02-9 Perfect Bind

ISBN: 978-1-958273-00-5 eBook

All rights reserved under International and Pan-American Copyright Convention. No part of this publication may be reproduced or transmitted in any form or by any means, electronic or mechanical, including photocopying, recording, or by any information storage and retrieval system, without prior written permission from the Publisher.

BWPublications.com – Florence, Alabama

This work is based on the authors' personal interpretation of research.

# Table of Contents

Acknowledgements .................................................................................................. 1

Chapter One .......................................................................................................... 3
    Warrior Mountains ............................................................................................. 3
    Aboriginal People of the Warrior Mountains ..................................................... 5
    Indian Inhabitants of the Warrior Mountains ................................................... 10
    Irish Indians of the Warrior Mountains ............................................................ 14
    Indian Treaties of the Warrior Mountains ........................................................ 17
    Indian Trails of the Warrior Mountains ............................................................ 20
    Early Roads of the Warrior Mountain ............................................................. 32
    Topography of the Warrior Mountains ............................................................ 37
    Wildlife Eliminated from the Warrior Mountains ............................................. 42
    Interesting Places of the Warrior Mountains ................................................... 47

Chapter Two ........................................................................................................ 60
Families of Range 6 West .................................................................................... 60
    Newt Hill Family of Buzzard Roost Mountain ................................................. 60
    Families of Beaty Hollow ................................................................................. 65
    Spears Family of Blowing Springs .................................................................. 73
    Families of Poplar Log Cove ........................................................................... 75
    Poole Family of Poplar Log Cove ................................................................... 81
    Chenault Family of Poplar Log Cove .............................................................. 86
    School at Hickory Grove CCC Camp .............................................................. 94
    Families of Hickory Grove Road ..................................................................... 96
    Walker Family of Piney Grove ...................................................................... 104

Chapter Three .................................................................................................... 107
Families of Range 7 West .................................................................................. 107
    Alexander Family .......................................................................................... 107

    Gillespie Family of Indian Tomb .................................................................................... 119

    Other Families of Indian Tomb ....................................................................................... 120

    Welborn Family of Pinhook ............................................................................................. 124

    The Simms Place of Pinhook Branch............................................................................... 127

    Naylor Family of the Spivey Gap Road ........................................................................... 130

    Osborn and Oden Families of Lindsey Hall .................................................................... 137

    Jenkins Family of Owl Creek ........................................................................................... 149

    Lewis Oden Family of Brushy Creek............................................................................... 152

Chapter Four ............................................................................................................................. 166

Families of Range 8 West ......................................................................................................... 166

    Treadway Family of Wren Mountains ............................................................................. 166

    Curtis Family of Montgomery Creek................................................................................ 177

    Families of Parker Cove and Borden Creek ................................................................... 181

    Families of Mountain Springs .......................................................................................... 187

    Families of Flanagin Creek .............................................................................................. 193

    The Wilkerson Family of McDowell Cove ...................................................................... 201

    The Blankenship Family .................................................................................................. 212

    Jack McDowell Family of the Cove ................................................................................. 230

    McDowell Cove Stories.................................................................................................... 233

    Families of the Black House ........................................................................................... 237

Chapter Five............................................................................................................................... 241

Families of Range 9 West ......................................................................................................... 241

    The Stephenson Family of the Ridge Road ................................................................... 241

    The Garrison Family of Sipsey River ............................................................................. 243

    Families of Gum Pond..................................................................................................... 253

    Boyles Family of Mattox Creek ....................................................................................... 255

    The Feltman Family of King Cove .................................................................................. 259

The Hubbard Family of Bear Creek ................................................................................. 271

The Will Spillers Family of King Cove ............................................................................... 287

Jane (Jenny) Brooks Johnston Family of Byler Road ....................................................... 308

The Riddle Family of Sipsey ............................................................................................. 316

BIBLIOGRAPHY ....................................................................................................................... 329

Index ........................................................................................................................................ 331

# Acknowledgements

In order to save a glimpse of the past before all was lost to the grave, I visited many elderly people who once made the Warrior Mountains their home. Through their eyes, I saw a lifestyle much different from that of today. Even though many of those old folks have died since my taped interviews, I wish to thank all these wonderful people and their families for sharing their folk stories and ways of life during the early settlement of the Warrior Mountains.

Without the help of many whom provided dear and precious pictures of families and friends, this book would not have been possible. I especially wish to thank the following people for their use of pictures and their help:

Edward Herring provided pictures of the Osborns, Odens, Hubbards, and Aunt Jenny Brooks' family; Mrs. Gladys LuAllen provided pictures of the Blankenships, Wilkersons, and Pates; Ms. Glen Hovator provided pictures of the Garrisons and McDowells; Ms. Faye Beaty provided pictures of the Beaty family; Ms. Eva Chenault provided pictures of the Poole family; Ms. Sudearia Garrison provided pictures of the Boyles family; Ms. Doris England provided pictures of the Riddle family; Ms. Doris England provided pictures of the Riddle family; Ms. Ila Wilburn provided pictures of the Curtis and Welborn families; Ms. Cathy Sloan provided pictures of the Borden family; Ms. Rhoda White Woods provided pictures of the White family; Don Alexander provided pictures of the Alexander family; Finnis Treadway provided pictures of the Treadway and Tankersley families; Ms. Reba Riddle for the Riddle and Feltman family pictures; and Lamar Marshall, of the Bankhead Monitor, provided many pictures and maps of the Bankhead Forest.

Many folks, too numerous to name, wrote letters of encouragement, called to thank me for all the articles, and stopped to tell me how much they enjoyed reading about the forest. To all those kind words, I say thanks to everyone who inspired and encouraged me during those five years it took to write this book. With their words of encouragement, Warrior Mountain Folklore has become a reality.

Many thanks are due to Steve Oden, who was the first person who asked me to write a series of articles about the forest. He was extremely supportive of my efforts and was always willing to provide that much needed encouragement. Again, thanks to Steve Oden.

In addition, without the help of Mr. Rayford Hyatt many holes in the story of the forest would have been void. Mr. Hyatt was always willing to share his vast knowledge concerning the people of the Warrior Mountains. Without his direction, I would have become hopelessly lost.

# Chapter One

## Warrior Mountains

For thousands of years, inhabitants of the Moulton Valley have looked south to see a beautiful range of mountains rising from the flat middle plain in the heartland of north Alabama. This east-west mountain range has represented many things to modern man, but probably was more important and sacred to our red ancestors than any of our European immigrants.

By the time of DeSoto's visit to our state in 1540, our Muscogee people recognized the range of mountains as a tribal and geographic boundary along the Continental Divide. The High Town Path or Ridge Path is a prehistoric east-west Indian trail that lies along the divide. The divide begins separating the Atlantic's coastal waters from those of the Mississippi drainage in Maine and continues through the upper Tombigbee watershed in the western portion of Alabama and into Northern Mississippi.

**Black Warrior**

Probably the most accurate and appropriate name for the Wm. B. Bankhead National Forest portion of this vast chain of mountains is derived from the Muscogee people who lived along the forest streams hundreds of years before white people came to our country. The Creek word "taskagu" or "taska and the Choctaw word "tashka" refer to the English translation of "warrior" with the Muscogee word "lusa" meaning "black." We know from reading Alabama history, DeSoto encountered a giant of a man known as "Chief Tuscaloosa" or the Black Warrior; therefore, the name was here long before the first European settlers claimed the land in the southern portion of Lawerence county, Alabama.

In early days, the stream forming south from the Warrior Mountains of Lawrence County also became known as the Tuscaloosa River. In a French map dated March 1733, Baron De Crenay, Commandant of the Post of Mobile, identified the southern drainage from these mountains as the Tuscaloosa River. On the other early maps, the main river, which drains south, was also called the Tuscaloosa. Later in 1814 a map of Alabama identified the river draining south from the Tennessee Divide as the Black Warrior River.

## John Bull

In 1829, a frontiersman and famous rifle maker by the name of John Bull engraved two of his masterpieces from the Warrior Mountains. According to information provided by Mr. Dan Wallace, the exceptional rifle is inscribed on a silver platelet in the stock, "John Bull for David Smith, Warrior Mountain." The inscription on the silver cheek piece is as the following:

"Ann"

This gun is named Charlotte,
from hills and mountains Came,
made to delight the heart of man,
with Joy, the laboring Swain,
And from the sportsmen of the day
Victorious bear the prife,
Away"

According to Old Land Records of Lawrence County, Alabama by Margaret Coward, David Smith entered 79.92 acres of land in Section 36 of Township 7 South and Range 7 West, near Indian Tomb Hollow on September 12, 1818, and 79.92 acres on September 28, 1818, in Section 35. He married Charlotte Ann Havens, who was the daughter of James Havens. According to the Havens family legend provided by Spencer Waters, James Havens was buried next to his Indian friends on the side of the Warrior Mountains where the magnolia blooms in the Spring.

## Warrior Mountains

In his 1899 book, Early Settlers of Alabama, Colonel Edmonds Saunders refers to Lawrence County's southern highlands as the "Warrior Mountains." Later in 1918, when the government began organizing our mountains into a national forest the area was called the Black Warrior. Today, the State Wildlife Management Area is still known as the Black Warrior.

It is a shame that our forest had a name that could be traced back for over 400 years and has been changed to honor a white politician. However, with the Indian pride that has grown strong in north Alabama, our mountains will never take second place. These mountains will always remain the Sacred Land of our ancestors, and be known as the "**WARRIOR MOUNTAINS.**"

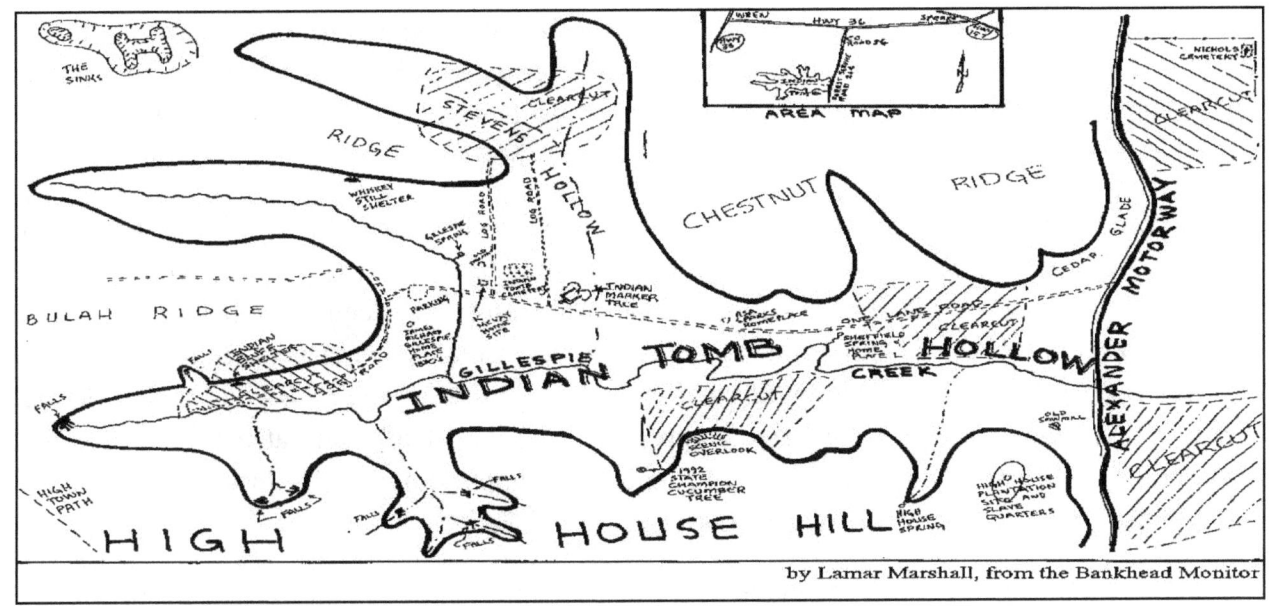
by Lamar Marshall, from the Bankhead Monitor

# Aboriginal People of the Warrior Mountains

## Prehistoric

The area of the Warrior Mountains features artifacts from the following four main periods of early American Indian pre-history: Paleo Pre-9000 BC; Archaic 9000-1000 BC; Woodland 1000 BC-900 AD; and Mississippian 900 AD to 1540 AD.

Some 12,000 years ago the first inhabitants of the Warrior Mountains area roamed the woodlands and streams hunting for wild game, their primary food supply. The nomadic hunters left behind some of the most beautiful chert (flint) spear points ever made by the stone age red men who were the first Americans.

## Paleo Period

The oldest Paleo examples of the chert points that have been found in north Alabam include the Dalton, Clovis, Beaver Lake, Cumberland, and Folsom. From personal observation of many local artifact collections, it appears that Dalton style points are most numerous and provide substantial evidence of Paleo occupation in our area. The Clovis and Beaver Lake styles appear to be equal in number, while the Cumberland and Folsom are a rare find in north Alabama. A Folsom point was found at the head of Spring Creek during archaeological survey of Wheeler Basin in 1939.

Many types and examples of Paleo points have been found throughout north alabama and into the Warrior Mountains. The *"Handbook of Alabama Archaeology"* suggests that Paleo points have an antiquity in excess of 10,000 years; therefore, as the last Ice Age began retreating, Paleo-people were living and hunting in the area of the Warrior Mountains.

It is clear from archaeological evidence found in local collections that by 10,000 years ago, Paleo-Indians had established a sizable population from the Tennessee River to the Warrior Mountains. Paleo evidence appears most numerous along the Tennessee River, but Paleo campsites also have been identified along the three main streams in our area, beginning on the northern slopes of the Warrior Mountains and including West Flint Creek, Big Nance Creek, and Town Creek. These streams have Paleo campsites along their banks and at major springs that feed these creeks. Paleo artifacts have been found in the upper drainages of these streams, along and into the northern edge of the Warrior Mountains.

The Paleo-Indian hunters were nomadic and moved from camp to camp in search of the big game animals that were utilized for food. These small family bands probably utilized the same campsites along Lawrence County streams for several years. Archaeological evidence, such as the stone points, tools, and camp remnants, provide a tantalizing glimpse at the lives of these Paleo nomads who lived in the shadow of the Warrior Mountains some 10,000 to 12,000 years ago.

**Archaic Period**

Much evidence of the Archaic people also exists near and in the Warrior Mountains. These hunter-gatherer people primarily utilized notched spear points such as the Plevna, Lost Lake, Decatur, Big Sandy, Pine Tree, and many others. The Big Sandy points provide the most numerous Archaic evidence found in local artifact collections. I personally observed a Decatur point and uniface duckbill scraper found in Poplar Log cove of the Warrior Mountains.

Archaic people used a spear with a throwing stick known as an atlatl. The atlatl had an end notched tip made from deer antler or bone. According to the *Forty-Fourth Annual Report of the Bureau of American Ethnology* of 1926-27, Gerald Fowke of the Smithsonian Institute excavated two bone atlatl tips from a shell mound at the mouth of Town Creek. Fowke was directing an archeological study prior to the impoundment of the Tennessee River by Wilson Dam. The shell mound, located on the line between Colbert County and Lawrence County, was a 9 ½ feet high, 25 feet wide and 120 feet long. This large mound of shells, deposited by the aboriginal inhabitants over the centuries, was started by Archaic people and utilized into the Woodland

Period. Fowke also excavated the Alexander Mound about one mile north of Indian Tomb Hollow and found evidence of Archaic occupation.

The richness and wealth of aboriginal artifacts in north Alabama is due to several geographic monuments: in large part the great Mussel Shoals located on the Tennessee River; the numerous streams flowing through the Tennessee and Moulton Valleys; and the vast Warrior Mountains in the southern part of the Tennessee Valley. In 1924, A.E. Ortmann reported an immense number of species of freshwater mussels found at the Shoals. A vast number of each individual species of mussels was also reported. Ortmann said, "There is no other place upon the whole wide world which could be compared with this one in this respect…I have tried to complete a list of naiads (mussels) known from Mussel Shoals, and have found that about 80 different species and varieties are represented, belonging to 29 genera."

As evidence from the large mounds of mussel shells left by the prehistoric Indians of the area, it is obvious that early aboriginal inhabitants of the Tennessee River depended heavily on the mussels as a staple source of food. Archaeological evidence suggest that large concentrations of prehistoric nomadic hunters would gather at the Shoals during the low water periods and feast on mussels gathered from the shallow water. The discarded shells would accumulate over areas larger than the size of football fields. Then high water, which forced the mussel gatherers back toward the woodlands of the Warrior Mountains, would place a layer of silt over the discarded mussel shells. Successive periods of high and low water levels allowed for the creation of large shell mounds containing alternating layers of mussel shells and silt.

The large size of three such shell mounds located on the Tennessee River were identified in the "Archaeological Survey of Wheeler Basin on the Tennessee River", by William Webb (1939) as follows: 7 feet high, 148 feet wide, and 330 feet long; 7 feet high, 195 feet wide, and 305 feet long, and 3 feet high, 110 feet wide, and 245 feet long. These tremendous mounds of shells are evidence of a considerable prehistoric Indian population in the north Alabama area. During high water, the early mussel eating Indians probably returned to the woodlands of the Warrior Mountains to harvest the bountiful mast supplied by nut and fruit bearing plants and trees.

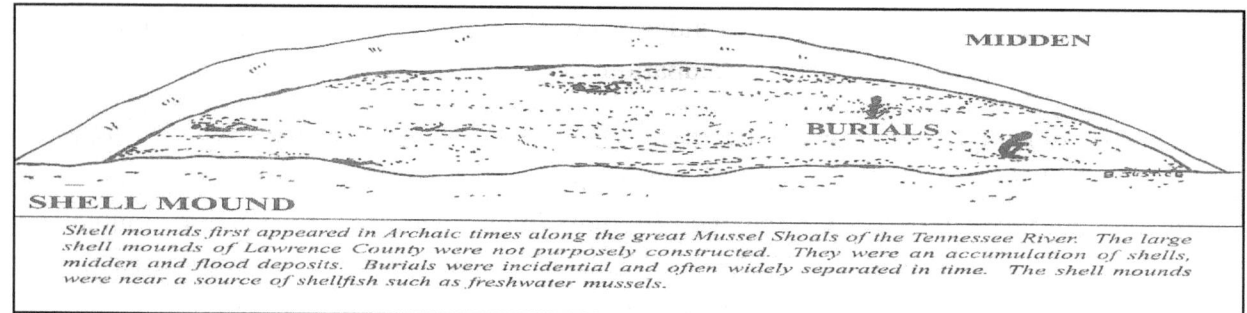

SHELL MOUND
Shell mounds first appeared in Archaic times along the great Mussel Shoals of the Tennessee River. The large shell mounds of Lawrence County were not purposely constructed. They were an accumulation of shells, midden and flood deposits. Burials were incidental and often widely separated in time. The shell mounds were near a source of shellfish such as freshwater mussels.

## Woodland Period

The Woodland lifestyle of Indian people inhabiting north Alabama occurred between 1,000 BC to around 900 AD. The Woodland Indians lived in more permanent settlements and are thought to be the people who began building burial and ceremonial mounds in the Tennessee Valley

The Oakville Indian Mounds are believed to be of Woodland origin. Within some 20 yards of the big ceremonial mound at Oakville, a charcoal pit was excavated by archaeologists from the University of Alabama. A radio-carbon analysis of the material revealed the time period of 40 AD, plus or minus 100 years.

In addition, a culture using copper and galena objects, known as Copena, existed to the northern base of the Warrior Mountains. On one ridge of Sand Mountain in eastern Lawrence County, the remnants of five small beautiful Indian mounds are found within 50 feet of each other. Pieces of galena were excavated from Sand Mountain mounds. In addition, a Copena mound, some four miles directly south of the Oakville ceremonial mound contained several large pieces of galena. The mound was located about two (2) miles south of Speake School and within one (1) mile of the northern edge of the Warrior Mountains. These as well as many other small Woodland mounds are found along the northern of the Warrior Mountains. In addition, Poplar Log Cove and McDowell Cove, within the northern edge of the Warrior Mountains, have small mounds located in their flat valleys.

Much evidence of Woodland Indian occupation exits throughout the rock shelters of the Warrior Mountains. Most of these sandstone shelters provided protection from the elements to the early aboriginal inhabitants. Many Indian rock shelters throughout Bankhead Forest contain numerous artifacts which were utilized by the Woodland Period Indians.

## Mississippian Period

The Mississippian lifestyle in north Alabama occurred from 900 AD to 1540 AD when DeSoto made trip through northern Alabama. Mississippian Period evidence is found from the Tennessee River through the Warrior Mountains and is characterized by small triangular points used on arrows.

The small triangular points found throughout Tennessee Valley are indicative of Mississippian campsites and villages. Located just west of the forks of Thompson and West Flint Creeks, one such Mississippian site contained many triangular points. Mississippian artifacts are found in rock shelters throughout the Warrior Mountains, but in the mountainous area, they do not appear to be as numerous as Woodland artifacts. The Mississippian Period Indians lived in farming communities and depended heavily on agricultural products; therefore, in general, the poor mountainous soils were not as conducive to large settlements of Mississippian people as were bottomlands of the Moulton and Courtland Valleys. In some instances, forest valleys such as Poplar Log and McDowell Coves provide the rich agricultural bottomlands on which the agrarian Mississippians depended; therefore, the immediate area of the Warrior Mountains were not utilized by these prehistoric Indian people for farming, but for hunting game animals and the gathering of mast crops for food sources.

Town Creek, Big Nance Creek, and West Flint Creek beginning in the northern foothills of the Warrior Mountains, teemed with fish and their resourceful bank areas provided an abundance of wildlife upon which these prehistoric hunters depended. The dividing ridges of these streams became primary routes that directed the red men of long ago through the Courtland and Moulton Valleys to the Warrior Mountains. Running from the middle of Big Mussel Shoals and Elk River Shoals on the Tennessee River, these highland ridges were free of rivulets, streams, and creeks and continued south toward the Warrior Mountains of present day Bankhead Forest.

The north-south streams from the Warrior Mountains to the Tennessee River were obviously utilized for aboriginal occupation as evidence of large numbers of prehistoric Indian village sites and numerous artifacts found along their banks. Many of the aboriginal settlements, however, were far removed from the great Tennessee River and located along feeder streams and limestone springs in the heart of the "Warrior Mountains."

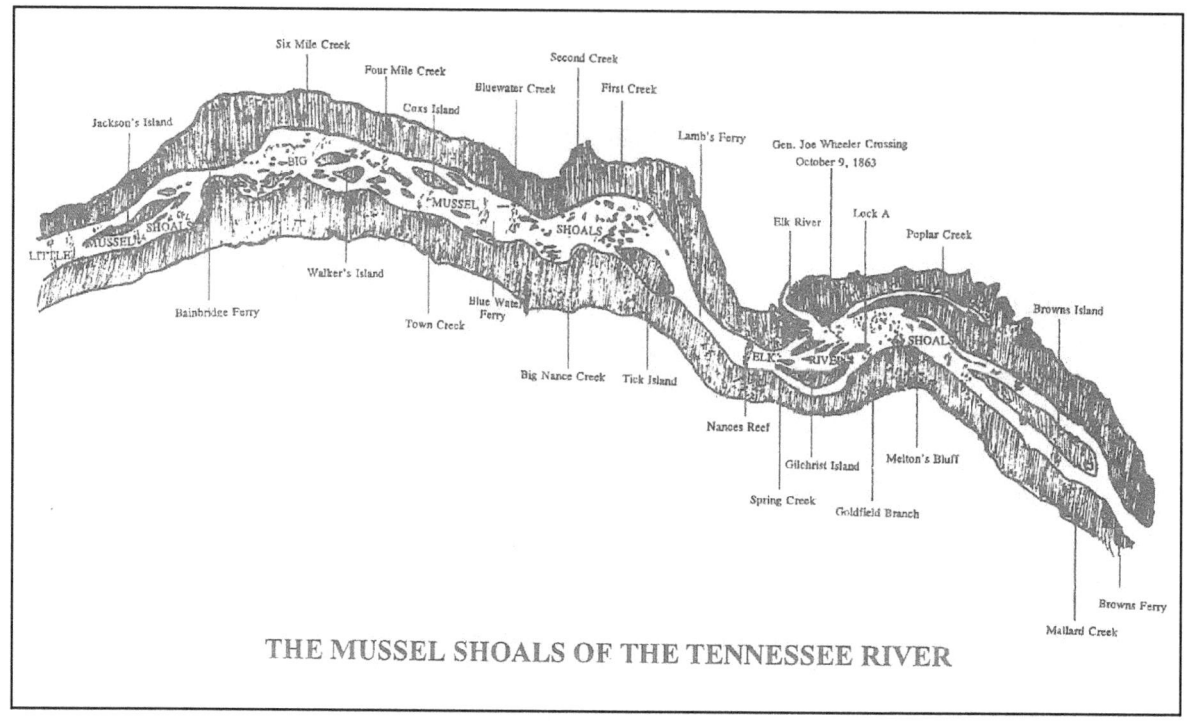

THE MUSSEL SHOALS OF THE TENNESSEE RIVER

## Indian Inhabitants of the Warrior Mountains

As soon as I hear the name Black Warrior, my heart swells with pride not only because I'm a descent of the noble Creeks and Cherokees, but also because of the beauty, peace, and tranquility of the majestic forest once known as the Black Warrior. In order to write about the majesty of the Black Warrior, now known as the William B. Bankhead National Forest, one must first explore the historic roots of such a land.

Probably the most powerful group of Indians ever known to exist was the great mound building society of Indians that once inhabited the land that became north Alabama. Their society spread east from the mighty Mississippi River, south to Florida, and north to the Great Lakes. At least 100 years prior to DeSoto's expedition into Alabama in 1540, the great society began to break up. Probably from this society arose the native historic Indians that inhabited the Black Warrior Forest in, the original Alabama Indians called the "Creeks."

## Creeks

Historically, the Creek boundary to the north in Alabama was the High Town Path. This was a ridge top trail that followed the Continental Divide between the Tennessee River drainage to the north and the Coosa River, Warrior River, and Sipsey River drainage South. The High Town Path went easterly from the Chickasaw Bluffs (Memphis) on the Mississippi River through Copper Town in Mississippi. From Copper Town to the French Landing (Cotton Gin Port), the path proceeded to Flat Rock in Franklin County then through Lawrence County to an area just north of Atlanta, Georgia. The High Town Path intersected the Great War Path near Willstown, an Indian village just north of present day Fort Payne, Alabama. The trail through Lawrence County followed what are now the Ridge Road and Leola Road in the northern portion of William B. Bankhead National Forest.

*Desoto and Giant Creek Chief Tuscaloosa, Black Warrior, as portrayed in 1838 in History of Alabama*

From pre-historic times, the Creek people inhabited the Warrior Mountains which was originally named after the great Creek Chief Tuscaloosa, Black Warrior, who was described in the DeSoto chronicles as being a giant of a man. Tuscaloosa's feet would just about touch the ground setting astride a Spaniard's horse. In later years, the forest was named after white politician, Wm. B. Bankhead.

## Battle of Indian Tomb

As the Chickasaw people established themselves along the Tennessee River and as the Americans began pressuring the Creeks from the east, conflicts arose between the tribes. Beginning in 1786, the Creeks started making raids into the Chickasaw Nation, probably because the Chickasaw supported the U.S. Government. Also, the Creeks and Cherokees were initially friendly with each other, both tribes warring against the Chickasaws. Finally in July 1798, a lasting peace was established between the Creeks and Chickasaws.

Even though the High Town Path was considered the Creek's northern boundary in Lawrence County, they used trails crossing the Moulton and Tennessee Valleys enroute to their buffalo hunting grounds near the French Lick (Nashville, Tennessee). Probably the only historic battle between the Creeks and Chickasaws to take place in Lawrence County was the Battle of Indian Tomb Hollow. The story, about a Creek-Chickasaw battle which occurred in 1780's, some seven miles south of Moulton, was published in the *Moulton Democrat* newspaper in November 1856.

**Cherokees**

In 1770, the Cherokee people began a massive movement into North Alabama under the leadership of Dragging Canoe and Doublehead. In 1769, the Cherokee engaged the Chickasaw in a vicious battle at the Chickasaw Old Fields (Hobbs Island) near present day Huntsville. Even though the Chickasaw claimed victory, they began giving up land to the Cherokees who moved into the Tennessee River's Mussel Shoals during the 1770's. According to Ann Royalle's letter originating from Melton's Bluff dated January 14, 1818, the Cherokee Indian village of Melton's Bluff was established between 1788 and 1793.

The Cherokees established towns along the Tennessee River at Brown's Ferry (Moneetown), Melton's Bluff, Courtland, and the mouth of Town Creek. Doublehead established a village near the mouth of Blue Water Creek in Lauderdale County, located on the opposite side of the river from the mouth of Town Creek. By the late 1770's, the Cherokee had pushed westward toward Mississippi and intermingled with the Chickasaws by marriage. To some degree, the Cherokee and Chickasaw were living cooperatively, claiming and occupying the same lands of north Alabama until the Turkey Town Treaty of September 1816.

Initially, the Creeks of the Black Warrior assisted Doublehead, a powerful Cherokee Chief of North Alabama, in establishing towns along the Tennessee River including Doublehead's Town. With the aid of Creek warriors, Chief Doublehead established his village at Doublehead Springs in 1790 near Natchez Trace just north of the town of Cherokee in what is now Colbert County. After the marriage of Chickasaw Chief George Colbert to two daughters of Chickamauga Chief Doublehead, the Chikasaws and Cherokees maintained peaceful relations.

However, in 1813, peace between the Creeks and Cherokees was soon forgotten when the U.S. Government demanded the Cherokees take up arms against the Creeks. As a result of Cherokee assistance, the once powerful Creek Nation fell to Andrew Jackson's forces. The Treaty of Fort

Jackson in 1814 relinquished all Creek Indian claims to the land south of the High Town Path (Tennessee Divide).

Prior to the 1800's, all Alabama Indian tribes were controlled by white-Indian mixed-bloods. After Jackson's defeat of the Creeks, the land of the Black Warrior (Bankhead Forest) was opened for settlement. In 1815, Richard McMahan became the first documented settler in the area near the present day town of Haleyville.

Only through intermarriage with white trappers, traders, and settlers, the Creek Indian blood of the Black Warrior was to remain in north Alabama's Creek Indian descendants. Presently, the Creek Indian blood still flows in the mixed-blood Indian students who attend public schools in Alabama.

As mysterious as the blending of a great mound building society from which the powerful Alabama Creek Nation arose, so was the vanishing of the Creeks of the Black Warrior. However, the Creek blood line became evident in the early settlers of the forest who testified of their Creek Indian ancestry.

As John Ridge, a great Cherokee leader, wrote 1835, "Our blood, if not destroyed, will win its course in beings of fair complexion, who will read their ancestors became civilized under frowns of misfortune, and the causes of their enemies," so lives the remnants of the mighty Creeks of the Warrior Mountains.

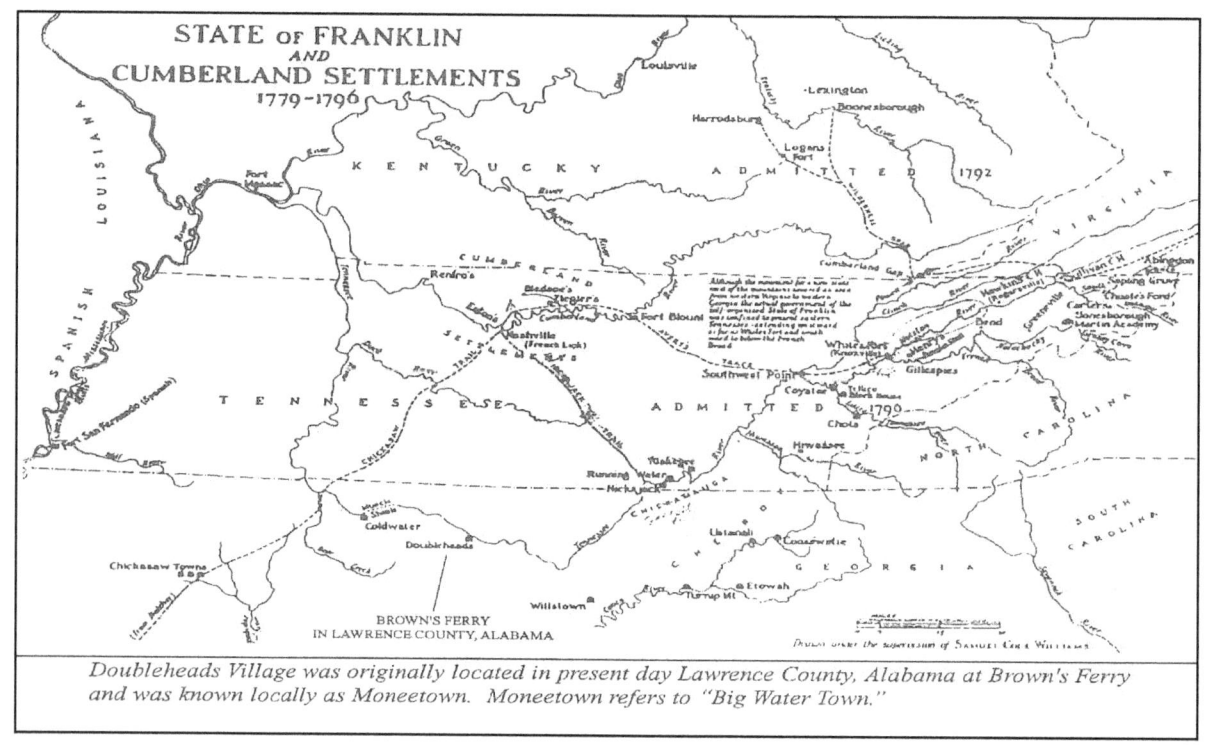

Doubleheads Village was originally located in present day Lawrence County, Alabama at Brown's Ferry and was known locally as Moneetown. Moneetown refers to "Big Water Town."

# Irish Indians of the Warrior Mountains

Between 1816 and 1840, thousands of the Southeastern Indians intermingled by marriage with Irish and Scot-Irish pioneers who rapidly moved into the Indian nations. Many of these mixed-blood Indian people were eventually forced into hiding or denial of their Indian ancestry because of their fear of removal to the west by the United States Government. The newly established southern states, still in their infancy in the early 1800's, refused the right of the Cherokee, Creek, or Chickasaw to establish Indian nations within the newly recognized sovereign states of Alabama, Georgia, Mississippi, and Tennessee.

**Jackson**

The "Documents on United States Indian Policy" written by Francis P. Prucha, on December 8, 1829, implicate that President Andrew Jackson said, "the Southern tribes, having mingled much with the whites and made some progress in the arts of civilized life, have lately attempted to erect an independent government within the limits of Georgia and Alabama. These States, claiming to be the only sovereigns within their territories, extended their laws over the Indians, which induced the latter to call upon the United States for protections."

Jackson went onto the say, "It seems to me visionary to suppose that in this state of things claims can be allowed on tracts of country on which they have neither dwelt nor made improvements, merely because they have seen them from the mountain or passed them in the chase." Jackson, the great Indian fighter of the Southeast, believed in the spoils of the system, "To the victor belongs the spoils of war." After the Treaty of Fort Jackson in 1814 and around the year 1815, Jackson laid claim to the Irish-Cherokee Indian farmland at Melton's Bluff in Lawrence County Alabama. As he stole from the local Irish-Indian people at Melton's Bluff prior to the time that any legal land claims could be made, Jackson had no reservations about eliminating all Indian lands east of the Mississippi River after becoming President of the United States.

During the turbulent times in the early history of the Southeastern United States, Irish people, who have always been somewhat rebellious freedom seekers, migrated into the Southeastern Indian farmlands, mingled with the native people, and married into their tribes. As the Federal Government forced the removal issue during the 1830's under Jackson's administration, mixed-blood Irish-Indians began moving from the Cherokee Nation in Alabama, the Carolinas, Georgia, and Tennessee into the Warrior Mountains of northern Alabama. The mountains provided isolation and protection as long as they denied their Indian backgrounds. The Irish-Indians, who were of dark complexion, would many times claim to be Black Dutch or Black Irish and deny their rightful Indian descent in order to stay in their aboriginal lands.

Those who question the idea of intermarriage of Irish and Indian people, who settled primarily on the poor isolated lands found in the Warrior Mountains as well as other isolated areas of northern Alabama, are merely misinformed. After looking into their eyes and examining the features of those who make efforts to reclaim links to their Indian past, many common threads appear which not only strengthen but confirm that the vast majority of these people are truly Irish-Indians afflicted with over 150 years of denial. Isolationism and intermarriage forced their complexions fairer through the genetic sieve of the Irish which transcends nearly two centuries. However, from within their hearts they speak with a straight tongue of their Indian ancestors who survived in the Warrior Mountains of Alabama.

One of the most common characteristics of the true Warrior Mountains Irish-Indians is the direct line of descent from the Cherokee or Creek originating prior to the 1830's Great Removal. Another common occurrence was the intermarriage within family units, where cousins married cousins, sisters of one family married brothers of another family, two different families intermarried over several years, and children from the same mother and different fathers took the mother's last name. One would be amazed at the number of people having the same great-grandparents on two sides of their family. An original Warrior Mountain Irish-Indian, who is at least a quarter blood Indian, will many times have the same great-grandparents on more than one side of the family.

Another common thread is the migration of their Irish ancestors from the Carolinas, to Georgia or Tennessee, and then into Alabama. Intermarriage between Irish and Indian people most often occurred in the Carolinas, East Tennessee, North Georgia, and Northeast Alabama which made up the Cherokee Nation until 1838.

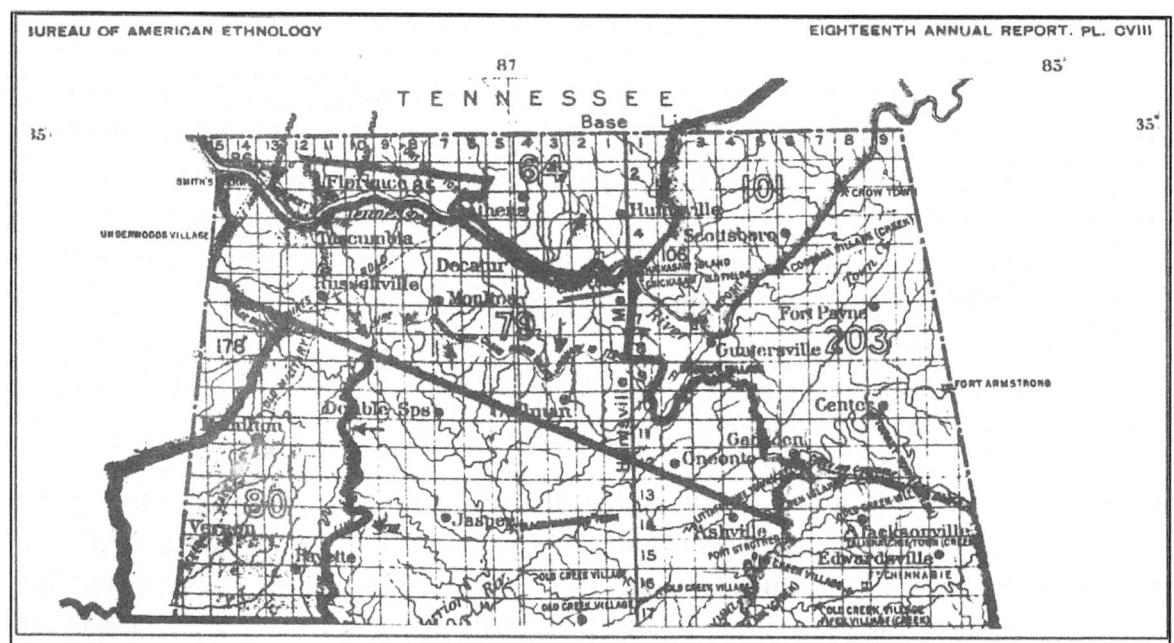

*The Chickasaw Boundary Treaty of January 10, 1786 is shown on this map of Alabama which shows the line of Chickasaw land claims until the Turkey Town Treaty of 1816. (Note: Arrows indicate the Chickasaw Boundary Line.)*

The remnants of the Warrior Mountain Irish-Indian mixed-bloods survive in the Warrior Mountains under common family names. Today, the most common occurrence of surnames of Indian children in Lawrence County Schools are: Alexander, Black, Blankenship, Borden, Bradford, Dutton, England, Gillespie, Green(e), Hill, Hood, Jackson, Johnson, Jones, Kerby, Kelsoe, LouAllen, Owens, Parker, Riddle, Rutherford, Smith, Terry, Walker, White, and many other family names not as prevalent.

# Indian Treaties of the Warrior Mountains

Indian people utilized the Warrior Mountains for years before the coming of the white man. Shortly before the first settlers arrived in the Warrior Mountains, many treaties had taken the last remnants of the native lands.

## Chickasaw Boundary Treat – 1786

The Chickasaw Boundary Treaty of January 10, 1786, recognized the High Town or Ridge Path along the Continental Divide in north Alabama as the Chickasaw's southern boundary and Creeks northern boundary. This early boundary between the Creeks and Chickasaws lay primarily along the present day Leola Road and Ridge Road of Lawrence County's portion of the Warrior Mountains.

The backbone of North Alabama or divide was also the boundary line between the Cherokees and Creeks. The boundary line along the divide with Chickasaw claims extending eastward to a north-south line drawn between the Path and Hobb's Island or Chickasaw Old Fields just south of present day Huntsville, Alabama. The north-south line lay along the Huntsville Meridian and formed the eastern boundary of the Chickasaw Nation until the Turkey Town Treaty of 1816. From Ditto Landing or Hobbs Island, the Chickasaw boundary crossed present day Madison County about 45 degrees toward the northwest to the Tennessee State Line.

## Cotton Gin Treaty – 1806

The Cotton Gin Treaty of January 7, 1806, was between the Cherokee Indians and U.S. Government. The treaty identified the tract of land that Moses Melton, the mixed-blooded Indian grandson of John Melton, lived on and declared the land to be equally shared property of Melton and Charles Hicks. Charles Hicks was noted in Cherokee history as being the first person to show Sequoyah how to write his name in English. In addition, Tahlonteeskee (the Overthrower) was the half brother to Sequoyah.

The treaty gave up Cherokee claims to Indian land north of the Tennessee River, except for Doublehead's Reserve, and placed a cotton gin at Melton's Bluff. Doublehead was killed because of the terms of this treaty. Doublehead's Reserve lay between Elk River (Chu wa lee) and Cypress Creek (Te Kee ta no-eh) in present day Lauderdale County. The Cotton Gin Treaty with the Cherokees did not relinquish the Chickasaws claims to the area; therefore, Ft. Hampton was established to remove squatters from Chickasaw land, located primarily in the area of Limestone County known as the Simms Settlement.

**Treaty of Fort Jackson – 1814**

The majority of the new frontier south of the Tennessee Divide that now makes up Bankhead Forest was taken from the Creeks at the Treaty of Fort Jackson in 1814. The Creeks did not receive monetary compensation for their vastly large tracts of land from Bankhead Forest to the south near Montgomery, Alabama. This large tract was taken after Jackson's defeat of the Red Stick Creeks at the Battle of Horseshoe Bend. This 1814 cession of land was from the High Town Path or Continental Divide in north Alabama and extended south for nearly 200 miles.

**Turkey Town Treaty – 1816**

The Turkey Town Treaty of September 14, 1816, gave up Cherokee and Chickasaw land in the Lawrence, Colbert, Franklin, and Morgan counties of the Warrior Mountains. Both tribes had legitimate claims to the land by previous treaties.

According to the terms of the Turkey Town Treaty, the last Indian lands of the Warrior Mountains were bought from the Chickasaws and Cherokees on September 14 and 18, 1816, respectively. The Chickasaws were paid $125,000.00 with the Cherokees being paid $60,000.00 for land that now makes up Colbert, Franklin, Lawrence, and Morgan Counties.

The Chickasaws and Cherokees had overlapping land claims with the Cherokees claiming land west to Natchez Trace some 10 to 15 miles west of Caney Creek in Colbert County. The Chickasaws claimed land east to the old official Chickasaw boundary, which runs from the Chickasaw Old Fields (Hobbs Island) south to the High Town Path then west along the High Town Path to Flat Rock in present day Franklin County. From Hobbs Island, the boundary ran northwest diagonally across Madison Counties.

The Chickamauga Cherokee Chief Doublehead and the Cherokees farmed and controlled the Tennessee Valley to Natchez Trace by agreement with George Colbert.

The Turkey Town Treaty signed by the Cherokees on September 14, 1816, ceded Colbert, Franklin, Lawrence, and Morgan counties; however, the U.S. Government established the Chickasaw's new eastern boundary from Franklin County's Flat Rock to Caney Creek in Colbert County until 1832. The High Town Path was recognized as the southern boundary of the cessions for both the Chickasaw and Cherokee, until the Turkey Town Treaty of 1816. The 1816 treaty identified the new cession boundary as a straight line drawn from Flat Rock in Franklin County to Ten Islands on the Coosa River. Previous treaties recognized the Continental Divide along which ran the High Town or Ridge Path.

**Indian Removal Act - 1830**

On May 28, 1830, congress passed an act authorizing the exchange of lands in the west for those lands east of the Mississippi River held by Indian tribes. President Andrew Jackson was intent on seeing all Indian people removed from the eastern United States.

**Treaty of New Echota – 1835**

On December 29, 1835, the Treaty of New Echota was signed by a small number of Cherokees. The U.S. Congress ratified the treaty on May 23, 1836. The treaty ceded the entire Cherokee territory east of the Mississippi River.

**Trail of Tears – 1838**

The Cherokee people were given two years to move at which time the forced removal known as the "Trail of Tears" began in the Spring of 1838. The forced march began in October 1838 and ended in March 1839.

An estimated 4,000 Cherokees died on the forced march to the west. Many of the Cherokees from the east passed through north Alabama during 1838 by railroad. By the time of the "Trail of Tears" in 1838, much of the land of the Warrior Mountains had already been claimed by the Irish/Cherokee mix-bloods who denied their heritage in order to remain in the "Warrior Mountains", the land they loved.

Many of north Alabama's Indian people were already mixed with white settlers and stayed in the hill country of the Warrior Mountains. They denied their ancestry and basically lived much of their lives in fear of being sent west. Full bloods claimed to be Black Irish or Black Dutch, thus denying their rightful Indian blood. After being fully assimilated into the general population years later, these Irish/Cherokee mixed-blood descendants began reclaiming their Indian heritage in the land of the "Warrior Mountains."

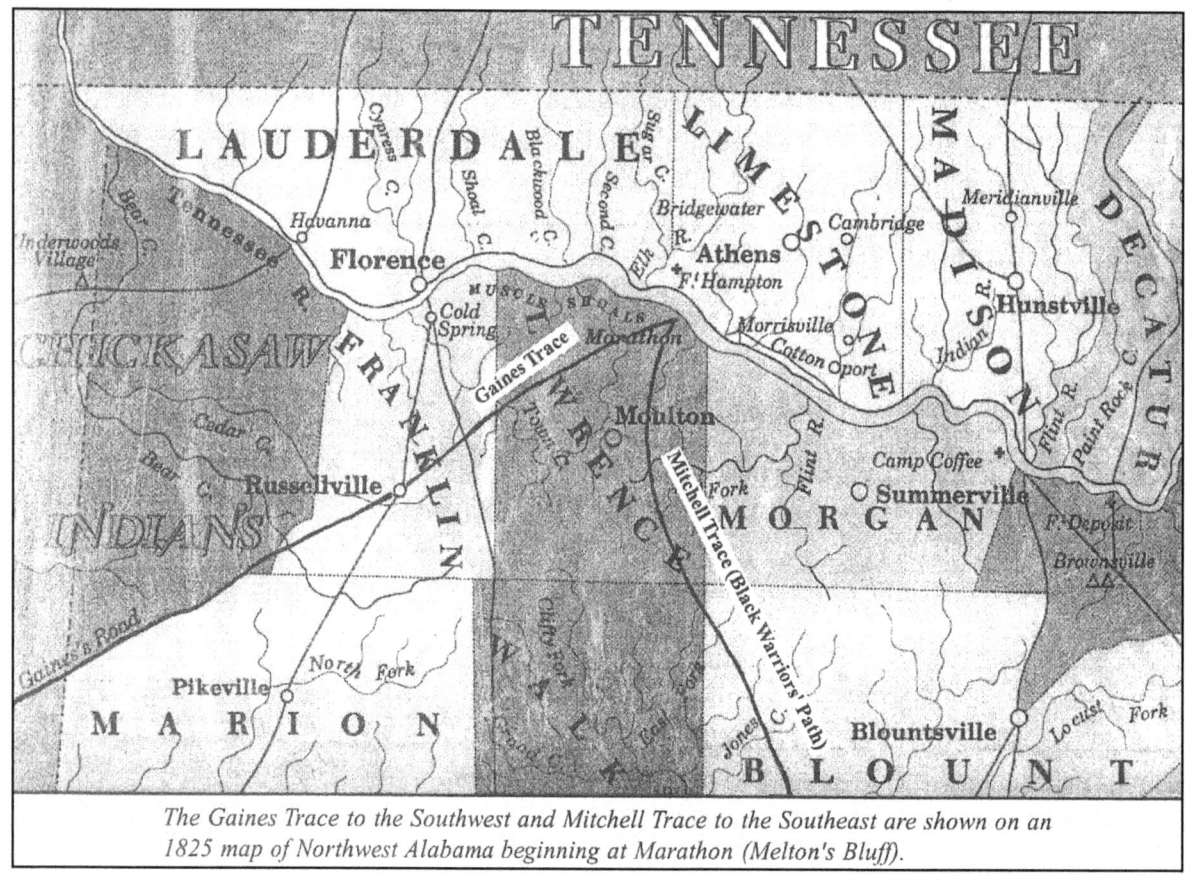

*The Gaines Trace to the Southwest and Mitchell Trace to the Southeast are shown on an 1825 map of Northwest Alabama beginning at Marathon (Melton's Bluff).*

## Indian Trails of the Warrior Mountains

Trappers and Indian traders came down the Tennessee River by flatboat to the head of Elk River Shoals at Melton's Bluff. At the Bluff as early as 1813, they could travel southwest and southeast by way of the best Indian roads known as Gaines Trace and Mitchell Trace (Black Warriors' Path).

These early white intruders on the Indian lands were allowed to remain because most had married into and were accepted by the Cherokee nation. Ann Royall gave an account of one such individual in a letter dated January 12, 1818. Ms. Royall called the white guide Rhea and explained that he had married one of John Melton's half-blood Cherokee daughters. John Melton, Irishman by birth, had a large plantation in Lawrence County at the head of Elk River Shoals. Rhea had lived among the Cherokees for 15 years (1803) and John Melton had established his plantation around 1790.

From Melton's Bluff two early Indian roads ran south through the Warrior Mountains. Gaines Trace went through the western portion and Mitchell Trace went through the eastern portion of the Warrior Mountains.

Many other Indian trails traversed the dividing ridges of the Warrior Mountains creating a north-south network from the Warrior River Valley to the Tennessee River Valley. In addition, one of the longest known Indian trails was the High Town Path which crossed the backbone of North Alabama as an east-west route.

## Gaines Trace

When reading the early history of Lawrence County, the first existing road mentioned, before our county became a county and our state became a state, is the Gaines Trace. Gaines Trace was a government road from Melton's Bluff on the Tennessee River, through the Warrior Mountains, to Cotton Gin Port, descending to St. Stephens Trading Post on the Tombigbee River.

Gaines' Trace was authorized in 1806 by Article IV of the "Wafford Settlement," a treaty with the Cherokees which primarily ceded Cherokee lands in central Tennessee and Kentucky. The road was named and laid out by General George Strothers Gaines about 1805. "Gaines' Trace" began approximately eight miles west of Mallard Creek at Melton's Bluff near the head of Elk River Shoals and proceeded southwest where it forked. One route continued west to Eastport, Mississippi with the other route passing through Russellville to Cotton Gin Port on the Tombigbee River. This trace route later joined or crossed a route laid by Edmund P. Gaines that passed through the Warrior Mountains in the western portion of Lawrence County.

## Edmund Gaines Trail

The other Gaines route was described by Captain Edmund Pendleton Gaines in a letter to the Secretary of War on January 29, 1808. As requested by the Secretary of War on July 31, 1807, Captain Gaines surveyed and marked a way for a road from the head of Muscle Shoals (Melton's Bluff) to Cotton Gin Port on the Tombigbee River.

Gaines said in his letter, "I have also explored the route, from the lower end of the shoals to the head waters of Bear Creek, near where the last will intersect the first mentioned route…From the head of the shoals to the northeast sources of Bear Creek, distance 35 miles, is nearly level as could be wished, either for making a good road for carriages by going near a straight course; but by waving the course in conformity of the slopes of the ridges all will be crossed without ascent or decent of more than 13 ½ degrees… The route for the greater part of this distance is on the dividing ridges, between the waters of the Tennessee and Mobile...Several Cherokees have designated different places, where they promise to settle in the course of the present year, along the way as Bear Creek Ridge, which they call their South boundary..."

As given in the <u>Territorial Papers of the United States</u> compiled and edited by Clarence E. Carter, the description above describes the dividing ridge in western Lawrence County between the Bear Creek drainage which flows to the Tennessee River and the Sipsey River drainage which flows to Mobile. The High Town Path which was the Chickasaw's southern boundary defined by the Treaty of January 10, 1786, also follows the same dividing ridge.

In his letter, Captain Edmund Gaines states that the Cherokee claim the Continental Divide of Bear Creek Ridge as their south boundary. In addition, Edmund Gaines identified two routes from the Shoals that joined on the ridge near the headwaters of Bear Creek, which remains in the western portion of present day Lawrence County. The two routes joined south of present day Mt. Hope and proceeded southwest along the Continental Divide toward Cotton Gin Port.

A portion of this dividing ridge in southwest Lawrence County also became the first legislative road in Alabama – the Byler Road. In addition, the closest route of 35 miles, from Melton's Bluff at the head of the Shoals toward the northeast sources of Bear Creek, would be just south of Mt. Hope approximately some four miles. Since the headquarters of Bear Creek and the headwaters of Sipsey River lie in southwestern Lawrence County, the Edmund Gaines Route lay along the portion of mountain ridges of the watershed divide that became the Byler Road by Act of Alabama Legislature on December 15, 1819.

**Black Warriors' Path**

An 1813 Melish map of Indian country shows two roads beginning at Melton's Bluff, which located at the head of Elk River Shoals. Of course, the two roads shown on the map are the Gaines and Mitchell Traces. The date of the map was three years before these Indian lands were given up by the Turkey Town Treaty of 1816.

The relationship of the Gaines and Mitchell Traces does not end with a common beginning point at Melton's Bluff. The trails were also connected on their southern ends by a trading route from Fort Mitchell to St. Stephens. Thus, an early Indian trading triangle was established in the area becoming the State of Alabama long before the area became a state.

The Indian trail known as the Black Warriors' Path or Black Warrior Town Trail lead from Melton's Bluff toward the Mulberry and Sipsey Forks of the Black Warrior River, and then traversed southeast to Fort Mitchell on the Chattahoochee River in present day Russell County, Alabama. The path ran from Melton's Bluff at the head of Elk River Shoals, across the Warrior Mountains, to the center of the Creek Indian Nation near the Little and Big Oakfuskee Towns, probably preceding Gaines Trace. The route became known as the Mitchell Trace and connected Fort Hampton in Limestone County to Fort Mitchell in Russell County, Alabama.

Mitchell Trace was probably named after the construction of Fort Mitchell in 1811. Mitchell Trace eventually became a post route which connected Fort Hampton, a Cherokee/Chickasaw Indian outpost (located near the forks of Elk River and the Tennessee River), to Fort Mitchell, a Creek Indian outpost. Fort Mitchell was named after David Brady Mitchell, who was listed as an Indian Agent or Governor.

The 1818 John Melish Map shows the Black Warriors' Path beginning at Marathon (Melton's Bluff), proceeding east of Courtland several miles and following closely to the present day Hillsboro Road to Fairfield Church. It continued, crossing the Fish Dam Ford on the West Fork of Flint Creek east of its junction with Elam Creek, passing just west of Oakville. The path was adjacent to the Oakville ceremonial mound, traveling into Beaty Hollow south of Speake, through Poplar Log Cove, and exiting Lawerence county near Basham's Gap at Piney Grove.

Remnants of the very old road were still visible on the west side of the ceremonial Indian mound at Oakville. In addition, just south of Lindsey Cemetery, the old road bed is clearly visible as it crosses U.S. Forest Service property into Beaty Hollow and on into Poplar Log Cove.

Beginning near the eastern end of Elk River Shoals on the Tennessee River at Melton's Bluff, the old Black Warriors' Path proceeded south into the foothills of Bankhead Forest, through the forest, and into the Black Warrior River Valley. The Black Warriors; path crossed the Warrior River just northeast of the junction of the Mulberry and Sipsey forks where it intersected another trail coming from the Tennessee River at Ditto's Landing near present day Huntsville. The trails joined and proceeded a few miles southwest of the road junctions and the river crossing to the Indian village of Black Warrior Town. This Creek Indian town was destroyed by the military forces commanded by General John Coffee and David Crockett.

*Black Warriors' Path at Oakville Indian Mounds Park.*

According to William Lindsey McDonald's article on Melton's Bluff, "The renowned pioneer and soldier, David Crockett, remembered two occasions when his military unit crossed at Melton's Bluff. The first instance was in November 1813. Actually according to Crockett, he crossed the Tennessee River twice on his first occasion in order to maneuver around the local Indians. After crossing at Huntsville, they moved westward to cross the river again at Melton's Bluff. Crockett described the river at this point as being about two miles wide. The rocky bottom of the river was rough and dangerous. While fording the river, several of the horses became stuck in the rocky crevices and had to be left there while the military command moved onto their destination. Crockett's second crossing at Melton's Bluff was in October 1814. Payroll and muster records reveal that he was a third sergeant in Captain John Cowan's company at the time." According to McDonald, the aforementioned information was obtained from the book <u>A Narrative of the Life of David Crockett.</u>

General Coffee and Davy Crockett crossed the Tennessee River at Melton's Bluff twice during 1813 and traveled the Black Warriors' Path (Mitchell Trace) to Black Warrior Town. In a letter from John Coffee to General Jackson, dated October 22, 1813, and belonging to Mr. Richard C. Sheridan, the following describes the crossing: "...I proceed to cross the river at the upper end of the Shoals, all my efforts failed to procure a pilot. I took with me one of John Melton's sons who said he knew not the road, he showed me a path that had been reputed the <u>Black Warriors' Path</u>..."

In 1813, David Crockett helped General John Coffey's forces burn the large, yet deserted, Creek Indian village known as Black Warrior Town. Crockett and General Coffee's forces traveled along the Black Warriors' Path to destroy the Creek town.

It is also highly probable that James Richard Gillespie from Indian Tomb Hollow also served with David Crockett. Gillespie served under Captain Cowan in 1813 during the same period of time as David Crockett. Gillespie attended the muster rolls in Blount County, Tennessee on January 1, 1814.

To confirm the existence of the Black Warriors' Path, one can just look at old maps showing the area known as Melton's Bluff in Lawrence County. The Black Warriors' Path or Mitchell Trace is clearly shown on the following maps listed by date: 1813, 1818, 1823, 1825, 1831, and 1842. Since the road is not shown after the 1850's, the route probably became a part of the vast Wheeler Plantation. Thus, the town of Marathon became one of the "ghost towns" of North Alabama. Furthermore, Marathon, at the head of Elk River Shoals, also died after the railroad around the Shoals was completed in 1834.

It does not appear accidental that the trail connected areas of cultural importance to the Indian people of the Tennessee River Valley, the Black Warrior River Valley, and the Chattahoochee River Valley. An Indian trail also ran from Ft. Mitchell to St. Stephens on the Tombigbee, thus completing a trading triangle.

**Old Buffalo Trail**

Along the western edge of the present day Black Warrior Wildlife Management Area, a trail running the divide was recorded by Captain Edmund Pendleton Gaines on January 29, 1808. According to the Territorial Papers, he described a route from the head of the Shoals at Melton's Bluff toward Bear Creek Ridge, then south toward Cotton Gin Port. This early route has been identified by old timers as the Old Buffalo Trail. The Old Buffalo Trail ran portions of the Byler Road and High Town Path along the ridge dividing Bear Creek and Sipsey River for some five miles and followed the route of present day highway 101. It later became Doublehead's Trace.

The trail was used by Creeks and Choctaws traveling north to the French Lick (Nashville, Tennessee area) in search of buffalo. It later became a trade route used by the Cherokees. Eventually, part of the approximate route of the Buffalo Trail became the Byler Road at Big Mussel Shoals leading from the Tennessee River to Tuscaloosa. The Old Buffalo Trail probably crossed the Tennessee River near Wheeler Dam and likely followed close to the route known as State Highway 101. Doublehead up graded the route to a road to Franklin, Tennessee, and therefore, became Doublehead's Trace.

**Freedom Trail or Braziel Creek Trail**

According to local folklore, the Freedom Trail or Braziel Creek Trail was an Indian trail which ran from the Elk River Shoals south toward Tuscaloosa along the creek and river bottoms. In

Lawrence County, the trail followed Braziel Creek to Borden Creek, to the Sipsey River, and to parts south. Portions of the trail of which I write may represent the escape route of some Cherokees during removal, as well as other Southern Indians and black slaves. The trail appeared untouched by the white man. According to Jim Manasco, the trail was a secret route, running through Bankhead Forest's Sipsey Wilderness Area in Lawrence County, Alabama.

The trail was strategically located between the Byler Road to the west, and the Cheatham Road to the east, both of which traverse the Warrior Mountains in north-south directions. Isolated from military movements and other traffic along the two major Bankhead roads, the trail offered protection to travelers over its long course from the south, to its junction with the High Town or Ridge Path on the northern border of the forest.

According to folk lore and Indian legend passed down for 130 years, snakes were drawn on beech trees along the trail by Indian people around the time of removal. According to Jim Manasco, his Indian ancestors passed through the area along the trail to settle on the Rocky Plains.

## Sipsie Trail

According to early historical information concerning the Indian inhabitants of the Warrior Mountains, most of the major dividing ridges of the forest served as trails, paths, and primitive roads from one part of the country to another. The dividing ridge which separates the watersheds of Brushy Creek and the Sipsey River was no different and known locally as the Sipsie Trail.

Archaeological evidence found in bluff shelters near the Sipsie Trail indicate that

*The Rattlesnake Tree, located near the Freedom trail, was drawn on an old beech tree by historic Indian people.*

the route was used as early as the prehistoric Woodland Period. One such bluff site, the McDougal shelter and mortar rock, was located not far from the dividing ridge. The McDougal Shelter lay close to the divide route and contains numerous prehistoric artifacts dating back to woodland times.

The High Town Path ran a portion of the Sipsie Trail from near the junction of the Leola Road to the Ridge Road. Local folklore indicates the north-south dividing ridge was one of many routes utilized primarily by Creek Indians in the early historic period, as well as providing use for the Creek and during late prehistoric times just prior to DeSoto.

The Sipsie Trail junction with the High Town Path was located on top of Wren Mountain some five miles south of Moulton. The route crossed the Sipsey River in Winston County, proceeded south to Lost Creek, and then traveled toward the Black Warrior River Basin near Tuscaloosa. In all probability, the route was utilized by southern Indians hunting buffalo in Cumberland River basin during the prehistoric and historic periods. Creek and Choctaw hunters also used this trail when traveling north from the Warrior River Basin toward the French Lick in search of buffalo.

According to an 1830's map of the Cherokee Nation, the route ran the dividing ridge of Brushy and the Sipsey River to the Sipsey River crossing about one mile southeast of the Sipsey and Caney Creek junction. Another 1850's map shows the route running from Pulaski, Tennessee, to the Rodgersville crossing of the lower Elk River Shoals of the Tennessee River at Lamb's Ferry. The route then passed through Courtland, Moulton, and Wren in Lawrence County, to Double Springs, to Rocky Plains in Winston County, and onward towards Tuscaloosa. According to local folklore, Rocky Plains was an Indian stronghold even after the 1838 removal known as the "Trail of Tears."

**High Town Path**

Another major route into the Warrior Mountains was by way of the High Town Path, also known as the Ridge Path. The path ran along the Continental Divide or Tennessee-Warrior River Divide, and followed portions of the Old Corn Road, Leola Road, Cheatham Road, Ridge Road, and Byler Road.

The High Town Path or Ridge Path, one of the most famous Indian trails in the Southeastern United States, traversed across the backbone of the William B. Bankhead National Forest. The Indian trail completely crossed the Southeastern United States in an east-west direction and traveled through Alabama along the dividing watersheds of the Tennessee River to the north and the waters that drain southward into Mobile Bay. The long Indian trail was some 1000 miles in length with the Indian village of High Town (present day Rome, Georgia) located somewhat near the middle of the route.

The High Town Path was probably most heavily used as an Indian foot path in prehistoric times was free of creek crossings as well as other water and wet weather barriers. Major portions of the High Town Path followed high lands which appear to be the general route of early Indian trails. It is thought that the trail ran from Charles Town or Charleston, South Carolina to Chickasaw Bluffs, located at the junction of the Wolf River and the might Mississippi known today as Memphis, Tennessee.

According to the *Annals of Northwest Alabama*, "The High Town Path was as Indian trail that extended from near the present site of Atlanta, Georgia, westward through the Cherokee Nation south of Sand Mountain, through the Creek Nation, and into the Chickasaw Nation and the present counties of Lawrence, Franklin, and Marion in Alabama before entering Mississippi. Settlers from North Georgia and South Carolina could migrate to Winston along this route having good roads until they turned southward to cross the mountains. After the building of the Cheatham Road and Byler's Road, they could have fair roads all the way." It should be noted that the High Town Path did not enter Winston County. Settlers traveled from the path along the Jasper Road (present day Highway 41), the Cheatham Road (present day Highway 33), and the Byler Road to get into Winston County.

*The deep, worn and old route of the High Town Path runs adjacent to the present day Ridge Road and along the Continental Divide in Lawrence County, Alabama.*

The following is two descriptions of the High Town Path as reported in *The Story of Alabama*, "High Town Path, from High Shoals on the Apalachee River to High Town in the fork of the Oostenalla and Etowah Rivers, the site of the modern Rome, Georgia, thence to Turkey Town of the Cherokee Country, to Coosa, then to Flat Rock in the Northwestern part of the state, thence to Copper Town of the Chickasaw Nation. Two great trails from the east united at Flat Rock in Franklin County, Alabama, and thence continued west to the Chickasaw Nation. One of these trails comes from the Chattahoochee to Little Oakfuskee then to Flat Rock. The other, High Town Trail, started from Tellico in Monroe County, East Tennessee, thence southward to Coosa Town, and from it to Flat Rock."

The book *Alabama History for Schools* by Summersell describes the trail in the following: "One example of a long Indian trail was the High Town Path. This was named for the Creek Indian village of High Town in present day Etowah County. This trail ran all the way across Alabama from the land of the Chickasaws in the west, through the Creek Country to Turkey Town. From Turkey Town it ran through the Cherokee Country and across the Chattahoochee River into Georgia."

According to the book, *History of Alabama* by Moore, "The Creeks had numerous paths radiating from eastern Georgia into Alabama, along which Carolina and Georgia traders, and later settlers, penetrated the interior of the state. The most notable of these were the "High Town Path" and the "Southern Trail". The former crossed the Chattahoochee at Shallow Ford, just north of the present city of Atlanta and extended by way of High Town (Etowah), Turkey Town, and other villages along the Cherokee border to the Chickasaw Country."

Furthermore, according to a report of the Alabama History Commission "the true Cherokee southern boundary, after following the ridge separating the waters of the Tennessee and Black Warrior to the headwaters of Caney Creek, ran thence down said creek to the Tennessee River."

As noted by the *Annals of Northwest Alabama*, "before the coming of the white man, the ridge generally separated the lands of the Chickasaws on the west from those of the Creeks to the east and the lands of the Cherokees on the north from the Creeks to the south. During the late 1700's and early 1800's, the ridge top path and the Continental Divide was referred to in treaties with the Chickasaw and Cherokee Indians. Later, the path was used to divide early counties in Mississippi Territory.

In identifying the Cherokees' southern boundary the *Manual for Writing Alabama State History* states, "Consequently we may conclude in a general way that from the lower end of Ten Islands the line followed the most prominent dividing ridge butting on the river in that vicinity, around the headwaters of Canoe Creek, until it reached the height of Blount Mountain, thence northward with said mountain along the ridge dividing the waters of the Coosa from those of the Black Warrior to the top of Raccoon or Sand Mountain near the town of Boaz in Marshall County. From this point westward to the Chickasaw boundary, wherever that lay, it is quite clear that the line was the ridge dividing the waters of the Tennessee from those of the Black Warrior."

Writing to the chiefs and headmen of the Creeks in 1794, Governor William Blount said: "In the original division of land amongst the red people, it is well known that the Creek lands were bounded on the north by the ridge which divides the waters of the Tennessee and Mobile."

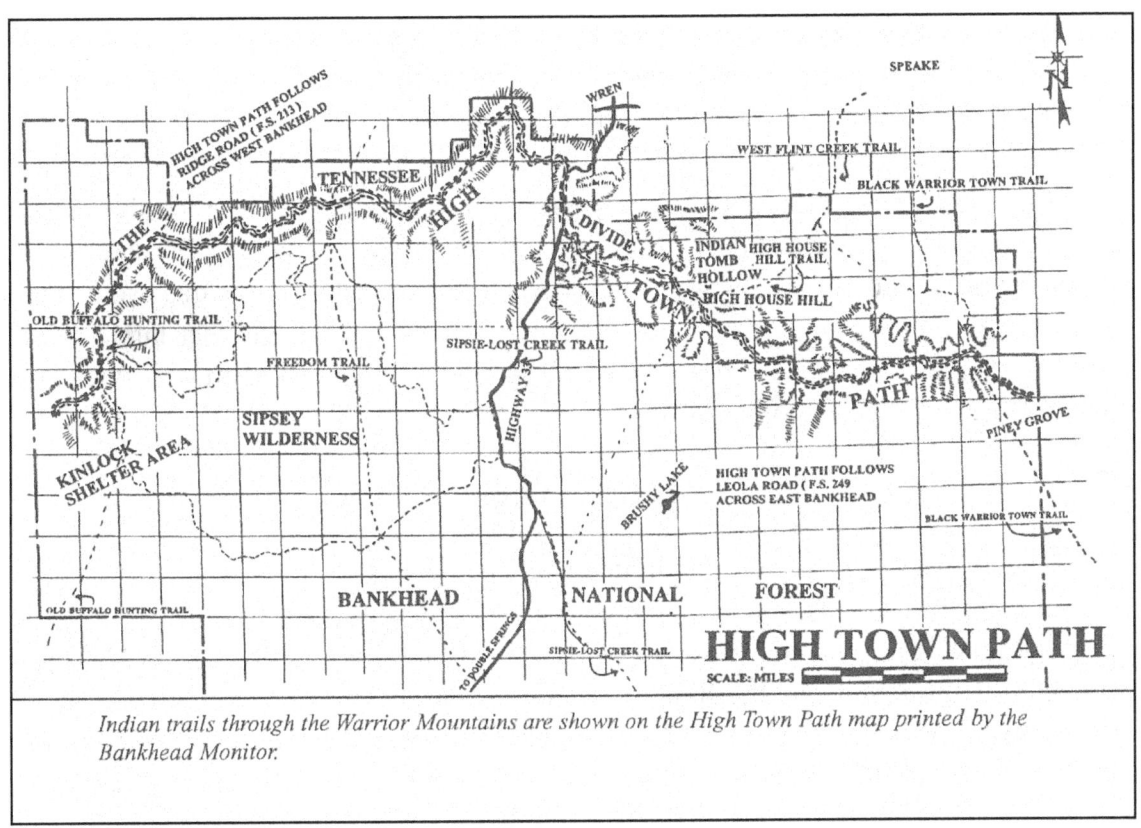

*Indian trails through the Warrior Mountains are shown on the High Town Path map printed by the Bankhead Monitor.*

In addition to being an Indian trail, the High Town Path became the line of the Chickasaw Land Claims under the Treaty of January 10, 1786. According to a map of Chickasaw boundaries, the Chickasaw claims line followed the Continental Divide through Lawrence County and Cullman Counties and turned north and east of the Chickasaw Old Fields on the Tennessee River near Huntsville.

In the Turkey Town Treaty of 1816 which ceded land from both the Chickasaws and Cherokees, the ridge top path (High Town Path) was used as the southern boundary for the land cession of both Indian nations including Franklin, Lawrence, and Morgan counties. Articles 2 of the 1816 treaty with the Cherokee states, "The Cherokee Nation acknowledge the following as their western boundary. South of the Tennessee River, commencing at Camp Coffee, on the south side of the Tennessee River, which is opposite the Chickasaw Island, running from thence a south course to the top of the Dividing Ridge between the waters of the Tennessee and Tombigbee rivers, thence eastwardly along said ridge, leaving the head waters of the Black Warrior to the right hand, until opposed by the West branch of Well's Creek down the east bank of said creek to the Coosa River, and down said river."

Indian people, including Indian mixed-bloods, and early settlers moving into north Alabama from east Tennessee and north Georgia, came in contact with the High Town Path and followed along its course. The Indian trail crossed Georgia just north of Atlanta and traversed diagonally across Tennessee southwest from the Knoxville area and through the area east of Chattanooga. Portions of the trail crossed Lookout Mountain and Sand Mountain as it proceeded toward the dividing ridges of Bankhead National Forest. High Town, which was near present day Rome, Georgia, and Turkey Town, which was near present day Gadsden, Alabama, were important Indian towns along the eastern portion of the route. It was by this route that numerous Indian mixed-bloods, settlers, and many north Alabama families can trace the western movement of their ancestors into the Warrior Mountains.

## Early Roads of the Warrior Mountains

Many of the early Indian trails were laid out to take advantage of the springs, the land divides between different watersheds, and the terrain. Many settlers, who came to Lawrence County from the Carolinas, Georgia, and Tennessee, once called Bankhead Forest home. Many of the families claimed the beauty of the hills and hollows for some 100 years – the early 1800's through the early 1900's. The United States government began buying the property from these settlers in the early 1900's in order to establish a national forest in Franklin, Lawrence, and Winston Counties.

Most of the early settlers were from similar hill country of the Appalachians; therefore, the low but rugged mountains afforded them all the comforts of their old home places. Most of these early settlers, who sought the Bankhead region as home, were poor folks of Irish and Indian descent. Many of the men, who were trappers, traders, or small farmers, were married to Indian women or intermarried with Indian families.

After the land of north Alabama was taken by treaty and opened for settlement, hundreds of people rushed into the area to claim the prized land. Madison County had been established about 1806 and many of the first settlers coming overland by way of Huntsville probably crossed the Tennessee River by ferry. Two ferries, Brown's Ferry from Limestone County and Lamb's Ferry from Lauderdale County probably carried people and supplies to the Lawrence County side of the Tennessee River.

Brown's Ferry, which was just east of Brown's Island, crossed the river between Mallard and Fox Creek. At one time, Chickamauga Cherokee Chief Doublehead lived in Lawrence County and settled near Brown's Ferry. He later moved to Blue Water Creek just one mile west of present day Wheeler Dam in Lauderdale County. According to William McDonald's version as given in the *Journal of Muscle Shoals History of 1981*, Doublehead is buried close to his Blue Water Creek home in Lauderdale County.

Lamb's Ferry crossed the river from now present-day Rogersville to a place some three to five miles west of Spring Creek in Lawrence County. Lamb's Ferry was located at the lower end of Elk River Shoals and was portion of a major North-South route from Pulaski, Tennessee to Tuscaloosa, Alabama, known in Indian days as the Sipsie Trail.

Prior to the late 1830's probably few settlers came from the east unless they were Cherokee mixed-bloods or connected to the Cherokee through marriage. Until the late 1830's, the Cherokee Nation controlled large sections of land from the eastern edge of Morgan County in Alabama, through the upper Northwestern third of Georgia, and into the southeastern third of Tennessee. After the Indian removal in 1838, all Indian lands in Tennessee, Georgia, and Alabama were opened for settlement.

With the invention of the cotton gin in 1793, cotton became the "Agricultural King" not only to the Cherokee people, but to the hundreds of settlers who would quickly claim Tennessee and Moulton Valley regions of Lawrence County. However, the forest to the south, the "Gem of Lawrence County," had an attraction for the Appalachian mixed-blood Indian descendants which they could not resist. All of my early ancestors, though poor by means of worldly treasures, found that early spot where peace, beauty, and tranquility abounds both in life and death in the eternal land of the "Warrior Mountains."

## Byler Road

The Byler road ran through the western portion of the Warrior Mountains from the Tennessee River to Tuscaloosa. The Byler Road was one of the first roads authorized by the Alabama State Legislature. The road was approved two days after Alabama was admitted into the Union of the United States of America on December 14, 1819. The road was named after John Byler, who is buried in Rock Springs Cemetery at Mt. Hope in Lawerence County, Alabama.

*John Byler — builder of the first road authorized by the Alabama legislature.*

The road ran from Bainbridge Ferry on the Tennessee River, across the western border of Lawrence County, and into the Warrior Mountains of present day Bankhead National Forest. The road went southward to the falls of the Tuscaloosa River and basically ran the divide between the Tombigbee and Warrior River drainages. The road followed the basic route of the Old Buffalo Trail, which was a north-south route for the Creeks and Choctaws to the French Lick (Nashville).

The mountainous part of the route between the upper portion of Bear Creek and Sipsey River drainages of Lawrence County was along the same route laid out by Captain Edmund Pendleton Gaines on July 31, 1807. The area was part of the Cherokee and Chickasaw territories.

According to an early map of Lawrence County, William McCain, son-in-law of John Byler, ran a toll gate on the Byler Road near its junction with the Northwest Road. The toll gate was located in the Southeast quarter of Section 18 of Township 8 South and Range 9 West.

The Moulton Fork of the Byler Road ran from Moulton, skirting the edge of the mountains through Youngtown, and up to the mountain at McClung Gap. The two Byler Roads joined at a site known as the 66 mile tree which was located about one-half mile west of the junction of the High Town Path and the Moulton Fork in the southwest one-quarter of Section 33 of Township 7 South and Range 9 West. The 66 mile tree was thought to be a designated tree at the forks of the two roads. The total distance, from the beginning of the Byler Road at Bainbridge Ferry on the Tennessee River, and the beginning of the Byler Road Fork beginning at Moulton, to their junction on top of continental Divide south of Mt. Hope, was supposedly marked on a tree designating the 66 miles of the Byler Roads north from that point.

Since prehistoric Indian times, the portion of Byler Road between Poplar Springs Cemetery and Aunt Jenny Brook's home place was utilized as a trail or route from prehistoric Indian times. This particular portion of the Byler Road was previously designated using various names; the

High Town Path, the Old Buffalo Trail, the Edmund Gaines Road. The road was also the tribal boundary of the Creeks, Cherokees, and Chickasaws.

During the Civil War, Union troops of Northern Aggression under the command of Colonel Abel Streight were attacked on the Byler Road near Aunt Jenny's place. In addition, Union General G.M. Dodge's scouting part utilized the Byler Road in the Spring of 1864. Later in March, 1865, one division of Union General J. H. Wilson's cavalry of 13,480 horsemen passed down the Byler Road in route to Tuscaloosa and the Battle of Selma. One division passed through Lawrence County and stayed the night at David Hubbard's Plantation located at Kinlock.

**Cheatham Road**

An Indian route known as the Sipsie Trail, the Cheatham's Turn-Pike, and the Wilderness Parkway is a road through the Warrior Mountains which has been traveled by many people. However, without a doubt, the most historical of all too ever use the road through the middle of Bankhead Forest was Wyatt Cheatham.

Due to a 1824 Act of the Alabama Legislature, Wyatt Cheatham was authorized to upgrade the trail and build the Cheatham Road. The actual upgrade of the road began seven miles south of Moulton and is the approximate location of the existing junction of Leola Road and Highway 33. The roadway was to be cleared 18 feet wide with 12 feet of roadway clear of stumps.

The old horse and wagon road through the mountains is still visible in many places. The original road ascended Wren Mountain along the west side of the valley, west of present day Highway 33. The old road reaches the mountain top some 200 yards east of the junction of Ridge Road with Highway 33. South from the Ridge Road on Highway 33, old roadbeds exhibit existing signs of the original roadway and are adjacent to the edges of the Wilderness Parkway.

According to the _Annuals of Northwest Alabama_ by Donald and Wynelle Dodd, Cheatham was directed by the Act to build the road toward Tuscaloosa. The point of beginning would be the approximate junction of the Leola Road with State Highway 33, presently known as the "Wilderness Parkway." This point would be the same as the High Town Path's junction with the Brushy-Sipsey Dividing ridge.

It appears that Wyatt Cheatham had assistance in his appointment over the construction of the roadway. Joseph Coe, who was Lawrence County's State legislative representative, was obviously a good friend to Wyatt Cheatham. The _Old Land Records of Lawrence County_ by Margaret Cowan, indicate that Joseph Coe (originally from Tennessee) had entered land some three miles south of Courtland in Section 7 of Township 5 South, Range 7 West on September 11, 1818. Cowart states that Wyatt Cheatham originally entered 160 acres of land at Wren and 160 acres near Spivey Gap on September 12, 1818. He also entered an additional 160 acres near Wren after moving to Winston County. On February 12, 1825, Wyatt Cheatham and Joseph Coe jointly entered 80 acres of land in Winston County where the (their) road crossed Clear Creek in Section 30 of Township 11 South, Range 8 West, according to the Dodd. Earlier on January 26, 1825, Wyatt Cheatham had entered 80 acres near the same location in Winston County.

Wyatt Cheatham is listed in the 1820 Census of Lawrence County, but is not found after that time in the county census records. However, Wyatt again entered an additional 160 acres of land at Wren on September 28, 1831, some six years after entering land in Winston County. According to the Lawrence County Census of 1820, Wyatt Cheatham and wife had nine boys under age 21, and two girls under age 21, along with the ownership of two slaves. In the 1830 Census of Walker County, Wyatt Cheatham is listed as being 55 years old with six boys under age 20, 3 boys over age 20, and one female under age 20, and one female over 20, and in addition, two slaves. It is obvious that Cheatham lost a daughter or his wife between 1820 and 1830. Again in the 1850 Census of Winston County, Wyatt Cheatham is listed as being a 72 year old native of Virginia. At the time of the census, Wyatt lived with Lavina, 29; George, 16; Francis, 12; Thomas, 11; and an infant girl, Elizabeth, 1. All are listed as being born in Alabama

According to a January 13, 1826, statement made by the Dodds, and election precinct was approved at the home of Wyatt Cheatham on Clear Creek where said Cheatham's Turn-Pike crossed the sand. In 1828, Wyatt Cheatham obtained a license to sell liquors at his place at the Clear Creek crossing. Wyatt and his son, Wyatt D. Cheatham, renewed their liquor license for $10 in 1833. Cheatham served in the War of 1812 as a sergeant in John A. Allen's Madison County Company. After the war, he moved to Wren where he entered a total of some 320 acres of land. Wyatt Cheatham had a strong alliance with Andrew Jackson.

It appears from historical records that Wyatt Cheatham moved from Madison County to live at Wren in Lawrence County from 1818 until he was authorized to build the Cheatham Road. By 1825, he had moved to Winston County and entered land at the Clear Creek Crossing of his road. In later years, he profited in trade from folks who traveled along his road and stopped by his tavern on Clear Creek.

The route through the middle of Bankhead Forest was known for many years at the Cheatham Road. The road officially changed to Wilderness Parkway after the establishment of the Sipsey

Wilderness Area. The present day route of Highway 33 going to the top of Wren Mountain is in its third location since the original road was built.

*Sipsie Trail or Cheatham's Turnpike at McLemore Cemetery.*

The Cheatham Road (which later became Highway 33) and the Wilderness Parkway was improved and parts were re-routed up the Wren Mountain in the late 1920's. The road was eventually paved and rerouted again during the late 1940's. Many portions of the original Cheatham wagon road are still visible today along Highway 33 south of Wren.

## Topography of the Warrior Mountains

Many springs with clear fresh water flowing from limestone crevasses are found throughout the southern portion of Lawrence County. Many of these springs erupt at the edge of the Moulton Valley where the land abruptly rises from flat land at some 650 feet in elevation to the rim of the hills at some 1,000 feet above mean sea level, thus creating the Continental Divide which separates the waters of Lawrence County in north-south directions. South of the rim, which creates the back bone of North Alabama; all the water eventually flows into Sipsey River to the Black Warrior River, and then joins with the Tombigbee River onward to Mobile Bay. On the northern slopes of the divide, all the runoff eventually flows northerly into the Tennessee River, the Ohio River, and the mighty Mississippi River.

**Sandstone over Limestone**

With thousands of years of erosion caused by the runoff of many rainfalls, the valleys of Bankhead have been cut deep through the massive sandstone formations overlying thick layers of limestone. At the edge of the limestone outcroppings are numerous caves and springs which once provided drinking water to native wildlife, Indians, and early settlers who made Bankhead their home.

Many sandstone bluff shelters are found throughout the Warrior Mountains. The shelters and overhanging rock ledges provided many early Indian inhabitants a home and protection from the elements. Probably the most well-known of these protective sites is the Kinlock Rock Shelter located in the southwestern corner of Lawrence County.

Over the centuries, the sandstone layers of overlying rock in the Warrior Mountains were eroded away creating some 400 miles of canyons or gorges in the Bankhead National Forest. These particular canyons are the sites of some one thousand waterfalls; thus, this area is known as the "Land of a Thousand Waterfalls." The majority of the falls are seasonal. Many of the deep gorges in Bankhead range from 60 to 100 feet high. The highest falls are some 60 to 70 feet in height.

**Typically Valley of the Warrior Mountains**

The following is a description of a typical valley in the northern portion of Bankhead Forest. A few years ago, Dr. Charles Borden and I guided a spring wildflower group into the beautiful valley of Montgomery Creek. This area is now protected under the Wild and Scenic Rivers designation for the valley portion of its watershed. As we progressed down into the canyon, massive layers of sandstone, composing the highest sandstone cliffs, abruptly stopped about midway into the beautiful valley. At this point, limestone formations started and continued to the stream bed of Montgomery Creek. These limestone formations are characteristic of all the upper tributaries of the Sipsey River.

In addition to a geological change within the rock formations that make up the hills and valleys, a noted change also occurs in the vegetation. The tree species varied from white oak, scarlet oak, mountain oak, post oak, black oak, hickory, red maple, sourwoods, and black gum on the sandstone hills, to the valley species which was orchestrated with eastern red cedar, chinquapin oak, shumard oak, swamp white oak, beech, sugar maple, sycamore, sweet gum, hackberry, box elder, yellow poplar, and black walnut that thrive in the limestone valley soils. One the rocky limestone glades within the valley slopes, eastern red cedars were the most abundant trees and dominant vegetation. During this spring time hike, a change was also noted in the herbaceous plants which cover the forest floor. On the sandstone hills and slopes, a minute variety of forest floor plants were noted with poison oak, green briar, mountain laurel, and viburnum being most abundant. As we moved into the limestone outcroppings midway into the valley, a vast array of spring wildflowers laid fairy before us. Lining the stream bank of Montgomery Creek, we saw many beautiful cow slips (Virginia bluebells). In addition to this endangered species, the valley was filled with Jacob's ladder, trout lily, fairy bells, wild ginger, hepatica, bloodroot, fairy wands, trillium, cohosh, may apple, may varieties of violets, and wild blue phlox.

## Caves of the Warrior Mountains

Within the limestone slopes and outcroppings, numerous caves and holes are housed within the massive limestone formations. The limestone appears to have been overlaid with a layer of sandstone rock ranging from 60 to 100 feet thick. The limestone in certain areas has eroded away leaving an extensive network of caves.

Tingling Hole is a unique limestone shaft which contains a waterfall that roars from the west of the rock shaft in the eastern portion of Lawrence County's Bankhead Forest. The vertical shaft appears to be in excess of twenty feet circular diameter, and the bottom is at least 80 feet down. A diagram of the cave shows the vertical shaft is some 30 feet wide and 80 feet deep. The shaft does not have any horizontal passages except for the water fall opening. Its splendor makes it easy to understand why the cave is known as the Tingling Hole.

The Lawrence County portion of William B. Bankhead National Forest has over 70 registered caves with approximately 20 that are 1,000 feet long or longer. The Borden Creek drainage has the densest concentration of caves with some of the largest and longest caves in our area. The exposed limestone outcroppings along the upper Borden Creek drainage are littered with numerous underground openings. Some of the more noted caves in the Borden Creek system are: the Devil's Well containing an underground waterfall over 100 feet high; Armstrong Cave which supposedly has blind cavefish; Saltpeter or Bunyon Hill Cave which contains many tunnels and rooms with the entrance near Borden Creek; Twin Springs Cave which contains speleothems; and Captain Jack's Cave which contains nodules, the Captain's Room, and Hoffman's Horrible Hole.

Caves have fragile environments and are extremely dangerous to the inexperienced. Remember, take nothing and leave only tracks in the caves of the Warrior Mountains.

**Waterfalls of the Warrior Mountains**

The overlying layer of sandstone in the Warrior Mountains has given away to erosion, thus creating some 400 miles of rugged sand rock walled canyons. Plunging into these canyons containing hundreds of waterfalls create the "Land of a Thousand Waterfalls."

The winter and spring seasons are the most ideal times to hike into the canyons of the Warrior Mountains to view the many spectacular waterfalls hidden deep within the forest. Most of our waterfalls are seasonal but during rainy seasons, these waterfalls are perhaps the most exquisite waterfalls and their surrounding scenery found anywhere in the world. The following is a brief listing of some of the most beautiful waterfalls in the Warrior Mountains of Bankhead Forest.

**Kinlock Falls** – Kinlock is probably the best known waterfall or cascading waterfall in Bankhead. Water flows over Kinlock for the entire year, but the many winter rains determine the waterfall's ultimate crescendo during the spring, thus creating a white cascade on a canvas of green leaves. Kinlock Falls is located on Hubbard Creek. To locate the falls, go north at the west end of the Cranal Road. Prior to reaching the Hubbard Creek Bridge, the falls can be discovered some 20 yards to the right of the road.

**South Caney Creek Falls** – Caney Falls are one of the most spectacular in the forest with a vertical drop of some 30 feet into a huge pool of turquoise water. This is probably the largest waterfall in the forest when comparing greatest volume of water. After crossing Sipsey River going south, you must turn west off Highway 33 onto Highway 2. Travel west on Highway 2 for 3.8 miles to a USFS road. There is a steel closure on the right and/or north of the road. It is approximately one miles out the FS road to the falls.

**Turkey Foot Creek Falls** – Two beautiful waterfalls are located in close proximity to each other on Turkey Foot Creek. At the Sipsey River Recreation Area on the Cranal Road, travel west along Turkey Foot Creek which enters Sipsey River a few feet of the north side of the west bridge abutment. As you walk up the creek, look at the Indian mortar and shelter under the north bluff. Within a half-mile west up Turkey Foot Creek from the Sipsey River Bridge, you will see the first beautiful waterfall.

**Collier Creek Falls** – Collier Falls are located just east of the Grayson Sawmill lumber yard. The waterfall was the site of a large gristmill. Two huge stone columns approximately 20 feet high held the waterwheel and are still presently intact. From the Grayson lumber yard, travel east about three-fourths of a mile and follow the hollow to the beautiful falls that plunge into a narrow box canyon.

**Sow Creek Falls** – Sow Creek flows off a rock shelter that completely circles the waterfall. You can stand in the shelter 20 feet behind the waterfall. The fall drops vertically approximately 40 feet into a beautiful pool of water. This waterfall is approximately two miles upstream from Brushy Creek Bridge located on Hickory Grove Road. The creek flows in from the west, thus falls are about 300 yards from Brushy Creek. Drive toward Moreland from Brushy Creek Bridge approximately one and a half miles and turn north on the gravel log road. Finally, one must walk north and travel into the hollow which will also lead to the falls.

**Holmes Chapel Falls** – The falls are located about one-fourth mile west of Rush Creek Bridge on the Mt. Olive Road. There are two routes leading to the falls. One route is the branch that leads to the falls enters Rush Creek on the southwest side of the bridge. Another route entails traveling one-fourth mile west of the bridge and stop at the first log road to the southwest. The falls are located about 200 yards south of the Mt. Olive Road.

**Parker Falls** – Parker Falls are located in a beautiful canyon through which the Parker Branch flows. The falls, which are stair steps, are absolutely beautiful. Parker Falls are in the Sipsey Wilderness near the point where the Winston and Lawrence County lines cross Parker Branch. The upstream portion of Parker Canyon is rugged, but below the falls lies one of the most spectacular old growth found anywhere in Bankhead.

**Indian Tomb Hollow Falls** – Three beautiful, but small waterfalls, are located in the southwestern end of Indian Tomb Hollow. These falls are seasonal but are worth the one mile hike up the canyon.

**Quillan Creek Cascades** – Quillan Creek flows through a rugged, extremely narrow canyon which has high vertical sandstone walls covered with eastern hemlock trees. One could easily throw a rock from one side of the canyon to the other. Near the middle of Quillian Creek Canyon are a beautiful set of cascades flowing through solid sandstone troughs. On the upstream side of the cascades is an Indian rock shelter.

Within the canyons of Bankhead, hundreds of small waterfalls plunge to the canyon floors, some ranging as high as 60 feet. Bankhead is known at the 'Land of a Thousand Waterfalls". During the wet season explore the canyons which bring peace, beauty, and serenity to the few who behold the "Land of a Thousand Waterfalls" in the Warrior Mountains.

*Soogahoagdee Falls, the Creek Indian name for Sow Creek Falls, flows into Brushy Creek in Bankhead Forest.*

## Wildlife Eliminated from the Warrior Mountains

It was the fall of 1890 and the brisk October air was chilled from the early morning frost. Brown's Spring (approximately 100 or more yards from the Old Looney's Tavern Historic Site in Winston County) was flowing with fresh cool water capable of satisfying the thirst of both the hunters and their dogs. Excitement was in the air as the hunting party gathered at the springs located in the eastern portion of Bankhead Forest, and began to organize their day of hunting.

Sidney Walker, my great grandfather, was standing with other members of the party and talking about the day's hunt. The stock of his rabbit-eared muzzle loading shotgun was resting on the ground with him leaning against it for support. One of the big bear and deer hounds stood up against my granddad for a pat on the head. As the big dog dropped back to the ground, one foot caught the rabbit-ear hammer causing the shotgun to discharge into my grandfather's stomach and chest. Sidney died shortly after the accident. He never knew the big game animals he longed to hunt would disappear from the Bankhead Forest within a few years.

This true account is a sad beginning to a story about the demise and disappearance of large game animals, beautiful birds, and majestic trees that once were a vital part of the primeval wilderness of the Warrior Mountains of Lawrence County.

Hunting parties, an important part of wilderness life, provided a means of obtaining meat for hungry families, hides and furs which could be traded for goods, and the thrill of the hunt along with the fellowship of friends and neighbors. However, unregulated hunting practices began taking their toll on the native wildlife. Between 1890 and 1910 big game species were eliminated from the Warrior Mountains by "overhunting". This tragedy is believed to have eliminated wildlife such as the whitetail deer, the black bear, the timber wolf, and the eastern cougar.

## Whitetail Deer

After the last original Warrior Mountains whitetail deer was eliminated from the forest, this herd was restocked with a northern subspecies of deer during the 1920's. Again in the 1990's, deer from South Alabama were restocked in the Black Warrior Wildlife Management Area.

Mr. Rayford Hyatt, past conversation officer of Bankhead, relates an interesting story about the last native deer to be killed in the forest. According to Mr. Hyatt, the last pure blood line deer was a small racked buck that was hunted for two or three days before it was eventually killed. The deer was killed by James M. Flanagin on Hagood Creek in early 1909. Mr. Amos Spillers, one of the first conversation officers of Bankhead Forest, had the antlers of the last known native Bankhead whitetail deer. Many people came to view the antlers of this beloved wildlife creature which was once taken for granted by many in the forest.

## Timber Wolf

According to Mr. Hyatt, the last known timber wolf of Bankhead was killed during snowy weather in the Hurricane Creek area in 1910 by William Straud Riddle. William Straud Riddle, the son of Jonson (Rake) Riddle and Martha, was at least ¾ Cherokee Indian. His father was a full blood and his mother was ½ Cherokee.

The wolf had killed several sheep owned by a Mr. Sewell who resided south of Grayson. After hunting and tracking the wolf in the snow nearly all day, the hunt ended without success. As Mr. Riddle started home toward the western side of Sipsey River, he found fresh wolf tracks in the snow. After tracking the animal a short distance, he saw the wolf standing next to a huge hollow log where it denned. Once the wolf was shot and killed, it was taken home and placed in a standing position before it became stiff. Many people came to see the carcass before it was finally discarded.

In the early days of the county, wolf scalps could be used in the payment of taxes. Notice in the following law:

*ACTS OF ALABAMA 1835 SESSION. ACT NO. 123 Pages 119,120*

*"After passage of this Act, it shall be lawful for Tax Collectors of Franklin and Lawrence Counties to receive all wolf scalps in payment of any county tax due from any person in the county, on prior affidavit made before an acting Justice of the Peace that the wolves were killed in Franklin or Lawrence County, as the case may be – Scalps received at the following rate; all scalps under one year $1.00; all scalps one year and upward $1.50; Tax Collector of each county to return affidavits with scalps to the County Treasurer as money for any county tax due from them as tax collectors – no money to be paid out for scalps; only receive scalps in payment of taxes."*

Three species of wolves were known to exist in Bankhead Forest; grey, black, and red wolves. This last known black wolf was shot in 1917 and is now considered extinct. The red wolf is recovering from the verge of extinction with one small pack re-established in Cades Cove of the Smokey Mountains National Park. The timber or grey wolf is found only in the northern portion of the United States.

**Bear and Panther**

The black bear and eastern cougar were eliminated from Bankhead as a breeding population in the early 1900's. Specific information about the demise of the last bear and cougar in Bankhead is unknown, however, many mountaineers tell stories of encounters their grandparents had with bears and panthers during the early 1800's. Reports of bears and cougars still persist to this very day, but no known population of either exists in the Warrior Mountains. It is estimated that some 30 wild eastern cougars still roam the swamps of Florida and rank as the most endangered animal in the Southeastern United States.

## Elk

The eastern elk migrated to the Appalachian Mountains into Alabama in the early 1800's. The elk were rapidly eliminated by Indian and early settler hunters. The eastern elk were killed out in the state of Tennessee by 1870. No known record exists on the demise of eastern elk in the Warrior Mountains.

## Eastern Bison or Buffalo

The eastern bison or buffalo ranged from the Great Lakes into Alabama. The eastern buffalo was much larger than the western buffalo was very black. The last known eastern bison were killed in West Virginia 1825. Herds of thousands of eastern buffalo roamed the Cumberland and Tennessee River Valleys during the 1700's.

## Passenger Pigeon

Passenger pigeons were beautiful birds that once filled the skies and woodlands of the Warrior Mountains. Old-timers have passed down stories of passengers pigeons. The birds were extremely abundant and flocks containing thousands of birds roosted in mature hardwoods. The passenger pigeons, much larger but similar to an oversize mourning dove, would use the same roost for years. One such roost existing in the northern portion of Bankhead was near the forks of Thompson and West Flint Creeks, at the site of the old Jake Alexander Place (now Dallas Yeager's farm). Other places in surrounding areas immortalized the name of the passenger pigeon by being named "Pigeon Roost."

The pigeons were smoked out at night while on the roost by huge bond fires. They were also shot and killed at their nesting sites. Eventually, this beautiful wilderness bird was eliminated from Bankhead Forest with the last verified flock appearance in Alabama in 1893. Eight of these birds were killed before this flock of some three hundred birds flew away never to return to our state. The last known passenger pigeon died while in captivity on September 1, 1914, at the Cincinnati Zoological Garden. This wilderness bird that once fed on the giant chestnut, oak, beech in Bankhead Forest is now extinct.

## Ivory-billed Woodpecker

The ivory-billed woodpecker, another large bird once native to the Warrior Mountains, is on the verge of extinction due to habitat destruction as well as needless killings. The last known ivory-billed woodpecker in Alabama died about 1906. The bird met its fate at the hands of a hunter who probably never considered his kill would be the last of the species reported from our state.

The ivory-billed woodpecker's form was mystic and immortalized by prehistoric Alabama Indians who engraved its image on stone plates, handles of axes, and other ornaments of the Mississippian culture. If our modern ancestors had cared that much for this bird of mystery, our children today might have been blest not only by sight of the bird but also by the sound of its hammering beak in the hills and hollows of the Warrior Mountains.

**Carolina Parakeet**

The Carolina Parakeet was probably the most colorful and beautiful bird to inhibit our county. In early 1819, Ann Royalle describes flocks of the birds in Lawrence County with their beautiful green and yellow plumage. The fatal flaw of the Carolina Parakeet was their love for ripening fruit and corn. When one bird was wounded, the others would hover to help. This endeavor caused the whole flock to become easy prey. Eventually, the Carolina Parakeet was totally wiped out, never to be seen again in the Warrior Mountains.

**American Chestnut**

The American Chestnut, the largest nut producing tree in North America, was once abundant in Bankhead. It is now sometimes found as only a small sapling or tree struggling for survival. With some documented to be 13 feet in diameter, these giant nut producers once claimed, if in a pure stand, millions of acres of timber land in the eastern United States.

In about 1910, Chinese Chestnuts, which carried the deadly chestnut blight, were imported into New York. The mistake proved to be very costly. By the late 1930's, the blight had spread like wild fire down the eastern coast killing all the American Chestnuts in its path. Chestnuts of the Warrior Mountains also fell victim to the terrible blight. The Indians, early settlers, and wildlife of Bankhead once utilized the bountiful production of nuts from the majestic chestnut. Today, the American chestnut survives as a frail sprout in the Warrior Mountains.

**Old Growth Hardwoods**

Today, the demise of our old growth southeastern hardwood forest continues at the hands of clear-cutting experts of the U.S. Forest Service and the timber industry. If changes are not soon forthcoming, our native old growth hardwood forest will be replaced by the pine plantations of modern free farmers. According to the original field surveys of 1817, the vast majority of the vegetation of Bankhead was mature old growth hardwoods of oak, hickory, and chestnut.

Now 100 years since the death of an early Bankhead hunter in 1890, I look back with grief and sadness at the devastation we have wreaked upon our beautiful forest and its wildlife. But as the mighty American Chestnut reduced to its frail existence as a lowly shrub returns year and year from sprouts of the life giving stump again to claim its glory, I hope new eco-warriors will arise to fight for the protection of our beloved land known as the Warrior Mountains.

## Interesting Places of the Warrior Mountains

**Sipsey Wilderness**

Sipsey Wilderness is found in the southwestern portion of Lawrence County. Many people enjoy the beauty of Lawrence County's greatest resource, the Sipsey Wilderness Area of Bankhead Forest that lies in the heart of the Warrior Mountains. Sipsey River Picnic Grounds are located on Sipsey River near the Cranal Road, the south border of the wilderness. Many people not only hike in the wilderness, but also drive along Highway 33 and the Cranal Road to enjoy the fall colors and splendors of the Sipsey Wilderness.

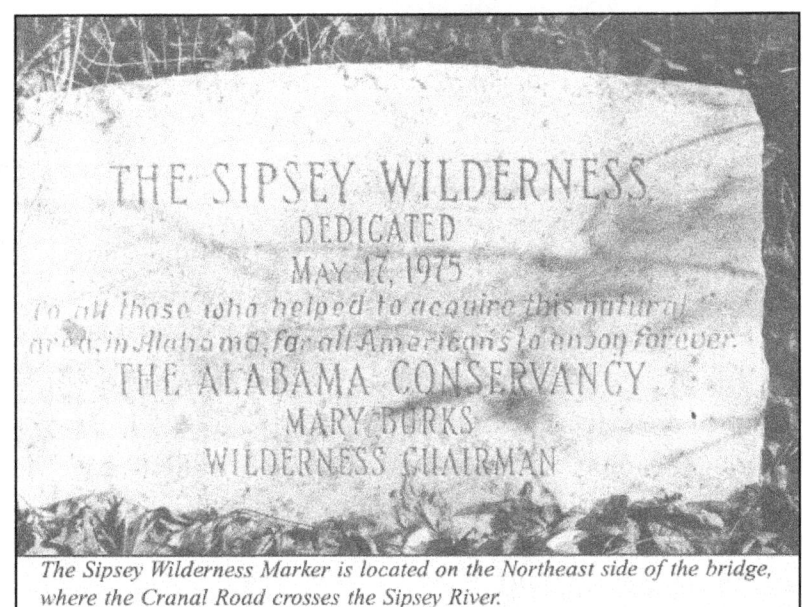

The Sipsey Wilderness Marker is located on the Northeast side of the bridge, where the Cranal Road crosses the Sipsey River.

*Bee Branch Falls in the Sipsey Wilderness Area are well worth the six to eight hour hike.*

Sightseeing, hiking, canoeing, and horseback riding are only a few of the many outdoor recreational activities available to Lawrence County residents, as well as visitors from all over the Southeastern United States. The Sipsey Wilderness is the place for those who want to get away from modern conveniences without the sound of traffic, telephones, and TV's, but instead listening to the songs of warblers, the hammering beaks of woodpeckers, the hoot of the great horned owl, the howl of a lone coyote, and the sound of water running over rocks and boulders in the many streams flowing through this portion of the Warrior Mountains. Avid outdoorsmen cherish the stimulating sounds, sights, and smells that only mother nature can provide to those who visit the Sipsey Wilderness.

The U.S. Forest Service has designated and established trails for hiking, horseback riding, and horse or mule drawn wagons. These trails and roads provide access to secluded sandstone cliffs, wonderful waterfalls, fantastic fall foliage, beautiful wildflowers, and tremendous trees. Designated hiking trails begin at Borden Creek Bridge on the Bunyan Hill Road, Sipsey River Picnic Area, and at Thompson Creek Bridge on the Northwest Road. A hiker can spend a few hours or a few days hiking the trail systems in Sipsey Wilderness. Mc Dougal Hunter's Camp is a campground for those hunting or hiking in the area. A system of horse trails begins at Owl Creek Horse Camp and contain many miles of connected riding loops. The new addition to Sipsey Wilderness can be used by horse or mule drawn wagons. The wilderness access to wagons could provide rides for young, old, and disabled individuals through the most scenic portion of our Warrior Mountains.

In addition to various types of trails and roads in the Sipsey Wilderness Area, primitive wilderness camping is available to those who really want to get away without driving for hours. Two sites which I would strongly recommend for wilderness camping is Bee Branch and Ship Rock a totally isolated area with great sandstone bluffs and shelters located on either side of the canyons.

# McDowell Cove

McDowell Cove of Bankhead Forest is located primarily in Section 4 Township 8 South and Range 8 West. McDowell Cove is on the upper drainages of Flanagin Creek and is one of the most beautiful canyons in the Warrior Mountains of Lawrence County. The Cove lies between Mountain Springs Road on the eastern ridge, Gum Pont Road located on the western ridge, and the Ridge Road on the northern ridge.

In the center of McDowell Cove, an Indian mound is found in the front yard of Jack McDowell's old log house. The flat level top of the mound actually lies immediately east of the dog trot style log cabin. The sides of the mound only rise some four to five feet at the highest point. Around the mound, numerous flakes of flint can be found. Throughout McDowell Cove, flint provides evidence of long term occupation of the cove by Indian inhabitants.

*Celeste Walker, daughter of the author, stands against the State Champion Yellow Poplar in Bee Branch Canyon.*

The area has been known as Wallis Cove, Wilkerson Cove and after many of the other families that inhabited the area in the past; however, since Jack McDowell was the first Forest Ranger of Bankhead and one of the last to make the Cove his home, the area is widely accepted as being McDowell Cove.

Wallis Cemetery, named after some of the Cove's first residents, contains the graves of four Civil War soldiers. Two old houses still stand in the flat valley – Jack McDowell's home and the Wilkerson home. The old Sally Ann House was sold to a Mr. Norman Tidwell from Winston County and moved during 1993. Open pasture or farm land located in the Cove is privately owned.

# Bee Branch Canyon

Bee Branch of the Sipsey Wilderness Area is located primarily in Section 26 of Township 8 South, Range 9 West. Bee Branch is a deep canyon located east of Sipsey River. The area is probably the most primeval site in the Warrior Mountains. Most of the canyon was protected by the U.S. Forest Service as early as 1919.

Bee Branch is a forked canyon with seasonal and beautiful waterfalls in each fork. The Bee Branch Falls plunge from 50 feet above the canyon floor. Both forks are virtually box canyons forming a small creek that flows into Sipsey River. The eastern fork of the canyon features the largest yellow poplar in the Southeastern United States. The whole canyon is a botanical garden of a virgin gorge in the Warrior Mountains.

**Tar Springs Hollow**

Located in the upper portion of Capsey Creek, once known as Capp's Creek, is a place not found elsewhere in William B. Bankhead National Forest. The creek begins at Cave Springs on Highway 41 and on the Leola Road at Basham Shelter and Spring. The area, not noted for the two head water springs, is unique because of the two springs downstream in the middle of the big hollow. This unusual site found on Capsey Creek is known as Tar Springs Hollow.

Capsey Creek is a tributary to Brushy Creek which empties its waters into Sipsey River on Smith Lake. The Tar Springs Hollow on Capsey Creek contains two mineral tar springs which are located about once quarter mile apart in the southwest ¼ of Section 26, Township 8 South, and Range 6 West.

According to the Alabama Geological Survey as reported by geologist Jonathan Hunter and made available by Mr. Leon Hightower, "These springs years ago were places of a resort for the afflicted who drank their waters and swallowed their tar or maltha, made into pills, and supposed that they were greatly benefitted thereby. The hotel and cottages for the accommodations of the visitors to these springs are said to have stood on the hill just south of this lower spring. Both of these springs, however, have been spoiled by blasting them for asphaltum."

The article also indicated that barrels of tar were collected in holes made in the floor of the springs and shipped off. In addition to the Tar Springs, oil wells were drilled in 1865 and 1867 that were between 700 and 800 feet deep. The geological survey reports that Jonathan Watson probably drilled and got oil out of the wells in Tar Springs Hollow.

According to material furnished by Mr. Rayford Hyatt, the Tar Springs Hollow Road was on route many settlers and visitors took to the Tar Springs Resort. The early road lead from Melton's Bluff to Oakville, then to Poplar Log Cove where the road forked. The eastern fork was the main route and was the Black Warriors' Path or Mitchell Trace. The south fork became known as the Tar Springs Hollow Road or Double Springs Road and traveled south up Wiggins Hollow. The road crossed the High Town Path east of Center Church and passed down a long ridge into Tar Springs Hollow.

From the 1800's through the early 19000's, prior to the National Forest status the land has today, many people lived in the area of Tar Springs Hollow. Cave Springs Cemetery and Center Cemetery contain the remains of many who called the Tar Springs Hollow area home.

It appears from examinations of the tombstones in Cave Springs and Center Cemetery, that many of the people were descendants of the Creek and Cherokee Indians, the earlier inhabitants of the area. Many of the family names of those who presently compose the Lawrence County Indian population are found in the old cemeteries.

The family names at Center Cemetery include Osborn, Smith, Williams, McVay, Hampton, Jackson, Steele, Holley, Looney, Wood, Eddy, Asherbranner, Poole, Burnett, Hogan, Rooks, Kelsoe, Johnson, Cooper, and many others. These family names still persist in the southeastern part of Lawrence County.

In the area of Tar Springs, the forest seemed eternal except for the destructive clear cutting activity. In the late evening as the eerie sounds of a screech owl were emerging from the forest, it was hard for me to imagine how the area might have looked when the hotel and cottages within the rugged canyon were alive with people seeking the healing powers of the Tar Springs in the heart of the Warrior Mountains.

**Poplar Log Cove**

Poplar Log Cove of the Warrior Mountains is located primarily in Section 10 of Township 8 South and Range 6 West. Poplar Log Cove is on the upper portion of the West Fork of Flint Creek in Lawrence County's northeastern portion of Bankhead Forest. Black Warriors' Path traversed through the Cove and passed by the Poplar Log Cove Spring which forms the headwaters of West Flint Creek.

Based on archaeological evidence, Poplar Log Cove was utilized by Indian people as early as the Paleo Period. A Paleo scarper and Decatur Point were found and identified near the center of the Cove. Poplar Log Cove was settled in the early 1800's by Indian mixed-bloods and white people. The Cove was flat with broad fertile valleys which were farmed in patches of cotton and corn. Today, most of Poplar Log Cove is privately owned but remains one of the most beautiful valleys of the Warrior Mountains.

## Indian Tomb Hollow

Indian Tomb Hollow is located primarily in Section 2 Township 8 South, Range 7 West on the northern edge of William B. Bankhead National Forest. In the distant hollows of Indian Tomb, the wood hen can be heard as the evening sun sinks behind the bluffs. Three gracious waterfalls of the southwest fork echo eternal sounds that formed the sandstone canyon containing vertical walls reaching to the sky. Looking down the canyon toward the northeast sandstone bluffs on either side of the canyon causes one to be in awe of the area because of its beauty.

Early settlers and Indian mixed-bloods settled to the north and west of the hollow's southwestern fork. Several folks lived for a while in the old High House located on a small knoll at the mouth of Indian Tomb. Families of the Warrior Mountains would enter the hollow from Chestnut Ridge, Beulah, and High House Hill not only to view and enjoy the beauty of the area, but to dig roots, herbs, and hunt. It was in this same tradition that I was first introduced by my granddad Arthur Wilburn, to the mysterious but beautiful Indian Tomb Hollow.

Mr. G. H. Melson tells of experiences he had as a small boy in Indian Tomb Hollow and is a wealth of information concerning an Indian fight occurring near the mouth of the famous canyon. He tells of his father working on the old plantation and passing down stories through many generations about the Indians of the area, the black slave cemetery, and the early settlers who called the area home.

Over many years, the Gillespie family has traditionally been drawn to Indian Tomb. Not only does the family consider the area a sacred Indian burial site, but their ancestor, James Richard Gillespie, a veteran of the Creek Indian War, is buried in the Gillespie Cemetery. In addition, Gillespie Spring and Gillespie Creek, which runs through Indian Tomb Hollow, are named after the Gillespie Family of Lawrence County.

The ancient beech trees of Indian Tomb are a record of family traditions which have spanned over 200 years of time. From early Indian drawings and settler names, the beeches of Indian Tomb bear record of visitation. The markings also indicate that much of the time spent in Indian Tomb was recorded in the numerous beech carvings located throughout the canyon. In addition, the Indian Marker Tree in Indian Tomb Hollow is a symbol considered sacred by the descendants of those who once roamed the beautiful valley.

A story called the "Battle of Indian Tomb Hollow" or "Ittaloknak" was originally printed in The Moulton Democrat in November 1856. The articles compose a beautiful love story that describes a fierce fight in Indian Tomb between the Creek and Chickasaw inhabitants of the Warrior Mountains.

*Rickey Butch Walker, the author, shows respect to the Indian Marker Tree in Indian Tomb Hollow.*

**Narrows Ridge**

Narrow Ridge is located in Bankhead Forest in Section 21 of Township 8 South and Range 8 West. While walking south on a ridge from the Northwest Road, suddenly a high narrow strip of land emerges between two beautiful old growth hardwood valleys. The valley to the east was the Borden Creek Canyon and the valley to the west was the Flanagin Creek Canyon. The old settler road along the top of the ridge continued along the slender natural bridge of sandstone rock connecting the two mountaintop ridges which divided the beautiful creek bottoms. To either side of the old road were the edges of bluffs which rose some 40 to 60 feet above the two hardwood valleys.

The narrow ridge runs in a north-south direction for approximately 100 yards narrowing to as little as some 12 feet wide. The unique and beautiful ridge is known to most local people as the "Narrows Ridge." Narrows Ridge is now in the Sipsey Addition to the Wilderness Area which will provide protection for the beautiful hardwood valleys on either side of this natural ridge.

It appears that early settlers in the area south of Narrows Ridge were also forced to use the connecting strip of rock to get to their valley farms and crops located near the forks of Borden and Flanagin Creeks. The Henderson Family and Parker Family, whose descendants still live in the Moulton area, have roots in the Borden Creek portion of the area. The Gooder Walker family had crops and farm land along the western portion of the area along lower Flanagin Creek.

The road leading to Narrows Ridge is about ¼ mile east of the Mountain Springs Road. The log road runs south from the Northwest Road's highest point between Borden Creek and Flanagin Creek. About ½ mile west of Borden Creek, the log road turns south and runs ¾ mile prior to reaching Narrows Ridge. Narrows Ridge is a unique but beautiful spot in the Warrior Mountains.

**King Cove**

*Celeste Walker sits next to the mortor rock of King Cove.*

King Cove is located in Township 8 South, Range 9 West in Sections 22 and 27 of the southwestern portion of Lawrence County. King Cove lies adjacent to the forks of Hubbard and Thompson Creeks which is the beginning of Sipsey River in the western portion of Bankhead Forest. The King Cove extends up Thompson Creek to the forks of Tedford and Mattox (Thompson). Ship rock is found at the southern end of King Cove and is just east of the forks of Hubbard and Thompson.

King Cove shows evidence of early Indian habitation. Mortar Rock, located to the north across the creek from Ship Rock, contains five mortar holes and a huge nutting stone used by early Indian people. Local folklore tells of numerous arrowheads and spear points picked up in the old creek bottom fields.

**Parker Cove**

Parker Cove is located in Section 30 of Township 7 South and Range 7 West and is named from the Parker family who settled the cove long ago. Parker Cove forms the headwater streams of Elam Creek on the north-central edge of Bankhead Forest. The cove still contains three old log houses that were used over 100 years ago. When going south on Highway 33, the main entrance to Parker Cove is along the first steep winding road turning east off of Wren Mountain. The deep cove is visible east of the Wren Mountain portion of the Wilderness Parkway which runs through the center of the Warrior Mountains.

**Blankenship Cove**

The lower portion of Blankenship Cove is still an active cattle farming site and is located primarily in Section 2 of Township 8 South and Range 8 West on the upper portion of Borden Creek. The cove was originally called Borden Cove, settled by the family of Christopher Borden. The upper portion of Blankenship Cove extends through the northeast part of Sections 34 and 35 of Township 7 South and Range 8 West. Some of the Borden Family originally settled along portions of the cove adjacent to Borden Creek. The cove is presently owned by Glenn Whisenant, who bought the property from the heirs of his Granddaddy Willis Blankenship. Two areas of the Blankenship Cove were known as the upper place and the lower place. Willis Blankenship lived on the lower place.

Ownership of land in the early days of settlement gave priority in naming some of the Coves of Bankhead. Many of the coves still found in Bankhead are beautiful isolated islands of open land nestled in the heart of the Warrior Mountains.

**Ship Rock**

Ship rock is located in the Sipsey Wilderness Area in Section 27 of Township 8 South and Range 9 West. The large rock is located some 200 yards east of the forks of Hubbard and Thompson Creeks in the heart of the Sipsey Wilderness. The site is known as Ship Rock, Herron Point, Boat Rock, Needle's Eye, or the Windows. The following text is a descriptive but symbolic version of the Ship Rock of Sipsey.

The mighty Ship Rock of the Black Warrior is sailing east dragging the mountains and canyons of unspeakable beauty through the universe. In front of her awesome sandstone bow is the Tugboat Rock of the forest leading the way and breaking the bonds of time to allow the Ship Rock to meet her destiny beyond the knowledge of humankind. The Tugboat Rock is always at her bow never allowing her voyage to be slowed by the forces of time. Near the stern of tugboat rock is the Needle's Eye which focuses the last easterly flowing rays caught from the westerly setting sun to provide the brief sailing light toward the east before darkness again dims the mighty ship's journey. Thousands of years ago, the forces of time blasted the hole called the Windows or Needle's Eye at the stern of Tugboat Rock yet undaunted the little sandstone tug maintains a true course guiding the mighty Ship Rock through the earth's celestial sphere.

*Brandy and Celeste Walker sit at the bow of the great Ship Rock of the Warrior Mountains.*

Out of Hubbard Creek Canyon, and through the middle of King Cove, she sails leaving a deep botanical trough and solid standing waves of sandstone which begin to close at the falling waters of Parker, Quillan, and Kinlock. The waterfalls of the Warrior Mountains send the melodious sound waves of the true wilderness lapping at her sides. At the bow of Ship Rock, the crest rises high, creating vast depressions of beautiful valleys through which the Sipsey and Thompson waters flow. Forever eastward toward the rising sun, dawns a new day for her forested sea. She plows and pulls the high bluffs as she churns constantly through the land of a thousand waterfalls. From the botanical gardens of the limestone valleys, to the hardwood ridges of the sandstone slopes, she has sailed from before the time of the dinosaurs toward eternity with the timeless canyons of the Warrior Mountains lashed firmly to her stern.

Ship Rock has a great deck nearly 1,000 feet in length and over 100 feet wide. Her bow is a sharp rising crest which rides high in the waves of the air reaching nearly 60 feet above first contact with her timbered and stony sea. Her stern is broad with the great force of Mother Nature driving her through the mountainous sea, always leaving the beginning of Sipsey in her wake. Her sides, adorned with big flowered trillium, Virginia bluebells, blue cohosh, and Dutchman's breeches, rise some 50 feet to the mountain laurel and Virginia pine covered deck.

*Celeste and Brandy Walker stand at the base of the Needle's Eye or Windows in King Cove.*

Ship Rock is a moment in time and a symbol of persistence before the age of the great reptilian dinosaurs, the age of the gigantic mammals, and the age of the red man who once inhabited her great forested seas. No time, force, or age is her master, for God is her pilot and only he knows her true destiny. As God spins the eternal swirl of the universe, Ship Rock holds steady while dragging the Warrior Mountains along with the rest of the world.

Where is the huge Ship Rock, the Tugboat Rock, and the Needle's Eye? These geologic wonders are woven into the fabric of Lawrence County's Warrior Mountains. The magnificent weaver left his Needle's Eye as a guide for those who may think they are lost to the great ship and the little tug. Now for directions: From the Byler road, turn east on the Northwest Road and go to the dead end at Thompson Creek Bridge. Take the wilderness trail which turns south down the east side of the beautiful Thompson Creek Canyon. You will hike about one and a half hours before you see a large hole in the face of the bluff just prior to reaching the forks of Thompson and Hubbard Creeks. You have arrived at the Ship Rock of the Warrior Mountains.

**Kinlock Rock Shelter**

Kinlock Rock Shelter is located in Section 31 of Township 8 South and Range 9 West. The shelter is one of the largest of its kind with an overhang of sandstone rock some 250 feet wide, 30 to 100 feet deep, and 30 to 150 feet high.

The Indian shelter is a premier petroglyph site of prehistoric Indian occupation. The sacred Indian shelter is still actively used by American Indians for ceremonies. Kinlock Bluff Shelter should be nominated to the National Register of Historic Places.

*Kinlock Rock Shelter is considered by many local folks as a sacred Indian site.*

**Pine Torch Church**

The oldest original log church in the State of Alabama is located on the Pine Torch Road in Bankhead Forest in Section 29 of Township 8 South and Range 7 West. The old poplar log church was originally moved from Holmes Chapel, east of Brushy Lake, and reassembled. The log church is 24 feet wide and 27 feet long, and is over 170 years old. The first logs were hand hewed in the early 1820's by the Holmes and Nicholson family (1820 Census of Lawrence County). It was originally used for worship services by the congregation known as "Hard-shell Baptists." Blazing pine knots were used to light the church at night. Thus, the church was named Pine Torch.

Dr. Charles Borden comments on the protection of the historic Pine Torch Church: *"The Pine Torch Preservation Society, of which I am president, was formed in 1981 to preserve and perpetuate the historical attributes and uses of this memorable part of our heritage."*

*Pinetorch Church and Cemetery*

# Chapter Two

# Families of Range 6 West

The Warrior Mountains extend from Highway 41 at Piney Grove in the southeastern corner of Lawrence County to the Byler Road area on the southwest side of the county. The mountainous territory where the families of Range 6 West lived extends through Townships 7, 8, and 9 West. Included in the central portion of this area is Buzzard Roost Mountain south of Speake, Poplar Log Cove, Center Church, and upper portions of Capsey Creek.

## Newt Hill Family of Buzzard Roost Mountain

**John Hill**

Recently, I visited with Mr. Newt Hill of the Speake Community, my distant relative. Mr. Hill's great-grandfather, John Hill, Sr., came to the Bankhead area from Georgia. John Hill, Sr., born in 1795, moved into the Sipsey River portion of Winston County. According to the 1860 Census of Winston County, the following children were living in the John Hill, Sr. household: Mary E., 25; Robert A., 21; Nancy., 6; and Samuel., 3.

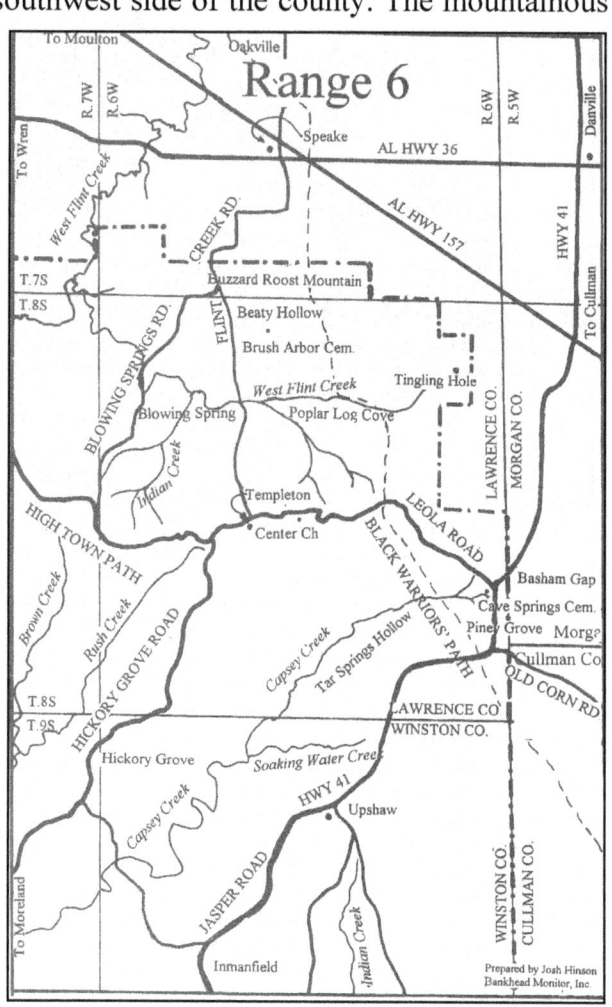

John Hill, Sr.'s son, John Hill, Jr., was born in Georgia in 1830, and also lived in Winston County near his father. John Hill, Jr. was the postmaster in Winston County and carried mail from Double Springs to Jasper, Alabama. He is listed in one of the old ledgers kept at Natural Bridge in Winston County.

In 1860, John Jr.'s family consisted of the following: his wife, Manervia C. ., Angeline Elizabeth (Betty), my great-great-grandmother, born on October 2, 1855; and William S. Hill who was two years old. Newt Hill's daddy, John Hill III was born about 1865 and lived to be 89 years, 6 months, and 20 days old. The other children of John and Manervia were Bob, Dallas, Julie, Martha, and Osa. Betty Hill married Jim Johnson and they were my great-great-grandparents.

*Elizabeth Angeline (Betty) Hill (1/4 Creek)*

Based on census records, it appears the John Hill family moved into the Bankhead Forest portion of Alabama in 1855. According to family legend, all of the Hill family were Scot-Irish and Creek Indian descent. My great-great grandmother, Betty Hill, and her brothers and sisters were one-fourth Creek Indians.

Mr. Newt Hill's daddy was a third generation of John Hill. John Hill III married Martha Allred who was one-half Creek Indian; therefore, Newt's family has strong ties to the Indian people of Lawrence and Winston County.

**Newt's Early Years**

Newt Hill was born January 6, 1902, at the foot Cedar Mountain just south of Highway 36 on the Henry Alexander place. Newt said his father, John Hill, was born, raised, and married in the same house on the Sipsey River between Highway 33 and Highway 278 in Winston County. He said the house was at the location of the singing Spears family. John Hill III owned some 200 acres of land in Sections 29, 30, and 32 of Township 10 South and Range 7 West. The land was located where Highway 278 crosses present day Smith Lake.

The Hill family migrated from Winston County to Lawrence County prior to 1900. Mr. Newt's older sister was born on Brushy Creek between the old Matt Pearson place and the Pine Torch Road. Originally, Newt's family lived near the Jim Wilson place west of the Old Man Rodgers place on Brushy Creek. The Rodgers home was on the Leola Road about ¼ mile east of the junction of the Pinhook Gap Road and the Leola Road. The road the Hills lived on turned at the Rogers place and wound downhill to Brushy Creek, past the Wilson home where it fords the creek. The road continued west by the old Matt Pearson place to join Pine Torch Road about two miles southeast of Highway 33. Today, part of the old road is just a dim log road hardly recognizable as an old country settler and wagon road.

Mr. Newt's daddy lived two years in the Brushy Creek area at the Jim Wilson place on the east side of Brushy Creek, and later between the Matt Pearson old place and Pine Torch Road. During that time

*Newt Hill (3/8 Creek)*

John Hill III was a share cropper and tenant farmer. From the Brush Creek-Pine Torch area, John Hill moved to the Henry Alexander place where Newt was born. After tenant farming on the Henry Alexander place for a couple of years, John Hill moved back to Winston County and later to Walker County. When Newt Hill was five years old, John Hill moved back to Lawrence County and lived in the valley.

Newt and Arthur Wilburn, who was my granddaddy, were cousins and use to stay together a lot. Newt helped Arthur and my great-grandfather, Sandy Wilburn, make a crop. Newt and Arthur stayed together many nights. For fun, Arthur and Newt would ride the family bull. They would tie a saddle to the big bull and hang on for dear life. Sometimes both boys would try to ride the bull at the same time. The boys were always thrown. At other times, Newt and Arthur would hunt many miles with a $1.50 rifle. Newt said the 22 caliber brass-line rifle shot awfully good. The young hunters would bring in lots of game taken with the little single shot rifle.

## Newt's School Days

Newt did not have the opportunity to attend school as a youngster. When he was eighteen years old, Ms. Pullar Alexander, a teacher at Pinhook, made a deal with Newt, Nobe Johnson, Buster Williams, and another friend. The young men had never attended school and could not write their names. Ms. Alexander promised them if they would start to school the following Monday, she would teach them to read and write their name. Ms. Alexander told the young men she would provide them a primer. Newt did not want to go, but told her he would attend. Newt, being a man of his word, got up Monday morning and went to school. The other boys who had made the promise never showed up. Newt said he would have given anything in the world to get back to the house that first morning. After completing the day, Newt said he enjoyed his first day of school.

*Newt and Ida Miller Hill (1/4 Cherokee)*

The old Pinhook School house was one big room with two teachers—one teacher at each end of the building. Guy Aldridge and Pullar Alexander were the teachers at Pinhook during Newt's school days.

Money ran out the first week Newt attended school. There were not enough students willing or able to pay the ten cents a day per scholar to complete the school term. Therefore, school was closed after Newt attended four one-half days of school. The last half day Newt played ball since he joined the team his first week of school. Mr. Newt said he liked school enough that he would have paid his fees if enough of the other students would have paid to continue school; however, in 1920, Newt was then eighteen years old and needed to work. Newt did learn to write his name but without practice soon forgot.

## Newt's Adult Life

Newt Hill married Ida Miller in 1923 at the Decatur Courthouse. Ida Miller was born and raised near the junction of Leola Road and Owl Creek Road, near what is now known as the Garvin Garrison place. Initially, Ida Miller attended Poplar Springs School. Poplar Springs School was located about one-eighth mile east of the junction of Leola Road and Pinhook Gap Road, which runs by Beulah Church. The school was located on the northeast side Leola Road, west of High House Hill Road. The school was near the beginning of Old Brushy Creek Road which went to the Jim Wilson and Old Matt Pearson place. According to Newt, Poplar Springs was a small log building used as an elementary grade school and had been closed over seventy years. Ida finished going to school at Lindsey hall, a one room school and church.

Ms. Ida's parents were Daniel Miller and Mary Jane Williams, who was ½ Cherokee Indian. They owned one hundred and twenty-five acres of land on Dillashaw Mountain between Leola Road and Lee Creek on the Alexander Motorway. After Ida's father died, the family lost all their land.

After Newt and Ida married, they initially moved to the Enon Road. Newt and his wife stayed at Enon until he purchased seventy acres of rolling land just north of Buzzard Roost Mountain in October of 1949. Newt and Ida had the following children: Felton; Grady Alton; Lois Essie; Hazel; Tollise; Johnny; Rayburn (R.B.); and Eloise.

## Hill-Kelsoe Connection

Three of Newt's daughters married three brothers, who were the sons of Eric Bradley Kelsoe and Mattie Lou Dover. The Kelsoe sons and Hill daughters were married as follows: Marlin married Lois, Eric Junior married Hazel, and Edward married Eloise.

Eric Bradley Kelsoe was the son of William Todd (Boss) Kelsoe and Mary Teague, who was ½ Cherokee Indian. Boss, who was also ¼ Cherokee, and Mary Kelsoe had the following children: William Riley (Will), John, Paralee, Claude, Lawrence, Ava, David Crockett, Clyde, Eric, and Grace.

In addition, the other two daughters of Newt's married brothers as follows: Essie married Sam Montgomery and Tollise first marked Hal Montgomery. Also, Newt's son, Grady Alton Hill, married the daughter of David Crockett Kelsoe, Celia Mae Kelsoe. David Crockett Kelsoe married Enzie Chaney whose mother,

*William Todd (Boss) Kelso, 1/8 Cherokee and Mary Teague, 1/2 Cherokee.*

Dora Hill, was also ½ Creek Indian; therefore, members of the Hill-Kelsoe families are mixed-blood Indian people of Creek and Cherokee ancestry.

**Newt's Working Days**

On his farm, Newt raised cotton, corn, and hay. He first worked his crops with mules and would make from nine to eleven bales of cotton per year working from 18 to 20 acres. During his early years of farming, he never used fertilizer. Later he traded for an old tractor which broke down after the first year; however, Newt planted more cotton and ginned twenty-five bales of cotton his first year using that old tractor. The great harvest gave Newt the fever for "big" farming. He bought a new tractor the next year and ginned fifty-five bales of cotton.

Newt worked at Tom Poole's sawmill after crops were laid by, and during the winter when he could not farm. Newt's last sawmill work for Tom Poole's sawmill, located in Poplar Log Cove, was in 1952.

Mr. Newt Hill is an avid hunter. When the wildlife refuge first opened in Bankhead Forest, Newt Hill was extremely disappointed in his fellow hunters. During the first part of the hunt, he found many illegal doe deer shot and left in the woods to rot. Newt also liked to hunt wild plants such as ginseng, star root, and golden seal. Coon, squirrel and deer hunting were Newt's favorite types of game to hunt.

Today, Mr. Newt Hill still lives on his farm some three miles south of Speake School. He still had the desire to hunt as evidenced by the several weeks he deer hunted this past season. Newt looks forward to many more years of hunting and enjoying life.

## Families of Beaty Hollow

Beaty Hollow is a beautiful isolated cove in the headwater drainage of McDaniel Creek located in the Northwestern portion of Section 3 in Township 8 South and Range 6 West. The cove was crossed by one of the first roads that was used as a post route through the Indian country. The route became known as Mitchell Trace but was earlier known as Black Warriors' Path or Black Warrior Town Trail.

Presently Lamar Marshall, owner and publisher of the Bankhead Monitor magazine, owns and lives in Beaty Hollow. Some 30 acres of the cove is still in open pasture land and is surrounded on three sides by U.S. Forest Service property within Bankhead Forest.

## Thomas A. Beaty

The family of Thomas Alexander Beaty, who was born in 1810 in North Carolina, moved to the northern edge of Poplar Log Cove in 1847. Thomas and his wife Nancy, who was born in South Carolina in 1822, came from Charleston, South Carolina. More than likely the family traveled along the High Town Path from Charleston to Lawrence County, since that is the basic route of the trail.

According to the Lawrence County Census of 1850, Thomas and Nancy had three children: Nancy C. born in North Carolina in 1846, John Jackson born in Alabama 1848, and Benjamin born in Alabama in 1849. At the time of the census, Mary A. Griffin, who was probably a sister to Thomas' wife, also lived with Thomas and Nancy Beaty. In the 1860 census,

Right: *Lamar Marshall, founder of the Bankhead Monitor, sits on a log in the middle of Black Warriors' Path near Poplar Log Cove.*

Thomas A. and Nancy Beaty had the following children: Nancy C., John J., George, Martha, and Frances Cornelia Beaty. Benjamin probably died between 1850 and 1860.

Prior to and during the Civil War, Thomas Alexander Beaty, a tanner of leather goods, accumulated a great deal of silver and gold which he had stashed away in Poplar Log Cove. For years, Ed Hogan reported his father John Hogan knew of the accumulated wealth of Thomas A. Beaty. A large timber fell on Thomas Beaty breaking his back. As Thomas lay dying, John Hogan asked John Beaty to find out where his father's treasure lay buried.

John J. Beaty, being of stubborn will, told John Hogan he had lived a good life without his father's wealth and could live the rest of his life without the money. John Hogan, unwilling to accept no as an answer, hired men to search for the elusive pot of gold. During the years following Thomas' death, people dug in a great portion of Poplar Log Cove. If Thomas A. Beaty had any money, John Hogan and his men never found the gold and silver.

Thomas Beaty's son, John Jackson Beaty entered land approximately ½ mile north of Brush Arbor Cemetery. Brush Arbor meetings were held on a regular basis during the summer near the cemetery. The area was prepared by constructing a pole frame over laid with brush to protect people from the heat of the sun. The meetings were similar to open air revivals.

The John Jackson Beaty home in Beaty Hollow, now known as Black Warriors' Cove. Lamender Sue Doss Beaty, wife of John Jackson Beaty, stands at the gate.

## Willis Watkins

Thomas' sister, Nancy., who was born in North Carolina in 1808, was married to Willis Watkins. Willis was born in South Carolina in 1850. Nancy Beaty, born in Virginia in 1783, was the mother of Thomas and his sister Nancy. The elder Nancy Beaty is listed in the household of Willis Watkins in 1850 along with Angeline, born in North Carolina in 1827, and James K. who was five months old and born in Alabama. James K. is thought to be the son of Angeline and probably the grandson of Willis and Nancy Watkins. According to the 1860 Lawrence County Census by Lester and Myra Borden, Willis Wadkins (Watkins) was listed as being 60 years old

*John Jackson Beaty and wife, Lamender Sue Doss Beaty with grandson, Ottis Beaty.*

from South Carolina; Nancy was 51 from North Carolina; and James, 10, from Alabama. In addition, A.M. Demastes, a female from North Carolina, was listed as 34 years old.

The Willis Watkins family settled on Washspring Mountain one mile west of Thomas A. Beaty. Willis' place was just east of the old Friendship Cemetery. Even though Mr. Stanley Newman's abstract lists Willis Watkins, Willis never officially entered or properly homesteaded the land from the government. It is theorized that Willis Watkins' father is buried on the east side of the road going to Brush Arbor on top of Washspring Mountain. People reported seeing the lone grave on the side of the old road.

**Doss Family**

John Jackson Beaty married Lamender Sue Doss on December 9, 1869. She was the daughter of Ezekiel Doss and Lamenda Hampton, a sister to Ephriam Hampton. As mentioned earlier, Ephriam Hampton's place was near the center of Poplar Log Cove. Ezekiel was the son of John David Doss and Frances J. Neal. Ezekiel Doss received land north of the Brush Arbor Cemetery as bounty for serving in the War of 1812. Ms. Faye Cash Beaty, who now lives on Ezekiel Doss's old home place near Poplar Log Cove, has on page four of her abstract deed information showing that Ezekiel received land in Section 34, Township 7 South, and Range 6 West, January 6, 1848.

According to Mr. Alton McWhorter, Ezekiel Doss entered the War of 1812 on August 24, 1813, and was released in Cincinnati, Ohio, on March 1, 1814. Ezekiel served with a Captain David McNair under the regiment leadership of Colonel Levi Barbee. After leaving the land near Brush Arbor Cemetery, Ezekiel moved to the Red Hill Cemetery area near the Five Points Community.

Ezekiel's son, James Doss, also a blacksmith, born in 1825, moved to his father's Brush Arbor home place with his wife Malinda Stover. After James' first wife died, he married her sister, Nancy Stover. The land around Brush Arbor and south of the Doss place was that of D.T. Stover who was probably related to Malinda and Nancy. D. T. had purchased the land surrounding Brush Arbor from Darius Lynch, who had originally entered the land in 1849.

## John Jackson Beaty

John Jackson Beaty, who was a carpenter, built and lived in a dog trot house not far from where he was born. The house consisted of two big rooms on each side of the hallway, a lean to on the front, a porch on the front and back, with a side room on the back porch hallway and a stone fireplace and chimney on each end of the house. The old John Jackson Beaty house burned down in the early 1980's. John Jackson Beaty obviously had some fine white oak timber on his land which he had sold to the "Holland and Blow Stave Company" of Decatur. The contract shows the stave company paid John Beaty $150.00 for the white oak on 80 acres of his property in 1910. John Jackson Beaty owned land in three sections: Section 3 and 4 of Township 8 South, Range 6 West, and section 34 of Township 7 South, Range 6 West.

According to old records provided by Ms. Faye Beaty, John J. Beaty had trouble with some neighbors over his hogs running loose. I must share the following letter:

*Feb 16-1912*
*Mr. John Beaty Dear Sir you*
*hogs ar stil using in my*
*fill your hogs has bin running*
*at large for some time if we hav*
*stock Law why not use it and*
*keep owr stock up and not let*
*them torment somebody else*
*I keap min up and wish the other man*
*to do the same, so good by from your*
*friend Lawrence Watkins*

John Jackson Beaty and Lamender Sue Doss had five children: Lucy, Edward, Thomas, John Tolbert, and Charlie. John and Lamender Sue had three children (Lucy, Edward, and Tommie) to die of the bloody flux within one week. Bloody flux was thought to be a severe form of dysentery. John Jackson and Lamender Sue Beaty, along with the three children who died of the bloody flux, are buried in a row of unmarked graves in the Brush Arbor Cemetery.

## Charlie Beaty

Charlie Beaty was the father of Ottis Verbon Beaty, who married Faye Cash. On a clear day in 1904, Charlie was struck and killed by lightning at the age of 23. He is buried at Friendship Cemetery on the county line of Lawrence and Morgan Counties.

Charlie Beaty married Clara Walker in January 1900. Clara was the daughter of Jim Walker and Victoria Roden. James W. (Jim) Walker and Victoria Roden were married on December 28, 1875. Victoria's brother, Martin, married her husband's sister, Janee. Victoria's dad, Archie, was killed while fighting in the Civil War at Athens, Alabama, and was buried at the location where he fell. Jim Walker lived near the sandpits located at the foot of the mountain west of McDaniel Branch; Jim raised and sold mules, and farmed cotton for a living. He kept more than 100 stands of honey bees to sell honey.

Ms. Clara Walker attended school at Beaty School with the McDaniel children. Charlie and Clara had two children – Ottice who married Faye Cash and Lucille who died as an infant and is buried at county line Friendship Cemetery. After Charlie died, Clara married Earnest Templeton.

John Tolbert Beaty

Charlie Beaty

## John Tolbert Beaty

Near the Beaty home place was a one room log school known as Beaty School. The school was made logs and constructed similar to Pine Torch Church. John Tolbert Beaty, who was the son of John J. and Lamender Doss Beaty, taught in the early school. John Tolbert never married and after dying of a heart attacked was buried in

Lebanon Cemetery. The family was unable to carry him to Brush Arbor because of the weather and road conditions.

John Tolbert Beaty attended the first Speake School when it was a one room log building about ½ mile south of highway 36 on the west side of the road. A three room school was later built across the road where the home of Bill Kelsoe is presently located. Jesseton was the post office located at the road junction with present day highway 36 and county road 81. After finishing school, John Tolbert Beaty began teaching at Beaty School near his father's home place and taught for at least 8 years.

John Tolbert Beaty, who was born on April 6, 1872, recorded the following children and their ages attending Beaty School during the class of the second term from January to April 1892.

## Beaty School Class of 1892

| Name | Age | Name | Age | Name | Age |
|---|---|---|---|---|---|
| DOLLY WALKER | 9 | WILLIE MCDANIEL | 12 | MOODY HOGAN | 11 |
| LIZZY JOHNSON | 12 | LENA HOGAN | 16 | JOHNNY SIMS | 11 |
| ARRIE JOHNSON | 7 | MAGGIE SOUTHERN | 11 | MONROE LOONEY | 15 |
| LULA MCDANIEL | 10 | ARRIE NORWOOD | 10 | G.W. NORWOOD | 16 |
| J.T. ROBERTS | 10 | LOUENDA HOGAN | 8 | LOU SOUTHERN | 1 |
| JOHNNY BEATY | 8 | VINIE LEDLOW | 17 | | |
| DAN SIMS | 7 | TOMMIE BEATY | 12 | | |
| | | | | | |
| ROBERT WALKER | 14 | CLARA WALKER | 7 | JAMES LOONEY | 9 |
| PHIL McDANIEL | 9 | ALICE JOHNSON | 10 | NAY SIMS | 10 |
| TOMMIE HOGAN | 14 | LILLY WALKER | 15 | DONNIE SIMS | 8 |
| JOHNNY NORWOOD | 13 | RUBE MCDANIEL | 8 | ANDRIAN BEATY | 7 |
| WALTER LOONEY | 7 | CARLIE BEATY | 9 | | |
| WILBURN LEDLOW | 13 | GEORGE LEDLOW | 8 | | |

John Tolbert Beaty left many letters and notes which were loaned to me by Faye Beaty. I truly enjoyed reading the material and I would like to complete my story on John Tolbert Beaty with the note I liked most of all. He wrote this note at the age of 18 and was already worried about getting old. This note is presently over 100 years old and the paper is turning dark brown with decay:

> *December 31, 1890*
> *This day ends the year 1890 As we pass from the old year to the new we should not forget to look back and think how swiftly time passes away Look H\how precious time is and see if you do not think we should improve our time in a way that will useful to us Time is precious. Improve it well while you are yet young Just a little while longer and our young heads will white with the frost of many winters*
>
> *J.T. Beaty*

## Spears Family of Blowing Springs

Whoa, gee, haw, and get-up are words which have been ringing through the trees during 1993 in the beautiful hollow of Poplar Log Cove in the northeastern portion of William B. Bankhead National Forest. The well trained mules of Mr. Ted O. (T.O.) Spears and Mr. Billy Henderson respond to the words of their masters without hesitation as they drag the heavy logs to the truck.

In the last two years, Mr. Henderson bought some 40 acres of land in the mountain valley of Poplar Log Cove. Located on his property was a stand of pines which had become infested with beetles. The pine beetles were killing the trees in two stands of timber. The pine stands were located in two old fields, which according to a ring count, had regenerated about 27 years ago. In addition, some of the hardwoods were intermingled with pines which needed to be harvested. T.O. and Billy were using the mules to skid the logs from surrounding timber land in order to prevent damage to the woodlands.

**Spears Family**

Mr. Spears got his start in the logging business in the 1930's. He first used trained steers to skid logs. Since no hard lines were attached to the steers, a bullwhip got their attention when voice commands were not obeyed.

T.O. Spears grew up just down West Flint Creek from Poplar log Cove near the Blowing Springs area. He first logged with his dad, L.R. Spears, selling dye wood to a mill in Decatur.

The Spears family cut mountain oak and dead American chestnut. The timber was ground up to make dyes. The logs were cut into four feet lengths and quartered before being sold to the dye mill.

Mr. Spears said his dad raised his family and also three nephews after his Uncle Gid Spears died. He said his family did not have a lot of money or did not make a lot of money, but back then, you could not starve a country family out. They always raised plenty of food and always had something to eat.

T.O. Spears and his dad did a lot of logging on forest property when Ranger Wilson was in charge of the Bankhead. He said Wilson was very protective of the forest and did not allow small saplings to be cut or destroyed. T.O. said, "You only cut the timer that was clearly marked or you paid."

*T.O. Spears & Billy Henderson*

Today, Mr. Spears does not agree with the timber practices which are now occurring throughout Bankhead Forest. He says his mules "do not do near the damage to an area as that of dozers and skidders." He also states that the only way loggers can make anything on U.S. Forest Service Property is cutting more timber than they actually buy. Presently, Mr. Spears gets from $108.00 to $140.00 per thousand board feet of lumber, depending on the length of the logs. When timber companies pay in excess of $125.00 per thousand board feet on the stump, then they have got to harvest more than they buy just to cover their costs.

The mule skidding loggers know their business when it comes to logging. They understand their mules cannot pull several logs at one time but the difference comes from the little damage done to the forest when compared to heavy machinery. Mr. Spears told me to come back to the woods where they are removing pines within two years and I would not tell the area had been logged.

When I asked Mr. Billy Henderson "Where is Mr. Spears' logging crew?" he kinda laughed and said, "The only person in this logging operation that T.O. Spears has to please is himself."

## Families of Poplar Log Cove

Poplar Log Cove is located in the northeast corner of William B. Bankhead National Forest in Lawrence County. The cove contains the headwaters of the West Fork of Flint Creek and a tributary stream which flows from the southeastern fork of the cove known as Wiggins Creek. Indian Creek, flowing in a northerly direction, is another tributary to West Flint which enters the western end of the cove about one mile west of the Chenault Road or Flint Creek Road. To the north of the cove lies Washspring, Hog Heaven, and Buzzard Roost Mountains with Flat Mountain to the east and Brindley Mountain to the south.

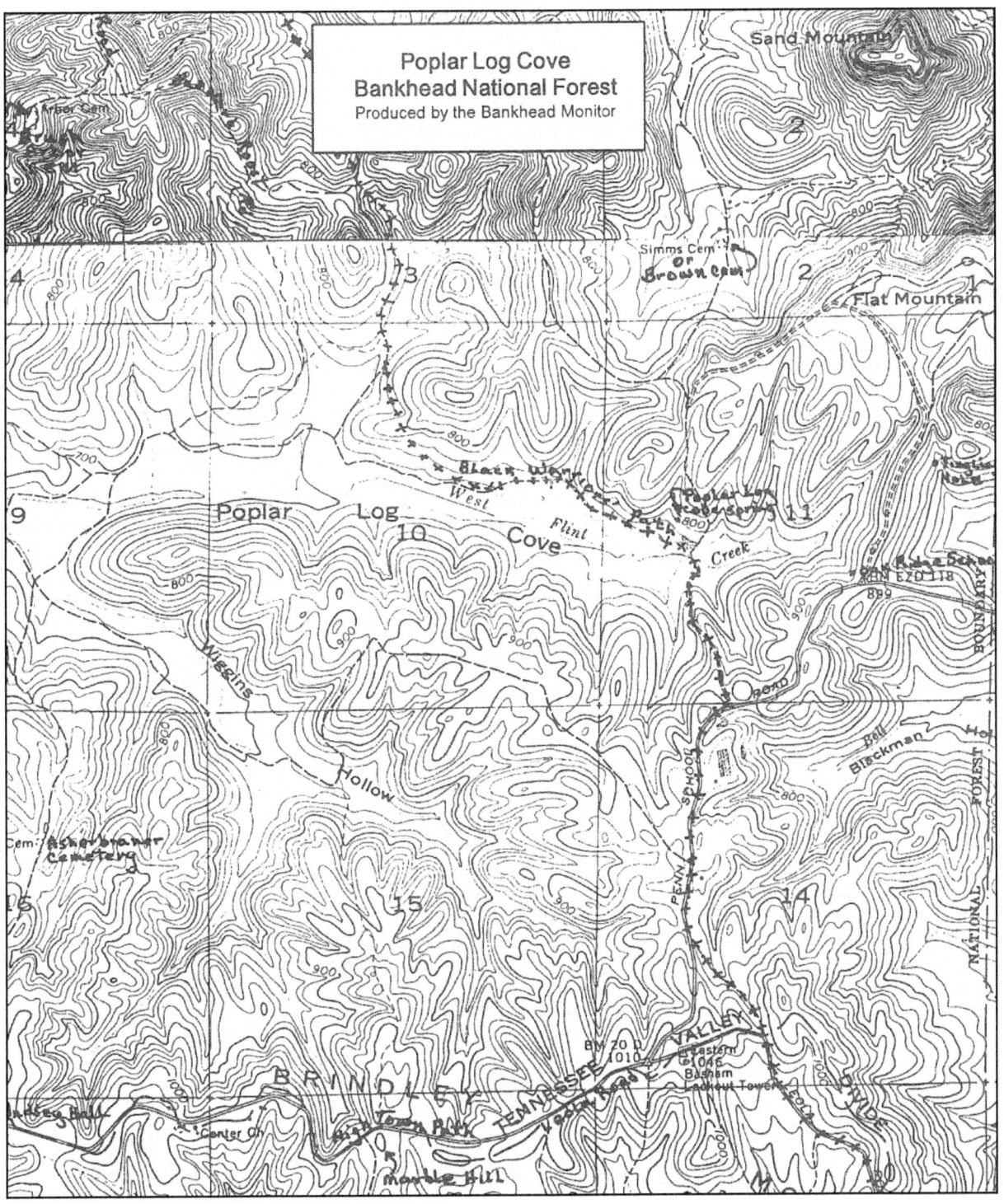

The Poplar Log Cove is located some five miles South of Speake School in Bankhead National Forest. Poplar Log Cove is a large flat valley containing open fields on both sides of the headwater streams. These cove headwaters contain some of the most diverse and abundant mixtures of beautiful wild flowers anywhere in Bankhead Forest. Many times I have hiked the Indian Creek and Poplar Log areas of West Flint Creek photographing the vast array of plant life. Much of the cove is now U.S. Forest Service property intermingled with private land holdings. Most Bankhead coves had some valuable flat valleys which were highly prized by the early families who settled the land. Some early settlers and their descendants who own the land refused to allow their property to be purchased by the government.

**Smith Family**

Presently, Mr. Ray Smith and his wife live on the north ridge of Poplar Log Cove and to the south side of the Buzzard Roost Road located in the northeastern portion of Bankhead Forest. The Smiths recently purchased land and built a home on the northern hills and slopes of Poplar Log Cove. The 126 acres of land encompasses the old Brush Arbor Cemetery (sometimes referred to as Doss Cemetery) and is surrounded on three sides by U.S. Forest Service property. The Smith home sites on the property's highest knoll and provides a magnificent view of the valleys and ridges of Poplar Log Cove.

In less than three years, Ray and Peggy Smith have developed a love for the beauty, history and isolated location of their mountaintop home. After walking around the cemetery, sandstone spring, and old home places on their property, it did not take long to understand how quickly and deeply roots could be established. They are very fortunate to have such a beautiful and private home place, in addition to a bountiful supply of water from an everlasting spring.

**Beaty Family**

Approximately 100 yards southeast of Brush Arbor Cemetery is the everlasting spring of water issuing from a sandstone bluff that rises some 30 feet high. The spring flows into a crystal clear pool of water which is surrounded by mountain azaleas, mountain hydrangea, dogwoods, and a mature stand of hardwood timber. Just downstream from the spring are the remains of two tanning vats and at least one moonshine still.

According to nearby resident Ms. Faye Beaty, Thomas Alexander Beaty used the tanning yard and vats to make leather goods. Since leather was in high demand during the Civil War,

Thomas A. Beaty made and sold leather goods and materials to the Confederacy for hard currency, gold, or silver. Local legend indicates Thomas became quite wealthy from the leather trade and buried most of his fortune. It is believed that his fortune still remains hidden to this day.

## Doss Family

North of the old tanning yard area and spring, old house place chimney stones are located some 75 yards south of the cemetery. In addition, a probably blacksmith shop was located near the cemetery. Evidence of this shop is provided by chunks of melted metal and the remains of a hand-welded eye hoe.

The blacksmith shop may have belonged to an early settler of the area, Ezekiel Doss. Ezekiel, born in 1792, was given a section of land for serving with Jackson in the War of 1812. He is listed in the 1850 Census as a blacksmith from Kentucky. According to Ms. Lillian McCaghren, Ezekiel's first wife was Frances Thurman who was a Cherokee Indian. After Frances died, Ezekiel married Lamender Hampton. In addition, Ezekiel's daughter by his first wife, Lucinda Doss married Ephriam Hampton. Ephriam's first wife was another Lamender Hampton. Thus, many of these early families became closely related through intermarriage.

## Ephriam Hampton

After much of the virgin timber in Poplar Log Cove was cut, cotton farming in the valleys and on the ridges of the cove activated all tillable soil into cultivation. Ephriam Hampton, born on January 12, 1802, lived just north of West Flint Creek and south of Brush Arbor Cemetery. He had a cotton gin and ran a general supply store. According to Colonel James Edmonds Saunders'; book, _Early Settlers of Alabama_, Ephriam Hampton was carrying cotton bales below the Mussel Shoals to Tuscumbia for shipment. During one muddy trip, his wagon was accidently bumped by another wagon driven by Mr. W. Winter Payne causing the wagons to lock wheels. Both men of powerful build climbed out of the wagons and engaged in a violent fist fight. The fight ceased after each man was unable to continue except to climb into their wagons and go their way. Later, at Oakville, Ephraim endorsed Winter Payne as the democratic nominee for congress.

## Sheets Family

On the western edge of Buzzard Roost Mountain is the headwaters of Sheets Branch which was named after the early Sheets family who also lived nearby. Archibald Sheets, born in 1784, was the first of his family to move to the Brush Arbor area. Archibald was a farmer and worked in the tanning yard.

## Other Cove Families

In addition, the Templeton, Doss, Beaty, and Hampton families lived and worked together in the early 1800's to establish themselves in the new wilderness of Poplar Log Cove. On page one of the *1850 Census of Lawrence County* compiled by Odalene Ponder, Johnson, Roling, and Ephriam Hampton are listed with their families. Other names important to Poplar Log Cove history include the families of David Templeton, Thomas Beaty, and Ezekiel Doss, all of which are found in association with the cove.

An old single lane wagon road which has been eroded down some five to six feet in some areas is still clearly visible as it winds its way by Brush Arbor Cemetery and into the Poplar Log Cove. The old wagon road and old ways are quickly becoming a fading memory of the older cove descendants.

## Cemeteries Surrounding Poplar Log Cove

Many cemeteries are on or near the ridges which surround the cove and are evidence of many settlers who lived nearby. Several cemeteries on the northern ridges of the cove are Old Friendship or Garrison Cemetery which is on Washspring Mountain to the north of the White Pine Road some 75 yards, McVay or Sheets Cemetery south of the White Pine Road approximately 1/8 mile south along the Lyge Wiley Ridge, and Brush Arbor or Doss Cemetery on a southerly ridge of Buzzard Roost Mountain. Simms or Brown Cemetery west of Flat Mountain located at the upper end of McDaniel Creek and Watkins Cemetery at the northern edge of Washspring Mountain are in the northern valleys just outside the cove. Friendship Cemetery on the edge of Blowing Springs Road about ¼ mile north of the junction of Blowing Springs Road with the Leola Road and Smith Cemetery just north of the Leola Road are on the ridges near the headwaters of Indian Creek. Four Friendship Cemeteries are located near the northeastern portion of Bankhead Forest. The southern ridges of the cove contain Cave Springs Cemetery, Asherbraner Cemetery, and Center Cemetery which is the largest cemetery in the area. These cemeteries contain many of the early settlers who lived in and around Poplar Log Cove. Only Friendship and Center Cemeteries appear to be used within the last fifty years.

**Schools of Poplar Log Cove**

In the early days, four schools were located near Poplar Log Cove. Lindsey Hall School was located on the Leola road about ½ miles west of the road junction with the Blowing Springs Road. Templeton School was located at the forks of the Leola Road and Flint Creek Road. Oak Ridge School was on the eastern side of the ridge which forms the east portion of the cove and was located just east of the forks of the Flat Mountain Road and Penn School Road. Lindsey Hall, Templeton, and Oak Ridge also served as churches and were made of rough cut lumber. Beaty School was located north of Brush Arbor Cemetery in the valley east of Buzzard Roost Mountain.

**Post Offices**

Two post offices located south of the cove served many of the cove's settlers. Poole Post Office was located at the junction of the Blowing Springs Road and Leola Road. Templeton Post Office was located at the junction of Flint Creek Road and Leola Road about 1/8 mile west of Templeton School.

**Wildlife**

Wildlife around the cove appeared to be quite abundant in the days when early settlers were making their way into the area. Two elderly people mention black bears were hunted and killed in the area. During the early years of the 1800's, bear, deer, turkey, and small game probably provided much of the winter's meat supply for the area residents. In addition, fur trade was one way many folks made extra money when farming and digging roots were out of season.

**Industry**

According to Mr. Johnny Burgess Poole, the earliest company to establish themselves near the center of Poplar Log Cove between West Flint and Wiggins Creek was the Holland and Blow Stave Mill. Many people mention the stave mill which processed white oak barrel staves. In addition to the stave mill, Mr. Thomas Alexander Beaty had a tanning operation consisting of a tanning yard and tanning vats. Several people indicated that Thomas used white oak, ash, and water in the tanning process. As mentioned in an earlier article, his tanyard was a few hundred yards south of Arbor Cemetery. Darius Lynch entered and homesteaded the area around Brush Arbor Cemetery on July 12, 1849.

After the old farm fields became gully washed and unproductive, cotton farming in the cove was virtually abandoned. Today, large piles of rock are found throughout the cove and are again overgrown in mature forest. The rock piles stand as monuments of the hard work and high demand cotton farming placed not only on the early settlers, but also on the land. Therefore after a few years of settlement, the impact of timber cutting and farming drastically changed the early wilderness of Poplar Log Cove.

*Popular Log Cove Spring is the main headwater spring of West Flint Creek. The spring was located adjacent to Black Warrior's Path and provided aboriginal people a fresh supply of*

Farm land, which was claimed from the virgin hardwood wilderness of Poplar Log Cove, became unproductive due to repeated planting of cotton and farming practices. Early farmers abandoned the sandy hills and valleys of the cove for more productive red land in the Moulton and Tennessee Valleys. As time passed, trees began reclaiming much of the land in Poplar Log Cove there by returning the area to forest land. Prior to the 1900's, mature stands of timber had replaced many of the old fields. Today, in the upper drainage of Poplar Log Cove some 200 acres adjacent to West Flint Creek is still open pasture land and is privately owned.

## Poole Family of Poplar Log Cove

### Lorenzo Poole

In the beginning of the 1880's, Lorenzo Poole and family came from Georgia and settled in the eastern end of Poplar Log Cove at the headwaters of West Flint Creek. He and his wife, Mary Hamilton settled near a large everlasting spring which is the beginning of West Flint Creek.

Lorenzo bought the isolated area from the John T. Hunter family. John Hunter was noted in Cove history as killing several black bears in and around Poplar Log Cove which had an abundance of wildlife. According to <u>Old Land Records of Lawrence County</u>, John T. Hunter entered some 200 acres of land in the Cove on March 17, 1855. In addition, William Hunter also entered 40 acres in the Cove on March 178, 1855.

Lorenzo and Mary had nine children: Tom, Harrison, Herschel, Wiley, Claude, Ellis, Addie, Lizzie, and Mamie. Addie married Gus Pike; Tom married Annie Garnett; Harrison married Bessie Asherbraner; Herschel (Hutch) married Mattie Doss; Mamie never married; Wiley married Haley Hampton; Lizzy married Jimmy Hampton; Ellis married Imogen Asherbraner; and Claude married Eunice Hampton.

## Oak Ridge Church and School

Some of the Poole children attended Oak Ridge School on the eastern ridge just outside the Cove. After Oak Ridge was consolidated, Ms. Eva had a younger brother and sister who went to Penn School for one winter and then started to Reed School. Ms. Chenault said the consolidation of the schools ended her education because of the distance to and from school.

Oak Ridge also served as a church for local residents. The church and school was a rectangular building some 20 feet wide and 40 feet long. The one room school accommodated children in first grade through seventh grade. During the winter time, the school was heated by a large wood burning heater. A single water bucket with a dipper provided the drinking water for all students. According to Ms. Eva Poole Chenault, Mr. Luther Morris was the school teacher at Oak Ridge.

## Tom Poole

Ms. Eva's father, Tom Poole, first lived just outside the Cove in the northeastern valley that forms the headwaters of McDaniel Branch at the Odell Place. Most of Tom's children were raised on the old Odell home place. Just a short distance from Tom Poole's home on McDaniel Branch was the Brown or Simms Cemetery. Mary Poole, wife of Lorenzo, is buried in the cemetery along with some ten to fifteen other people.

Tom Poole farmed some cotton and corn in the fertile valleys along McDaniel Branch, but his love was the lumber business. Later, Tom bought his father's home place in the Cove. Lorenzo's old home place was a large log house with two big rooms on each side of a dog trot hallway. The house, also, had a side room, used as a bedroom, a kitchen, and one large bedroom upstairs. After moving into his father's home, Tom piped water into the house from the spring under the bluff. The spring was uphill from the log house and water issued from the bottom of the bluff.

Tom ran a steam operated sawmill and planer to smooth the lumber; therefore, Tom's mill would produce dressed lumber. The lumber mill and planer was located in Poplar Log Cove. Tom worked with steam engines until the late 1950's when he changed to a gasoline engine. In the mid 1900's, the Tennessee

*Tom and Annie Garnett Poole.*

Valley Authority (TVA) assured people all over North Alabama that power would be provided to all residents in the Tennessee Valley. Supplying power to Tom Poole's home in Poplar Log Cove during the early days of TVA became a tremendous job of stringing electrical power lines over the Flat Mountain Range into the east end of the West Flint Creek area.

## Harrison Poole

Harrison Poole ran a shingle mill and a grist mill located at the foot of Flat Mountain at the headwaters of McDaniel Branch. The shingle mill was steam operated and was used to produce shingles for roofs of houses. The cornmeal mill was also operated by steam. Tolls were charged for making shingles or grinding corn. Tom and Harrison Poole are buried at East Friendship Cemetery located on the Lawrence-Morgan County Line.

## Hutch and Mattie Doss Poole

Mr. Johnny Burgess Poole said his family lived in the area of Poplar Log Cove for many years. Johnny's parents were Herschel (Hutch and Mattie Doss Poole. Mattie was the daughter of Walter and Ezibell Doss, who lived one-half mile north of Buzzard Roost Mountain just outside the northern edge of Poplar Log Cove.

Hutch and Mattie's family lived at the Jim Asherbraner Place located at the junction of the Johnson and Chenault Road about one-half mile north of the Leola road. The Jim Asherbraner house was made of planks and consisted of three rooms and a side room with a dug well in the yard. Just a few yards from the house was a barn and corn crib.

1st Row Seated L-R: *Walter Poole, Tom Poole, Annie Garnett Poole and 'Bertha Poole Hamilton.* Standing Seated L-R: *Buford Walker (Annie's sister's boy), Calvin Poole, Lorene Poole Wilbanks, Lewis Poole, Eva Poole Chenault, Ethel Poole Jarrett.* Floyd Poole is missing from the photo.

Hutch moved from Jim Asherbraner place east of Oak Ridge Church and School where he lived until his death.

## Jimmy and Lizzie Poole Hampton

North of the Jim Asherbraner Place about one-half mile was the Ike Chenault home place. Lizzie, another of Lorenzo's children, and her husband, Jimmy Hampton, lived on the Ike Chenault Place for a while. The Chenault Place was on top of the hill south of the Chenault Bridge on West Flint Creek and about one-half mile north of the Jim Asherbraner Place. Both the Asherbraner and Chenault home places are mature stands of timber and the land presently belongs to the U.S. Forest Service. Very little evidence remains of the old settler homes on the south ridge of Poplar Log Cove.

## Jackson Templeton

On the south edge of Poplar Log Cove was Center Church and Templeton School and Post Office. Mr. Johnny Burgess Poole attended Templeton School while he was growing up. Templeton School and Post Office was named after the Templeton family who lived south of the cove on the Leola Road. Jackson Templeton lived just west of Center Church and ran the Templeton Post Office located near the junction of the Chenault or Flint Creek Road and the Leola Road.

*Tom and Annie Garnett Poole.*

## Johnny Burnett

Center Church is located three-fourths of a mile east of the junction of the Leola Road and Flint Creek Road. Johnny Burnett built a house near Center Church on the north side of the Leola Road. After Johnny moved west to Arkansas his father, Henry bought Johnny's home place. Henry Burnett's family and his son, Bill Burnett, lived around Center Church for several years.

## David Asherbraner

Just north of Center Church was the David and Staymee Asherbraner Place. David's son, Noah Asherbraner, who married Emaline Pearson, also lived at the old Asherbraner home place. The Asherbraner family cemetery is located on the ridge near the Asherbraner home.

According to the *1860 Lawrence County Census* compiled by Lester and Myra Borden, David Asherbraner was a farmer from North Carolina. He was listed as being 43 years old in 1860. His family in 1860 Census are given as the following: Sarah, 26; John L., 8; Noah H., 6; Mary E., 4; Henry, 3; Miriam C., 1.

**Buttermilk Bill Johnson**

William Franklin "Buttermilk Bill" Johnson lived west of the Chenault Road about halfway between the Ike Chenault home place and Matt Pearson home place which is south of Blowing Spring. Buttermilk Johnson's old home place was just southeast of the end of the Johnson Road. Buttermilk later moved west of the Hickory Grove Road on the Leola Road near the Sandbar Hill in a house on the south side of the road. Lee Miller worked cotton around the old Buttermilk Johnson house place at the junction of Indian Creek and West Flint Creek. The old place is now grownup in mature timber.

*Henry Asherbraner and wife, Sarah Fulmer, the sister of Lucy Fulmer Oden.*

**Other Poole Neighbors**

Dick Johnson lived just off the Leola Road between Templeton School and the Hickory Grove Road. Leamon Williams lived off the Leola road to the right. Wesley Hampton's place was located at the junction of the Leola Road and Hickory Grove road.

Many other people lived and owned land in and around Poplar Log Cove. Most of the old settler home places are only identifiable by a few remaining sandstone corners, chimneys, or old dug wells with each passing year slowly erasing all members of days gone by.

## Chenault Family of Poplar Log Cove

During 1993, I had the pleasure of meeting a noble descendant of a distinguished Bankhead Forest family – Mr. Prince Chenault. At 84 years of age, Mr. Chenault is an impressive gentleman who can grab your attention by weaving a life' story which is uncharacteristic of other Bankhead families in that his family

*The chimney of Matt Pearson's original cabin at Basham Gap still stands within 20 yards of the Basham Indian Shelter.*

became highly educated and very successful. Prior to talking to Mr. Chenault, I had learned that he came from a highly motivated and hardworking family. His mother, Callie Johnson Chenault, had impressed many people by her hardened work ethic. Prince Chenault was born on April 25, 1907, just ¼ mile south of West Flint Creek on the south ridge of Poplar Log Cove. Prince's father and mother were Issac and Callie Johnson Chenault.

**Buttermilk Bill**

Callie's family came from Tennessee in a covered wagon. The Johnson family drove their cows and hogs along behind the wagon. Callie's father, William Franklin "Buttermilk Bill" Johnson, was a Civil War veteran. Buttermilk Bill and his wife, Mary Jane, also had two sons: Harvey and Manley. The two Johnson brothers moved south near Birmingham to work in the coal mines. They eventually went missing never to be heard from again.

*Matt Pearson and wife, Mary Johnson*

Buttermilk originally lived south of Blowing Springs at the Matt Pearson place. Matt and Mary Pearson were Prince's great uncle and aunt. Mary was a sister to Issac Chenault's mother, Marge Johnson. Matt and Mary never had any children. They lived, died and were buried near their Blowing Springs home place. Buttermilk later moved to the Issac Chenault place near the end of the present day Johnson Road. The old home place was southeast of the junction at Indian Creek and West Flint Creek.

Grandpa Bill Johnson had his old brown jug next to his bed and it was kept filled with moonshine. Buttermilk always took a good swig of moonshine at night before bedtime and a good drink first thing in the morning. Prince said that moonshine finally killed his grandpa Buttermilk Bill at 103. Buttermilk Bill and his wife, Mary Jane, are buried in Center Cemetery which is located on the southern ridge of Poplar Log Cove.

**Issac and Callie**

Issac Chenault married Callie Johnson about 1900. They had three boys and five girls. The children were: Price; Louise; Mary, who died of membranous croup or diphtheria when she was two; Prince, Icy Mae; Pleas; Paralee; and Jewel.

Issac and Callie owned 320 acres of land in Poplar Log Cove and along the southern ridges. Issac, who was named after his mother's brother Issac Johnson, Sr., would run 40 to 50 head of cattle. He farmed over 100 acres, raised hogs, chickens, a garden, and all the food the family needed.

Issac and Callie lived in a nice plank house on the ridge south of West Flint Creek. The house had a tin roof and contained three bedrooms, a kitchen, and two fireplaces. Two dug wells were located close to the house and served as the family's drinking water.

Callie would boil clothes in the pot and take them out and beat them with a slat. Callie lived to be 93 years old and is buried in Hartselle Cemetery.

**Sharecroppers and Neighbors**

Two sharecropper families lived on the Chenault place for some fifteen to twenty years. The head of the families was Charlie Partridge and Gordon Mattox. They used teams of mules to farm the mountainous land of Poplar Log Cove.

*The Issac Johnson Home. 1860 Lawrence County Census: Issac Johnson, 32; Elizabeth, 29; Margaret, 7; Issac, 6; Jesse, 4; Sallie, 3; Derias, 1*

Charlie Partridge, one of the tenant farmers on the Chenault place, took Mr. Leon Moody possum hunting. They got lost in the mountains and walked all night. Leon made it back to his boarding room at Issac Chenault's the following day.

Holland-Blow Stave Mill was the only nearby industry and operated in the cove. The mill was located in the valley of West Flint Creek. Prince and his friend, Shorty Long, hauled stave bolts to the mill during the summer months.

The Jim Asherbraners were neighbors to the Chenaults. Mrs. Noah (Emaline) Asherbraner, Jim's mother, knitted socks all the time. Price said it was amazing to watch Ms. Emaline Asherbraner knit as she was walking down the road.

Jackson Templeton ran the post office at Templeton and the Hawkins family ran the post office at the Lindsey Hall Community. Mr. Matt Carter lived between the Chenault place and the Jim Asherbraner place. The closest doctor was Dr. Crow at East Friendship on the county line. Dr. Burch, who was a friend of the Chenault family, lived at Danville.

**Issac Chenault**

Issac Chenault's father was William Chenault who lived in the Speake Community. William's wife was Margie Johnson. Issac had three horses which were used to farm cotton and corn. Issac brought corn to a grist mill located across the road from Speake School west of where Mr. Bill Kelso lives.

The Chenault family left Poplar Log Cove after the land was sold to the U.S. Forest Service for $30.00 per acre. After World War I, the cove area just being to disintegrate. Issac Chenault bought 320 acres in the valley. He paid for the farm during the depression of 1929 through the 1930's by farming.

*Issac and Callie Johnson Chenault.*

Issac Chenault was a gifted musician. He played the fiddle, organ, accordion, guitar, and banjo. Issac and Prince entered the county music contest at Lawrence County Courthouse. Prince played the banjo, and his dad played the fiddle. They won the contest with their string instruments. Prince and his family loved country music. They had a string band at Speake and would play at singings and decorations.

**Farm Boy Days**

When Prince was small a lot of the cove was open fields. At least 150 acres of 320 acres the family owned was in cultivation and pasture. Prince hunted squirrel, quail, and turkeys.

Prince's daddy gave him two young bulls when he was seven years old. Prince was told he could sell the two bulls or let them grow and make a yolk of steers. By the time Prince was twelve years old; his steers were included in most of the daily activities. Prince would use the steers to ride, pull a sled, and haul many different materials.

Prince swapped his steers with his father for a roan colt. One day, Charlie Hardrick, a cattle trader, stopped at the Chenault farm to look at some cows. Charlie liked the pair of steers and talked to Issac about trading the animals. The next morning after staying the night with the Chenault family, Charlie bought the yolk of steers that Prince had raised and trained.

Prince raised pigs to buy a saddle for his horse, which he named Billy. Prince loved the horse which became a daily part of his activities. He trained the horse to pace and fox trot. Billy eventually became an excellent buggy horse. He rode and raced his horse at social gatherings and even took the horse to a race in Decatur.

Dr. Burch at Danville took a fancy for Prince's horse. At first, Prince would not sell his horse for any price. After visiting and staying the night with the Chenault family, Doctor Burch left word with Issac, he would pay handsome price for the horse. Doctor Burch told Issac to tell Prince to come to Danville with the horse, and he would make it worth his time.

*Prince and Pleas Chenault with the fish they caught one day.*

Prince had a trading nature and decided to ride Billy to Danville to see what Doctor Burch would offer for his horse. Prince decided to trade Billy for a fancy buggy and harness, a western horse, a mare, and a mule colt. Prince also got to keep his saddle. Two months later, Prince traded the western horse and buggy with $20.00 to boot for 40 acres of land. He traded the mare for three more yearlings. Prince kept the mule for a farm animal.

**School Years**

As a small child, Prince Chenault attended Templeton School which was one teacher log school containing six grades. Prince's first teacher at Templeton School was Ester Thomas. She, as did most all the Templeton teachers, boarded with the Issac Chenault family. Ester eventually married Byron Young from Mt. Hope.

Leon Moody was Prince's teacher about the third grade and later became Superintendent of Lawrence County Schools. Another teacher who taught Prince at Templeton School was Jim Edmundson. Coach Grady Elmore, who coached at LCHS two different times, eventually married Jim's daughter.

After completing the six grades at Templeton, Prince attended Speake School where he completed the eighth and ninth grades. Speake School was a three teacher school located at present day Bill Kelsoe's house. After attending Speake School for two years, Prince started the ninth grade at Morgan County High School in Hartselle. Prince lived with Dr. Vaughn Booth when he attended school in Hartselle. Dr. Booth was a close friend to the Chenault family. He told Issac and Callie he wanted Prince to live with him while he went to high school, and he would treat him like his own children.

*Issac and Callie Johnson Chenault at their home in the valley.*

Prince's oldest brother, Price, was smart and set pace for the rest of the Chenault children. Price had vowed he would never make his living farming. Price played football at Hartselle and later for the University of Alabama. Price played tackle and guard.

During his last year of school, Prince lived with his brother, Price, at Tuscaloosa. Prince graduated from Tuscaloosa High School. During his stay at Tuscaloosa, Prince's work included waiting tables, cleaning, and sweeping part-time. Price Chenault moved to New York and attended graduate school at Columbia University where he was received his Master's Degree. Prince followed his brother Price to New York to attend college with his brother. While in New York, Price married the sister of Price's wife, Alba L. Pruitt, in 1935. Prince and

Alba were married at "The Little Church Around the Corner." One of the most famous churches in New York City. On June 28, 1991, Prince and Alba will celebrate their 56th wedding anniversary. Alba's family was from Pine Hill, Alabama.

Prince received his Master's Degree in Commerce and Business administration from Columbia University and was six hours away from his doctoral degree. Later, he received his certification in education.

Prince taught school in New Jersey and coached the line in football for 15 years. While in the north, Prince got involved in real estate and received his real estate license. Prince left the north in 1950 and came back to Moulton. He went into the Ford dealership with his brother, Pleas, and stayed in the business for 14 years. Pleas that started the car business in 1942 has one of the oldest dealerships in Alabama.

**Prince's Log Cabin in Parker Cove**

Recently, Mr. Prince Chenault began restoring an old cabin in Parker Cover of Bankhead Forest for his children and grandchildren. His four children include John, who was killed in a car crash in 1963, Rick, Carol, Christine, and 11 grandchildren. One hundred acres will be set aside for their use. Prince bought the old homestead to restore for his children.

The following is a detailed description of the house which was built around 1850 and completed in early 1900. The old log cabin is a pole and beam structure. The foundation of the older portion of the house is large hued sandstone rock spaced on approximately eight foot centers. One top of the supporting stones are perimeter beams or logs approximately twenty-four feet long which have been flattened on both sides.

Sleeper logs still containing their rough bark are half timbers with the bark portion turned toward the ground. The sleeper logs were split in half with each half notched to fit evenly to the exterior perimeter log. The old logs which make up the walls are hand hued and flatten on both edges with bark still remaining on all the cracks. The logs, which appear to be of yellow poplar, are still very solid and show no signs of decay or damage.

The house contains three sandstone fireplaces. Homemade brick were found in the north flue which came from the kitchen cook stove through the roof. The back fireplace contains the initials JTA on the outside hip stone. The fireplaces were constructed on a cantorliever step like foundation. The sandstones are hand hued and made to fit in place. The backside of the fireplaces is of full stone width.

A block of sandstone which was found on the southwest chimney contains the engraved name Riddle. The chimney was probably made by James Calvin Riddle. James Calvin Riddle was considered the best rock mason in the Warrior Mountains. His mother was Samantha Parker, daughter of William Parker.

Two huge logs squared all the way around make up the top of the walls and provide support for the rafters and roof. These top logs extend past the outside edge of the home some two feet. The logs on the older structure appear to be cut with a cross cut saw. Rafters in the upstairs attic portion were made of stripped or peeled poles of cedar or pine.

The back portion of the house is an addition based on the battan system. The only rough cut sawmill lumbers is found predominately on the addition which was added in the early 1900's. Newspaper print on the walls was dated in 1905.

The east bedroom of the older portion of the house contains a staircase with a 90 degree turn which is approximately midway up the wall. The southeast room is going to remain as it was when the original cabin was built.

Mr. Prince Chenault was a teacher to Roger Harville in the ninth grade. Roger, a third generation carpenter, was hired to remodel the old log house. Mr. Chenault taught Roger while he was attending Lawrence County High School. Prince taught at the high school for ten years and was assistant principal under Lewis Watkins.

*Buttermilk Bill's Tombstone in Center Cemetery.*

Mr. Prince Chenault, his brother, and sisters still visit the graves of their grandparents, Buttermilk Bill and Mary Jane Johnson, who are buried at Center Church in Bankhead Forest. He plans to leave the old restored log house in the forest for his three living children and eleven grandchildren to enjoy. Truly, Mr. Prince

Chenault has never forgotten his Bankhead heritage or lost his love for the area he was born in the "Warrior Mountains."

# School at Hickory Grove CCC Camp

FIRE! FIRE! Screamed a running student. "You children stay in your seats and do not listen to such foolishness," said a teacher trying to calm her class. Within seconds black billows of smoke started entering the classroom and panic stricken students began looking for an escape route from a fiery inferno. The smoke was accompanied by the heat and flames of the large timbers of the frame school building going up in blazes.

## The Burning of Speake School

The scene occurred about 1934 or 1935 while students were sitting in class at Speake School. Ms. Sedenina Gillespie Suggs said she "jumped" a student who was taking time to retrieve books from his desk. After retreating to the outside, students stood and watched as their school burned to the ground before their eyes. Many students with tear-dimmed eyes were saddened by the disaster, while others appeared to be happy to be outside, even if it was to watch their school burn to the ground.

After the destructive fire, Speake High School students were literally sent to Bankhead Forest to complete their year of schooling, while the elementary students used the Lebanon Methodist Church near the destroyed school.

## Hickory Grove School

According to Ms. Suggs, Cave Springs School on the drag strip road closed when she was in the seventh grade. On rainy days Mr. Wes Dutton carried Ms. Suggs and her daughter, Ms. Dot Dutton Waits, to the Negro Hall at Oakville in a covered wagon to catch the bus to Speake. After the school burned, the older children were transported by way of the Flint Creek Road to Hickory Grove Road CCC Camp in Bankhead Forest to have school until Speake School could be rebuilt.

After the buses arrived at Speake and let the elementary students off at the church, the older students were transported to the CCC Camp. Located at the school camp, just off the Hickory Grove Road, were some four or five large buildings, including a large ball hall used as a basketball court.

The large hall, equipped with basketball goals, was also used for teaching some classes when students were not playing ball. Ms. Willie Wallace was the girls' basketball coach. Ms. Suggs said they had a real good girls' basketball team.

Located at the Hickory Grove Camp site was a well-kept spring which was "rocked-up." Ms. Suggs said it provided some of the best and coldest water in the area. Some 40 steps lead down the hill to the big spring, which produced an ample supply of water. The rocks were stacked and cemented around the spring entrance forming a wall about six feet square.

The Hickory Grove Road CCC Camp did not have electricity and very few windows in the large buildings. After the depression, the camp had been abandoned. At the time Speake School utilized the facility, there were not any CCC Camp soldiers stationed at this site.

*Speake School children at Hickory Grove CCC Camp Spring. L-R: Wilbur Blankenship, Dual Hampton, Euliss Oliver, Girl ?, Myrtle Blankenship (left of straw hat), Victoria Chenault (with hat), Alvin Curtis (with cap), Annie Mae Lowery (with button-up skirt), Mable Hampton Anders (right of cap), Sedenia Gillespie Suggs, Helen Stephenson (arms across body), Dot Dutton Waits, Boy ?, Edith Hampton (front right), and Ruth Hampton Lawrence (far right). The little boy is the son of the teacher, Ms. Etta Horton. Buddy Clemons is in front on his hands and knees.*

**Rebuilding of Speake School**

Speake School had a very endangering rough early history. The original log school was blown away in a tornado. The second wood frame school burned as did the third floor frame and sandstone rock school building. The building that now stands has caught fire one time.

The children attended the CCC Camp School, utilized for one school year, until the new school building at Speake School could be completed. Mr. Leldon Kelsoe said he helped haul sandstone rock from Blowing Spring Mountain to build the school. Some of the rock was hauled by sleds or wagons pulled by mules, while other loads were brought to the building site by trucks. According to Mr. Kelsoe, people donated timber which was cut and hauled to Dick Vest's sawmill at Oakville. Mr. Vest owned a sawmill and cotton gin in the Oakville Community. He cut the timber into lumber and used it in rebuilding Speake School.

Some of the Sapp brothers helped lay the sandstone rock used in the building's outside construction. The Sapp boys included Tommy, Howard, Blaxton, Allen, Willis, and Charles. They had built several stone houses, including the rock house in which their family lived.

Today, the area that once afforded many young men employment and a place for students to attend school is but a memory in the minds of many who still remember the camp's days of glory. Now, the old CCC Camp has been reverted to the timberland from which it was carved some 60 years ago in the "Warrior Mountains."

## Families of Hickory Grove Road

The Hickory Gove Community was located along a road that ran the ridge between the Capsey Creek and Brushy Creek drainages. The road crossed Brushy Creek just ¼ mile west of the junction of Capsey and Brushy Creeks. The Hickory Grove Road joined the old Cheatham Road at Moreland Church in Winston County. Presently the Hickory Grove Road crosses the eastern portion of Bankhead Forest.

As a small child entering first grade in 1956 at Speake School, I rode a big yellow school bus which was driven by Mr. Manco White. Ten years later my family became his next door neighbor with my father and mother still living in the same location. Mr. Manco White and his wife became extremely close and dear to my family.

*Manco White (3/8 Cherokee) and Olga Hampton White.*

Today, I realize the hands of time are taking a toll on older Lawrence County residents, such as Manco and Olga Hampton White, who were early settlers of William B. Bankhead National Forest. Since the writing of this story Manco and Olga White died.

Even though the only pay I receive from writing historical information is an occasional than you from a reader, I see the importance of sacrificing trying to preserve a small chapter in the life and times of people who once called home the land of the "Warrior Mountains."

## White Family

Left: *Bob White and Evie Sims White (3/4 Cherokee) at the old Jim Walker homeplace near the mouth of Beaty Hollow. Bob White died on April 1, 1942 and Evie died April 5, 1951. They are buried at County Line Friendship Cemetery on the Lawrence-Morgan County Line.*

Manco White was born September 23, 1899, on top of the mountain in a double log house which was located just one-half mile south of Blowing Springs. Manco White died on October 22, 1994. Manco White had four brothers and six sisters with two sisters still living. Ms. Ida White, never married, but always visited Manco. During my last visit, she was 99 years old and was still getting around. Ms. Ida lived in Cullman County with her sister. Ms. Rhoda White Woods, who is some seventy years old. Mrs. Ida white died on September 8, 1995.

The old house place, where Manco was born, is presently a part of the William B. Bankhead National Forest. Manco's parents were Bob White and Evie Simms, a Cherokee Indian from Georgia. After Manco was born, his family moved some four miles further south to the Lawrence and Winston County line on the HickoryGrove Road. At that time in the early 1900's, houses were every four to five miles along the Hickory Grove Road.

*Ida White (age 99) and Rhoda White Woods, the daughters of Bob and Evie Sims White.*

L-R: *Nora (Hutson) Johnson, George Johnson (son of Tom and Mary), Mary White Johnson (sister to Bob White), Elizabeth Johnson (daughter of Tom and Mary), Manco Johnson (son of Tom and Mary), Leroy Johnson (top of photo), Manco White (bottom row), Tom Johnson (top row), Ida White (middle row), Elizabeth (Lizzy White) Summerford (1st row), Evie Sims White (3/4 Cherokee) with baby Porter White, Phil White (bottom row), William (Will) White (top row), Robert (Bob) Greene White (middle row) and little girl on bottom row, Leavie (White) Vest. Two more children were born later: James S. White and Rhoda White Woods.*

Manco's family lived at the Will Minor place which they had bought from Mr. Minor. The Minor place was located on the Hickory Grove Road about four miles south of its junction with the Leola Road. The homestead consisted of 40 acres of the land located in Winston County and 80 acres of adjoining land located in Lawrence County. The White's home was located on the Lawrence County portion of their farm.

The Whites lived in a log house with a board roof of home-made wooden shingles. The house contained two main rooms with a side room that was used as the kitchen. Yards were kept clean and were swept with brush brooms. Some brooms were made from broom sage and were used to sweep the floor.

The family had one horse that was used for transportation and farmed about 60 acres with three mules. They raised sugar cane, corn, cotton, and some tobacco for personal use.

The family kept possum and squirrel dogs. They would sometimes sell possum hides and eat the squirrels. Mr. White said there were no deer in the area where he lived. He did seldom see a black bear near his home place.

Mr. White remembers eating the wild Americans chestnuts. A lot of people would use the chestnut wood for split rail fences.

The family obtained all drinking water from a large dug well. The livestock got water from a large spring located at a nearby bluff. The family had at least two or three cows. In case one cow would go dry, the family would still save a supply of milk.

In the early days, most of the rough land along the Hickory Grove Road was cut over open range pasture land. The fields were fenced with split rails made from chestnut, oak, poplar, or any wood available. All stock were turned loose on open range. All cows and horses wore bells around their neck so they could be found. The mules were kept in the barn and were hardly ever turned out. The livestock were fed corn and fodder. The hogs were allowed to go wild and when the family needed meat they would go out and kill a fat one. Hogs were killed with a rifle or a double-barreled shotgun. Cotton was packed in the gun barrel to hold the powder.

*The Bob White family. L-R: Will White, Bob White, Manco White, Evie Sims White (3/4 Cherokee), Elizabeth (baby) and Ida White. All the children were 3/8 Cherokee.*

The family raised their own sugar cane which was converted to molasses. Mr. Bob "One-Armed" White owned and helped operate the syrup mill. Bob lost his arm in a cotton gin when Manco was one year old. Manco fed the syrup mill with sugar cane seven days per week during syrup season. It would take a family from seventy-five to one hundred gallons of molasses per year to last the entire winter. They sometimes would eat molasses three times a day with cornbread. Mr. Manco White claimed it beat going hungry. The White family tried to complete syrup making before cotton picking time.

After the cotton was picked, it was carried some thirty miles to Cullman in a wagon pulled by a pair of mules. It took three days to carry a wagon load of cotton to be ginned and return. The trip required one day to get to Cullman, one day to gin and sell the cotton, and one day to get back home. The cotton would sell for about $100.00 per bale or twenty cents per pound. The family made approximately ten bales of cotton per year on about twenty acres of land. Manco never remembers making a bale of cotton per acre with the harvest usually averaging one-half per acre.

Family Picture House And Mules, Polk County, GA. L-R: *Nora (Hutson) Johnson, George Johnson, Manco Johnson, Leroy Johnson, Tom Johnson, Mary Johnson, Elizabeth Johnson, Ida White, Elizabeth (Lizzie White) Summerford, Little Girl, Leavie (White) Vest, Evie (Simms) White (Cherokee), Porter White (baby in arms), Phil White, Bob White, Manco w/mule, Will w/white mule.*

## Hampton Family

Fiddling George Hampton, who became Manco's daddy-in-law, was owner of a grist mill. The family used ground meal made at the water mill to make cornbread. Manco, who ran the mill for his father-in-law, could make some mighty fine meal. The grist mill would grind about one bushel of corn per hour. During milling, corn was placed in a skillet and parched. The men would sit and eat the parched corn while the cornmeal was being made.

The water mill was located on West Turkey Creek, east of the Hickory Grove Road and one-half mile from their houses. During the direst season of the year, the grist mill could not operate because of low water levels. Mr. George Hampton built the dam and mill. The dam was five to six feet high and was made from split oak and pine. The dam would backup an area of water in excess of one surface acre. A water gate was raised or lowered in order to turn the water wheel. The water wheel was about twelve feet in diameter. Fan boards of the water wheel were more than one foot wide. A large wooden axle, about eighteen inches in diameter had wooden cogs which interlocked with the water wheel. The oak axle came up into the mill house through a large hole in the floor and turned a mill rock some three feet in diameter. For grinding a bushel of corn into meal, the family got about one half a gallon of shelled corn. The Hamptons lived between West Turkey Creek and the Hickory Grove Road one and one-half miles north from Hickory Grove Church and School.

Some lumber for buildings could be obtained from a nearby steam powered sawmill. Mr. Wesley Hampton, a cousin to George, ran the sawmill which was about three miles north of George's home place. The sawmill was located at the southwest corner of the junction of the Leola Road and the Hickory Grove Road. Scrap slabs were used to fire the steam sawmill. The mill ran for about seven years and ceased running in about 1920 when Wesley died.

Hickory Grove was a log and plank building which served as both a church and school. Mr. White attended the Hickory Grove School for approximately one month when he was fifteen years old. He quit to help his family clear land for row crops and to attend to other farming chores.

*George Hampton, ? Hightower (Syble's sister), Syble Hightower Hampton (George's wife) and Olga Hampton White (baby).*

Mr. George Hampton and his daughter, Olga, chewed tobacco raised on his Bankhead farm. Ms. Olga Hampton White, now deceased, was George's oldest daughter. Olga Hampton was born on July 29, 1900. She helped pick tobacco worms each morning to prevent them from destroying the tobacco crop.

Hickory Grove Church was everybody's church and did not belong to a single denomination. Mr. Hampton and his wife, Syble Hightower, were devote Christians and attended the church every Sunday.

*William Warren White and Sally Galloway, parents of Bob White.*

George had four steers which pulled his wagon and plow. Manco and his wife, Olga, plowed the fields with the team of steers and also with mules. Much of the land north of Hickory Grove was originally entered for homesteads by both the White family and the Hampton family. Mr. Warren White, Manco's grandfather, entered two thirty acre tracts for his homestead. Later around 1923, the two thirty acre tracts along with some of the Hampton homestead was sold to the U.S. Forest Service for $1.00 per acre. Mr. George Hampton owned 470 acres which Manco White later sold for the family. The land was sold to Mr. Columbus Lackey for $4,500.00.

**Manco – The Cherokee**

Manco White was proud of his Cherokee Indian bloodlines. His mother, Evie Sims, was the daughter of William Sims, who was ½ Cherokee, or more, and Mary Davidson who was a full-blooded Cherokee Indian. Mr. White quickly reminded me that his mother was a Cherokee Indian from Georgia.

## Manco White

Manco White and Olga Hampton were married on December 19, 1920, at Piney Grove. They were married while setting in a one horse buggy which was pulled by a fine mare. They were married by Mr. Frank Turrentine. Manco and Olga were married for some seventy years. When he did not have farm work of his own, Manco plowed for the other fellow for 50 cents per day. Mr. White also worked on a seasonal basis for the Danville rock crusher.

*William Sims (1/2 Cherokee) and Mary Davidson (full Cherokee) were the parents of Evie Sims White.*

He helped put rock on the dirt road from the county line to Hartselle, Alabama, now Highway 36. Local men had to work at least eight days per year on the road. Every man between 20 years old and 40 or 50 years old were required to work free of charge.

On his first regular public job, Manco drove a school bus which was pulled by four fine mules. The mules were the best that could be bought. Mr. White drove the mule bus for four years for $2.50 per day. Manco owned the mules and bus. He later sold one pair of mules for $800.00 to Mr. Jack Steele. Later, Manco drove the gasoline wheel bus for fourteen years for Speake School. He made $60.00 every school month which was a total of 20 school days.

Before his death Manco White lived in the Speake Community. The Whites had three boys and one girl, all of whom live in the Speake Community – Calvin, James, Seborn, and Marie White McLemore.

*Mary Davidson Sims (full Cherokee) was the mother of Evie Sims White*

Recently, a new Forest Service road has been built in the area of Manco's and Olga's old home places in Bankhead National Forest. The road turns south just before reaching the old Hampton house place. The grist mill, home places, and farms are now converted back to forest and pine plantations.

Sadly, evidence of these early mountain farms will only be in writing or memories of a time in the past. During my last visit with Mr. Manco White he asked if it would be possible for him to buy forty acres of his old home place. It made me feel proud to know that these people never forgot their roots and cling to those memories of a time gone by in the land they loved – the "Warrior Mountains."

## Walker Family of Piney Grove

Sidney Walker's family was from the north Georgia and southeast Tennessee area. According to some of the family, Sidney Walker's family were direct descendants of John Walker, Sr. family who lived in the Cherokee Nation south of Cleveland, Tennessee. John Walker Jr. was assassinated due to circumstances related to the Treaty of the New Echota.

### Sidney Walker

Sidney Walker and his brother, Jim Walker, traveled west with their dad. According to family history, Sidney married Vicey Stevens in the late 1860's in Joiner, Arkansas. Sidney and Vicey lived for a while in the Choctaw District on the Red River at the junction area of Oklahoma, Texas, and Arkansas.

*Brady Walker: father of the author and 5/16 Creek/Cherokee.*

After living in the Red River area for a while, Sidney and Vicey moved with the rest of the family to Alabama, and settled in the Piney Grove area. Sidney was a white-Indian mixed blood of ¼ Cherokee ancestry. Vicey was considered by family members to be a full blood Creek Indian. Sidney and Vicey had six children – Bell, Lou, Cindy, James, Will, and Dan. Will and Dan were the only two children to return to Alabama. Will was the oldest son and Dan was the youngest.

After moving back to Alabama, Sidney got killed in a hunting accident at Brown's Spring just south of Piney Grove in the northeast portion of Winston County. Brown's Spring is ¼ mile west of Looney's Tavern historic marker on present day Highway 41 and some 4 miles south of the Lawrence-Winston County lines. Sidney was accidentally shot while preparing for a hunt with a large party of settlers gathered at Brown's Spring.

**Vicey and Family**

The year Sidney died was 1890, just two years after Dan was born. Right after Sidney's death, Vicey moved her six young children back to the Red River area near the state junctions of Texas, Oklahoma, and Arkansas. According to Oklahoma Indian District Maps, the area where the family settled was part of the old Choctaw District of Indian Territory.

Since Will had one son born in Texas in 1914 and another son born in Cullman County in 1916, he made his way back to Alabama sometime around 1915. Will Walker settled some three miles south of Piney Grove. Probably, the family move west by Vicey and her small children in 1890 was with Sidney's brother, Jim and their dad. Vicey returned to the Piney Grove area with Will's family in 1915.

It is not certain that Dan came back to Alabama with Will in 1915, but it is for certain that Dan settled just a few miles south of Will's place. Since Dan married in Cullman County, Alabama, in 1907, it is obvious he was in Alabama earlier than Will. Will Walker settled on Soakingwater Creek just north of present day Upshaw. Dan settled on Indian Creek just south of Upshaw in northeast Winston County.

Some relate that the Walker family moved from Oklahoma to Alabama on several occasions from 1890 to 1915. Two sons of the family group were settled in the Piney Grove area by 1916. Vicey lived the remainder of her life with Will's family and made occasional visits to Dan's family. Vicey died in the 1930's and was buried next to Sidney at Old Emus Cemetery in east Cullman County. James, the other son of Vicey and Sidney, was shipped back to Alabama when he died and is buried next to his mother and daddy. My dad, Brady Walker, has vivid memories of his grandma Vicey smoking her corn cob pipe, chewing tobacco, and dipping snuff. She loved her tobacco.

## Dan Walker

*The Dan Walker Family Front Row L-R: Kenneth, Violin, Lucille, Brady, Oliver and Paul. Back Row L-R: Ida, Thurman, Roy, Vady and Lodine. Far Right Corner: Dan Walker (5/8 Creek/Cherokee). The children of Dan and Vady Legg Walker were 5/16 Creek/Cherokee.*

Dan Walker married Maudy Nevady (Vady) Legg, on January 31, 1907, in Cullman County, Alabama. Dan and Vady were married on the front porch of an old plank house located, just inside of Cullman County, about ¼ mile east of the Jasper Road (highway 41) at Piney Grove. The house was on the Old Corn Road which was earlier known as High Town Path. Vady was the daughter of Addison and Elizabeth Speakman Legg of the Upshaw area. Dan and Vady had a dozen children, two of whom died young. Dan and Vady are buried at Friendship Cemetery just one half mile north of Upshaw.

For years, Dan worked at a sawmill located in Tar Springs Hollow in the upper drainage of Capsey Creek in Bankhead Forest. In addition to sawmill work, Dan also farmed cotton, corn, and raised livestock. At about 32 years old, Dan became a hell fire and brimstone Baptist preacher. In the early 1900's, he was a noted preacher along the northern edge of the Warrior Mountains.

When Brady Walker, the son of Dan and Vady, was a young man, he moved to the West for a while and lived with his cousin, Dan Walker, who was the son of James. While living in Oklahoma with Dan, their aunt, who lived across the Red River in Texas, died. Dan and Brady crossed the Red River by boat to get some of their aunt's belongings. After arriving at their house, they found the surrounding people had already taken or stolen everything in their aunt's dwelling. Dan died a few years ago but his family still lives in Oklahoma.

# Chapter Three

# Families of Range 7 West

The families of Range 7 West and Townships 7, 8, and 9 South lived in the area from Pinhook Community on the northern boundary of Bankhead National Forest, Indian Tomb Hollow, and Brushy Lake in the southern portion of the territory. Families in this region ranged from the very wealthy plantation owners, to very poor one room cabin settlers who seeked out a living on the poor mountain soils.

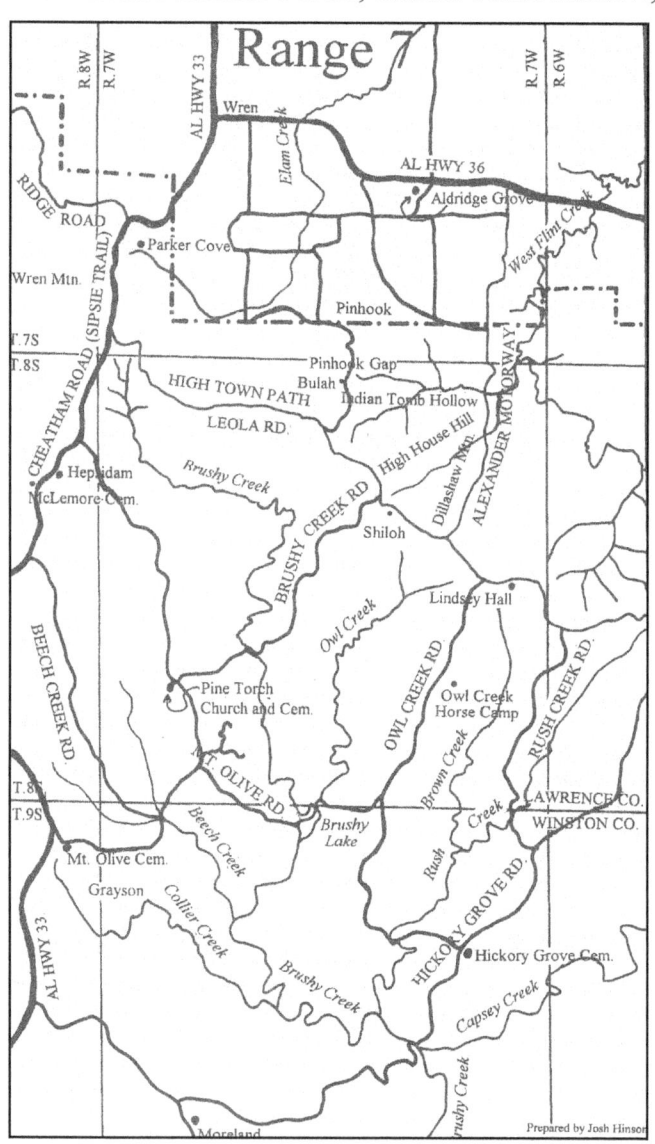

## Alexander Family

On the afternoon of August 22, 1990, I sat on a large flat sandstone rock located at the point of the ridge which separates the watersheds of Lee and Gillespie Creeks in the northeastern portion of the Warrior Mountains. I listened to the breezes, which were emerging from both canyons; rattle the leaves as if these winds were in a struggle for dominance. Here on the rock, I felt extremely close to the land which I loved. There seemed to flow a nurturing element from Mother Earth to soothe my spirit and make me keenly aware of the tranquility I was experiencing. As I gazed off into the valleys of the two watersheds, a feeling of power and grandeur, as if bound in the winds which lift the wings of the mighty eagle, came to me in a gentle flowing wind. What a privilege it was to feel what many people have sought through countless ages. It was a feeling that one would struggle to hold on to. This place seemed eternal and unchanged as if existing hundreds of years ago; not one sound of human existence, but the feeling of peace that men seem to never find. This area is a place many people take for granted, but I know it is the land of God. This spot in Bankhead Forest is a place where the heart can speak, even without a tongue. Then I understood that my beloved forest could provide something that money could never buy nor physical forces never control, but is there for those who seek what is bound in the sacred land of the "Warrior Mountains."

## Alexanders

The eastern vantage point of High House Hill Ridge was at one time part of the vast Alexander Estate. Here I thought back to the time when I was a small child living in a sharecropper's house on the "Jake Place". The house in which I lived was about one mile north of the High House Plantation Home. My right big toe is a constant reminder of those days in the old plank house on the Plantation. I lost my toe nail hanging the back of the nail on a steel nail head which had worked loose from one of the boards on the front porch. The toe nail never grew back properly; thus, the old clapboard house we lived in has left a mark that will remain with me the rest of my life.

At one time the Alexander family controlled an area that covered part or all of some 25 sections of land containing in excess of 10,000 acres. The land lay west from Pinhook to present day Highway 33 including Downing Hollow, east to the Flint Creek Road, south of the Leola Road, and north beyond Highway 36. Thus, the Alexanders controlled the largest area of land in the Warrior Mountains. Their control of this vase area of land was either maintained by direct ownership or through relatives. Today, much of the land lies within the northeastern boundary of William B. Bankhead National Forest and belongs to the U.S. Government.

The Alexanders had a large extended family. Many early generations of Alexander men were married twice, having a set of children by both wives. The 1820 census of Lawrence County indicates seven Alexander families were reported from the area. At that time, the Alexander family did not list any slaves.

The first known Alexander to settle in Lawrence County area probably moved in with the Cherokees in the late 1700's. Family legends of Cherokee origin support the family's early appearance into the area when it was still an active part of the Cherokee Nation. In addition, it is well known that family members married Cherokee mixed-bloods.

## James Alexander

James Alexander was born in Pennsylvania in 1770 or 1772 and died on August 26, 1851. James is found in all Lawrence County census records from 1820 through 1850. The 1850 census lists his age at 80 years old, making his date of birth 1770. This is supported by all Lawrence County census records prior to 1850.

James moved into Alabama from North Carolina in the late 1700's. Thus, he was probably related to the Cherokee people through marriage. James' first wife, Kitty Walker, was born in 1782 and died May 5, 1823. His second wife, Elizabeth, was born in October 1807 and died December 5, 1846. Kitty is buried to the right of James with Elizabeth buried to his left. James and his wives are buried in the old Alexander Cemetery. All three graves are denoted with marble tombstones, an unusual and generous tradition during the early eighteen hundreds.

## William Alexander

William Alexander was born to James and Kitty Walker Alexander in North Carolina on November 20, 1803. William died on April 4, 1873, and is buried in the Welborn-Alexander Cemetery in Pinhook Community. William married Mary Aldridge, who was born December 22, 1801. They were married on May 15, 1823.

William's children were: Jane Caroline, born 7/24/1824; Eliz Louisa, born 4/25/1826, and married Brian Kelly; Mary Belinda, born 8/19/1828; James, born 4/10/1830, and married Louisa Stover on 2/19/1857, and died 7/8/1906; Kitty Eleanor born 7/23/1833 and married Fletcher McKelvey on 6/3/1860; Thomas (Tom) Jefferson, born 8/7/1835, and married Sarah C. Warren

*Tombstones of Elizabeth, James, and Kitty Alexander in the old Alexander Cemetery at Pinhook.*

and later Sally Fitzgerald, and died 8/3/1890; William C., born 5/18/1838; David Walker, born 11/22/1844, married Sally Sherron; Sarah Ann, born 3/13/1844, and married N.G. Dillashaw on 11/4/1869; John Tyler, born on 5/25/1846, and married Fannie Johnson; and Henry Clay who was born in 1848.

**Tom Alexander**

Thomas (Tom) Jefferson Alexander, son of William and Mary, was the grandson of James and Kitty Walker Alexander, who are buried in the old Alexander Cemetery. Tom's first wife, Sarah Caroline Warren was born July 22, 1829, and died September 3, 1872. His second wife, Sallie A. Fitzgerald was born April 28, 1845, and died August 3, 1909. Tom Alexander and his wives are buried in the Wilburn-Alexander Cemetery about two miles east of Pinhook and about 200 yards south of James and Kitty.

*Thomas Jefferson (Tom) Alexander, the son of William and Mary Aldridge Alexander.*

Tom had two sons who lived in plantation style houses, Henry and Jake. Henry's mother was Sarah Warren and Jake's mother was Sallie Fitzgerald.

**Jake Alexander**

After Tom died his house was given to his youngest son, Jake Alexander. The Jake Alexander plantation house, later known as the "Jake Place," was located on a hilltop west of the forks of Thompson and West Flint Creeks. Jake Alexander married Sally Lindsey, the daughter of Jim Lindsey. Jake and Sally are buried in Aldridge Grove Cemetery.

Jake Alexander, along with his older half-brother Henry, and Henry's brother-in-law, Pope Warren, all had houses built exactly alike. The plantation style houses were all "L"-shaped with the bottom of the "L" being the front. The entire inside of the "L" had a large porch. The front of the house had a large downstairs porch as well as an upstairs porch with a picket railing. All the houses were two storied with nearly all rooms having a fireplace. Each was built of four inch yellow poplar drop siding with yellow poplar logs as floor joists. The houses had lightning rods on every ridge. They also had gutters with all down spouts leading to a large brick lined cistern. The three identical plantation style houses were the finest homes of that time.

I played in the old "Jake" house many times with my cousin. My uncle, Curtis Wilburn, was the last person to live in the Jake Alexander house. He eventually helped tear the house down for Mr. Dallas Yeager, the present property owner.

Sarah Laura Willis Alexander (1/4 Cherokee).

Henry Alexander, the son of Tom and Sarah Warren Alexander.

**Henry Alexander**

Henry Alexander's house place was bought from Silvanus Gibson. Gibson completed the back part of the house in the 1830's. Henry Alexander ended the completion of the plantation style home after he obtained the property from his father, Thomas, in the 1870's.

Henry Alexander married Laura Willis who was ¼ Cherokee Indian. Her mother was Margaret Roberts who was a half-blood Cherokee Indian. Laura had a brother Will Willis and a sister, Lucy Willis, who married Pope Warren.

Margaret Roberts Willis (1/2 Cherokee), who was born in 1832 and died in 1913, was the mother of Sarah Laura Willis Alexander.

Howard Roberts, who was the father of Margaret Roberts Willis, was born in 1804 and died in 1884.

Henry's house has been recently renovated by Don Alexander, Henry's grandson. The house is in Speake Community, located on the north side of Highway 36 about one half mile east of the West Fork of Flint Creek. Today, the beautiful home is a vivid reminder of days gone by.

**Plantation Products**

According to Mr. G. H. Melson, the old Tom Alexander plantation (which later belonged to the Jake) was erected using building materials which were hand-made or taken from the natural resources of the surrounding area. On the Alexander farm, bricks were mixed and molded by slaves and then fired in three large brick kilns. The kilns are approximately 5 feet high, 8 feet wide and 20 feet long. The kilns were heated by hickory and oak wood with each kiln being able to hold hundreds of bricks. The three kilns were built side by side facing a north-south direction with the open end facing south. The kilns were located about 150 yards due west of the main barn which was built seven years prior to the Civil War. All bricks were made by slaves prior to the Civil War. However, after the war, brick making ceased. These bricks could only be formed from intensive skills mastered by the slaves. The clay for making bricks was dug from the edges of nearby rocky glades.

The lime kiln was an open pit approximately ten feet deep. A huge fire was built with limestone rocks laying on top of the burning oak and hickory timbers. The ash from the timber and from the burned limestone was used as lime. The lime which was applied to cotton fields and other row crops. Other grades of lime were used for whitewashing, and while some grades were used as mortar when mixed with sand. The whitewash was used on barns and buildings and would last approximately one year.

Livestock manure was used as the major source of fertilizer for all row crops. At one time, Jake had about 40 head of hogs, 35 head of horses or mules, and 15 head of milk stock. The farm usually had five to eight cows which were milked each day.

William Todd "Boss" Kelso was in charge of the tanning yard for Tom and later his son, Jake Alexander. Boss made leather shoes from the hides that were tanned on the farm. His boys helped make shoes for the Alexander family or anyone who had 25 to 50 cents for a pair. Boss Kelso was also in charge of the blacksmith shop. According to family history, Boss and his wife, Mary Teague, were Cherokee Indian mixed-bloods. Mr. Gray was primarily responsible for most of the actual blacksmithing work.

The Alexander Cotton Gin could process about two bales of cotton per day. Mr. George Harvey Melson's first work was riding the ginning horses that pulled the large lever which ran the saws operating the cotton gin. It took six horses to work the gin-two abreast and three deep. The circle they pulled in was some 50 feet in diameter. After ginning, the horses were hooked to an auger press so the cotton could be made into a large bale. The bales were shipped from the Alexander place by wagons.

According to Mr. G. H. Melson, people did not work for money; they worked for what they wore and what they ate. Mr. Melson commented, "One thing wrong with people today is if they work they expect to get rich."

*George Melson and Nancy McVay, 1/2 Cherokee. George was the son of James Melson and Martha Osborn. Nancy was the daughter of Gilbert Zudock McVay and Catherine Brazell, a Cherokee Indian.*

A bridge crossing the West Fork of Flint Creek on the Alexander Plantation was made of five chestnut logs at least 50 feet long. A solid plant floor was nailed across the logs. The abutments of the bridge were made of cedar pole pens filled with rock. The bridge was an important crossing to reach Alexander property east of West Flint Creek. Mr. G. H. Melson helped replace the bridge that crossed West Flint Creek three times in his lifetime.

G. H. Melson's father and mother lived and worked on the old Alexander Plantation for years. His parents were George Melson and Nancy McVay who was ½ Cherokee Indian.

**Alexander Plantation Trench System**

Around the old Alexander Plantation site east of Thompson Creek and south of Gillespie Creek in the northern portion of Bankhead Forest is a long series of trenches that appear to have been hand dug. The trench system extends over one mile in length and is found on the uphill side of old fields which are now mature pine stands. The trench system was brought to my attention by Carl NeSmith, a local squirrel hunter who was puzzled over their purpose.

*Author Rickey Butch Walker, Carl Nesmith and Ray Hunkapiller examine a hand dug hillside trench which was utilized by the Alexander Plantation as a water diversion device.*

The trenches are some five feet deep in several places and run the contour around the hillsides. The downhill side of the trenches are mounded up and have all the dirt piled on the downhill side. The uphill side of the trench system is even with the rise of the land. At two springs located along the trench system, the ditches turn downhill to divert the water along the stream leading from the springs.

From close examination of the trench system and from observation that most of the trenches were built at the edge of old fields, it appears the trenches functioned as water control devices. In some places, the trenches appear to have been used to divert water around the hillside in order to slow the runoff. This would reduce erosion across the old fields that now stand in mature pine trees.

It is obvious that many people worked for days and possibly years to create the elaborate ditches. It is highly probable that slave labor was used to excavate the ditches. In all probability, the trenches were dug with hand tools because of their narrow width and depth. Part of the trench system crossed a ravine which had a stone dam that was used to divert water from the stream around the hillside. The diversion techniques kept the tillable soil from washing away and also provided a type of irrigation system which would allow the water to be soaked into the soil on the uphill sides of the fields.

After examining some American beech trees along the trench system, we located markings on a beech dated 1852. The close proximity of the 1852 beech markings to the trench system could lead one to believe the date of the tree and the trench could have been the same time period.

According to Mr. G. H. Melson, whose folks grew up working on the Alexander Plantation, the hillside ditches were used in places for terraces. They were built on contours and kept water running as slow as possible. In the mouth of Indian Tomb Hollow, a rock wall was also built from the rocky glade to Gillespie Creek to keep the water from rushing across the fields. Mr.

Melson said, "When I was a small boy, the rock wall was over waist high. I was told some 40 to 50 slaves worked at the digging of ditches and building the flood walls. The ditches and rock walls carried runoff water which drained off the land to the lower edges of the fields."

According to Mr. Melson, Jim Monk Alexander probably had part of the ditch system constructed prior to the Civil War. Jim Monk had several slaves and a lot of gold. Jim Monk had the fields on the lower side of the trench system farmed by his slaves. He was said to have been extremely rough with his slave labor and demanded they obey his every command or face his wrath.

The contour ditches went from High House Hill up Indian Tomb. In addition, they were built east of Thompson Creek for over a mile. Later, Jake Alexander bought some of the trenched fields from his uncle, Nobe Dillashaw, and farmed the area for several years. John Alexander, who lived on the mountain between West Flint and Thompson Creeks, also worked for some of the hillside fields. The McVay field east of Flint also belonged to John Alexander who was a cousin to Jake.

Many years have passed and many leaves have fallen in the old ditches. We may never know who labored long and hard to construct such an elaborate system of hillside trenches, but one thing is clear: If left undisturbed, the evidence of labor in the ditches can still be seen long after we have pushed up many years of daisies.

**Alexander and Stover Families**

James (Jim Monk) Alexander, who was the son of William Alexander and Mary Aldridge, probably inherited the old High House Hill home and lived there until his death. William Alexander entered the land on High House Hill on February 12, 1833. James was born on April 10, 1830, and married Louisa M. Stover on February 19, 1857. James died on July 8, 1906.

Louisa M. Stover was the daughter of Elijah Stover of Virginia and Delphia Logan. The Elijah Stover family settled in the Speake Community of Lawrence County about 1818. Elijah, who served in the War of 1812, was thought to have passed through Lawrence County while enlisted with the East Tennessee Regiment under the command of Andrew Jackson. It is highly probably that Stover passed through the Speake area along the Black Warriors' Path (Mitchell Trace) during his time of service from September 1814 until March 1815. It is documented in the book "A Narrative of the Life of David Crockett" that the East Tennessee Volunteers crossed the Tennessee River at Melton's Bluff in October 1814, and traveled along the Black Warriors' Path through the area of Speake Community. Stover could have returned to the beautiful area he had seen during his time of service.

James W. Alexander and Louisa M. Stover had the following children: Artimsey (Ms.Timm), born December 1958; Sarah Ann (Sallie), born December 1859; James, born 1862; Eliza Bell, born 7/7/1864; Nettie, born 1875; Ider Mae, born 1875; Mattie, born May 1879; and John L., born October 1880.

James W. Alexander enlisted in the Civil War at Hillsboro, Alabama on May 24, 1861, in Company "C" of the 9th Alabama Infantry. He was captured in Decatur, Alabama on May 18, 1864.

**High House Hill Plantation House**

At least three large Alexander homes were located within the Thompson Creek watershed. The James W. (Jim Monk) Alexander Plantation house, later known as the "High House," was located at the ridge point of High House Hill halfway between Gillespie and Lee Creeks. Another Alexander house owned by John Alexander, known at the "John Alec Place," was located on the ridge east of Thompson Creek and south of West Flint Creek. Ms. Tim Alexander's house, known as "Ms. Tim's Place," was located between James and John on the west side of Thompson Creek. Her house was located between Lee and Gillespie Creeks and east of the Alexander Motorway. Ms. Tim, daughter of Jim Monk, never married and lived to be some 80 years old. As a result of these strategically located plantation homes, the overseers of the family had control of the large Thompson Creek watershed and all its tributaries, as well as a large portion of West Flint Creek.

High House Hill is a mountain ridge which is now part of the William B. Bankhead Forest. The ridge is located west of Alexander Motorway and north of the Leola Road. Two small creeks, Lee and Gillespie, are tributaries to West Flint. The creeks begin on the western slopes of High House Hill and contain rich fertile valleys. These valleys, now containing mature trees, were large open fields prior to, and after the Civil War. Located on the hill top ridge above these fertile valleys was a large plantation house which was known locally at the "High House."

The High House may have been designed and built by James W. (Jim Monk) Alexander's daddy, William Alexander. The "High House" was on the last bench of the ridge prior to the top of the hill. Some 100 yards downhill from the edge of the bluff line on a small knoll, Jim Monk's house provides an excellent view of the fields in the fertile valleys of Lee and Gillespie Creek. The large two storied plantation house contained sixteen rooms with nine outside doors. The house was made of typical four inch yellow poplar drop siding. The floor joists were built with large yellow poplar timbers. Nearly every room contained a large brick fireplace. The top of the house was covered by a slave observation deck. Mr. G. H. Melson helped tear down the old High House for the lumber to be used on the Jake Alexander place.

The yard of the High House contained approximately three acres and was enclosed by a split rail fence about waist high. Three guard dogs were trained to protect the place. Supposedly, one of the dogs guarded each of the two gates leading into the yard with the other one staying near the house. No one could pass along the road unless Jim Monk "called off the dogs."

Just outside the yard, but nearby, were seven slave cabins. According to local history, Jim Monk owned some forty slaves who worked the rented cotton fields. Jim Monk owned from forty to eight acres, thus, renting most of the land his slaves farmed. His wealth, most of which was gold, had to be traded for confederate currency during the Civil War. For years after the war, his children played with the worthless money. Legend has persisted for years that Jim Monk buried most of his gold near his house. He was said to have a pouch containing over

$400.00 of gold coins when he died. People have searched for the hidden treasure for over 100 years.

North of the High House was a spring with the best drinking water in the country, The High House Spring still issues a good stream of flowing water during the driest season of the year, late August.

**High House Hill**

As I sat listening to the trickle of water flowing from the lower layers of a massive sandstone bluff, I thought about the slave times of long ago. I imagined what it would like to drink this cool water after a long day of work. The spring actually flows from a sandstone rock wall at the bottom of the bluff at about the same elevation or slightly higher than the house place. It has been told that the house had a source of natural flowing water piped from the spring.

Between the spring and house is a rock shelter that appears to have been modified by the early settlers. Unfortunately, pot hunters had dug deep into the soil on the floor of the shelter. A trail from the top of the ridge passed through the sandstone bluff. The passageway was just large enough for a person to pass and exit at the bottom of the bluff line within five feet of the shelter. I walked up to the top of the ridge through the narrow sandstone trail. The passage was stair step like and rose approximately 50 feet above the shelter to the ridge top. The gap was obviously a footpath from the ridge top fields on High House Hill to the spring.

*The Henry Alexander Plantation Home.*

The old wagon road came off the Alexander Motorway and up the hill close to the High House. The road turned southwest and intersected the High Town Path (present day Leola Road) about a mile west of

Shiloh Church. The High House plantation house sat just northeast of a high rocky crest which sloped enough to allow wagon passage up to the top of the ridge. The edge of the bluff line was within a few feet of the road as it passed between the bluffs on either side. The road was at one time a part of old mail route three from Moulton.

The bluff line from the gap is continuous northwest into Indian Tom Hollow. The bluff line on the other side of the road continues into Lee Creek Canyon. Human skeletons once lay under the bluff line west of the gap. The bluff, with skeletal remains, was just over the ridge from the High House Plantation. Many people had seen the scattered skeletal remains, which may have been a disturbed burial.

The High House Hill area was a type of primitive mountain village located in the northern edge of Bankhead Forest east of Old Beulah Church between the Alexander Motorway, Leola Road, and Spivey Gap Road. It is obvious that High House Hill was once a thriving settlement with as many as twenty-five residents claiming the surrounding area as their home. These families probably came from the east into Lawrence County along the High Town Path, an early Indian trail leading from Northwestern Georgia into Lawrence County, to settle in the area. Some families, besides the Alexanders were the Gillespies, Naylors, Sheffields, Eddys, Browns, McVays, Sparks, and other families who still have many descendants living in Lawrence County today. Most of these families were mixed-blood Indian of Cherokee and white ancestry.

## Gillespie Family of Indian Tomb

Located about one-half mile north of the High House was the home place of James Richard Gillespie and Lucy Johnson Gillespie. Gillespie Spring and Gillespie Creek was named after these early Bankhead people who settled in the area in the early 1820's. The old Gillespie home site is located about 100 yards southeast of Gillespie Spring.

According to Mr. Bobbie R. Gillespie, Lucy was the daughter of Henry Johnson who fought and was wounded in the Revolutionary War. Henry Johnson and his brother had immigrated from Ireland. Henry's brother was killed in a conflict with Indians shortly after his arrival to the United States.

**James Richard Gillespie**

James Richard Gillespie fought in the Creek War of 1812-14 with the East Tennessee Volunteers from September 23, 1813, to December 23, 1813. He served in Captain Cowan's Calvary and was armed with two pistols and a sword. A Colonel Porter was in command of the troops. James Richard Gillespie received $60.30 for his three months of service. His horse received more money for service rendered than did James.

James Richard Gillespie served in Captain John Cowan's company during the same time that David Crockett served as a third sergeant with Cowan. It is highly probable that James Richard Gillespie from Indian Tomb knew and fought with the famous frontiersman David Crockett, "King of the Wild Frontier."

On January 1, 1814, James attended the muster rolls in Blount County, Tennessee, where he received an honorable discharge. After returning from war, James married Lucy on September 9, 1818. They were married at Cotaco by Justice of the Peace Menafee. They had five children with their daughter Mary marrying John Alexander. Mary died shortly after the birth of their son, Henry Johnson Alexander. According to the 1850 census, John Alexander and his son Henry were living with his mixed-blood Indians. After James Richard Gillespie's death, Lucy filed for two pensions. She eventually received 80 acres near the Liberty-Morris Chapel area.

James Richard Gillespie is buried about 300 yards northeast of Gillespie Spring. The Gillespie or Indian Tomb Hollow Cemetery contains some forty graves with James Richard Gillespie and his family having the only engraved tombstones. The rest of the people buried in the cemetery have only rock markers and are thought to be Indian, black, and white.

## Other Families of Indian Tomb

Many other early house places of families who settled near Gillespie Spring are located in Indian Tomb Hollow.

**Eddy Family**

At the junction of Alexander Motorway and the Indian Tomb Road is the old Roof Eddy place. Mr. Eddy lived on the rocky glad at the beginning of the old wagon road into Indian Tomb Hollow. At a party and bonfire at the Eddy Place, one of Mr. Eddy's daughters got too close to the fire and her dress caught on fire. She began to run, but family members overtook her and put out the flames. She later died of the burns. After the death of their daughter, the Eddy family moved from the Indian Tomb area.

**Minor Family**

After the Eddy family moved, Mr. John Norman Minor's Cherokee Indian family moved to the old house place. John Norman Minor, one-half Cherokee, was born in 1880 and died in 1957. He was the son of Henry Butler Minor and Cadzy Cadiza Coluda Caco, a full-blooded Cherokee. John Norman Minor married Ella Allred who was also one-half Cherokee.

John and Ella had eleven children: Dola first married Hayes Wilhoite, later she married Wallace Sapp; Nola married Ernest Hill; Rena married Levi Adair; Lena married Roy Millwood; Eunice married Jim Shaddix; Worda Minor married Irene Mays; Lewis Minor married Mary Strickland; Dona first married ? Adair, second ? Johnson and third time Frank Sapp. They had an infant that died at childbirth; and twin boys that died at birth with their mother, Ella.

Top Standing L-R: Ella Allred Minor (1/2 Cherokee), John Norman Minor (1/2 Cherokee) Seated: Jane Childers Allred - Ella's mother (1/2 Cherokee) Twin Babies L-R: Dola Minor, Nola Minor. Date of picture: 1911.

The Minors were Cherokee Indians from east of Indian Tomb. Most of the Minor family still live within a few miles of their old home place and retain their community identity as Indian people.

**Sheffield Family**

The next place west along the Indian Tomb Hollow Road is the Sheffield home place. Member of the Sheffield family intermarried with the Gillespie family. Mr. Sheffield ran a blacksmith shop near his home which was located just west of his spring, Sheffield Spring flows from a limestone outcropping nine months a year and is about one-quarter mile west of the Alexander Motorway. The Indian Tomb Road now makes an uphill curve around the old spring site.

## Sparks Family

About one-fourth mile further west along the new road between Sheffield Spring and Gillespie Spring is the old Asa Sparks place. Mr. Sparks is buried at Pinhook in the old cemetery located on a wooded hillside. Some of the graves have large hardwood growing from the burial site.

## McVay Family

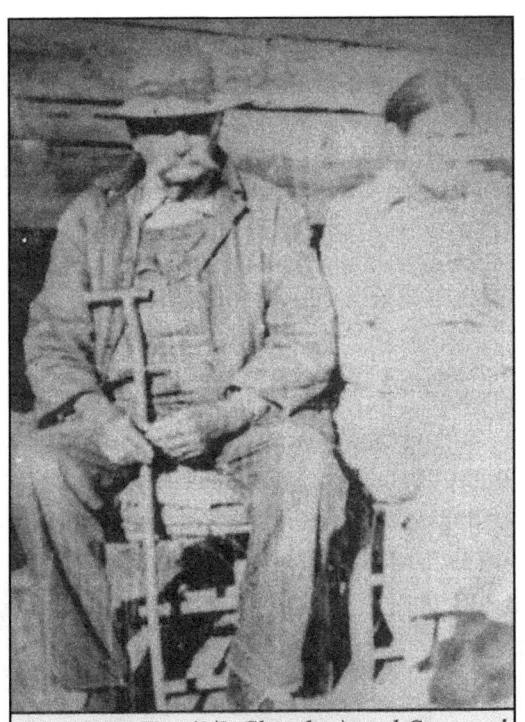

*Kay C. McVay (1/2 Cherokee) and Savannah Brannon. Note their log cabin in the background.*

K. McVay lived in the old Gillespie house and Tom McVay lived in the old Sparks house. Mr. G. H. Melson said, "Uncle K McVay set up with Jim Monk before he died. Uncle K said Jim Monk talked about the gold he had and that he kept $450.00 in gold in a pouch under his pillow. After he died, Uncle K said the gold under his pillow went missing."

## Ferguson Family

In addition, Mr. John T. Ferguson lived in the old house near Gillespie Spring for a long time. For several years, Mr. J. D. Ferguson lived in Indian Tomb just a few yards from the upper fork of Gillespie Creek. The Ferguson home was a log cabin with a dirt floor. Located on the south bank of the creek, it was just a short distance from where Gillespie Spring Branch enters Gillespie Creek. According to Mr. Ferguson, no more than 20 acres were cleared from the Alexander Motorway up the creek. Near the forks of the creeks, a long narrow field of about three acres lay along the south bank. Two to three other patches lay adjacent to the creek downstream from the forks toward the Alexander Motorway. Most of the canyon was considered virgin timber by Ferguson. He moved from the area in the 1930's.

## McMillan Family

The Emmett McMillan family also lived in Indian Tomb for a while. Ms. Bessie McMillan remembers having small patches of corn surrounded by the tall timbers of Indian Tomb.

**Dillashaw Family**

South of Lee Creek, the largest area of land was owned by Nobe Dillashaw who married Sarah Ann Alexander, daughter of William and sister to Tom Alexander. Today, that area is known and recorded on maps as Dillashaw Mountain. According to Jack McDowell, Nobe was from a homestead on Borden Creek near the creek's junction with Horse Creek. Nobe's parents were Joseph and Beckie Dillashaw.

**Other Families of Lee Creek**

Within the Lee Creek Valley was the Camedy, Squalls, Wakefield, and Nichols home places. Mr. Squall ran a cedar mill. The cedar was cut from the many limestone glades in the surrounding areas. The Wakefields and Nichols were intermarried and ran a large syrup mill. Mr. William Nichols was a revolutionary war soldier and is buried on Forest Service property in the mouth of Indian Tomb Hollow, east of the Alexander Motorway. The Nichols Cemetery is located on Forest Service property at the edge of the present day Dallas Yeager farm in Section 1 of Township 8 South and Range 7 West.

Nearly all of the land that lies within the Lee and Gillespie Creek watersheds is now part of the U.S. Forest Service property. The valleys have a limestone base with the hillsides containing beautiful sandstone cliffs, some of which contain vertical rock walls over fifty feet high. One of the most historical areas in Lawrence County, the beautiful Indian Tomb Hollow, is located in the valley portion of Gillespie Creek and is situated with Gillespie Spring near the center of the hollow. By way of the improved Indian Tomb Hollow road into the area, the U.S. Forest Service harvested the four blocks of timber before their clear-cutting was finally stopped. Thus, it is hopeful that the old growth timber of Indian Tomb Hollow surrounding the majestic sandstone box canyon was saved.

*William Nichols, a Revolutionary War soldier, is buried in the mouth of Indian Tomb Hollow near Thompson Creek.*

As I started this story on the point of a large sandstone bluff, I again take a long and enduring look into the beautiful valleys. I behold what the red men of long ago beheld. However, my heart is now without words, but is filled with feelings of sadness of what might happen to the land that I love – the "Warrior Mountains."

# Welborn Family of Pinhook

On December 25, 1893, my great, great, grandfather, Gustavius (Gus) T. Welborn, became one of the prominent citizens of the Pinhook Community. The land he bought consisted of 160 acres located in the northwest ¼ of Section 35 of Township 7 South and Range 7 West. According to the old deed, Gus purchased the property from J. M. Doss, who had acquired the property from R. M. and Pandora Simpson on November 6, 1893, for $800.00.

Originally, Gus, who claimed to be from Winston County, entered 160 acres of land in Section 24 of Township 8 South Range 7 West on January 15, 1890, according to Old Land Records of Lawrence County, Alabama by Margaret Cowart. The land was located on property now owned by the U.S. Forest Service and lies just south of Leola Road near Lindsey Hall Church some 30 yards. Later Gus moved to the Pinhook Community just north of Indian Tomb and lived there until his death.

Gustavius (Gus) T. Welborn (1/4 Cherokee).

### Census Records

Gus was the son of Lockey B. and Martha Segars Welburn, who were from Jackson County, Georgia on November 16, 1848. The Pascal name was probably for SandyPascal Segars, since my great-granddaddy was Sandy Pascal Wilburn and my grandfather was Authur Pascal Wilburn. Lockey was the son of Martha Welborn who was born on June 20, 1797, and is buried in Cave Springs Cemetery at the junction of Leola road and highway 41.

According to the 1870 Winston County Census, Wood P. Welborn was a 43 year old boot maker from Georgia, and Lucinda was 44 years old from Georgia. Also listed in 1870, Thomas Welborn was a 25 year old farmer from Georgia and his wife Francis was 24. According to the 1870 Lawrence County Census, Martha Welborn, 70, lived with Thomas's family. Martha was listed as being born in North Carolina. In addition, the 1870 census also lists Lockey B. Welborn and his wife Martha who were 35 and from Georgia.

## Naylor Kinfolks

Gus had married Sarah Mandy Segars, the daughter of Mary E. Welborn (Segars) Naylor. Mary, known as Granny Naylor, had at least two children before her first husband died. She married the second time to a Jeremiah Naylor from the Sand Mountain area. Mary (Granny Naylor) had three known children: Thomas Segars; Sarah Mandy Segars (Welborn), born September 10, 1858, and died March 25, 1937; and Thomas and Sarah Mandy's half-brother, George W. Naylor, who was born November 3, 1866, and died May 23, 1943.

*The home of Gustavius T. Welborn in Pinhook Community.*

My great, great, great grandmother, Granny Naylor, was born on May 2, 1838 and died on December 24, 1913. She was the matriarch of the Bankhead Forest Naylor Family. The George Naylor family settled on the ridge just west of Indian Tomb Hollow with a lot of their land lying in the upper drainages of Gillespie Creek. Mary settled along with her son George and his family about two miles from Gus and Mandy near Old Beulah Church. Gus and Mandy were first double first cousins. Mandy's parents were Sandy Pascal Segars and Mary E. Welborn. Mandy and Lockey Welborn were brother and sister, and Sandy Pascal and Martha Segars were brother and sister.

George Naylor, Gus's brother-in-law, and his family made regular visits to the home of his half-sister, Mandy Welborn. Most of George's sons helped Gus and Mandy farm and gather their crops. Mandy was married to Gustavius "Gus" T. Welborn

*Sandy Welborn (3/16 Cherokee)*

on October 23, 1879. Gus was born on December 7, 1861, and died on October 20, 1920. He was a farmer and old herb doctor. Many people would call on Gus when they got sick.

**Welborn Family**

Gus and Mandy Welborn were the parents of my great granddaddy Sandy Welborn and the grandparents of my granddaddy Authur Wilburn. According to the 1880 Census of Lawrence County, Gus, who was 18, and Mandy, who was 20, had a child one year old named Luther.

Gus and Mandy had ten children: Luther who married Mattie Ellenburg; Josh married a Tucker woman; Martie married Tranny Morgan; Sandy married Dora Johnson; Howard married Minnie Curtis; Nellie married Terrance Ledlow; Celie married Frank Johnson; Lynch married Fanny Johnson; Nelly died at five or six years of age; and Monroe died at four years old.

My great grandparents were Sandy and Dora Johnson Welborn. The children were: Authur, Mamie (Harden), Nathie (Proctor), Monroe, Nola, Willie Myrl (Proctor), and Willard. Nathie and Willie Myrl married brothers, W.D. Proctor and Ira Proctor.

**Gus**

Gus Welborn farmed for a living and sold cured meat from his smokehouse. The closest store was about ¼ mile west of Gus Welborn's home. The local grocery store in Pinhook Community around 1900 was owned and operated by Lee Revis.

*Gus and Mandy Welborn's family*

Gus had severe asthma which contributed to his death and Mandy died of pneumonia. Mandy was a big boned redheaded and freckled woman and claimed all the redheaded grandchildren belonged to her. Mandy never worked in the fields because she had a ham of cured meat stolen the only time she went to the field.

Gus's boys mostly worked the crops and took care of the livestock. Gus also hired his nephews, Thomas, Mile Jack, and Kir Benjamin Naylor, to help with the crops. The Naylor boys were the nephews of Gus and Mandy. Gus raised a lot of alfalfa for hay. He also raised more corn than any other crop to feed the livestock. He had fine mules and all types of farming equipment. He had a big barn built just for storing hay and corn. Gus kept several head of hogs and cows. The family depended on stock for food, transportation, and for their income. Gus raised hogs, cured the meat, and sold the meat for profit.

Gus gave land joining the northwest corner of the Alexander Plantation for the Welborn Cemetery. Gus and Mandy are buried on their old home place in the Welborn-Alexander Cemetery.

## The Simms Place of Pinhook Branch

Nestled against the northern edge of William B. Bankhead Forest is a small community known as Pinhook. In the early days of Lawrence County, the thriving farm community of Pinhook was the site of large plantations and wealthy landowners. The area was dotted with clean clear limestone springs, beautiful timbered ridges and valleys of the Warrior Mountains, and the vast flatland and farms stretching into the Moulton Valley. Three families, who were prominent in the area around Pinhook, were the Alexanders, the Aldridges, and the Simms.

### Pinhook

As a small boy growing up near the Pinhook Community, I knew the Simms Place as the historical center of the Pinhook Community. It seemed as though everyone knew of the Simms Place, the old Pinhook School, and Pinhook Church.

A large plantation style house, the home of Doctor Thomas D. Simms was located near the center of the Simms Place. A heavily flowing limestone spring was located some 100 yards southeast of the plantation house. Today, four huge sandstone chimneys, sandstone foundations and steps, and a sandstone-lined well marked the site of the historic place.

According to the abstract of Mr. Hoyt Adair, the land that became the Simms Place was first entered by Jacob Boren on September 1, 1818; Samuel Elliott, September 12, 1818; and

William Wise in 1831. Probably sometime around the 1840's, Thomas D. Simms acquired the property at Pinhook and built the huge plantation house. In addition to the land around Pinhook, Thomas also purchased the large farm along West Flint Creek and highway 36 known as the Kelly Place, now owned by Mr. G. T. Hamilton. According to <u>Old Records of Lawrence County, Alabama</u> by Margaret Cowart, Dr. Simms entered most of the land near highway 36 and West Flint Creek in November 1850.

**Doctor Thomas Simms**

Doctor Thomas D. Simms was born in Madison County, Virginia on October 12, 1813. According to a letter written by Thomas D. Simms on March 31, 1873, he was the first child of seven children born to Col. Ruben C. Simms from Orange County, Virginia and Francis Graves of Madison County, Virginia. They were married on November 11, 1812. Francis Graves was the daughter of Captain Thomas Graves and Mourning Burrus. Ruben was the son of Major James Simms (1755 and 1811) and Mildred Durrette. The Simms family ancestors can be traced back in Virginia to the year of 1619.

Thomas D. Simms came to Alabama and began teaching school near Danville. He married Martha Hodges of Oakville in 1842. Thomas and Martha had four children before she died in 1851. According to the 1850 census, four people were living in the Simms household: Thomas D., age 36; Martha E., age 24; Edgar, age 1; and Sarah Hamilton, age 24.

Many stories have been told of Doctor Thomas Simms riding his horse from Pinhook to Oakville without getting off his land. Since he owned land at Pinhook and the Kelly Place, and his wife's family owned land at Oakville, it could have been entirely possible for him to ride a horse from Pinhook to Oakville and never get off their family property. Dr. Thomas Simms had several slaves who worked, farmed, and lived on the Simms Place. Many of the black people in Moulton are probably descendants of the farm laborers who once worked in the Alexander, Aldridge, and Simms plantations in the Pinhook Community. The Simms Place had a total of three cemeteries: one cemetery for the slaves; another cemetery now in mature forest for the white sharecroppers; and third cemetery, west of the old Simms plantation home, for members of the Simms family.

Dr. Thomas D. Simms married the second time on October 15, 1857, to Frances Preuit. Frances was born on January 15, 1836, and died January 22, 1896. Thomas and Frances had two children. Dr. Simms died on July 16, 1891.

**Robert and Panola Simms Simpson**

The daughter of Thomas and Frances Simms was Panola Eugenia Simms who was born January 29, 1859. Panola's half-brother from her father's first marriage was Doctor Edgar T. Simms. Dr. E.T. Simms' understudy for about two years was a young man by the name of Robert Murphey Simpson. Probably during the understudy, Miss Panola and R.M. Simpson became acquainted and eventually married on April 15, 1877. After their marriage, Robert and Panola settled on the Simms Place at Pinhook for some seven years. Robert and Panola Simpson owned some 800 acres of land with approximately 250 acres for cultivation.

In 1884, R.M. Simpson began attending medical school at Vanderbilt University in Nashville, Tennessee and graduated in 1885. After graduating from Vanderbilt, Doctor Robert and Panola Simms Simpson moved back to Pinhook Community for approximately four years before moving to Moulton about 1889. Dr. R.M. Simpson pursued a large and successful medical practice for some eight years before his death on April 24, 1897. Dr. Robert M. and Panola Simpson had six children: Frances Mildred Ann – September 14, 1878, to April 19, 1893; Robert Emmett – July 5, 1880, to November 6, 1948; William Lawrence – February 25, 1883, to November 30, 1929; Edgar Murphey – July 19, 1885, to March 12, 1933; and John Preuit – January 20, 1896, to December 18, 1968.

**William Lawrence Simms**

In addition to Panola, Thomas D. and Frances Preuit Simms had one son William Lawrence Simms. William Lawrence Simms married Forrest Rose Preuit and lived near the Pinhook Community in his early days. Shortly after his youngest child, Annar Rose, was born William Lawrence moved his family to Moulton.

I recently had the distinct pleasure of talking to Mrs. Annar Rose Simms Vester, a delightful lady. According to Ms. Annar, who now lives in Nashville, Tennessee, her mother and father had eight children: Thomas, Preuit, Willia, Frank, Bluit, Minnie, Frances Panola, and Annar Rose.

Today the Simms Place remains one of the most historical and beautiful places in Lawrence County. The old limestone spring still gushes cool crystal clear water as it probably did when the red men lived and roamed the area known as the Simms Place of the "Warrior Mountains."

# Naylor Family of the Spivey Gap Road

Beulah land, sweet Beulah land of the Warrior Mountains in Bankhead National Forest is the cemetery where Bular Naylor lies buried along with many of his Naylor family kinfolks. The Naylors can claim Beulah as their mountaintop family cemetery since only two other people who were not directly related or married to the Naylors are buried in the graveyard. The beautiful and peaceful place is the true Beulah Land of all the deceased brothers and sisters of Bular Naylor.

## Bulah

The Old Bulah Church and Cemetery are located on the Pinhook Gap Road about ¼ mile north of the Leola Road. According to the sign above the door of the old church, the site was established as a Missionary Baptist Church in 1893. George W. Naylor deeded three acres of land and helped construct one room log building which initially served as the church. The church was covered with wooden shingles and had wooden shutters to close over the open windows. The first log church burned down and was reconstructed, while the third building was made of cement blocks.

Bular Naylor, the first person to be buried in the adjoining cemetery, was the young son of George W. and Lousia Simmons Naylor. Bular was born on August 16, 1905, and died on December 22, 1905, and the old log church building and cemetery was named Bulah in his memory.

## Granny Naylor

According to family history, Mary E. Welborn's (Granny Naylor's) first husband, Pascal Sandy Segars, was killed in the Civil War at the Battle of Cedar Run or Slaughter Mountian in Virginia.. Granny Naylor's husband, along with some 70 Confederate soldiers, were killed in the battle and were buried in a mass grave. Since so many Confederate soldiers were killed, it was impossible to allows families to claim and bury their dead.

After Mary's first husband died, she married Jeremiah Naylor from Sand Mountain about 1867. After their marriage, Mary gave birth to George W. Naylor. After her husband evidently moved back to Sand Mountain, Mary was left with small children to raise. Since George was born after his daddy had left the family, most people believed George had powers to cure diseases such as the thrash which effected small children. George would read in the bible and then blow in the children's mouths. Many people claimed George would cure their children.

Granny Naylor lived in a small one room log cabin at Old Bulah near her son George and his wife Louisa. Granny's cabin was just west of George's home. Near the Naylor homes was Naylor Spring that provided water for the nearby family and church.

**Ruthie Naylor Pruiet**

Recently I talked to Ms. Ruthie Naylor Prueit who is the youngest child of George andLousia Naylor. She was born in the family's log cabin, located just north of Old Bulah Church on the west side of the Pinhook Gap Road on July 14, 1911. Ruthie was delivered by the help of Ms. Liz Smith, the mother of Mr. Shirley Smith. When Ruthie was young, she was told by her mother and daddy, they found her by a stump on the road going up the mountain to Old Bulah. For years, Ruthie would look by each stump as she would walk up the mountain with her family to see where she was found.

Ruthie also told of Granny Naylor dipping snuff with the aid of a black gum brush. As a small child, Ruthie always wanted to get Granny's snuff brush. One day Granny sopped up a big wad of fresh snuff and on her old brush and let Ruthie place it into her mouth. The snuff made Ruthie so sick she thought she was going to die. From that day forth, Ruthie never wanted to try dipping snuff.

**The George Naylor Family**

The family's cabin was a two room log house with a dogtrot hallway through the middle of the house. All eleven of George andLousia Naylor's children were born at Old Bulah and are listed as follows:

Thomas, born on December 30, 1883, and died on June 17, 1968, married Lula V. Brooks; Pearl Lee, born on August 10, 1886, and died September 11, 1924, married Jones Rodgers; Mile Jack, born on April 29, 1888, and died on March 17, 1955, and married Myrtie Brooks, second marriage to Nellie Ledlow; Tilda, born May 19, 1889, and died October 21, 1971, married A.J. (Bud) Demastus; Lillian is buried at Jasper and married Will Smith; Kir Benjamin (Ben), born on January 30, 1894, and died on January 25, 1978, married Janie Morgan; T. Wash, born on January 6, 1898, and died on November 11, 1961, married Eva Riggs; Jim Mat, born on October 28, 1990, and died June 10, 1944, married Martha Adair; W.C. (Buster), born on March 3, 1902, and died on December 20, 1964, married Minnie Morgan; Bular, died of diphtheria five months after he was born in 1905; Theral, born on May 19, 1907, and also died of diphtheria on November 18, 1909; and Ruthie.

George entered over 300 acres of property at Old Bulah. Later his daughter, Tilda Demastus and her husband entered land High House Hill. Tilda's land joined Mr. Shirley Smith's property to the south. Thomas got land next to Tilda and later took the land that belonged to Tilda and Bud. Will and Lillian Naylor Smith lived in the old High House after they got married. A total of four of the Naylor family members lived in the High House. At one time, George Naylor and his children owned nearly all the property in the Old Bulah area.

*The George Naylor family.*

When the Naylors lived at Bulah, most of the older children walked about one mile to Poplar Springs School on Leola Road. The Naylor family attended church services at Bulah which were held at least two Sundays per month. Mr. Green Towers, one of the early preachers at Old Bulah, would ride a mule to church each Sunday he preached. They did not have Sunday school but had singing and preaching.

During the early days after the family moved from the mountain, their dead relatives were transported to the mountain cemetery in a wagon pulled by mules. Only two people not directly related to the Naylor family are buried in the Bulah cemetery. Ms. Florence Williams, who was a member of the church, asked the Naylor family to be buried at the cemetery when she died and J.T. Rodgers had a baby that was buried in the cemetery.

The Naylor children use to attend singing schools at Pine Torch Church and other nearly locations where singing schools were held. The singing schools were a major social event during the early days of Lawrence County. Ben and Buster Naylor met their wives at a singing school held at Shiloh Church on the Leola Road. Shiloh was located about a mile and a half from Old Bulah.

The neighbors to the Naylors were old man Rodgers, the father of Jones Rodgers. Mr. Rodgers lived on the Leola Road about ¼ mile east of Pinhook Gap Road. An old wagon road turned southwest at the Rodgers place and crossed Brushy Creek. Mr. Tom Gailey lived on the Pinhook Gap Road north of Bulah just off the mountain west of the Simms Place. Did Robbins live near Mr. Tom Gailey. The Spivey family also lived near the foot of the mountain.

**Louisa Simmons Naylor**

The closest store was on top of a hill about one mile east of Pinhook Church. The store was owned and operated by Lee Revis. Mr. Revis would swap groceries for ginseng, pink rook, grub root, and various other herbs which could be resold. Lousia Naylor would take her children out in the woods to dig all kinds of herbs for trade. Louisa always kept her family in groceries during the root digging season and would always get more groceries for the ginseng. After a very successful digging trip, Louisa had enough roots to get the family a clock. Ms. Ruthie said the whole family was tickled to death over their first clock.

Medical doctors never came to the mountain, because Lousia would treat her children. During the winter, Louisa would take a jug of whiskey mixed with ginseng, pink root, and other herbs and give her children a dose of the tonic each day. The tonic did not taste too bad as compare to Louisa's mixture of whiskey and strong roots called the "bitters". For some bad ailments, Louisa would give the children a dose of the "bitters". Bitters were made from whiskey, yellow root, and other bitter herbs. The children were also forced to wear strong smelling poultices for some respiratory ailments.

Louisa would also work all day for Dave and Julie Alexander who lived just west of the Simms place. She would take Buster and Ruthie to the Dave Alexander place and stay all day and night patching clothes, making soap, and quilting. After two days of work, Dave and Julie would give Louisa a side of meat, bucket of lard, dried beans, and other goods. Lousia would sometimes bring all her children to pick peas and beans for half of what they gathered.

Lousia Naylor did not can food for winter but would dry everything. She would peel pumpkins which would be cut into a continuous ring to be hung out until it was bone dry. Lousia would place her quilt frames outside on four straight chairs to hang her pumpkins rings in the sunlight. After the pumpkin rings were dry, they would be placed in cloth bags where the rings would last all winter. When she was ready to cook dried pumpkin, Lousia would cut it up into pieces and soak it like dried beans before cooking. She also dried peaches and apples in the same manner.

Lousia would place dry peas and beans in the hulls on a large quilt. She would fold the quilt over the peas or beans and have the kids beat them with a stick to knock them out of the hulls. After being knocked out of the hulls, the children would help pick out the beans or peas. The dried peas and beans would be placed into cloth bags and hung in the sun each warm day. Sassafras limbs were broken up and placed in the sacks with the peas and beans to keep them fresh.

**George and Lousia**

Each fall George would kill hogs and make a lot of sausage. Lousia would make little cloth bags about two inches in diameter and stuff each one full of fresh sausage. The little bags would then be hung in the smokehouse to dry.

When they were ready to fix breakfast, Lousia would take the bags of sausage and cut the meat to be fried. In addition, the Naylor family also dried beef strips to make jerky which was also soaked before being fried.

George and Lousia would also raise chickens for food. All the roosters were placed in a coop and fed until they were real fat. When the family wanted chicken for dinner, they would go to the coop and get a fat young rooster. The hens were depended upon to provide the family with fresh eggs and new supplies of roosters.

Mr. Will Willis at Wren would trade groceries for herbs and other goods. Mr. Jake Alexander also had a store from which he would give goods, such as meat and meal, to the sharecroppers on credit in return for their work on his farm.

All the Naylor children worked at their father's sawmill when they got old enough to work. The sawmill was located on the east side of the Pinhook Gap Road about a ¼ mile north of the church. The mill was situated on George Naylor's property but was close to the property boundary of the Jake Alexander Place. Next to the sawmill, George had a big orchard.

**Naylors Leave the Mountains**

After George got into financial trouble with his sawmill and lost the land at Old Bulah, the family first moved to the east side of the Jake Alexander Place. Part of the Naylor children were already on their own and stayed at their own home site for a few years, after their father moved the remainder of this family to the valley. George worked as a sharecropper for the Alexanders for several years.

Buster and Jim Mat attended school at Pinhook when the Naylors lived on the Alexander place. Ms. Ruthie said a big thrill for her was to meet her brothers each afternoon at the old West Flint Creek Bridge and walk back home with them. She said they would always have a piece of cornbread in their lunch pails which they saved for her. Ruthie would eat the old cornbread as she walked home with her two brothers. She said that old cornbread was the best she ever ate. With a little sadness, Ms. Ruthie confessed those were the good old days.

The Naylor children moved off the mountain around 1920 and would always move to be near their other family members. In no other family have I seen such strong family ties to each other and to an old home place. After leaving the mountaintop home, Thomas Naylor found a farm that needed enough hands to take care of the place. The other Naylor children agreed to help and work on the Early Farm near Fairfield Church and School. George moved his family from the Jake Alexander Farm to the Early Place to help older children with the farm work. The whole Naylor family moved just west of Fairfield to work and stay together.

After moving to Fairfield, the Naylor family continued to return to Old Bulah for Sunday services and family funerals. The family would get up real early on Sunday morning and begin the long wagon ride to the mountains. After getting to Pinhook Church, the old wagon road turned south up the mountain just east of the Simms Place. The hill was so steep the family would have to get out of the wagon and walk about one mile to the top of the mountain. With everyone walking, the old mules would still strain to pull the wagon up the steep incline. The old road was just a rock bed and so rough that the mules could hardly stand up much less pull a wagon. Ms. Ruthie said, "There would just be a string of family members during the climb which was hard on everyone. Later the road was re-routed up Pinhook Gap west of the Simms Place."

Ruthie and the two young boys attended school at Fairfield, the only school she ever attended. The school was a large one room building. The children had their own drinking cups and the water bucket had a little faucet for filling each person's cup. Each day before class, the school boys carried water from a nearby spring.

**Ruthie marries Robert**

While living at Fairfield, Ruthie met her future husband, Robert Preuit, who she married on March 10, 1934. Robert grew up on the old Preuit Place which was located about one mile west of Speake and just south of present day highway 36. Most of Robert's family, including his deceased baby boy, are buried in the Preuit Cemetery at the old Preuit home place.

At one time, Robert's parents, Tolbert and Carrie Hampton Preuit, owned all the land from the foot of Washspring Mountain to the road that is now highway 36. Both Tolbert and Carrie had children from previous marriages. Tolbert had been married to an Orr from Danville and they had one boy and some girls.

Carrie had a husband and a daughter to die in Texas. After the death of her first husband and daughter, Carrie returned to her old home with Inez who was her other daughter. After Tolbert and Carried married they had five children; Robert, Essie, Mabel, Allen, and Sadie.

The Preuit home was located just south of the Preuit Cemetery. While trying to have a well drilled for Tolbert Preuit, the well driller, and Mr. Mahoney, struck a gas well. The property is now owned by the Glenn family. After Mr. Tolbert Preuit died, his children by his first wife received the property which they later sold to Mr. Shirley Smith.

After Ruthie and Robert married, they lived in the house with Robert's mother and daddy for two years and seven months. While living with Tolbert and Carrie, Robert and Ruthie built a small house on a hill just north of the Preuit Cemetery. Robert and Ruthie had five children; Billy who died of diphtheria, Jackie, Jerry, Carolyn, and Barbara Ann. Mrs. Ruthie Naylor Preuit said she will be buried next to her husband in Lebanon Cemetery near Speake School.

Now at Old Bulah, the first Sunday in June is set aside for decoration and dinner on the ground. Mr. Willie Delshaw sometimes preaches revivals at Old Bulah, and he also preaches at most of the decoration days.

To the Naylor family of Bankhead National Forest and Lawrence County, Bulah Land sweet Bulah Land still draws family members from far and near to the old home place. The Naylor heartstrings are still tied to Old Bulah in the beloved land of the "Warrior Mountains."

## Osborn and Oden Families of Lindsey Hall

Ada and Irene are sisters born and reared in Lindsey Hall Community of the Warrior Mountains in the William B. Bankhead National Forest during the early 1900's. Ada Mae, Luther, and Lucy Irene are the children of the late Will and Sarah Osborn Oden.

Edward Herring, grandson of Ada and great-nephew of Irene, accompanied me on a visit to hear the Bankhead stories about the sisters, their ancestors, and their families. All three members of the family provided details about their family's struggles, hardships, and the "good old mountain life" which was an important part of Lawrence County's heritage. In the next pages, I will share their story about the life and times of Lindsey Hall Community as it was lived by members of the Osborn and Oden families.

The ancestors of the Osborn and Oden families migrated into the Lindsey Hall area of the forest during the mid-1800's to face the hardships of wilderness life. According to early land surveys beginning in 1817, the forest area was wilderness containing magnificent tress of oak, hickory, chestnut, maple, beech, and numerous other hardwoods species. These first families began clearing the woodlands for crops and pastures, but found that survival on the poor sandy soils was difficult even during the best growing seasons.

Edward Herring, a descendant of these noble forest families, provided me with the background information of both the Osborns and Odens whose descendants still claim Bankhead Forest as their home.

*Bulah Church & Cemetery*

**Oden Family History**

Will Oden was the son of William Houston (Hughes) and Mary Isabell Roberts Oden. "Hughs", born on December 23, 1860, was the only child of William D. and Mary E. Milligan Oden and was probably named after his mother's father, William Houston Milligan.

William D. and his brother, Andrew J. Oden, enlisted in the first Alabama Calvary, USA, on July 21, 1862. Their brother, Lewis S. Oden, enlisted in Nashville, Tennessee on September 14, 1862. The Oden brothers were the sons of Lewis and Rosannah Jenkins Oden who were married on February 26, 1822, Morgan County. While fighting for the North during the Civil War, William D. Oden died on March 15, 1863 in a hospital at Murfreesboro, Tennessee, and Andrew died January 5, 1863, at Nashville, Tennessee.

William's wife, Mary E. Milligan, applied for a pension for her son "Hughs" in 1866 and received $8.00 per month. Mary remarried Joseph P. Roberts and lived about one mile east of the Cave Springs Cemetery at Basham Gap near the Morgan-Lawrence County lines.

William Houston (Hughs) Oden

"Hughs" and Isabell Roberts Oden homesteaded land on the Winston-Lawrence County line between Brown and Rush Creeks. They entered the land in the southwest quarter of section 36, Township 8 South, and Range 7 West in 1890 and received final proof of their claim on December 10, 1897. "Hughs" got to enjoy his homestead only a short time before he died on November 22, 1899. He was buried within a mile of his homestead at Hickory Grove Cemetery near his mother, Mary E. Milligan Oden Roberts.

Mary Isabell Roberts, who was a Cherokee Indian mixed-blood according to family, had lived in Georgia until her father died in the Civil War. Her mother, who was already sick, died upon hearing the news of her husband's death. Isabell's Aunt Elender and her husband, Reverend Soloman Cline, brought Isabell to Alabama and reared her in the forest. Soloman Cline is buried in Hickory Grove Cemetery located in the eastern portion of William B. Bankhead Forest.

In the early days when Isabell first settled in the forest, timber wolves were very numerous. The log cabin they lived in had a dirt floor and they continually worried about wolves digging into their home.

**Osborn Family History**

In the same area of the "Hughs" Oden homestead, James E. (Jim) Osborn established a grist mill near the forks of Brown and Rush Creeks. According to Ms. Ada Oden (England) Smith, her grandfather built a dam which backed up an acre or more of water to power his water wheel. Jim would grind meal for his surrounding neighbors in return for a small amount of cornmeal for the toll. Ada, who was born on her granddad Jim's place, remember the old grist mill in operation.

According to Herring, Jim's parents were James Ingram and Orlena Eddy Osborn who moved from Marion County to Lawrence County in the 1850's. James Ingram Osborn moved to the forest with his brother Alexander. James Ingram and Alexander Osborn's father was also named Alexander, who was born on March 16, 1805, and died June 6, 1887. James Ingram and his wife Orlena Eddy Osborn are buried in the Center Cemetery on Leola Road.

**Nick Eddy**

According to Ada and Irene, and also an article provided by Spencer Waters, Orlena's brother Nick Eddy, got into a confrontation with Sam Brooks. According to both accounts, Sam Brooks' throat was slashed open with one quick move of Nick's knife. Brooks fell dead almost instantly. The Oden sisters say their mothers' great-uncle, Nick Eddy, was a mild natured man but did not like to be pushed around. According to their account, Brooks knocked Nick's hat off his head in front of several of Brooks' friends. The first time Eddy replaced his hat, on which occasion, Sam Brooks again knocked the hat to the ground. Knowing he was in trouble, Eddy came out with the only weapon he had, a pocket knife, and cut Brooks' throat. The ultimate result was the quick death of Sam Brooks. As far back as Ada and Irene could remember, their mother, Sarah Osborn Oden, did not like anyone to touch her head. Sarah's parents were James E. (Jim) and Louisa A. Roberson Osborn. Louisa was born May 16, 1861, and died March 1, 1900. Louisa's father, John J. Robertson, served with Company E, 11th Regiment, Georgia Volunteers, CSA, and died as a private in the Civil War. Louisa's mother, Zeila or Zillar G. Roberson, never remarried.

## Osborn-Oden Bond

After William Houston (Hughs) Oden died in 1899 and Louisa A. Roberson Osborn died in 1900, Hughs' wife, Mary Isabell Roberts, married Louisa's husband, James (Jim) Osborn. After the marriage of Jim and Isabell, both the Osborn and Oden families became closely bound.

*James E. (Jim) Osborn and Isabell Roberts Oden (1/2 Cherokee)*

Jim and Louisa's children and their spouses are: Sarah married Will Oden; George Washington (Wash) married Eula Partridge; Jasper E. (Jake) married Cathrine Asherbranner; William R. married Pearl Baggett; Frank married Mary Dobbs; John Ed married Maggie Little; Anzy married Johnny Asherbranner and later Tom McVay; and Lena (Lenny) married John Brannon. John M. Brannon entered 80 acres in the South ½ of the Southwest ¼ of Section 25 and 40 acres in Section 36 in Township 8 South and Range 7 West on November 21, 1900.

Isabell and Hughs Oden's children were Renee, Charlie Monroe, and Will. In addition, after Jim Osborn and Isabell Oden married, they had one daughter of their own, Ziller.

Jim and Isabell, father of Will and mother of Sarah, moved to the Jenkins place one mile south of Shiloh Church. After living on the Jenkins place several years, Jim and Isabell moved to where Wesley Burnett now lives, which is about one quarter mile east of Shiloh Church on the Leola Road. Both Jim and Isabell lived at their Leola Road home place when they died.

## Will and Sarah Osborn Oden

Will and Sarah Osborn, who were brought together by the marriage of Will's daddy to Sarah's mother, fell in love and married. Will and Sarah Oden, while living at the old Osborn home place at the forks of Brown and Rush Creeks, had their first child, Ada Mae, who was born on January 29, 1910.

Will and Sarah helped Jim Osborn operate the gristmill while living at the old homeplace. Will and his family moved to the old Mat A. Parker place south of the Leola Road about two miles on Rush Creek Road. The old Parker home place was on the east side of Rush Creek Road.

Prior to the birth of Sarah's third child, she stayed with her mother who served as a mid-wife during the delivery of her baby daughter, Lucy Irene. Isabell not only served as mid-wife to her three grandchildren, but also to all the local families living in the Lindsey Hall Community.

After the birth of three children, Will and Sarah also moved to the Jenkins' place. Will and Sarah's children were mischievous like all small kids. Ada and Luther like to break the fruit jar lids to get the pretty white class inside the metal tops. The two young ones also liked to get on the foot of the bed and jump into the feather mattress. Every time their mother would get out of sight, Ada and Luther would jump on their bed. One day, Ada jumped a little too far and caught her backside on a nail sticking out of the wall. Ada says she carries the scar today and her momma never had to tell her to stop jumping on the bed. From then on, Ada hated to see children jump on the bed.

Front Row L-R: *Amon Osborn, Hubert Osborn and Eva England.* Second Row L-R: *Sarah Osborn Oden, Maggie Osborn (John Ed's wife), Ada Oden England (1/8 Cherokee).* Third Row L-R: *Averene & Imogene (twins of John Ed and Maggie), Irene Oden.* Back Row L-R: *Monroe Cooper, Will Oden, John Ed Osborn.*

When Ada was 10 years old, she got typhoid fever and nearly died. She said all her hair fell out and she was extremely sick. Ada said she liked to starved to death, an if it had not been for buttermilk and raw eggs she would not have lived. The only way they could cool her fever was to take buckets of water from the well and pour over her head.

The Will and Sara Oden home was a plank house which had a wooden shingle roof. Will made his own roofing shingles by placing the timber between a forked tree and using a froe to work off the board. The house had to large rooms, a side-room kitchen, and a porch all around the house. Between the two rooms was a large chimney with a fireplace in each room.

**Hard Mountain Life**

During the winter, the family would stuff rags and other materials in the cracks to keep out some of the cold air. The big feathered beds were essential in keeping everyone from getting cold. As the old saying goes, they could count their chickens without going outside or looking out the windows.

The three children had many chores which included helping with farming, cutting wood, piling and burning cornstalks, plowing, bringing drinking water from the spring or well, washing clothes, cooking and milking the family cow. Still the family was thankful to have enough food to eat and a shelter over their heads.

The Oden children helped sharecrop with their parents and grandparents on some 60 acres with two mules and a horse. Irene said one day when she was cutting ground with an old disk pulled by the pair of miles, the mules were not minding, and Irene hollowing out "haw you son-of-b----s". She did not think her dad could hear over the noise of the disks, but he stopped the animals and asked what she had said. Irene started crying and told her dad the old mules would not mind. After a little corrective dialogue, Irene was glad to get back to plowing.

In addition to a garden the family raised cotton, corn, potatoes, a little tobacco, and sugarcane. The family usually raised a large patch of sugarcane which was harvested and run through a mule powered sugarcane mill press. Jim Osborn operated a syrup mill while he lived at the Jenkins Place. Molasses was a big part of the daily diet all during the year.

A small patch of tobacco was an important part of most mountain farms. As the tobacco was growing the children had to pick tobacco worms to keep them from eating up the crop. Each year the tobacco was cut, hung in the barn until the leaves were real dry. On damp days the leaves were stripped of the large veins, cleaned, folded, and rolled into real nice twists. One day Irene was helping roll twists and got so sick she could not get out of chair.

Coffee was one of the most important drinks to be served at mealtime. Coffee beans were brought by the sacks. The beans were placed into a pan and parched before being ground. Many mornings the children would awaken to the noise of the coffee grinder. The family would boil the coffee grounds in a big kettle in front of the fireplace. The coffee was poured into the coffee pot for serving into the cups.

According to Ada, the family never got ahead in their sharecropping activities because they usually owed more than the poor mountain soil could produce. During the year, the family borrowed on their credit until harvest time. It seemed as though the crops would never be good enough for the family to have extra money.

Everyone in the mountains had a smoke house and a bunch of chickens and hogs which provided much of the meat for the winter. The pork was usually smoked or salted down immediately after the hogs were killed. All the dwelling places in the forest either had a spring or dug well near the house.

Everyone usually had just two sets of clothes which were washed about twice per week. Washing would take about a half a day, since they would build a fire and boil their clothes in the old black pot. After being boiled, the clothes were placed on a rub board where they were rubbed up and down in the lye soap water. The clothes were rinsed and hung on bushes, fences, or clothes line to dry.

**School Days**

The children of Will and Sarah Oden attended school at Lindsey Hall in the Fall of the year after the crops were gathered. Lindsey Hall was a two storied school with the first four grades on the first floor and grades five through seven on the second level of the building. The school got water from Brown Spring just east of the school 200 yards. The spring forms the head of Brown Creek. All of the students drunk water out of the same bucket and used the same dipper. The bigger students toted the water each morning before class.

Instead of having a restroom at Lindsey Hall, the girls went to the bushes in one area and the boys went to the restroom in another area. In order to get to the bottom of the issue concerning toilet paper, I inquired as to the common practice. Without hesitation Oden sisters pointed out the importance of Sears and Roebuck catalogs to the mountain people. The old book was hunt over a limb and only one page at a time could be used. The sisters said the paper was not near as soft as the paper we use today.

A typical lunch to carry to school consisted of cornbread, molasses, and a piece of meat. When all three of the children were attending school, they shared lunch out of the same pail. Ada said that back then, they did not know much about biscuits and were practically raised on cornbread. Ada had to walk three miles to the "Hall" to attend school. One morning when Ada was late for school, she dropped her bucket scattering all her food. She grabbed it all up and placed it back in her bucket all mixed up.

Some of their teachers at the "Hall" included Bart Herd, Mr. Parker, Inez and Eunice Thompson. Silas Black lived at the fire tower located on the north side of the Leola Road between the Hickory Grove Road and the Flint Creek Road. Silas' two sisters also taught at the "Hall".

On Sundays the family attended church in the same building. Some Sundays they would have old fashioned "foot-washing." One Sunday everyone was getting their feet washed and having a big time in worship. As the foot washing crew was moving through the congregation, they came to an elderly gentleman and asked to wash his feet. He politely told the washers he had washed his feet before leaving home and they did not need washing again.

**Mountain People Can Survive**

All the local shopping was at Floyd Looney's store at the forks of the Leola and Blowing Springs Road, or Lee Revis' store at Pinhook. During the years of the depression, many people in the mountains nearly starved to death. Even if you had money, there was not a whole lot a person could buy. There was no use to go to town because many of the store shelves were empty.

Many of the mountain folks survived by picking blackberries, blueberries, huckleberries, and any other natural fruit that was available. Lee Revis would buy a lot of natural mountain products for resale. Ada said they would get ten cents per gallon of blackberries.

They also picked up hickory nuts, walnuts, and chestnuts before they all died out. In addition to berries, fruits, and nuts, the family dug ginseng and other roots which were shipped to the Block Brothers in Tennessee. During the depression, they got very little money for their roots. People raised their own chickens, hogs, and gardens.

Prior to 1953, the Lindsey Hall Community did not have any electrical power at all. A typical evening consisted of lighting the kerosene lamps and setting in front of the fireplace. When oil was not available, the family would use rich pine splinters which were placed on top of the portable oven. The portable oven was set near the fireplace and was used to cook the bread.

**The Old Mountain Trade**

In addition to farming, most of the mountain families learned to survive by helping make moonshine whiskey. Many times the local moonshiners were supported by financial backers who eventually would get most of the money from the illicit whiskey trade. On some occasions, the poor mountain farmers went on their own, but were unable to pay for the protective services which the money people usually provided.

The independent shiners had to stay continually alert for the law enforcement authorities who were many times tipped off to prevent the independent trade. Sugar was a major ingredient in making moonshine and was usually bought in 100 pound bags. Sugar became the weak point in keeping the mountain trade a secret.

Will Oden, as many other mountain dew distillers eventually did, had to pay the price for his moonshining activities. His daughters were gracious enough to share this important part of most Bankhead families' heritage. Will and Mr. George Rainey were working a whiskey still in the Cole Branch area west of Charles Borden's present home place. The night before they were to make a run of wildcat, Will had a dream that he and Rainey would be caught. At breakfast that morning, Will confessed his dream to his children and Mr. Rainey. He told everyone he was not going to the moonshine still today. After eating breakfast at Will's, Rainey left for the still before daylight. About lunchtime, Will got to worrying about old man Rainey working the still by himself and decided to ride to the still on his white horse, Fred, to check the distillery.

Will arrived at the still and tied Fred to a sapling on the nearby ridge. After arriving at the whiskey still, the lawmen yelled everyone was under arrest. Will tore out through the woods with Sheriff Compy Ayers hot on his tracks. Will, a tall lanky man who was swift on his feet, quickly out-distanced his pursuers. While looking on his backtrack, Will ran smack into a tree and was knocked off his feet and hit the ground flat on his back. In the meantime, the Sheriff and his men started back to the still to destroy and confiscate the illegal brew. Will, who was nearly knocked unconscious, regained his feet and still fearing the lawmen were giving chase, tore out to running again; however, the encounter with the tree had him so disoriented he ran right into the middle of the law enforcement officers. Seeing the surprised lawmen and not knowing he was surrounded or which direction to run, Will just surrendered. The lawmen brought Will back by his home in their late 1920s automobiles and let the family know they were taking him to jail. The family members went to the still and brought ole Fred back home. Within a year or so of his arrest in the late 1920s, Will began serving a year in the penitentiary.

**Ada gets Married**

Just before reaching 15 years of age, Ada and Neil England, who were classmates at Lindsey Hall School, ran off and got married. Neil was in the upstairs classes and Ada was in the downstairs classes. Neil was son of Uranis (Tirey) and Mary Lou (Dusky) Pearson England. According to Cathy B. Sloan, Tirey and Dusky's family included: Walter, who married Bertha Higgins; Dellie, who married Leamon Williams; Pearl, who married Robert Carl Higgins; Lessie, who married Henry Alexander; Mallie, who married George Hill and Will Culver; Mildred, who married Thomas Borden; Claud, who married Miladean Hill; and Louis, who married Alma Dutton and Glenna Miller.

Tirey and Dusky England, who were of mixed Indian ancestry, lived at the head of Owl Creek about a half mile southeast of Shiloh Church on Leola Road. A trail ran from Earl and Eugene Jones' home which was located about a quarter mile south of the Leola Road on the Owl Creek Road, to the Tirey England home, and continued west to the old Jenkins Place a mile south of Shiloh Church, Ada, Luther, and Irene would use the trail to walk to Lindsey Hall School.

When asked why she ran off to get married, Ada laughed and said she just did not have better sense. Ada and Neil went to the "Hall" on Sunday for a singing and hired Lester Burnett to carry them to Pulaski, Tennessee where they got married. The trip to Pulaski took all day long.

The couple returned to Neil's parents where they lived a short time. After moving in with Tirey and Dusky, Neil bought a brand new T-Model at Hartselle and began the old mountain distillery trade. Ada said she used to drive the T-Model to Looney's store and fill the car up with gas with an old hand pump. She said you could tell exactly how much gas you were getting because you would pump the gas into a glass bowl on top of the tank and then put it into the car.

Neil and Ada moved from the England home to a house on the Holmes Chapel Road just southeast of Brushy Lake. The house the newlyweds moved to was about one quarter mile west of the Mt. Olive Road on the Holmes Chapel Road.

The house was the location where Doctor Crow got killed while eating breakfast after being an overnight guest in the mountain home. Some say the man of the house suspected Doctor Crow of getting too friendly with his wife, while other claim he was killed because of the death of the family's young child.

According to reports, Doctor Crow was setting at the table eating breakfast when he was shot at close range with a shotgun. The man loaded Doctor Crow in his wagon and hauled him out to the mountains. When he reached the Wesley Hampton home at the forks of the Leola and Hickory Grove Roads, he stopped and got Hampton to examine the body which was covered by a white sheet. As told by one already deceased, Mr. Hampton removed the food still in Doctor Crow's mouth.

Top Row: *Hodge Jackson & Irene Oden Jackson (1/8 Cherokee)*. Middle Row: *Almon Jackson, Will Oden and Willis' mother Isabelle Roberts (Oden) Osborn (1/2 Cherokee)*. Bottom Row: *Sarah Oden, Dennis Jackson, Martha Jackson*.

The old plank floor of the house where Ada and Neil moved was darkly stained with the blood. Every time Ada tried to remove the spot it seemed to be more visible. After living at Holmes Chapel for about a year, Neil and Ada moved just south of the Cooper Place on Owl Creek Road. Ada kept house and Neil worked at his distillery.

Neil and Ada had one daughter, Eva, who was born in a log cabin located on Leola Road about a half-mile east of Shiloh Church. Eva was only one year old when Neil and Ada separated.

Ada left Neial and went to Arkansas to live a short time with her uncle, Monroe Oden. On December 25, 1930, Neil and his brother-in-law had a fight in Higgins' home. Higgins went after his gun and Neil hit the door running. As Neal neared the road, the bullet caught him solidly in the back, killing him almost instantly.

Ada moved back to her parents' home south of Shiloh Church. She later married Dyke Smith. Dyke was the son of Dave and Lamender Penolia (Sis) Hampton Smith. According to many family members, Sis, who was the daughter of Ephram and Lucinda Doss Hampton was one-half Cherokee Indian on her mother's side. Dyke had a half-brother, William Smith, and a half-sister. Dyke's first wife was Tressie Smith.

Dyke and Ada lived at the forks of Leola and Owl Creek Road. They had four children: Willard, who married Charlene Strickland; Mable, who married Holbert Jackson; Huey, who married Dorothy Way; and Lucy Ordean, who married Norris Herring. Doctor Byars and Doctor Price Irwin helped deliver some of Ada's children.

Dyke was a good fiddle player. Monroe Oden and Frank Osborn were good singers. At big gatherings and parties, nearly everyone would participate in the square dances. The mountain people attending the dances would stay all night and return home about daylight. Different people in the mountains would host the all night dances which turned out to be the largest social entertainment gatherings in the area.

Dyke and Ada eventually separated after their house burned. Dyke passed away on December 25, 1972, thus, both of her husbands died on Christmas Day.

Irene married Quill Jackson who was 30 years her senior when they married. Quill already had ten children before he and Irene married. Quill and Irene had four children of their own: Hodge, Dennis, Almond, and Martha. Irene still goes to church at Lindsey Hall and was baptized in Brushy Lake.

In the 1920's and 1930's, Ada and Irene said the forest was a beautiful place with large hardwood trees and small isolated farms. To hear them tell the story, the forest was a paradise to be loved-the "Warrior Mountains."

# Jenkins Family of Owl Creek

## Lillie M. Jenkins Sparks

From the old dug well flowed memories of her early childhood which had deep roots within the mother earth of the Warrior Mountains. The grand old woman, who sat near the water supply of her previous mountain home, allowed the sweet memories to flow from her mouth as she told the childhood stories that touched her very soul. To her the place was scared and she would tarry at the old well as long as her folks could allow. She would then leave the memorable spot to come to her home in the valley, but each time she had to leave, her heart strings would tug the tears and the emotions she felt for the small clearing in the area known as the Warrior Mountains of Bankhead National Forest. Her father and two sisters died at the old forest home. They, along with her mother and brothers, were always remembered each time she returned to her childhood world.

*Ms. Lillie M. Jenkins Sparks at her old family well located in Bankhead Forest.*

The noble forest lady is now gone but her children fondly remember the mountain stories that lived so vividly in the memory of their mother – Lillie M. Jenkins (Sparks) . In her latter days, Ms. Lille loved to sit at the old dug well and tell of her early childhood. Over the years prior to her death, she got to visit the old home place. Her children made sure she had the opportunity to return to her mountain home before the end of her days.

The old well, all that remains of her original home site, is located in an isolated glade on top of our Warrior Mountains. Today, the beautiful home place belongs to Charles and Anna Borden, who were married and now live in the forest opening near the old well. You have to wonder if that old well could talk, what stories would it tell of the hard times and happy mountain people.

**Jim Jenkins**

Ms. Lillie's father, James (Jim) Jenkins, settled on a forest farm of some 320 acres which was located on Owl Creek approximately one mile directly south of Shiloh Church in the Lindsey Hall Community of the Warrior Mountains. According to the Old Lands Records of Lawrence County, Alabama by Margaret Cowart, James J. Jenkins entered 80 acres of land in Section 14 of Township 8 South and Range 7 West on November 13, 1900. On the same date, Jim also entered 40 acres in section 23, 80 acres in section 22, and 80 acres in section 15. In addition, Mary F. Jenkins entered another 40 acres in section 23 on October 25, 1906.

Jim, his wife Mary Frances Lester, and their family came to Alabama in an ox drawn covered wagon. They were part of a wagon train of families moving toward the Warrior Mountains of North Alabama in search of land on which they could settle and homestead. The family stopped for about one year in the Sand Mountain area of North Alabama where one of their daughters died. No doubt they followed the old and famous route of the High Town Path into the mountainous area of south Lawrence County from the Sand Mountain area. Within one mile of the Path, the Jenkins family made Lawrence County their home.

**Jim Jenkins Family**

People of the Warrior Mountains had to work hard and struggle trying to survive on the poor mountainous land. Often was the case when the struggle for survival was lost, even for the children of the mountain families. So was the life of the James (Jim) Jenkins family of Lawrence County's southern highlands.

While working on cattle drives to Mississippi, Jim got pneumonia and later died at this forest home. While on one of the long cattle drives, Jim had an infant daughter to die. Allie, a beautiful and very sensitive 18 year old lass, also died at the old mountain home because of a broken heart over one she deeply loved. Jim and his daughter Allie Jenkins are buried in the Shiloh Cemetery, but family members are not sure where the infant child was laid to rest.

Some years after Jim died, Mary Jenkins moved her family to the Conway Community which is located a few miles east of Moulton. The poor mountain soils and the isolation of the mountains probably loomed great in the decision of the family to eventually settle in the Moulton Valley. Other problems arose when Ms. Mary Jenkins was abruptly faced with the task of managing a mountainous farm and trying to raise her family. After Mary reached her elderly years, her daughter, Ms. Lillie Jenkins Sparks took care of her mother during her final years of life until she died in 1936.

**The Dug Well**

During her early childhood, Ms. Lillie remembered sitting with her youngest brother, little Jim, on the edge of the old well watching her older brothers, Jeff, John, and George, digging the well in their backyard. Lillie and her little brother sat there many days with their feet dandling into the hole watching the boys digging the well. With the temptation so great, occasionally the young children would knock dirt on their big brothers. After a strong warning of punishment from their brothers, the small children would still kick dirt into the well. When the brothers would come out of the dry hole for dinner, the two mischievous dirt kicking children would be placed into the hole as part of their promised punishment. The boys would leave their younger siblings in the hole until they finished lunch.

*Guy Sparks, son of Ms. Lillie Jenkins Sparks, carries on the traditions of his mother. Guy is renowned for the vast array of wildflowers he has established in his garden.*

After realizing they were trapped, the scared children were always proud to see their mother at the top of the hole. Ms. Lillie's mother would talk to her little ones and provide them comfort during their sentence in the hole. After their big brothers finished dinner and removed them from their hole of doom, the little kickers would be satisfied for only a short while before the urge to see into the hole became too great. Ms. Lillie never forgot the experience of being in the well and passed along the childhood story so her children would understand why she so loved to sit near the old dug well.

**Lillie's Family**

At age seventeen Ms. Lillie M. Jenkins, born on April 19, 1892, in Henry County, Georgia, married BD Sparks at Conway Church. They were married by Marion Hitt on November 17, 1909, in the church that also served as a school. Lillie and BD Sparks reared six boys and two girls: Britt, born on 1/30/1911; Guy, born 3/26/1913; Parker, born 4/26/1915; Leo, born 5/28/1917; Dempsey, born 8/24/1919; Delomer, born 7/30/1921; Lola Terry, born 8/26/1923; and Lillie Roden, born 1/22/1927.

Ms. Lillie, who died at 94 years old, was a remarkable woman. She had acquired pioneer survival skills from her parents which transcended many generations. She was noted for her arts and crafts abilities, making clothes for her children, farming and preserving what she had raised, making lye soap, embroidering and quilting, masonry and carpentry, but her first love was working with her flowers and vegetables. Ms. Lillie M. Jenkins Sparks had those skills needed for self-sufficiency, the skills which are quickly being lost in our present day society.

One of the great tragedies of life is not only the loss of our loved ones, but also the loss of our precious heritage, culture, customs, and traditions. May the way and lifestyles of our elders survive until we develop a concern to protect the heritage of our grandparents before it is forever lost in that eternal land – "The Warrior Mountains."

## Lewis Oden Family of Brushy Creek

On a cool overcast night, I drove to the heart of Bankhead National Forest to visit some of the nicest people I know. As I traveled nearly 20 miles of the lonely rock roads of Alexander Motorway, Leola, Brushy Creek, and Mt. Olive Roads, I thought of the struggles and hardships of the early settlers who made Bankhead Forest their home.

I finally arrived at the home of Mr. and Mrs. Robert Lewis Oden. I had known Mr. Lewis Oden when I was a student at Speake School. Mr. Oden drove a school bus for 28 years before retiring in 1989. Lewis, who has spent all of his life in Bankhead Forest, made many trips down the mountain to Speake School prior to his retirement. Since my first visit, Mr. Robert Lewis Oden died on August 12, 1995. He was buried at Pine Torch, a few miles from where he spent his entire life.

## Lewis and Lou Annie Borden Oden

Lewis and Lou Annie Borden Oden were married on January 24, 1949, and have been living about one mile west of Brushy Lake since 1967. I have passed their home many times in the past, but I finally made the opportunity to visit the Odens for a long and enjoyable talk. For the next few pages, I wish to relate the wonderful mountain stories shared by Lewis and Lou Annie Borden Oden.

After Lewis and Lou Annie got married, they lived at the Edley and Mildred Borden home place, just south of the forks of Leola Road and Alexander Motorway. The house was south of the Leola Road just over the hill from Mr. Tom Hall's home place. The Oden's moved from the Borden home to the Haynes place which was just a little piece from Lindsey Hall Church.

*Lewis (1/8/ cherokee) and Lou Annie Borden Oden (5/8 Cherokee).*

After living at the Haynes place for a while, Lewis and Lou Annie moved to the Stewart Place for about eight months before moving to their present home. The old house on the Stewart Place was located south of Leola Road, just one quarter mile west of the intersection of the Blowing Springs Road. The house was known as the old Hollaway home and now belongs to the Charlie Stewart family. Also located near their home at the intersection of the two roads was the old Tommy Rooks home place.

## Charlie and Lucy Fulmer Oden

Charlie and Lucy Fulmer Oden had three sons and one daughter: Lewis, lived west of Brushy Lake; Curtis who lives in South Carolina; Herman and Versie who live three miles south of Speake Community. Robert Lewis Oden was born on October 26, 1914, one mile south of Shiloh Church which is located on the Leola Road in Bankhead National Forest. Charles Borden now lives on the home place where Lewis and his brother Herman Oden were born. At least four houses were located in the area south of Shiloh near Lewis' old birthplace. When Lewis was born, his parents, Charlie and Lucy Fulmer Oden, who lived in a house which was one quarter mile south of Charles Borden's present home. Jim Osborn, who was Charlie Oden's stepfather, owned the property and also had a house just east of Charles' present home. Tom McVay or Wash Osborn lived in the house on the east side of Jim Osborn's property. North of Charles Borden's place was a home that belonged to John Ed Osborn. Farther north toward Shiloh Church is a small opening where a walnut tree now stands and was the home of old man Tom Herd.

At the intersection of Charles Borden's driveway with Leola Road is Shiloh Church. The first Shiloh Church built on the site was a log building. The second building was a plant structure that got eaten by termites and rotted down before it was completed. According to Lewis, the present Shiloh Church is a block building, the only other church built on the site.

Lewis was born in the old home located near the woods close to the south property line. The house was a log cabin with several side rooms and belonged to Mr. Jim Osborn, Lewis' step-granddad. The original log house just about rotted down during World War I, and the family built a new plank house. Jim Osborn bought or traded for the land from a Mr. Jenkins who actually entered the property from the government.

Charlie Oden moved his family from Lewis' birthplace about 1920 and during the next four years moved several times around the Lindsey Hall area. Charlie and his family finally settled down near the forks of Leola Road and Rush Creek Roads.

First, the Oden family moved from the Jim Osborn place to the Abe Paul Tanksley Place which was located just east of the West Flint Creek Bridge on Blowing Springs Road. Mr. Tanksley's old house place was about one half mile north of the Matt Pearson home on the ridge between Indian Creek and Blowing Springs. The road to the Tanksley place turned east off Blowing Springs Road (Forest Service Road 265) and followed the property boundary of the Pearson place north about one mile to Mr. Tanksley's farm. Two houses were located on the Tanksley Place which now belongs to the U.S. forest Service. During the time Charlie Oden's family lived on the farm (in the early 1920's), Mr. Tanksley lived in Hartselle and operated a gin cotton.

In about 1924, the Oden family moved to the Bud Higgins place on Rush Creek Road. The house was on the right side of the road with the barn on the opposite side. The home place was located about 200 yards south of the junction of Leola and Rush Creek roads. Lewis lived with his folks at the Higgins place until he married in 1949.

The Higgins place, where Lewis lived most of his younger life, belonged to a woman in Illinois. Charlie Oden wanted to buy the place through a lawyer in Cullman, but found it had so many mortgages he could not get a clear deed; thus Charlie never bought the land. According to Lewis, if his father "would have gotten land" where he could make a living, he would have kept the land until he died.

**Charlie Oden's Life**

Some three generations of Lewis Oden's family are born from the Lindsey Hall and Hickory Grove areas of Bankhead National Forest. Most of the Oden family were of Cherokee Indian descent with Isabell Roberts having a high percentage of Indian blood.

Charlie Oden was reared on his family's place which was between Rush and Brown Creeks on the Rush Creek Road. Charlie's parents, Hughes and Isabell Roberts Oden, owned the farmland on Rush Creek Road south of the Miller Place. Lewis's great-granddaddy, Oden, died of pneumonia while serving in the Civil War.

As a young boy, Charlie Oden attended Hickory Grove School and was taught by Mr. George Hampton. George boarded with the Hughes and Isabell Roberts Oden's family when he first began teaching at Hickory Grove. Mr. George Hampton later taught at Holmes Chapel School just east of Brushy Lake where he taught Lou Annie Borden Oden's mother, Elizabeth Hooper Borden.

After Hughes Oden died, the land along Rush Creek Road belonging to him was divided among his three sons. Will and Monroe Oden received some level tillable land as part of their inheritance; however, the two brothers bought some more land and let the inherited land stand good for new property. Will and Monroe eventually lost all of their property and the land now belongs to the U.S. Forest Service.

Charlie also inherited 53 acres which had only three acres of land level enough for row crops and cultivation. In the late 1920's, Charlie Oden sold the land to the government for $4.25 per acre, with most of it only bringing $2.50 per acre. Mr. Jack McDowell was the forest ranger over Bankhead when Charlie sold his land to the Forest Service.

Shortly after Charlie sold the land, sawmills and stave mills began coming to the mountains buying up timber. Lewis said his father could have sold the timber for more than the government gave for the property. One of the closest stave mills was located on Owl Creek just south of the home where Lewis was born. The Owl Creek stave mill was operated by the Holland-Blow Stave Company of Decatur. Another stave mill was located between Thompson and Flint Creek.

Most of Lewis' family is buried at Hickory Grove Cemetery located at the junction of Hickory Grove Road and Rush Creek Road. His grandmother, Isabell Roberts Oden, who married Jim Osborn after her first husband Hughes died, is buried at Center Cemetery on Leola Road.

Lewis said when he was a boy his father would take the family to Hickory Grove to clean off the cemetery. As the family rode past particular areas, Charlie would tell the family about seeing cotton and corn planted where stands of hardwood tress were growing along Rush Creek and Hickory Grove Roads. Lewis was amazed that the area had grown up in trees; however, Lewis said he now understands what his dad was talking about because he now sees areas that were once cultivated in mature timber. One example Lewis referred to was the Waters Place, which was located about a mile south of Leola Road on the Owl Creek Road. Mr. Monroe Cooper cultivated the place when Lewis Oden was a young boy. Now the place contains a stand of mature timber.

In order to make a living, Charlie Oden farmed about 12 to 15 acres of cotton and corn with two mules. Most of the cotton was taken to Hartselle to be ginned. Charlie and his sons would also carry some of the cotton to Upshaw or Templeton to be ginned. The ginned cotton would then be transported to Cullman to be sold.

Mr. Stephenson ran the gin at Upshaw, located just northwest of Friendship Church on present day highway 41. Transporting the seed cotton to Upshaw in the wagon was a tremendous job. Charlie and his boys hauled their cotton in a wagon pulled by two mules. The route to Upshaw was down the lower Capsey Creek Motorway by the Hampton Place and up the steep mountain on the southeast side of the creek.

Charlie would try to haul some 1200 to 1500 pounds of seed cotton at one time. The team of mules would always have to be rested to make it up the long steep hill. The old wagon road which crossed Capsey Creek south of Tar Springs Hollow came out on present day highway 41 at the Lawrence and Winston County line. Even though the trip was rough, the shorter distance was still better than transporting the cotton around the Leola Road to Cave Springs Cemetery and then south along present day highway 41.

Lewis said his family always had a large garden just to survive the winter. They grew corn, peas, and potatoes. Lewis said his dad was a real potato raiser and would make more potatoes than any one he had ever seen. Charlie would sell the surplus potatoes to neighbors and local folks.

The Oden family bought very little food at the store and traded for items such as soda, cole oil, and flour. The family would travel from Lindsey Hall to trade with "Steward and Bennet" General Merchandise of Hartselle on a yearly basis. They had about anything the family would need and would allow Charlie to buy on credit from Spring until Fall when the crops would be harvested.

In addition to farming, Charlie and family members would hunt ginseng and other roots during the summer. Lewis remembers a root hunting trip into Tar Springs Hollow with his dad, Charlie, Gus Pike, and Mel Fulmer. Lewis was about 15 years old and did not carry a lunch. After a long day in the woods digging roots, Lewis was about "starved to death, completely give out, and awfully proud to get back home."

## Lewis Oden's Early Days

Lewis attended Lindsey Hall School through the fifth grade, the highest grade offered. Lewis's mother, Lucy, told him that Lindsey Hall School was built around 1908. The original Lindsey Hall School was located northwest of the present building. Lucy told that dogs could crawl through the cracks of the old original Lindsey Hall.

Old man Will Hollaway bought the land and wanted the second building named Hollaway School; however, the community wanted to keep the original name of Lindsey Hall. The second Lindsey Hall was first built as a school and was later used as a church. The new building had an upstairs, but was eventually modified to a single level building. The school served the mountain children in the Lindsey Hall Community until around 1954.

After completing all the grades at Lindsey Hall, Lewis said he had gotten old enough to think he did not need any more education. Curtis, Herman, and his sister, Versie, continued their schooling at Speake.

All the children attending Lindsey Hall School lived nearby and had to walk to school. The school was a large one room building that accommodated children through the fifth grade. John T. Rose from Punkin Center was one of the teachers Lewis had while attending school.

Mr. Rose taught at Lindsey Hall for several years. Lewis said Mr. Rose taught him more than any teacher he had at Lindsey Hall. Lewis said they only had about a five and one half month school term because the tax to operate would last only that long. When the tax money was gone, the school would close. School would open for six weeks during the summer and would be completed during the winter.

Casting back to around 1927, Lewis Oden furnishes this photo of Lindsey Hall School. The teacher is Imer Teeters. The students include, from left, (front) Alvarine Osborn, Christine Alexander, Verbie Smith, Irene Alexander, Cora Jackson, May Fulmer, Imojean Osborn, (middle) Walter Looney, Herman Oden, Mildred England, Gertrude Smith, Felton Looney, Alice Looney, Curtis Oden, (back) Coy Jackson, Lewis Oden, Irene Oden, Lolle Osborn, Wesley Burnett, and David Smith.

While attending Lindsey Hall School, Lewis played ball but enjoyed the bear game. They would form a ring and try to remove each other from the center by forcing the other person out. The play was similar to wrestling and would leave Lewis going home many afternoons with his clothes torn in the scuffle. Most of his overalls had the galluses sewed back on several times from the game. He was careful, however, to never get in the ring with his coat. He knew what would happen if he ever got his only coat torn or lost.

Many of the children went to school barefooted during warm weather. Lewis said he remembered men and women going barefooted during warmer days. Most all the mountain people were poor but got by with the small farms and gardens. Lewis said some of the corn patches were used for making whiskey, but he never made moonshine. Lewis figured if he ever got into moonshine, he would end up in prison and the best thing to do was never get involved in the trade.

In the late 1920's, the government had a work crew to build the Leola Road. The crew was stationed on Leola Road, about two miles east of Cheatham Road. The pay for clearing, grading, and widening the road was pretty good for those days. Instead of placing culverts in the low spots, the road crews would split white oaks for bridges for the water to run under.

Lewis remembers the state stocking deer in the forest in 1924 and 1925. He said at one time the herd built up until there was a lot of deer in the area. Then something happened to the herd and they began to die out in the 1950's. Lewis does not believe the deer herd has ever recovered and that we have very few deer in the forest today.

**Lewis Goes to Work**

After finishing Lindsey Hall School, Lewis Oden began working at sawmills. One of the first mills where he worked was owned by Mr. Tom Poole. He started stacking lumber at the mill on Owl Creek just south of where Charles Borden lives today. They sawed logs on Owl Creek for about two years. Walter Poole did the sawing and Floyd Poole worked at the mill until he had to go the army.

In 1936, Lewis worked at Shirley Smith's old sawmill just north of Pine Torch Church on the Shirley Sawmill Branch. Shirley's mill was run by a gasoline engine, a straight eight Buick motor. The old engine had enough power to run the largest logs through the sawmill.

Lewis Oden.

Shirley selectively cut about 40 acres of timber at the site. According to Lewis, sawmills would be set up at the logging site and would be moved after the timber was cut. Jack Letson and Willie Smith were marking logs for Shirley on Saturday. Willie got into a large yellow jacket nest and ask Jack to retrieve the marking pole and ax without telling him about the yellow jackets. Jack got the ax and marking pole, but was covered with yellow jacket stings. Lewis said Willie got the cussing of his life from poor old Jack.

In 1937, Lewis worked at the Poole Sawmill just north of Blowing Springs Bridge. Instead of riding his contrary old mules, he would walk from his old home place on Rush Creek Road to Blowing Springs, a distance of some five miles. The old sawmill was steam operated with a huge boiler. The boiler set on the right side of the road with the log carriage setting in the middle of the old road. Lewis said they cut a tremendous amount of lumber right in the middle of the road. Being in the middle of the main road provided for easy handling of the logs.

One day when Lewis was working with the old steam sawmill, the spring, which operated the governors and provided the constant rate of power, broke causing the steam engine to begin running away. The old steam engine was about to leave the ground and had begun to vibrate up and down. Finally, Mr. Tom Poole come running around to shut the boiler down. Mr. Poole told everyone it was real dangerous and must be shut down or it would blow up.

Lewis and James Asherbranner also cut timber near the fork of Leola and Owl Creek Roads on the Jones place and between West Flint and Thompson Creeks on the John Alexander Place. The man who hired the timber cut was the most cussing man Lewis had ever heard. After learning that the man finally "got right and become a preacher," Lewis said he really would have loved to hear him preach since he was the best cusser he had ever heard. "If he could've preached half as good as he cussed he'd been the best in the country."

When Lewis' uncle enlisted in the Army, he and Lewis rode with Mr. Osteen (who took pictures in Moulton) to Hillsboro to catch the train. It was the Fall of the year and Lewis said it was the first time he ever rode in a car. At Hillsboro several of the local boys were leaving for the war and the crowd was the largest Lewis had ever seen. The large rail station platform was huge, used for holding cotton to be loaded on to the railcars. Only one well was located at the station and everyone was gathered around to get a drink of water. The hand pump was continually working to provide enough water for the thirsty crowd on a hot autumn day. Many people were on hand to see the local boys off to World War II. Shortly after in 1942, Lewis got his first car.

Lewis also sawed logs on Payne Creek Road just south of Grayson, for several years before World War II. The timber was cut for the Illinois Lumber Company and run by a man named Mr. Rawls. At Payne Creek, the timber cutting crews were using wooden wedges to place behind the cross-cut saws after the cut was made deep enough to allow space for the wedge. The wedge would lift the tree pressure off the saw blade allowing the crosscut saw to be pulled much easier and also to prevent pinching. Most of the time the trees were so huge that three big wedges would be driven behind the saw blade. Many of the real big trees were sent off to be made into lumber somewhere else, because they could get much more money for the tree than the rough sawmill lumber.

Lewis worked on Payne Creek with Henry McVay, John Fuller, Marvin Eddy, and Louie Melson. When Henry McVay first came to work, he wanted to know what the wooden things were used for. With a big grin on his face, Lewis told Henry "that was what they called wedges in Winston County."

All the logs the timber crew cut were snaked out with mules that were trained to go to the log pile. In Bankhead, Lewis said they never lead the mule to the log pile.

Lewis worked for the U.S. Forest Service during the war from 1943 to 1952. He worked out of the work center at Central Tower. Lewis set out a lot of pine trees and helped build roads. He also fought several forest fires in Bankhead some even until midnight. He helped fight many fires around the Houston area in Winston County. Now he says the Forest Service burns many acres of forest land each year and he does not understand why the Forest Service burns so much timer land each year.

During Lewis' time with the Forest Service, they did not clear-cut any timber, but did selective cutting. A bunch of men would work for the Forest Service for a while then they would lay off nearly everyone. Mr. Tom Wilson, the second ranger of Bankhead, was in charge of the forest when Lewis worked for the Forest Service.

Lewis helped clear timber for electrical power lines when electricity was finally run to the mountain in 1953. Lewis, Ammon Osborn, Austin Kelsoe, and Bill Kelsoe worked clearing the power right-of-ways for the power company. While working with the power company, Lewis relates the story of a fellow setting the crosscut saw teeth with a sledge hammer. The fellow would hit every tooth on the saw blade but the correct one. Needless to say the old crosscut was so dull it would wear the men out who were trying to cut the timber. Ammon told the fellow he would bring him a pick to set the saw. At least he would not hit but one tooth at a time.

Another time the same fellow brought a wide crosscut saw to work. The saw was so wide it would require a three foot diameter tree before it could be wedged. While trying to wedge the big saw with a steel wedge, a big gash was accidentally cut into the back of the saw. The next day, Lewis and Bill Kelsoe grabbed the big saw to cut a tree and broke it right where the wedge had cut the back of the saw. Lewis always used a small cross cut on smaller timber so they could be wedged without damaging the saw.

Lewis said he worked in timber most of his life and really loved to listen to the old sawmills run. For years after quitting the sawmill, Lewis still liked to hear the mills sawing timber.

## Lindsey Hall Grist Mills

Several grist mills operated in the forest around the Lindsey Hall area. One was located on the Blowing Springs Road about 200 yards north of the Leola Road toward Friendship Cemetery. Floyd Looney and Les Holley had both a sawmill and gristmill. Both mills were steam operated by water from a well. The well provided enough water supply to both the grist mill and the sawmill.

Dyke and Floyd Looney used to have another steam operated gristmill southeast of Lindsey Hall about 200 yards, at a spring on top of the bluff. At the time the Looney's had the mill, the springs had a lot of water.

The Roberts also had a water operated gristmill located on Rush Creek close to its junction with Brushy Creek. The dam was made of logs and backed up several acres of water. Hughes Oden used to have his corn ground into meal at the Roberts's Gristmill. The mill also served the settlers who lived in the Holmes Chapel and Brushy Creek areas.

## Poole Post Office

The Poole family, and later the Hawkins family, operated the post office at Lindsey Hall just south of the forks of Leola Road and Blowing Springs Road. Lewis still remembers the old log building where the post office was located. The old post office building was setting north and south and had two rooms divided by a little hall. An old dug well was located near the post office.

## Lou Annie Borden Oden

Lewis and Lou Annie Borden met at a dance at the home of Johnny England. Lewis was quick to point out the he did not do any dancing. Claude Dean England had been in military service and was home on leave.

Lewis and Lou Annie now own 25 acres which was originally entered by Josh England. The land was then bought by Dock Adley Borden, the father of Lou Annie. At one time, Dock could have bought more land for one dollar per acre. When Dock was young, he lived near Pine Torch for a while, but lived most of his life around where the Odens live now.

Lou Annie's parents were Dock Adley and Elizabeth Hooper Borden who were both of Cherokee Indian ancestry. Dock and Elizabeth had seven children: Evaline (MeHerg); Edley;

Thurlow; Mannie (father of Charles Borden); Roscoe; Lou Annie; and Walter. All the children were born in a little house which stood in front of the Oden's present home. The house had one room, a kitchen, and an upstairs with a porch.

Dock's parents were: Thomas Phillip Borden, born in 1855 and died in 1890; and Minnie England, daughter of Joshua and Susan Hooper England, born in 1853 and died in 1931.

Tom Borden was shot and killed near Pinhook when Dock was a young boy. Doc and Tom are buried in Pine Torch Cemetery. The Dock and Tom Borden's family are direct descendants of one of the earliest settlers of Lawrence County, Christopher Borden. Borden Creek in Bankhead is named in honor of Christopher who is buried somewhere along the beautiful stream.

William and Melvina McVay Hooper, Lou Annie's grandparents, were high percentage Cherokee Indian. They owned about 120 acres of land not far south of where the Oden's now live. William and Melvina had nine children: John, Grover, Roof, Elizabeth (Borden), Hattie (Yeates), Mary (Dobbs), Onner (Hill), Winnie (England), and Darthula (Dotson).

Elizabeth Hooper's uncle, Dock McVay owned land where Brushy Lake is now located. Just upstream from Brushy Lake was the Yeates Place. Hattie Hooper, sister of Elizabeth, married Joe Yeates who lived on the Yeates Place on Brushy Lake.

L-R: *Hettie Hooper (3/4 Cherokee), Doctor (Dock) Ada Borden (1/2 Cherokee) and Tabitha Elizabeth Hooper Borden (3/4 Cherokee) standing in front of Pine Torch Church.*

Lou Annie has lived in the same place she was born, with the exception of the first twenty years she and Lewis were married and lived around Lindsey Hall. Lou Annie has lived in the forest all of her life and attended school at Pine Torch.

Pine Torch School was located about one quarter mile south of the present day Pine Torch Church. The school was about fifty feet in length and went through the seventh grade. Some of Lou Annie's teachers were: Ms. Simms; Ms. Lucy Craig; Claude Sandlin; and Robert Sanderson. Both Lindsey Hall and Pine Torch Schools closed during the 1930's.

After Pine Torch School closed, the first bus driver to pick up school children in the mountains was Mr. Charlie Allred. Allred Hunter's Camp is located at the Old Allred home place and is named after the Allred family. Mr. Charlie Allred is buried in Shiloh Cemetery.

*William Rufus Adley Hooper (3/4 Cherokee) and Melvina McVay Hooper (3/4 Cherokee)*

## Pine Torch

As described by Dr. Charles Borden:

*"Pine Torch Church, nestled deep within the Bankhead National Forest, is thought to be the oldest log, church in Alabama. Believed to have been built between 1830 and 1850 by local Baptist settlers, the single-room structure doubled as a school house well into the early 1900s. My father, uncles, cousins, and other relatives living in the area attended classes there. Two of their teachers were Harvey Sims and Hershel Leigh. Hershel later taught me math at Moulton.*

*The name Pine Torch may derive from the burning of pine knots for light. Construction was typical for the period. Termite resistant poplar logs, roughhewn inside and out, formed the walls. Wooden shingles over pine log rafters sealed out the rain while the floors were covered with poplar puncheon said to have measured some 2' x 4' and being 4". Puncheons and shingles have long since disappeared and have been replaced by a tin roof and pine floor."*

## Lewis' Story Concludes

Mr. Lewis Oden has lived in the forest all his life and says "the forest has been set out more in pines than it used to be." He said clear-cut areas looks ragged when first set in pines, but some of the areas grow much better pine timber than hardwoods. His old home place on the Rush Creek has the same old hardwoods that have been there since 1924 and appear to be about the same size. Lewis said the timber at that site was still not worth fifteen cents and believes the stand has always had worms.

Lewis also believes the pines that have beetles should be cut and utilized. He does not like the idea of allowing beetle timber to rot down. Some good lumber has gone to waste close to his house. Lewis believes that beetles will always be a problem where loggers are not careful and damage or skin the bark off of the trees during the harvesting process. The forest ranger should not allow damage but one time, and the logger would be in trouble. Loggers who are careless about timber harvesting should be forbidden to cut anymore timber.

Lewis still likes to witch for water for people who need to dig a well. Lewis has witched over 100 wells most of which had a good supply of water. Robert Lewis and Lou Annie Borden Oden still love their mountain home and will probably be buried in their beloved hills – the "Warrior Mountains."

*Pine Torch Church*

# Chapter Four

# Families of Range 8 West

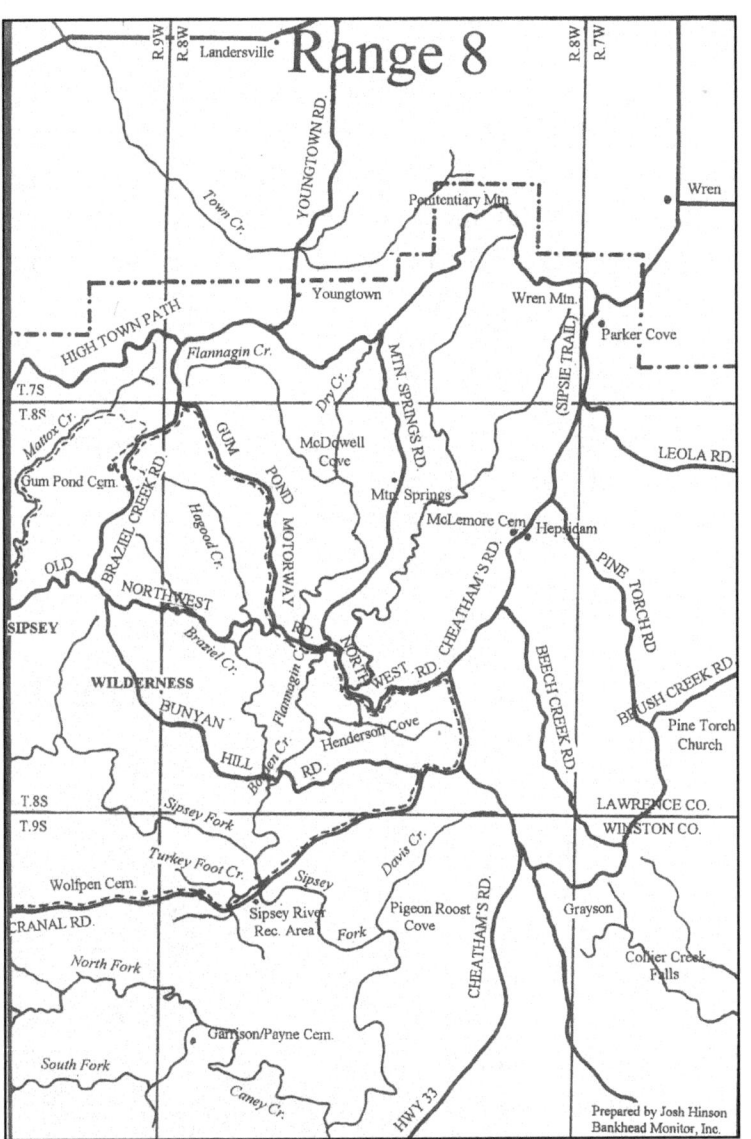

The families of Range 8 West lived in Townships 7, 8, and 9 South which extended from the Youngtown, McDowell Cove, to Pigeon Roost Cove which is south of Sipsey River picnic grounds. Some families move from one area of the forest to the other; therefore, some have lived in more than one range. Most of these families settled in the deep coves and the high ridges of some of the roughest portions of the Warrior Mountains. The area also contains some of the most beautiful coves found in the Warrior Mountains.

## Treadway Family of Wren Mountain

In the early days, the wagon route along or near the existing Leola and Ridge Roads were an Indian tail known as High Town Path. Many of the very first settlers to move into the Warrior Mountains of Bankhead Forest from north Georgia followed the High Town Path. The trail was named after the Indian Village of High Town, located near Rome, Georgia.

The High Town Path basically followed the continental divide between the Tennessee River drainage and the Mobile drainage system. It ran southwest down the Lookout Mountain and Sand Mountain areas into the hill country of Lawrence and Winston Counties. The High Town Path was the same general route the Treadway ancestors followed into Lawrence County, Alabama. They probably discovered the northern Bankhead area of Wren Mountain where the family settled via the High Town Path.

Since modern maps and surveying equipment was not available, Finnis Treadway said, "he was amazed how well the early wagon trail that lay along the High Town Path route was laid out by Indian people and early settlers." Portions of the Leola, Cheatham, Ridge, and Byler Roads in Lawrence County now exist where once lay the prehistoric Indian trail which many Lawrence and Winston County folks followed from North Georgia, the Carolinas, and east Tennessee into Bankhead Forest.

**Dan Treadway**

One of the first of his family to settle in the Warrior Mountains of Lawrence County was Dan Treadway. Dan Treadway, was a huge man who weighed some 270 pounds and was as strong as a bull. Dan was so strong that he would grab the spokes of the old wagon and help his steers move it out of mud holes, or pull the wagon up steep hills. Dan's family migrated from the Smoky Mountains of North Georgia into Alabama in the late 1800's. Dan and his wife, Janie White, moved from Georgia to Alabama in a covered wagon pulled by steers.

The route they followed was the High Town Path, passed close to Gadsden where they lived for about two years. After living for a while near the Gadsden-Sand Mountain Area, Dan Treadway and his family moved west into Lawrence County. The Treadway family settled on the High Town Path in the Wren Mountain area of Bankhead National Forest where Dan entered 40 acres. Thus the Treadway descendants have claimed the area as their home for over 100 years.

*Dan Treadway & Janie White*

Dan Treadway was born April 22, 1861, and died October 27, 1952. Janie White Treadway was born June 18, 1870, and died October 22, 1956. Janie's father, John Quincy White, fought in the Civil War of Northern Aggression with the Confederate States of America. Finnis Treadway said, "John rode a mule to Mississippi to recruit troops to a battle taking place in Georgia." The fight was leading up to the Battle of Atlanta.

**Henry and Maggie Treadway**

Henry Treadway, the son of Dan and Janie White Treadway, was born July 5, 1892. Maggie Tankersley, who became the wife of Henry, was born March 20, 1901. Henry and Maggie Tankersley Treadway had a total of 13 children with Finnis D. Treadway being their third child. Finnis was born in a small log cabin on December 24, 1919, at Clayton Cove, near the Blankenship Cove of Bankhead National Forest.

Henry and Maggie were sharecrop farmers and lived in the mountains of Bankhead all their lives. Maggie's daddy was Steve Tankersley and her mother was Leona Demasters. Steve had one brother, Ed Tankersley, who entered several hundred acres of mountain land along what is now Highway 33 and Ridge Road. Steve Tankersley farmed much of his brother's land located on top of Wren Mountain.

In addition to farming, Steve ran a blacksmith shop and worked at the limestone quarry on top of the mountain. Steve's blacksmith shop on Wren Mountain was on the eastern side of the Cheatham Road, about one-quarter mile south of Ridge Road.

Maggie's parents and grandparents were also raised in Bankhead Forest. Both the Tankersleys and Demasters lived near the Wren Mountain area for a long time. At 15 years of age, Maggie Tankersley married Henry Treadway, 22 years old. Henry and Maggie Treadway had 13 children who are:

Front Row L-R: *Steve Tankersley, Ennis Tankersley, Leona Demasters, Susan Demastus.* Back Row L-R: *Lucy Demasters, Maggie Tankersley, Jesse Demasters, Lillian Demasters, Ernest Tankersley.*

Irene Treadway, born September 5, 1917; Evelyn Treadway, born October 3, 1918; Finnis Treadway, born December 24, 1919; Willard Treadway, born September 20, 1921; Mitchell Treadway, born September 22, 1922; Cleo Treadway, born July 16, 1924; Ozell Treadway, born July 29, 1926; Odis Treadway, born April 20, 1928; Betty Ruth Treadway, born May 14, 1930; Quincy Ray Treadway, born September 26, 1932; Hazel Treadway, born October 8, 1934; Lennon B. Treadway, born June 4, 1937; Levona Treadway, born March 19, 1940. Irene and Willard died when they were very young and were buried in Montgomery Cemetery. After Henry and Maggie married, they share cropped a two mule farm of some 40 acres of land in the Clayton Cove area. In the early days, the crops planted in the mountains had to be fenced in because the stock animals were allowed to roam free.

Some two years after Finnis was born, his family moved from Clayton Cove to the foot of Wren Mountain, near the present day Deer Run Golf Course. They sharecropped a farm, known at the Stewart Place, and based on a 3$^{rd}$ of corn and a 4$^{th}$ of cotton. After approximately seven years at the Stewart Place, Henry and his family moved to the top of Wren Mountain near the junction of Cheatham Road and Ridge Road. Finnis was about nine years old when his parents moved to the mountain top. Their home was located southwest of the junction of Cheatham Road and the Ridge Road where a large stand of pines now grow on public forest property.

Henry Treadway bought four 40 acre blocks and one 20 acres block of land around the Wren Mountain area. After each block was bought, the family would clear the land and sell their firewood and stove wood. The wood was cut with crosscut saws and axes. After the stove wood was transported to Moulton, it was sold for $2.00 per cord. Initially, the family hauled wood in a wagon, and later it was transported to Moulton in a 1935 Ford truck.

In order to feed and raise a family of ten children, Henry farmed the local fields, blasted rocks and stumps from roads, worked at the Henderson Cove limestone quarry of the Northwest Road, mined coal in the Penitentiary Mountain coal mines, and was involved in the old mountain trade of processing the upland corn into the liquid gold that makes some men crazy.

Henry's family had 2 or 3 cows, kept 4 or 5 hogs, and farmed corn, sugar cane, and cotton. The family usually kept a brood sow and raised three and four hogs which were killed for meat. The Treadway children plowed and helped farm the poor sandy land on top of Wren Mountain.

**Penitentiary Mountain Coal Mines**

Henry Treadway worked the coal mines for some fourteen years. The miners worked the mines with picks and shovels by light from caps, which had carbide lanterns attached to the front. The carbide lights were usually recharged two or three times per day. The miners biggest problem in the shafts was called "Black Damp" which were areas where the mine contained no oxygen. The only sign of these oxygen problems was due to lanterns going out. Occasionally, a miner would go unconscious and would be pulled by his heels out of the mine shaft. There were no fans or air circulation in the mine and the miners would pass out if the oxygen problem could not be detected soon enough. Therefore when lights started going out, the miners knew to move quickly away from the area.

Bill Wilhoite, Jack Wilhoite, and Mance Hamby were working the coal mines on the mountain's southern slope. After the Wilhoites and Hambys quit mining coal, the Treadway shaft was eventually dug through the coal seam into their neighbors shaft on the other side of the mountain. In other words, in narrow strips where the mines joined, the coal seam was removed all the way through Penitentiary Mountain.

The Treadway miners actually dug into the mine shaft which originated on the south side of the mountain. With both the mine shafts joined together, the tunnel system was over a mile in length. The Treadway mine entrance was sloped downhill from the coal seam and the seep water easily ran out of the mine; however, the mine entrance on the south side mountain was higher than the coal, creating water problems for the miners coming in from the south. In the southern shafts, the miners would have to dig drainage ditches to keep the mine from filling up with water.

During the winter and spring rainy seasons, the mountain would become heavy as it was saturated with water and press downward on the seam of coal. The increased pressure would squeeze out clay and mud from under the layer of coal into the mine shaft.

The coal shaft was dug about 4 feet high. The bottom of the shaft was laid with board like cross ties and two inch by two inch rails were nailed on the ties about two feet apart for the coal wagons to be pushed in an out of the mine. It would take three wagon loads of coal to equal approximately one ton. At the face of the coal, side shafts would be dug so as to expose the layer of coal. Hand augers were used to drill approximately two feet deep under the coal. A stick of dynamite was then cut up into three sections with a portion placed into the series of holes which were also spaced about 2 feet apart along the face of the coal. The solid face of coal ranged from 18 to 24 inches thick. Once the charges were placed, the mine was cleared and the dynamite was set off.

The coal seemed to be a solid layer which spread out once the tunnel was well into the mountain. Within the tunnel system, pillars of coal and rock would be left to support the top of the mine shaft. In addition to the pillars of rock and coal, oak posts were placed in the shaft and tightened with wooden wedges and a sledge hammer. Since the layers of coal were overlaid with soft sandstone, a pick was also used to tap the roof to check for loose rocks. If loose rocks were found they were either supported with a post or removed from the roof of the shaft. After dynamite charges were set off, the mine shaft was inspected and roof support timbers were placed where necessary. Then the hard work of shoveling the huge pile of loose coal began.

If the miners could remove three tons of coal per day they were doing a good business; therefore, fifteen dollars per day was good money for the Treadway coal business in the early 1930's. Finnis's granddad, Dan, made fifty cents per day for hauling coal to Moulton. Many of the businesses and homes in Moulton depended upon the Penitentiary Mountain coal for their winter energy supply.

**School Days**

Henry and Maggie's children attended Wren School, located about one mile west of the junction of highway 36 and 33. Finnis and his sister, Evelyn, walked from the top of the mountain to the school in the valley. The old Cheatham Road did not wind its way down the ridges as does the Highway 33 of today, but instead followed a valley from near the Cheatham-Ridge Road junction to the flat land at Wren. Presently, the original Cheatham route up the mountain is only a dim wagon road. The route up the mountain, which highway 33 presently follows, is actually the third road from Wren to the mountain top. Finnis said he and his sister got scared several times while walking up and down Wren Mountain to school. They walked to school for some two years before school bus transportation to Wren was provided for the mountain children.

The first person to haul the children from the forest to Wren School was Mr. Ralph Knox. Some of the Knox family are buried in the Tapsville Cemetery near Central Tower. The family lived about one mile east of the Cheatham Road on Pine Torch Road, and owned several acres of land west of the road.

Ralph built a small bus out of his T-model truck. The top of the bus was covered with an oil cloth and always leaked if it rained very much. The bus would haul about a dozen children to Wren school. When returning home, the children would get out and help push the school bus up Wren Mountain.

The Knox family were thought to be the most wealthy people living in the forest. When folks had to turn in gold during the depression of the 1930's, it was told that Ralph Knox's father had to turn in $800.00 in pure gold.

After Ralph Knox, quit driving the bus, Mr. Charlie Allred, who lived where Allred Hunter's Camp is now located, carried the mountain children to school.

Mountain View School, a short distance south of the Treadway home place, was already closed when Finnis started to school. Mountain View was between Leola Road and Cheatham Road. Finnis's mother, Maggie Tankersley, attended school at Mountain View before it closed, around the 1920's.

After Mountain View School closed, the building was opened for a short time as a second-hand dry goods store. After one of the stores at Wren had closed, Mr. Freeman Armstrong bought all the merchandise and moved it to Mountain View. The store was operated for some three years, or until Freeman had sold most of the merchandise. After Freeman's folks died, he moved near Hepsidam.

**Finnis Treadway**

Finnish had quit school in the sixth grade to help his family make a living. One of Finnis' first jobs was loading rock at the limestone quarry in Henderson Cove, near Borden Creek and Northwest Road. The rock crew could load about one yard of rock per hour. While working in the rock quarry on the northwest road, Finnis was employed by the U.S. Forest Service and was paid twenty-five cents per hour. Initially, the limestone layers were drilled and blasted. The men used sixteen-pound sledge hammers to bust the rock into gravel.

Finnish said, "the biggest problem was the bruises and cuts on his shins and lower parts of his legs." Finnis' legs always stayed "beat up" due to flying rocks and hammers. Finnis worked in the limestone quarry with the Forest Service for about two years.

In addition, Finnish helped his father, Henry Treadway, mine coal on Penitentiary Mountain. The coal mine was on the northeast side of the mountain consisted of a low, narrow tunnel which ran south under the mountain. Henry leased the coal mine from Bill McCarty and worked in the mine for some fourteen years.

When Finnis was about 13 years old, he started working in the coal mine. Finnish worked for three years in his daddy's coal mine and claimed it was the hardest work he had ever done. After the coal was dug from the mine, it was hauled from the mountains in a wagon pulled my mules to Moulton where it was delivered to purchasers. They sold coal in Moulton to shops and homes for about $5.00 per ton which included hauling.

*Finnis Treadway at the entrance of the old coal mine where he used to work.*

Finnis and Mitchell were the only Treadway boys to work in the coal mines. Mitchell worked in the mines just over one year. The old mine entrance was on privately owned land, with the Treadway mine shaft starting on the northeast side of the mountain. The shaft eventually went all the way through the mountain and came out on the southwest side; therefore, the tunnel passed under the Ridge Road. The entrances to the old coal mine shafts are still visible.

Mr. Finnis Treadway said they left lots of coal, not only in the coal support pillars, but also in the areas where the seam of coal narrowed. Finnis was glad the coal mine eventually closed because of the extremely dangerous and hard work.

## Forest Service Early Days

During the early 1930's, a Forest Service work camp was located on Wren Mountain across from the old Treadway home place, on the east side of the Cheatham Road. The housing for the work camp consisted of a half dozen or so canvas tents. The tent crews cut right of ways, built roads, and up-graded existing wagon roads.

At the camp, the Forest Service had an old grader and tractor for making and maintaining the forest roads. The old tractor had a small gasoline motor on the side, which assisted in starting the diesel engine. After the small gasoline motor started, it would be placed in gear and turn the large diesel tractor engine until it began running on the diesel fuel. After the tractor began, the small engine was taken out of gear and cut off. The big tractor was used by the road crew for making and upgrading the Forest Service roads.

Finnis can remember when the Leola and Ridge Roads were just primitive wagon trails leading through the woods before the Forest Service began upgrading the roads for motorized vehicles. Finnis' father, Henry Treadway, was in charge of blasting stumps out of the right of ways on the Leola, Ridge, and Cheatham Roads. In addition, he worked on many other Forest Service roads blasting rocks and stumps.

## The Rock House

After 1940, after Finnis finished his duty with the Civilian Conservation Corps, he helped his dad build a rock house at the very back of their old log house. The rock house is still located on the west side of highway 33 about a mile south of the Ridge Road. Finnis and his dad built outside walls of the house out of sandstone rocks. They are about a foot wide and are made of layers of sandstone rock. The rocks were gathered and pried out of the ground from around Wren Mountain. They were cut into shape with an old ax and a sledge hammer. After the rocks were shaped and ready to use, scaffolds were made to carry the cut stones to the top of the walls. The sandstone rocks were cemented together by placing a layer of wet cement then placing a layer of rock on the top of the cement layer. The process was repeated over and over until the rock house walls were completed.

The ceiling, roof, and inside walls of the house were then framed with rough sawmill lumber. The floor of the rock house was later poured with concrete after the original flooring rotted out. The back porch of the original log house actually became the location of the front porch of the rock house.

The house was completed around 1941 with Henry, Finnis, and Mitchell working together to complete the house. Odis Treadway, Finnis' brother, still lives in the old rock house. When Henry Treadway died, his wife, Maggie, inherited the rock house and land. Maggie willed all of her children equal shares of the Treadway property.

*Finnis Treadway sitting on the front porch of the old rock house on Wren Mountain.*

Two big springs were located near the rock house: The Ed Tankersley Spring was located at the head waters of Montgomery Creek, and the Parker Spring was located west of the Cheatham Road in Parker Cove. The Parker Cove Spring was about one mile southeast of the junction of Ridge Road and Cheatham Road and forms the headwaters of Elam Creek. The Ed Tankersley Spring was due west about one mile southwest of the junction of Ridge Road and Cheatham Road and is the head water of Montgomery Creek. However, the Treadway family used their well, located near the porch of the rock house, for drinking water.

**Hunting – A Tradition**

Once when deer hunting and traveling through the woods toward home, Finnis was real hot and thirsty. He could hardly wait to arrive at the big Tankersley Spring to get a drink of water. Upon approaching the spring, he noticed a few blue jay feathers lying near the water. The feathers may have been the only thing to save his life. Upon closer examination, Finnis saw the head of a large timber rattlesnake lying in the edge of the water. Forgetting about his thirst, Finnis got a stick and killed the deadly snake, which had already killed and swallowed a feathered, thirsty spring visitor.

Not only did Finnis love to hunt, but his father was also an avid turkey hunter. Henry Treadway was considered one of the best turkey hunters in Bankhead National Forest. Henry learned to turkey hunt on his own by trial and error. He made his own turkey callers and killed as many as nine Black Warrior gobblers in one season. He was allowed to harvest ten gobblers that particular year; however, he fell one short of his legal limit.

**Finnis**

About 1947, after returning from World War II, Finnis began working with the Forest Service and became a registered forester. While with the Forest Service, Finnish marked timber, set out pine tree seedlings, worked in timber stand improvement, and fought forest fires.

Finnis also helped set out some white pine seedlings. The Forest Service thought white pines would do well in Bankhead since, at one time, the forest contained the state champion white pine on Caney Creek. The huge white pine was thought to be naturally occurring in Bankhead. The old white pine, which lived to be some 170 years, died several years ago. However, the white pine plantations were very susceptible to disease and insects and did not do well in the soils of Bankhead.

Finnis said he remembered one crown fire occurring in an old pine field. The fire was driven by high winds as it burned up a ridge, out of a big cove. Anybody who could fight the fire was recruited to help extinguish the crown fire, occurring in the late 1930's.

Finnis worked with the Forest Service until 1955, then moved to Georgia and worked ten years as an auto mechanic. Finnis and his family moved back to Lawrence County in 1965. He worked as an auto mechanic in Decatur for several years before getting into the carpentry business.

Finnis D. Treadway married Lorene Smith on September 28, 1946, and they have the following children: Dyann T. Roberts, Finnis O. Treadway, Janice T. Johnson, Ricky F. Treadway, and Randy D. Treadway. Finnis Treadway said his wife was of Cherokee Indian ancestry.

When asked how he felt about the forest today, Finnis' reply was, "Nothing can take the place of the old Wren Mountain home place. It is one of the most special places I have ever been and lived. Growing up in Bankhead Forest is like no other place in the world as far as its special meaning to my family. The better the forest is preserved for our future, the better off our county will become."

The last hope Finnis conveyed to me was, "The old rock house should always be preserved as a reminder to everyone who passes the way of those hard times but wonderful days in the land of the "Warrior Mountains."

## Curtis Family of Montgomery Creek

L-R: *Jonathon Bird Curtis (1/4 Cherokee), Robert (Bob) Curtis, Lydia Jane Allen Curtis, Mary Curtis, Tom Curtis, Cora Curtis. Jonathon Bird and Lydia Jane Allen Curtis are the parents of George B. Curtis.*

On Montgomery Creek is the footing of an old bridge which in earlier days was used as a creek crossing for wagons. Very little remains of this long ago reminder of those hardy settlers who lived in the area. Two stone walls, one on each side of the creek, were still intact with the eastern stone formation containing pieces of long iron rods, probably made in some settler's nearby blacksmith shop. At one time, it appeared the rods secured timbers to the footing; however, the wood has long since rotted.

As I stood there looking at the remains of the old bridge, my thoughts raced back to my great grandparents who probably crossed the bridge many times since their homestead was located just upstream. I then wondered about the extreme difficulties my ancestors must have had trying to establish a new home a long way from the hills of North Georgia and North Carolina, an area they claimed as home early in life.

In those early days of Lawrence County, it was reported that malaria, which was carried by mosquitoes, was quite common and a major reason many settlers sought out the hills and higher mountainous land, now composing the Bankhead National Forest. Even though much of the Tennessee Valley was fertile farming land, the low lying land of the swamps, creeks, and streams contributed to a heavy infestation of mosquitoes which were the primary culprits carrying malaria. Regardless of the mosquitoes, my folks settled in the forest because the land was free for homesteading. The hilly and mountainous land was made up of rather poor sandy soils, but offered isolation that many of the mixed blood Indian families sought. After openings were cleared in the forest through a lot of hard back breaking work, the small fields were plowed and planted in small patches of cotton and corn.

### George Curtis

My great-grandfather, George B. Curtis, was the grandson of Elizabeth Bird, from North Carolina, who was one-half Cherokee Indian. George was among the early settlers in 1900, who sought out a beautiful area in the Montgomery Creek Valley to homestead land and build his log cabin. George's parents were Jonathan Bird Curtis and Lydia J. Allen. Jonathan Bird Curtis, the son of J.A. Curtis and Elizabeth Bird, was born in Monroe County, North Carolina in 1846. According to Old Land Records of Lawrence County by Margaret Cowart, George entered 160.3 acres of land in Section 25 of Township 7 South and Range 8 West on July 1902. When they moved to Bankhead, they had two small girls, Minnie and Bessie.

*George and Mary Ellen Parker Curtis.*

### The Warrior Mountains Farm

With the help of neighbors, the family built the double log house containing two large rooms with a big open hallway through the middle of the house. The house was made primarily of yellow poplar which was cut near the house site. As with most homes of that time, yellow poplar was used as floor joists because termites would not eat that particular wood. Poplar was also used to make shingles because wide, water resistant boards, especially suited as roofing material, could easily be split from the wood. A palening fence, also split from surrounding white oak trees, enclosed a clean sandy yard which was kept in neat condition by a brush broom.

The cabin was located on Montgomery Creek west of present day Highway 33. A few yards from the cabin was a barn and rail fence enclosing a small pasture. The family owned two oxen used for plowing, two hogs for meat, and a cow for milk. Most local families owned similar livestock with some owning mules or horses instead of oxen. Nearly all families in the area had a cherry tree and a small orchard with apples and peaches.

**Curtis Family**

After George married Mary Sparks, they had four children; Minnie, Bessie, Johnny, and Ila. My grandmother, Ila Curtis Wilburn, was the fourth child born into the family after her brother, Johnny. On September 1, 1905, my grandmother was born in their log cabin located near Montgomery Creek. Shortly after my grandmother was born, her mother, Mary Elean Sparks Curtis, died from complications from childbirth. Death of this nature was common in the early days of Lawrence County. Mary Elean's funeral was at Fairview Methodist Church, the nearest church located just a few yards north of the old Hepsidam store site. Fairview Methodist was a long white washed building with one door and was the only building in the area of that time. My great-grandmother was buried across the road in McLemore Cemetery.

*George Curtis (1/8 Cherokee).*

In 1908, George, who had left his parents several years earlier, planned on visiting his folks. George was going to sell his two hogs in order to get enough money for the trip to Texas where his parents were then living. George's wife planned on keeping the six children they had at that time. George talked with a neighbor about buying the hogs. The neighbor agreed to meet George the next morning with the money. After a long night of worry, George met the man early the next morning at the split rail fence which enclosed the hog pen. He told the man that he had decided his family must have the meat in order to make it through the winter. George never made the trip to visit his folks. He never saw his parents after moving to Lawrence County, Alabama. George lived here until he died in 1968 at 89 years old.

**Neighbors**

While living on Montgomery Creek, George had several neighbors who lived on the old Cheatham Road and only three neighbors who lived in the Montgomery Creek Valley. Blue Will Singleton, Arie Hall, and Uncle Good Legg were neighbors who lived in nearby hollows Ed Tanksley, Steve and Leona Tanksley, Dan Treadway, Ben Legg, George Montgomery, Mullican Sparks, Jetson Demasters, Henry Parker, Sid and Alice Parker, Luther and Frances Parker, and Dee and Ester Parker were neighbors who live up on the ridges near Cheatham Road. The Parker boys were brothers to Georges's second wife, Mary Ellen Parker.

The children of George Baxter Curtis and Mary Elean Sparks are: (L-R) Ila Curtis Wilburn, Johnny Curtis, Minnie Curtis Welborn, and Bessie Curtis Smith. The little boy is the son of Ila, Cadle Wilburn.

The Cheatham Road, present day Highway 33, was a dirt road just wide enough for two wagons to pass. During rainy weather, the road was extremely muddy and had large holes which were cross laid with poles to prevent the wagons from sinking. The Cheatham Road was on mail route five from Moulton. All the families in the area had to pick up their mail at the road.

Most of the early mountain people began selling the land to the United States Government about 1918 for the eventual development of a national forest. Most of all the early settler families had moved to the edge of the Moulton Valley by the 1920's.

Now within the valley of Montgomery Creek is little evidence of the trials, work, and life of these early people. The buildings, fields, and roads have reverted back to the natural state. The forest of Montgomery Creek has again returned to the woodland it once was with very little trace of human existence.

The information about the early 1900 families near Montgomery Creek is from the vivid memory of my grandmother, Ila Wilburn, who was 90 years old the first day of September, 1995. But as the old bridge foundations erode away by natural forces, so do the memories of the early settlers who lived on Montgomery Creek in the peaceful land of the "Warrior Mountains."

## Families of Parker Cove and Borden Creek

On June 5, 1991, I visited with a wonderful lady who has never lived over five miles from where she was born in Parker Cove. Her name is Ms. Fannie Parker Montgomery, who lived about two miles southeast of Wren. Ms. Montgomery's has lived in her present house for over forty years. She was born on September 12, 1898. Since the writing of this story, Ms. Fannie Parker Montgomery has passed away.

**Parker Cove**

Parker Cove is a beautiful valley which can be seen from Highway 33 about ¼ mile south of the Ridge Road. The entrance to the cove is a steep narrow road that winds downhill to the valley, nearly 300 feet below the elevation of Highway 33 on the mountaintop. The cove forms the headwaters of Elam Creek. At one time, the cove had nearly 300 acres of cleared farmland and pastures.

Only three log cabins were in Parker Cove during the first years of 1900. During these early years, Fannie's family lived in a cabin near the east end of the cove; Cousin Dee Parker, his family, and daddy lived in a cabin on the south slope of the cove; Uncle Bill Johnson lived at the west end of the cove prior to going up in the mountain. Ms. Fannie was born in her family's old homestead cabin east of Parker Cemetery. She was the fourth child born to Henry and Minnie Lou Dutton Parker.

**Borden Creek Parkers**

According to Mr. Rayford Hyatt, William D., Lewis, and John T. Parker were brothers who moved with their families to Bankhead Forest during the 1830's. The Parkers first settled in the Borden Creek and Northwest Road area of the forest. Probably, William D. Parker and some of his family, along with one child of John T. Parker, are buried in the early Parker Cemetery near Borden Creek.

Sometime around 1850, John T. and Lewis Parker moved their families in or around Parker Cove. John T. and Lewis, along with several family members, are buried in the second Parker Cemetery in Bankhead in Parker Cove; however, no graves in either Parker Cemetery are marked. Some descendants of the Parkers say they do not have any Indian blood at all, even though other Parker descendants claim strong Indian ancestry. Several Parker family members have tribal membership through their family bloodlines. I personally have no desire to discuss the issue and leave the decision as Indian ancestry with members of the Parker family.

*Jane Parker Smith, daughter of John T. and Mary Polly Neely Parker (1/2 Cherokee).*

**John and Polly**

The first of the Parker family to live in Parker Cove was John T. and Mary (Polly) Neely Parker from Tennessee. They moved to the area around 1830. According to some family members, John and Polly were mixed blood Cherokee Indians. The blood lines appear obvious after looking at some pictures of John and Polly's children, whom their descendants claim part Indian.

John and Polly had 12 children with 11 being listed in the 1850 census of Lawrence County. The census list the children and their ages as: William Carroll Parker, age 20; Sarah Ann Parker (Chenault), age 19; Henry Parker, age 18; Elizabeth Parker, age 16; Lewis C. Parker, age 14; Mary (Polly) Parker, age 12; Washington Wilshire Parker, age 9; Martha Parker (Tankersley), age 8; Jane Parker (Smith), age 6; Lona (Zeeny) Parker, age 4; Elijah Parker, age 2; and James D. Parker who was not listed in the 1850 census.

## Washington Wilshire Parker

Washington Wilshire Parker, Ms. Fannie's grandfather, fought the Civil War with his brother. The Parker brothers were fighting side by side when Wilshire saw his brother killed in action during heavy fighting in Tennessee.

After the Civil War, Wilshire came back to the area and established his home just east of Parker Cove near Bogar Cemetery. He married Maranda Bogar and they established their home at the old Bogar home site. After his death, Wilshire was buried in Bogar Cemetery near his home place.

Washington Wilshire and Martha Maranda had the following children: Eliza, Henry Washington, Dora (Willis), Lucy who married uncle Bill Johnson, Addie (Dutton), Charlie, Horace, Sally (Dutton), Willie, Mattie (Simms), Letha (Simms), Ellie Vera (Robinson), and Nellie (Ellis).

Wilshire, a Baptist preacher, was the uncle to my grandmother's stepmother, Mary Ellen Parker Curtis. Wilshire married my great-grandfather George Baxter Curtis and Mary Ellen Parker on December 3, 1905. Mary Ellen's father was James B. Parker, Wilshire's youngest brother.

## Henry Parker

Henry Parker, the son of Wilshire and Maranda Bogar Parker, married Minnie Dutton. Henry and Minnie lived in the lower end of the cove about one mile east of Uncle Bill Johnson's log cabin, Mr. Fannie said she loved to eat the watermelons that Uncle Bill grew.

Later, Henry bought Uncle Bill's house in the western portion of the cove. Before moving in, Henry did some remodeling to the old log cabin. Henry Parker sawed down a big poplar tree to seal the cabin he had bought from Bill Johnson. After the big poplar was cut down it took 12 head of oxen to snake the log to the saw mill on top of the mountain. The poplar lumber was enough to make it a kitchen and to seal the whole house.

## Henry and Minnie Parker

Henry and Minnie Dutton Parker had nine children: Maggie and Minnie Mae, who were twins; Emmitt; little Walter, who died as a child; Fannie; Frank; Bessie; Elise; and Edna. Ms. Fannie, along with all but the two youngest girls, was born in the two room log house in the eastern portion of the cove.

Minnie's mother was Mary Plant Dutton. Mary's husband had died and she made the crop with the help of her sons.

Henry and Minnie owned 240 acres of land with a log cabin, a barn, and a smokehouse. They worked cotton, beans, peas, corn, and sugarcane. All the children had to hoe cotton and milk cows. They had their own milk, butter, and killed hogs. Henry traded in Hartselle because he could buy goods cheaper. He bought coffee, sugar, and flour by the barrels.

Sometimes they would buy seven to eight barrels of supplies at a time. Henry would carry several weeks of supplies in his wagon pulled by mules. In addition, all the farming was done with horse and mules.

Henry used Mr. Steve Tankersley as the family blacksmith. Steve lived on top of the mountain and made his crops with a steer. One day Mr. Tankersley had loaded a half bale of cotton on his wagon when the steer spooked and ran down the mountain with the cotton flying. He could not catch up with the steer because he was a real healthy fellow.

**Food for Survival**

Henry Parker had a molasses mill. They grew their own sugarcane and made their own syrup. The family used ash hopper to run lye to make their soap.

The Henry Parker family ground their own corn for meal at Wren. The grist mill was close enough to the cove to have meal ground when they ran out. The family cotton was carried to Moulton to be ginned.

Henry made just enough money to live on through the year. Ms. Fannie said we were just poor country folks. The family never used any fertilizer at all on their crops except manure. After the fields would get poor, Henry would buy some guano. They never poisoned any crops or vegetables. The vegetable garden or fruits were never poisoned because they did not have to worry about insects. In addition to raising cotton, corn, and vegetables of all kinds, the family also raised chufas, similar to peanuts.

Henry, Minnie, and the rest of their family stored apples in sawdust to eat on all winter. They would also place peaches in 40 gallons of brine water and have pickled peaches all winter.

They placed pears in the attic loft so thick there would be only small places where they could step between the fruit. The pears would weigh two or three pounds and were kept spread out so that they would not touch. The heat from the fireplaces kept the attic warm and helped keep the pears fresh all winter.

Henry's two older twin daughters always got to do the cooking while Fannie helped her brothers and daddy split and haul wood in the wagon drawn by two mules. Fannie also cut stove wood and fire wood and loaded the wood in the wagon. The family burned wood for both cooking and heating purposes. Ms. Fannie visited the coal mine located on the north side of Penitentiary Mountain. Even though coal was plentiful and coal mines were nearby, Ms. Fannie's folks always used wood.

**Fannie's Early Years**

One night Fannie decided to go opossum hunting with the boys. It was so dark that she prayed to God for help to get back home. Ms. Fannie said the problem with the night hunt was she did not have a light and her brothers stayed so far out front she could not see. That night she vowed to never go opossum hunting with her brothers again. Henry's sons, Emmitt and Frank, hunted everything they could shoot at. They always had meat on the table.

Fannie's brother built a bird house and placed it high in a nearby pine tree. One day Fannie decided to inspect the birdhouse and climbed the tree to peep into the box. She was unable to see into the little house, and, after all she had already climbed the tree. Therefore, she reached in the nest to check for birds. Suddenly a severe pain shot through her finer and hand. A flying squirrel had bit clean through her finger and held on as Fannie scattered pine bark sliding down the tree. Fannie's maw answered the cry of distress and rushed out to see what was wrong. Fannie was screaming with the little squirrel holding on for dear life. Fannie's mother had a hard time getting the little squirrel to turn loose. Even though the incident happened when she was a little girl, Ms. Fannie will never forget being bit by a flying squirrel.

**Fannie Remembers**

Fannie's family had one of the few telephones on the mountain. They would buy the telephone box and would be on a party line with all their neighbors. They had the telephone long before they got electricity.

Ms. Fannie said she never saw a car until she was grown and already had two or three children. The first car she ever saw was Doctor Price Irwin's car. He used the car to make house calls. Before cars came into use, Ms. Fannie remembers doctors riding horses to visit the sick.

Fannie said her family attended church at Old Elam, about two miles from Parker Cove. The Old Elam Church and School had benches which were hued out of huge logs. The church and school consisted of only one room.

**School Days**

The Gum Pond would freeze over thick enough that all the school children would get up in the mornings before school and skate on the ice. The pond was located in front of Rayford Hyatt's present house. The water was full of huge sweet gum trees and made a perfect winter playground. During the summer, the gum pond was always the home of numerous snakes.

Mag Massey taught at Old Elam when Fannie was in her first years of school. Ms. Fannie said an old man taught over there, but he was awfully lazy. Fannie walked to school during her school days. She had to buy her own books and used the Blueback Speller. The school children got water out of an old dug well lined with rock at Old Elam.

In addition to attending Old Elam and Wren schools, Ms. Fannie attended her last years of school at Mountain View. Mountain View School was located at the corner of Leola Road and Cheatham Road (Highway 33). John Day was Ms. Fannie's school teacher at Mountain View. Mr. Day played ball with the children; however, he would not turn school out until every lesson for the day had been completed. Sometimes the children would not get home from school until after dark.

Ms. Fannie played ball every time they had a game. Fannie loved to play ball and would be the first one picked every time. One day she knocked the ball so far that it was never found:

Around a 100 children went to school at Mountain View. Loggers came in and built a lot of houses that were just one-half mile south of Ridge Road. The people worked at the sawmill and their children attended to Mountain View School.

A logger by the name of Beryl Smart had a base fiddle and left it with the Parker family. Years later, he came back and got his fiddle which the Parker family had taken care of for him.

One morning when Ms. Fannie attended school at Mountain View, Mr. John Day came in shortly after she had started a fire in the heater. He told Ms. Fannie to stay at school until 9:00 and tell all the children not to come back to school until he got them word. Nine days after Mr. Day left school, Fannie also came down with the measles. Within a few days, every student that attended Mountain View became sick; therefore, school was closed for several days because the teacher had given everyone the measles.

**Fannie Gets Married**

Ms. Fannie was married on December 26, 1915, to Ellis Montgomery, her classmate at Mountain View School. Ms. Fannie said there "was no such thing" as honeymoons when she got married.

After Fannie married, she moved out of the mountain cove to George Montgomery's place on Wren Road. Later she and Ellis moved to the Chitwood Place, and then back to grandpa Parker's place near Bogar Cemetery. Coal oil lamps and fireplaces were the only light Ms. Fannie had until about 1950. At first, Ms. Fannie used her hands to rub their clothes together. Ms. Fannie said it was not long until rub boards came along and were used to wash clothes.

Fannie and her husband farmed all their lives. Ms. Fannie said she has had a life and enjoyed all the good old days. She admitted that she was the tomboy of the Parker family. Ms. Fannie has eight children, a bunch of grandchildren, a lot of great-grandchildren, and three great-great-grandchildren. Ms. Fannie had a strong love and devotion to the rolling hills which are clearly in view just south of her home located near the "Warrior Mountains."

## Families of Mountain Springs

On April 21, 1913, Ambros Milton Spillers entered a tract of land of 80.5 acres on the Mountain Springs Road. Mountain Springs Road is located in Bankhead National Forest about two miles west of Cheatham Highway or state Highway 33 and runs parallel to the highway. The northern end of Mountain Springs Road is Ridge Road, with the southern end being the Northwest Road. The road is approximately five miles in total length.

According to Ms. Birtie Mae Spillers Wilkerson, who is now deceased and provided most of this information before she died on March 14, 1993, her father, Ambros, paid the taxes on the land five years before it became his. Ambros, the son of Jim Spillers and Martha Flanagin, was born October 22, 1875, on Threlkeld Ridge, which is on the Gum Pond Road about 1 ¼ miles north of the Northwest Road in Bankhead Forest. The family lived close to the Riggs School House, just east of Gum Pond Road on Threlkeld Ridge.

Jim Spillers' daddy and mother were Amos J. and Mary Ann Armstrong Spillers. According to Ms. Gladys LuAllen, Amos J. Spillers was born on January 12, 1836, in Georgia and died September 28, 1902. A.J. and Mary (Polly) had three boys and six girls. The boys were William (Will), James (Jim), and Robert (Bob). The girls were Martha Jane (Made), Betty Ann, Kate, Georgia, Dolia, and Caldonia.

*Home of Ambrose Spillers*

The Jim Spillers family lived on Threlkeld Ridge in the Warrior Mountains. Threlkeld Ridge was named after the family that lived in the middle of the ridge. Captain Phillip Threlkeld, who was a Civil War veteran, died in 1900 and is buried in the Wallis' Cemetery in McDowell Cove. Born in 1820, Captain Threlkeld served with Company A, 4th Regiment, Alabama Calvary of the Confederate States of America.

According to local legend, the Threlkeld family lived about halfway between Gum Pond Road and present day game plot number 32 in a slight saddle between the ridge tops. Prior to the war, the Threlkelds had slaves which were forced to hold window panes in the house during storms. After the war was over, the Threlkelds lost their slaves and their fortune. Today, some Threlkelds blacks in Lawrence County get their name from the old Bankhead family.

**Ambros Spillers Family**

After Ambros got old enough, he served as the teacher at Riggs School close to this home on Gum Pond Road. Ambros married Elmira Richards on February 14, 1904. Ambros and Elmira Spillers had eight children: Junior Lee born 12/03/1904; died 10/06/1982; Percy Clark born

01/08/1907, died 04/28/1984; Cliaronee O'neal born 11/10/1910; died 04/10/1975; Birtie Mae born 03/16/1912; James Curtis, born 07/31/1915; Bessie See, born 02/24/1922.

Shortly after they were married, Ambros and Elmira began building a house on the Mountain Springs Road approximately 1 ½ miles south of Ridge Road. While their new house was being built, they lived in a small log cabin just below and west of Mountain Springs Cemetery. After Ambros completed and moved in the house, he began clearing timber and preparing the new grounds for spring crops.

Ambros farmed about 20 acres of cotton on the sandy ridge tops along the Mountain Springs Road. Ms. Birtie Spillers Wilkerson said, "from their house were fields along the road as far you could see." Her father farmed with two small mules called Pete and Sam. Ambros Spillers made about four to five bales of cotton per year.

The family also had a garden about ½ acre in size which was planted in beans, peas, squash, corn, and potatoes. They had two good pear trees next to the garden, apple trees, and an excellent Indian peach tree. During the summer and fall, the vegetables were canned, fruit was dried, and meat was salted down. Two hogs were killed each year during the cool days of December. The family had several chickens from which they collected eggs and occasionally killed young frying chickens for dinner or supper. The family also had three or four cows and calves. Ms. Birtie said this was "good ole country living."

Ambros M. Spillers built his family's log house out of eastern red cedar logs which is still standing today. Built in 1904, the house consisted of one big room, a kitchen, a side room that was used as a bedroom, and a front porch. Shortly afterward, a well was dug. The well only produced about two buckets of water per day during the fall of the year. However, the well provided a cool place to keep the milk fresh for a couple of days. The milk was lowered into the cool part of the well with a rope. During the driest time of the year, a good spring of water just below the house provided the drinking water. In addition to spring water, tubs were set in the drip of the house to collect water for washing clothes with the old rub board.

Located between the Spillers house and Mountain Springs School was a large dipping vat. The settlers in the surrounding area brought their cattle to run them through the dipping vat in order to kill the ticks. The process of running cows through the dipping vat was carried on for several years.

Ambros Spillers and his family lived in the cedar log house for all but two years of his life. For about two years the Spillers family lived on the Harley Turner place on Hillsboro Road near Harmony Church. During that time, Ambros worked on the farm and his children went to Harmony School. About 1918, Ambros moved his family back to his old home place on the Mountain Springs Road. Ambros lived the rest of his life at Mountain Springs and died in 1924. Ambros was buried in Mountain Spring Cemetery. After Ambros Spillers died, his sons lived in the house for a while before moving to the valley for work. The house was rented to Low Spears for a few years; no one has lived in the house for over 30 years. The house and land is now owned by Glen Whisenant.

**Other Families of Mountain Springs**

Ms. Birtie Spillers Wilkerson says her father was one of the earlier settlers to farm on the ridges along the Mountain Springs Road. Shortly after Ambros and Elmira moved into their ridge top home, the area began to be settled very quickly. The Arch McCay family, Willis and Sally Blankenship, the Hamby Parker family, the Pink Garrison family, Hechahans, Mchathey and Mandy Turner, Crave and Toni Spillers, and Cleve and Zora Spillers settled along the road in just a few years.

With many families and small children, the community built Mountain Springs School just a short distance from the Ambros Spillers' home. After school opened and began classes in the fall, a lot more families moved into the area. These families included the Walter Perry family, the Jess McCarty family, the Tom Flanagin family, and Will and Florence Whisenant. During the first fall opening, some 50 to 60 students enrolled at Mountain Springs School.

Early teachers at Mountain Springs School included Jack McDowell, Mr. Burch, Jim Counts, Bettye Lock, Sovola Lamon, Bessie See, Vivian Moffitt, and Leon Moody.

**Birtie Spillers**

Ms. Birtie Mae Spillers attended the school when she was a small girl. After she and her husband, Jim Wilkerson, had a family, their children attended Mountain Springs School. At the time the children were attending the school, Birtie and Jim lived in Sanko Wilkerson's old home in the Cove. One day in 1940, her children walked from the cove to attend school only to find it had burned down overnight. School was continued at Mountain Springs Church for a couple of years before being discontinued.

## Mountain Springs Church

Mountain Springs Church and Cemetery have been at the same location for over 100 years. The church has burned down at least twice since it was originally established. The last time the church burned was in October 1973. The church was built back with blocks. Ms. Birtie Spillers Wilkerson said her son-in-law and Roy Oliver did most of the block work and the neighbors pitched in to rebuild the roof. Since being rebuilt, Mountain Springs has been used for preaching and singing every third Sunday evening of the month. The third Sunday in May is the annual decoration day with preaching at 11:00 A.M. and dinner on the ground at 12:00 noon. Most of all the people of the old Mountain Springs Community return to the church on decoration day to visit with friends and clean off the cemetery which lies in the heart of the "Warrior Mountains."

*Birtie Mae Spillers Wilkerson stands in front of the original Log Cabin which belonged to the Sanko Wilkerson family.*

## Mountain Decorations

Each day many descendants of old Lawrence County families come to the many cemeteries in Bankhead Forest. The annual cemetery decorations in the forest are to pay tribute and respect for deceased parents, grandparents, and great-grandparents. Each May, the tug on heart strings of Bankhead descendants draw people to the graveyard clearing that once were a place of sadness for many families. There is also a desire to briefly relive what many consider the good ole days. Even though past times in the forested wilderness were tough on the early settlers, the desire to show respect and admiration for those old family members many years past has not diminished. People of all ages, from babies to the elderly, become a part of the Bankhead decoration days. Small ones are taught through stories and legends from their elders about their relatives, their way of life, and the location of their homesteads. The only link to the forest for most families are the old cemeteries which dot the vast forest.

On May 11, 1991, my daughter, Celeste Walker, and I traveled to the Bankhead National Forest to attend cemetery decorations at McLemore Cemetery on Highway 33 and to Wallis Cemetery in McDowell Cove. At the McLemore Cemetery, I photographed my grandmother, Ila Wilburn, and my daughter, Celeste, placing flowers on the grave of Mary Elean Sparks Curtis. Mary was the mother of Ila Wilburn and lived on Montgomery Creek at the time of her death.

L-R: *Clare Nell Wilkerson LuAllen, Maxine Spillers, Clezell Wilkerson Oliver, Birtie Mae Spillers Wilkerson, Dale Oliver, Josh Oliver, Andy Oliver. All family members are of Cherokee ancestry.*

**Tribute to A.J. Spillers**

Later in the morning of May 11, 1991, Ms. Birtie Mae Spillers Wilkerson, along with several family members and friends of the Spillers family, paid tribute to Civil War veteran, A.J. Spillers, who is buried in the Wallis Cemetery.

Ms. Birtie Wilkerson, along with her two daughters, Clarinell LouAllen and Clezell Oliver helped place the Civil War marker on their great-grandfather's grave. Ms. Gladys LuAllen, historian for Lawrence County Historical Society, read the following tribute to Mr. A.J. Spillers descendants and friends:

"Friends and descendants of A.J. Spillers, we have gathered this day May 11, 1991, to honor one of our ancestors who was a veteran of the Civil War and who fought for the Confederate States of America. Private A.J. Spillers and three brothers – Craven, Silas, and William (Bill) – came to Lawrence County from Georgia. On January 20, 1848, A.J. married Mary Ann Armstrong, the daughter of Patsy Wallis Armstrong Blankenship. On April 1, 1863, A.J. joined Company A, 10$^{th}$ Regiment, of the Alabama Cavalry at Mt. Hope. He was sworn in by L.B. Lyndon and served for three years with the army of the Confederate States of America. Mr. Spillers lived to be 80 years old. The marker was secured with the help of Mr. Douglas Pate of Muscle Shoals."

After Ms. LuAllen read the tribute, I thought of how often we take life for granted and view ourselves as permanent fixtures upon everlasting landscape. While visiting the graves of those deceased for some 100 years, I realized that we are as temporary as the once cleared fields of the old forest that no longer grow with cotton and corn. After years since the old bottoms and new-grounds were farmed, large threes have reclaimed and returned the old homesteads to mature forest.

As my youngest daughter Celeste and I paid tribute to those hardy Bankhead settlers who are many years deceased, it was extremely hard to hold back those feelings of sadness and fear for not what has happened in the past, but for those short years regardless of how long we have in the future. Regardless of the time we have left, I hope my descendants will always cherish the land that I love which is the "Warrior Mountains."

*This original Mountain Springs school burned in 1942 and was also used as the meeting place of the Church of Christ.*

## Families of Flanagin Creek

A winding and partially graveled dirt road turns south off the mountain from Ridge Road. The road goes off the ridge at an elevation of 940 feet and declines toward the bottom of the hollow to Flanagin Creek at an elevation of 600 feet. The 340 foot drop occurs within one-half mile off the road and descends quite rapidly into the depths of McDowell Cove. The cove is surrounded by beautiful sandstone bluffs some with vertical drops in excess of 50 feet. Just below the bluff line begins characteristic limestone out croppings which extend to and across the valley floor. Cedar glades mark the appearance of the limestone rock formations which continue to the cove's two creek bottoms. Dry Creek makes up the northeastern fork of the cove with Flanagin Creek making up the northwestern fork. Flanagin Creek leads out of the cove down a narrow canyon with extremely steep sides and bluffs to the east and west. The majority of the cove is surrounded by beautiful sandstone cliffs. The elevation is not comparable to that of Cades Cove in the Smoky Mountains, but the vertical sandstone bluffs provide interesting features just as spectacular as those of Cades Cove.

This isolated cove, the Cades Cove of Lawrence County and Alabama, could very easily be worth millions of recreational dollars someday. Most of this beautiful cove in Bankhead National Forest has been sold to Mr. J.O. Simms and Doctor Williams. Most of the land that makes up the vast portion of the bottom land in the cove is still under private ownership; however, it has a history of all its own.

**Indian Days**

Beginning in the early days, the cove was used by a group of Indians known at the Mound Builders. These Indians built a small mound within the cove. The mound was eventually plowed but evidence of its existence lies in the front yard of the McDowell cabin. The sides of the mound are still identifiable.

*The old log home of Jack McDowell still stands in the beautiful cove that bears his name.*

The cove was located south of the High Town Path or Ridge Path which followed Ridge Road and later became established as the boundary between the Creek Indians of the mountains in Lawrence County and the valley tribes of the Chickasaws and Cherokees. The land once belonged to the Creek Nation and was given up at the Treaty of Fort Jackson in 1814. In September 1816, the rest of Lawrence County was sold by the Cherokees and Chickasaws. Rapidly, early settlers began seeking places to establish their homesteads in Lawrence County's "Warrior Mountains."

**Wallis Family**

Early in the 1830's, Joseph Hall Wallis was a member of a hunting party which entered the cove after black bear. A huge black bear was killed by Wallis near the forks of the two creeks—Dry Creek and Flanagin Creek. When the bear was shot, it fell into a nearby spring which still goes by the name "Bear Spring." Wallis was so impressed by the area he set up a permanent camp and built a log cabin.

According to Cowart's Land Records, Joseph Hall Wallis entered a total of 160 acres of land in the Cove during 1832, 1833, and 1836, in section 4 of Township 8 South and Range 8 West. The Wallis land made up the southern portion of the cove. His land extended from his southeast corner near the forks of Dry Creek and Flanagin, and northwest along Flanagin Creek.

The Wallis family had a significant role in settling the cove. Jonathan Wallis, father of Joseph Hall Wallis, was born on July 25, 1766, and died on September 11, 1832. He was a Christian (Church of Christ) preacher and is buried in the Wallis Cemetery.

In the 1840's, it is probably the Wallis family had some of their folks die of disease, epidemic, or some other causes. The 1850 census records show Joseph Hall Wallis living with Irwin Paul McCrary and his wife, Mary Jane Killian, who was not Joseph's daughter as I had expected.

According to Ms. Frances Corum, Irwin P. McCrary was the son of Matthew and Mary O. Holland McCrary. Matthew was the son of Thomas and Cassandra Adair McCrary who came to Lawrence County from Duncan's Creek in Laurens County, South Carolina, November 1819. Thomas McCrary and his two sons, Matthew and Joseph, are listed in the 1830 census of Lawrence County. The McCrary family settled near the Masterson's Mill area.

Prior to 1850, it is speculated that Joseph H. Wallis moved from the cove to the McCrary farm where he was employed in farming. Probably some of the Wallis family moved with Irwin P. McCrary to Van Sandt, Texas in 1867. Descendants of the Wallis family confirm that members of the Wallis family left the cove and moved to Texas where some of the men became famous preachers.

Joseph Hall Wallis was first listed in Lawrence County Census Records in 1830. At that time Joseph Wallis had one son under five, one under 10, and one daughter under five years of age; however, in the 1850 census Joseph Wallis was living with Irwin P. McCrary. Joseph was listed as being 44 years old with his place of birth being Kentucky. It is not known what happened to the Joseph Hall Wallis family, however, the Wallis Cemetery in the cove contains many of his family members.

**Flanagin Family**

According to Old Land Records of Lawrence County, Alabama by Margaret Cowart, Thomas Flanagin entered 120 acres of land for a homestead in Section 4 of Township 8 South and Range 8 West on November 15, 1854. Thomas Flanagin claimed land south of the forks downstream along Flanagin Creek. Thomas entered a 120 acre tract in Section 9 in 1836 and three tracts of land in Section 4 in 1854. One large block established in 1854 was north of Wallis and took up the Northwestern portion of the cove. Another block of land extended further south down Flanagin Creek near the point of Dry Hollow Ridge Road.

Thomas Flanagin was first listed in the 1830 Lawrence County Census. According to the 1840 census, Thomas Flanagin had five boys under 15 years of age and five girls under 20 years of age. The 1850 census indicates Thomas was born in South Carolina in 1793. His wife Jane was born in Tennessee in 1798. Thomas and Jane had only seven children listed in their household in 1850; Parthena, 30; Sarah, 25; William, 21; Thomas, 19; James, 17; Joseph, 15; and Nelson, 8.

**Pate Family**

Probably around 1833, the Thomas Pate family moved into the cove. According to Cowart, Thomas first entered 40 acres in Section 5 of Township 8 South and Range 8 West on October 5, 1832. He also entered three other tracts between 1833 and 1856. Thomas and Christiana Pate are first listed in Lawrence County Census in 1840. According to the 1850 census, Thomas Christiana had 11 children: Stephen, 28; Mathew, 23; Jeremiah, 21; Lucinda, 19; Thomas, 17; Sarah, 15; Mary, 18; Mary, 13; William, 11; Nancy,

L-R: *Mary Jane Pate Wilkerson (1/4 Cherokee) and Nancy Pate (1/4 Cherokee) are the daughters of Thomas Pate and Christiana Borden Pate.*

9; and David 4. Thomas Pate and his wife were born in Tennessee. His date of birth was 1794 and his wife was born in 1804.

Originally from Tennessee, Thomas and Christiana Borden Pate married in Morgan County on May 7, 1822 and lived for a while near Somerville, Alabama. Records indicate they entered land and settled in the cove in 1832. According to the 1850 census records, Thomas and Christiana had 11 children. Three of the Pate children intermarried with other families in the cove: Nancy, Sarah Jane ("Mame"), and William F. (Bill) Pate. The Pate family were Cherokee Indian mixed-bloods since Christiana Borden was ½ Cherokee Indian on her mother's side.

According to census records, Nancy Pate, born in 1841, never married but had twin daughters. Sara Dale Pate and Mary Jane Pate. Mary Jane Pate married Andrew Jackson (Sanko) Wilkerson. Sanko was the son of Thomas Wilkerson, a confederate soldier, buried in Wallis Cemetery which is located within the cove. Thomas Wilkerson married the older sister of Nancy, Sarah Jane (Mame) Pate. Sanko's sister, Mary Ann (Sissy) Wilkerson married Henry M. McDowell. Mary and Henry had one son, Jack McDowell. The Wilkerson family moved to the cove from the Sand Mountain area and will be discussed later in further detail.

William F. and Dolly Flanagin Pate had one son, William Dale (Roddy) Pate, born on February 22, 1865. Six years after Roddy's daddy died in 1878, Dolly Pate married Tobe Blankenship on July 13, 1884. A little over one year after his mother remarried, Roddy married Missouri Jane Vines on December 19, 1885. The Vines family also lived in or near the cove.

Before Roddy died on November 9, 1939, he left many of his personal stories about the cove to his Lawrence County grandchildren—Madgie Campbell and Junior Pate (children of Johnny Pate). I owe these Pate descendants many thanks for the wonderful stories they shared with me while writing of the cove's history.

**William Pate**

One of the most well-known members of the Pate family was William who was only 11 years old in 1850. At the outbreak of the Civil War, William was married to Dolly Flanagin. William was in some very fierce fighting during the Civil War and was wounded at the Battle of Shiloh. William Pate died in 1878 and was buried in the Wallis Cemetery located in the cove. In the last few years, William (Bill) Pate was remembered as a Civil War veteran and had a Civil War

Marker placed at his grave site. Many of his family and relatives were present at the dedication.

William Pate was shot through the lung at Shiloh and was never the same after the war. He returned to his Bankhead home and his wife, Dolly Flanagin Pate. On February 22, 1865, Bill and Dolly had their only child, William Dale "Roddy" Pate. After William F. Pate died in 1878, Dolly married Tobe Blankenship. Even though Dolly and Tobe had two sons, Henry and Charlie, Dolly was buried in Bankhead's most beautiful cove next to her first love, Bill Pate.

**Wallis Cemetery**

After talking with descendants of the Pate Family, I felt the calling of the Warrior Mountains. As if lead by an unknown power, I was heading into McDowell Cove, one of the original settlements of the Pates. I passed unlocked gates and "No Trespassing" signs all along the narrow winding road. I did not know what to expect, but I knew I must visit Wallis Cemetery in the cove.

Arriving at Flanagin Creek, I met Mr. Dean Simms and part of his family enjoying a Thanksgiving afternoon. Mr. Simms was gracious enough to ride with me to Wallis Cemetery. As we passed the Jack McDowell home, a large whitetail doe bounded across the narrow one lane road that leads to the graveyard. The road followed along a narrow flat bench, with the creek just to the left, northeast of the road some 20 yards below.

The Wallis Cemetery, sometimes called the Sally Ann Cemetery, is midway up a short ridge with Flanagin Creek some 75 yards downhill. Mr. Simms and I began looking at all the tombstones and identifying the people whose graves is now part of the beautiful valley. To my amazement, four confederate soldiers who fought in the Civil War are buried in the cemetery: Captain Phillip Threlkeld, Company A, 4$^{th}$ Regiment, Alabama Calvary, CSA, 1820-1900; Thomas Wilkerson, Private, Company A, 11$^{th}$ Alabama Calvary, CSA, 1830-1863; and William F. (Bill) Pate, Company E, 16$^{th}$ Alabama Infantry, CSA, 1838-1878; and Amos Spillers.

After seeing his marker and talking to other family members, I learned Thomas Wilkerson was shot at the Battle of Shiloh. He returned home wounded and died on year later due to complications of the wound.

I also want to identify others who call the cove their family name – Wallis, Flanagin, and Wilkerson. However, I will continue to refer to the valley as "McDowell Cove" since Mr. Henry Jack McDowell was the last permanent resident of the cove. Of course, Wallis Cemetery is named after the Wallis family, while Flanagin Creek is named after the Flanagin family.

**Roddy Pate**

After introducing over some 150 years of the cove's history, I turn my attention temporarily to Roddy Pate. Roddy, nicknamed after General Roddy, claimed the cove in his younger days as his domain. He was born to Bill and Dolly Pate in the cove on February 22, 1865. He played and hunted along the valleys and bluffs in and around the cove. His room was in the attic portion of his home. A tree which grew close to his upstairs window became an easy escape route when he wanted to get out of the house without his parents being aware he was gone.

After Roddy got to be a good size boy, he would slip out the window at night and go hunting with his two beloved possum dogs. One night, Roddy was possum hunting on a nearby ridge. Not paying close attention where he was going, he came too close to the edge of the bluff line. As he slipped and fell from the cliff, Roddy caught on a sapling growing out from the side of the bluff. The night was extremely dark and he could not see the rock bottom. Roddy knew how high the surrounding buffs were and was sure he would die on the rocks below. He made his peace with God and prayed for deliverance. After holding on until being exhausted, Roddy finally turned loose to fall less than a foot to a narrow ledge. Roddy worked his way around the ledge in the dark until he was able to climb back to the safety of the ridge.

Roddy, like other children in the cove, had to help his mother wash their clothes in a nearby spring. In addition to helping with family chores, Roddy earned a little money by picking up sacks of wild American chestnuts. He would walk uphill one and one half miles to the Ridge Road and the same distance downhill to Young Town. If Roddy could not sell the nuts at Young Town, he would walk to Landersville trying to make a few cents.

On days Roddy could get the mule, he would ride over the mountain not only to sell or trade items, but also to visit his young girlfriends. On one such visit, Roddy returned home after dark. After he put the mule into the stall, Roddy decided to check the chicken nest in a nearby trough. Instead of getting an egg, he was hit between the eyes by a large snake. Immediately he felt something running down his face. Scared half to death, Roddy made a mad dash to his mother screaming he was dying. After his mother got a cloth and wiped egg from his face, they took the lantern to the barn to find a chicken snake swallowing the last egg.

## McDowell Cove – resources, schools, wildlife

In the early 1800's, most of the cove was probably mature hardwoods. It is obvious that white oak timber was at one time quite abundant since a stave mill located within the cove utilized white oak to make barrel staves. Many stories of Bankhead and the cove indicate the American chestnut trees were also very common.

In addition to the stave mill, early settlers mined saltpeter (used for making gunpowder) on the eastern slope of the ridge which separates Dry and Flanagin Creeks. The saltpeter mine was south of the Blankenship Cemetery. Also in the early 1900's, a limestone quarry was located on the western slope of the same ridge. The mining of other minerals in and around the cove is unverified.

Three schools were located not far from the cove. To the east was Mountain Springs School. It was a one room log school located about one mile north of present day Mountain Springs Church and Cemetery. Another school was located west of the cove about a mile from the forks of the present day Dry Hollow Road and Gum Pond Road on Pinnacle Ridge. The school was called Riggs School because of the family who owned the property also lived nearby. The third school was to the north on Ridge Road. The Ridge Road School eventually burned down.

During the early years, some 400 acres of the mature hardwood forest within the cove were eventually converted to farm land. Row-crops were located along the flat fertile area within the Dry Creek and Flanagin Creek valleys. Today it is estimated that less than 100 acres of land is still open with some areas becoming over-gown with shrubs and saplings.

Most of the families that lived within the cove farmed small patches of corn, raised their own meat, obtained milk from the family cow, gathered fruit from small orchards, depended on their own remedies and cures for sickness, and lived in harmony with the forest. Some families survived seldom visits and threats by mountain lions, devastation of the corn crops by black bears when the corn was in the roasting ear stage, and the fear caused by numerous timber wolves that inhabited the area in the early 1800's.

Mr. Herman Whisenant, longtime resident of Bankhead, relates a story passed down through many generations about the infestation of timber wolves. As one early forest resident was returning home after a day of hunting, a large pack of timber wolves became very interested in the lone hunter. The wolves started encircling the man who began shooting the animals. He forgot about placing patches into the muzzle-loading rifle, but instead just poured powder down the barrel, packed a ball, and fired. After killing three wolves and wounding several others, the remaining wolf pack left a shaken hunter proud to be alive.

Many years have passed and time has healed some scars made by the early settlers of McDowell Cove. Stories have been told of struggles and trials faced by some Lawrence County's earliest settlers. Some stories have survived the test of time while others have faded away with the people who inhabited one of Bankhead's most beautiful valleys.

Before turning to other families within the cove, we must remember this was an isolated forest community in the early 1800's and many of the cove's families inter-married; therefore, many of the people share family bonds through marriages of Pates, Wilkersons. Flanagins, Wallis, Blankenships, Bordens, and McDowells. All these families are not only bound by the cove's common ground, but also by blood which was of the original Indian inhabitants of the "Warrior Mountains."

## The Wilkerson Family of McDowell Cove

In order to recognize where we are today, we must look back and re-examine the past. Our generation has benefitted from the lifestyles of our parents and grandparents who preceded us. In this light, it is good to look at ourselves to determine what good things we can leave to our children and grandchildren. Many times we wait too long and sadly we realize too late to record how our parents and grandparents lived. Ultimately, our future descendants are the real losers without knowledge of their roots.

Today, many Lawrence Countians proudly claim their unique heritage and are willing to give the present and future generations a glimpse of their Lawrence County families. Recently, I had the pleasure to talk with and record the life of a fourth generation resident of Bankhead's beautiful McDowell Cove before her death – Mrs. Lucy Irene Wilkerson Devaney.

**The Wilkerson Family**

Mrs. Lucy Devaney was one of eleven children born to Jerry Maury Andrew Jackson Sanko Wilkerson and Mary Jane Pate Wilkerson. Since three of the Wilkerson children died at a young age, only eight are listed as follows: John Jackson, born 3/11/1885, married Cora Blankenship on 8/1/1919, died 2/7/1960; Lillie, born 4/15/1888, married Verge Nelson on 11/6/1913, died 10/9/1968; Lottie born 4/14/1890 married Cliff Bridges 9/19/1913; Julie, born 7/4/1896, married Ed LouAllen on 5/30/1915, died 12/23/1982; Lucy Irene, born 11/15/1899, married Archie Devaney on 4/3/1928 and died 5/28/1993; Savannah, born 10/25/1901, married William Oliver on 4/9/1939, died 4/8/1983; James Jackson (Jim), born 11/24/1904, married Birdie Mae Spillers on 4/10/1926, died 2/28/1944; Ethel, born 3/2/1908 or 1909, married Elbert Blankenship on 11/27/1925, died 37/1990.

*Sanko Wilkerson (1/8 Cherokee) and Mary Jane Pate Wilkerson (1/8 Cherokee).*

Sanko and Mary Jane Pate Wilkerson were first cousins and 1/8 Cherokee Indian from the Borden Family. Christiana Borden, who was ½ Cherokee married Thomas Pate. They had two daughters: Mary Jane who was the mother of Sanko who married Thomas Wilkerson; and Nancy Pate who was the mother of Sanko's wife, Mary Jane Pate.

## Wilkerson Neighbors

When I wrote this story, Ms. Lucy was the only surviving member of her family who was born and raised in the cove. She was related to most of the families that lived within the cove. Ms. Lucy's double first cousin, Jack McDowell, was her family's closest neighbor. Jack lived about ¼ mile south of the Wilkerson home. Other house places in the cove included the Sally Ann Wallis place, south ¼ mile from Jack's house. On down Flanagin Creek was Tom Flanagin's home place, Bill and Donnie Slayton's home, and the home of the Hose and Jess Flanagin.

Tom Blankenship, Tobe Blankenship, Henry Blankenship, Charlie Blankenship, Jim Spillers, and Arie and Cathlene Barkley had homes on the ridge which separates the cove into Dry and Flanagin Creek valleys. Cleve and Zora Spillers, Hathey Turner, Bill McCarty, Arch McKay, Josh Blankenship, the Hendersons, Willis Blankenship, and Walter Perry had homes on the Mountain Springs Road. To the west of the cove lived Bill Camp, John Riggs, and Little John Riggs. Clifford and Lottie Wilkerson Bridges and Verge and Lillie Wilkerson Nelson lived in the Dry Creek Valley. Lottie and Linnie were sisters to Ms. Lucy.

Ms. Lucy was related to the Borden family since her great-grandmother was Christiana Borden Pate, who was half Cherokee. The closest Borden relatives were Jesse and Rosie Borden who owned land in the upper end of the Mattox and Flanagin watersheds. Jesse lived in a house located north of the Ridge Road across from its junction with Brazil Creek Road.

The Spillers family were intermarried with Ms. Lucy's family. Ms. Lucy fondly talked about Crave Spillers. She said, "Crave used to be a mean little ole booger and was taught by his brother – Ambros. When he got a whipping at school by Amber, Crave's daddy, Jim Spillers, would get a hickory and give him another whipping at home. So every time he would come home crying about getting a whipping, he daddy would give him another one."

The southern tip of Pinnacle Ridge extends south about one mile from the Gum Pond Motorway on the eastern side of Hagood Creek. Mr. Buddy Hagood lived in the Hagood Creek bottom just south of the ridge. He had some kind of disease that made him swell up real big. Further south lived Anth and

L-R: *Sanko Wilkerson, Mary Jane Wilkerson, ? Spillers, June Spillers, Savannah Wilkerson, Clarence Spillers (with hat), Lucy Wilkerson (just face), Maury Richards Spillers, Clark Spillers, Female ?, Luke Flanagin (second hat, with fiddle), Elbert Blankenship, Floyd Wilkerson (baby), Jim Wilkerson and Birtie Spillers Wilkerson (banjo).*

Martha Elkins. Elkins Spring on Braziel Breek is named after the Elkins family who lived in the area.

**Deer Stocking**

After Ms. Lucy got to be a young lady, she and some friends went to an area where whitetail deer were being released. The state had brought a lot of deer to the Belcher Place on the Northwest Road. Ms. Lucy, Sally McDowell (Jack's wife), and Nellie Nelson went to the old Belcher home where the state had penned one load of deer. The first load was kept in the old house until another load was brought in the next day.

Ms. Lucy and her friends watched several deer unloaded and turned out of the old house. When all the deer were turned loose, the bucks would begin fighting. The men would take long sticks the size of hoe handles and separate the fighting bucks. Ms. Lucy said they walked around through the deer like they were dogs or cats. The deer were not afraid of humans.

**Schools**

Three schools were located on ridges above the cove: Mountain Springs School; Ridge Road School; and Riggs School. Riggs School was located on the road down Pinnacle Ridge. Amber Spillers taught school at Riggs School. Ms. Lucy attended the school located on the Ridge Road. After the school burned, Ms. Lucy started to Mountain Springs School. Mr. Jack McDowell taught Ms. Lucy for two school terms at Mountain Springs School. Ms. Lucy went to school from the first through the ninth grade. She had to quit school to help farm when her daddy got sick. Ms. Lucy and Savannah had to plow and make a crop. Therefore, Ms. Lucy did not have time to complete her education.

**Springs**

There are several limestone springs located in the cove. Bear Springs was located close to the Wallis Cemetery. A black bear was shot out of a tree by Wallis and fell in the spring. Blowing Spring was where Uncle Bill and Aunt Doll Pate lived. A cool breeze constantly issued from the spring which could be felt some 20 feet from the spring's opening. Wilkerson Spring was located Sanko Wilkerson's home. The Wilkerson Spring was a round cavity about three feet in diameter. The spring opening had a rock that appeared cut with a two inch groove to hold the milk bucket bail. The milk was kept cool for at least three days after milking without spoiling. The "Black House Spring" is underground spring with a cave like opening about four feet in diameter. To get water, a person would get on all fours and crawl into the cave. A small pool located inside held the water which had to be placed in a bucket with a dipper. McDowell Spring was also cooled by a slight breeze. The spring opening was large enough to provide space to keep a side of beef even during hot weather.

**Sanko and Mary Pate Wilkerson**

Ms. Lucy's mother and daddy were born and raised in the cove. After getting married, Sanko and Mary bought about 460 acres in the Flanagin Creek portion of the cove. They farmed corn, cotton, and raised hay for their cattle. They had about 60 acres of farm land on their property. They cultivated the flat, fertile bottoms with a yoke of steers, two mules, and also two horses.

Prior to the "Stock Law," all cattle and hogs roamed on open range with crop land fenced to keep the animals out of the fields during growing and harvest seasons. At the time the stock law came into effect, Sanko sold over 100 head of hogs and 30 to 40 head of cattle at one time. Ms. Lucy said her father never bought any meat, since he raised his own chickens, hogs, and cattle.

**Wilkerson Home**

Recently, I visited the pine log house located on Flanagin Creek portion of the "Cove" where Ms. Lucy Wilkerson Devaney grew up. The house, built about 1905, replaced a two storied house which was east of the present house about 50 yards. The Wilkerson house has front and back porch with a dogtrot hallway separating two large rooms and a small kitchen. One large room on the east side of the house has a large sandstone chimney.

*Sanko Wilkerson (1/8 Cherokee)*

The Wilkerson family had peach trees, apple trees, and pear trees. They had some of the best pear trees in the country with some still alive. Sanko Wilkerson had over 100 stands of honey bees at one time. Ms. Lucy used to rob the bee gums and cut out honey. She said her daddy's bees could really sting. She used a sifter with cloth sewed around it to keep from getting stung. The little black bees would sting you bad.

Andrew Jackson and Mary Jane Pate Wilkerson had a total of 11 children with eight of those living to adulthood. When the Wilkerson children were real small, their grandmother Mame kept them while their mother went to the field to help their daddy with the crops.

Sanko Wilkerson (1/8 Cherokee) and wife, Mary Jane Pate (1/8 Cherokee).

After buying sacks of flour, their daddy would pour the flour into the bin. Their grandmother would take the empty flour sacks, wash them, and then make the girls aprons to wear. The young girls would wear aprons while helping their grandmother cook meals. The girls always wore their aprons and bonnets everywhere they went.

When the children were little, their mother and daddy would always doctor them. Ms. Lucy said, "They sure did not run to the doctor every time they had an ailment. Daddy would get some calomel and herbs to threat his children."

Sanko used to go to Mattox Creek, west of the cove to get the tag alder, a small shrub which grows on the creek banks. They would take the shrub and boil it to make tea. They would drink the tea as a medicinal agent for arthritis and also for aches and pains. In extreme emergencies, the family could call on Dr. Fennel, the closes medical doctor, at Landersville.

**Churches Surrounding the Cove**

The people in the cove attended churches which were located on the surrounding ridges. Mountain Springs was the church most people in the cove attended. It was built as a community church, and later became a Baptist church.

Sanko and Mary Jane carried their children to Mountain Springs Church when they were little. The folks got into a big argument as to what kind of church it would be. After Ms. Lucy and her sisters got big enough to go by themselves, they went to church at Owen Chapel where a shooting took place.

On Sunday afternoon the girls would take their hatchet up toward the bluffs, where they would cut small pieces of sweet birch bark. They would scrape off small shavings and mix honey with the bark. Ms. Lucy said, "It was real good and now I do not get any birch bark and honey to eat."

One church, always called Camp's Church, was located close to the western end of Therkeld Ridge. Brother Bill Camp used to preach there all the time. Gum Pond Church was located just east of Gum Pond Cemetery. The church was located about ½ mile west of what is now Braziel Creek Road that leads into the wilderness. The church was on a road approximately ¼ mile before the wilderness road closure on Braziel Creek Road.

Ms. Lucy and her family would walk from the cove to Gum Pond Cemetery for the decoration. The family would carry dinner in a little box. Aunt Sally McDowell always carried a bucket of milk and good things to eat.

**First Store Bought Drink**

The closest store was run by Joe and Arthur Young and was located not far from Owen Chapel at Youngtown. The Youngs eventually moved their store from Youngtown to Landersville.

Ms. Lucy was 17 years old before she ever had her first cold drink, an orange drink. Ms. Lucy said she would never forget her first nickel cold drink. Prior to orange, all she ever had to drink was water, sassafras tea, spice wood tea, and milk.

**Farm Work**

Ms. Lucy use to have to always churn to make their own butter. The family raised their own meat-chickens, hogs, and calves. The family kept meat and lard all the time.

As a small child growing up in the cove, Ms. Lucy and her brothers and sisters were responsible for hoeing, plowing, gathering corn, pulling fodder, cutting tops, and cutting and hauling wood. After her daddy got down sick, all the children were required to do the farming; even the girls would have to plow just like the men folks did.

L-R: *Jim Wilkerson, Ethel Wilkerson (Blankenship), Lucy Wilkerson (Devaney), Savannah Wilkerson (Oliver). These children of Sanko and Mary are 1/8 Cherokee Indian.*

Ms. Lucy's sister plowed with ox and two big steers which weighed 1400 lbs. One steer was red and was called "Old Red." The other steer was black and white spotted and was called "Old Buck." When the steers would get around the creek in the hot summer time, they would take off to the creek when they felt it was time to cool off. After laying in the creek until they got cool, the steers could be driven back to continue plowing. Ms. Lucy plowed with mules and horses.

Manure was taken from the barn and placed on the cotton fields. They also bought a little commercial fertilizer from Haleyville and strewed it in the cotton rows. "We never knew to fertilize our corn 'cause it always made good corn."

**Independent Mountain Life**

Forest families in the early 1900's lived an independent existence based upon their initiative to grow, produce, and meet other necessities for survival. People devoted time and energy to live in a forest community isolated from the convenience of town or nearby stores.

The families living in the cove built their own log cabins, raised their own food, made medicines and medications for illnesses and infections, cut pine splits and firewood for light and heat, carried drinking water from nearby springs in homemade buckets, split boards and railings for shingles and fences, cleared land for crops with axes and grubbing hoes, gathered hay and corn for their livestock, made their own clothes, and washed their clothes in the cove's creeks and springs.

**Grist Mills**

Youngtown had the closes grist mill run by John Harvey Austin. The mill was about three miles from the cove, and about ¼ mile from Owen Chapel Church. Ms. Lucy Devaney said that her daddy, Sanko Wilkerson, always went to the Austin Mill to grind his corn. John Harvey Austin's mill was run by water in the early days and was located on Town Creek, about ¼ mile north of Owen Chapel Church.

Kerby Grist Mill was located on Flanagin Creek, below where Cleve and Zora Spillers lived. The mill was water powered and had a small dam which backed up a pool of water. Ms. Lucy use to go by the mill each time she walked to her sister's home, which was located close to Northwest and Cheatham Roads. Ms. Lucy does not remember the mill grinding corn. It had ceased operating when she was real small.

Ms. Lucy heard her daddy talk about Stephenson Mill located on Brazil Creek. Another grist mill on Mattox Creek, to the west of the cove, was known as Jones Mill.

L-R: *Sanko Wilkerson (1/8 Cherokee) and Mary Jane Pate Wilkerson (1/8 Cherokee) who was the daughter of Nancy Pate.*

**Homemade Products**

The folks bathed in a wash tub and used homemade lye soap. They would pour up a tub of water in the morning and let it warm in the sun. That evening they would have warm water to take a bath in.

Folks back then would use an ash hopper to make their lye, used in soap making. They would take split palenings and make a "v" shaped wooden box with the bottom of the "v" in the trough. At the bottom of the "v" they would place sage grass to prevent ashes from getting in the lye. The sage grass would act like a strainer. Ashes were placed in the "v" frame box and covered until folks were ready to make soap.

At soap making time, water was poured or dripped through the ashes and the lye would run down the trough into a pot. The lye, along with meat scrapes, animal fat, and rendered hot lard were heated to a boil in a large cast iron pot. If the lye would cause the vane of a feather to turn loose it would be weakened down with water. Pine rosin was sometimes placed in the pot to make the soap smell good. As the mixture cooled it formed a jelly like soap. When commercial lye was used, the soap would be cut into wedges and bars.

Many families heated rich pine knots to retrieve the pine tar to treat animals and themselves. Glade pine knots, rich in rosin, were placed on a large flat rock which had a downhill groove. An iron pot was placed over the pine knots and then covered with wood. The wood was burned to heat the pot enough to make the pine rosin run down the groove where it could be collected. The pine rosin in rich pine splinters would burn readily and were used to make pine torches for a light after dark.

A lot of meat was salted down and stored in a large wooden box to prevent spoilage until it was needed. Even after being salted down, the meat would sometimes get "skippers" (meat maggots); therefore, in February, Ms. Lucy would take the salted meat out of the salt box and wash it. She would then put a skipper compound that looked like soda in the meat. The compound would keep skippers out of the meat. When only a few skippers were boring holes through meat they would be cut out of the pieces of meat cooked well done. If the meat started looking like hoop cheese and had skippers real bad the meat would be thrown away. Ms. Lucy said they used to grind up a wash tub of sausage and spice it with sage and hot peppers.

*Archie and Lucy Wilkerson Devaney*

**Archie and Lucy Devaney**

Ms. Lucy and her sister were gathering corn one day during the fall of the year. As they came to the end of the corn row, they saw a young man watching them work. Savannah and Lucy pulled corn out to the end of the row where she and Archie Devaney struck up a conversation. He commented to Lucy about her being a good cook since she was wearing an apron.

Arch came to the cove from Russellville to find work at the stave mill. Giles Lumber Company made barrel staves out of white oak timber. The stave mill was located on the northeast side of Flanagin Creek across from the Wallis Cemetery close to the Sally Ann House.

The Sally Ann House was a two-storied house that was used as a boarding house. Several people who worked at the stave mill stayed at the Sally Ann House. Oak staves were piled up everywhere around the mill and the Sally Ann House.

Archie was staying at Henry Scoggins (Coggins) boarding house at the foot of Pinnacle Ridge. The Scoggins boarding house was also called the "Black House" and was on the extreme northern point of Pinnacle Ridge on the Wilkerson property.

Archie had to pass the Wilkerson place on his way to work at the stave mill. When Archie saw Lucy, he knew she was a fine cook because of her apron, and when Archie first saw Lucy, he commented, "There goes my wife cause she's got an apron on."

*Ladies of McDowell Cove:* (L-R) *Birtie Spillers Wilkerson, Savannah Wilkerson Oliver, Lucy Wilkerson Devaney, and Ethel Wilkerson Blankenship. The Wilkerson ladies were 1/8 Cherokee Indian.*

Ms. Lucy and Archie Devaney married at the courthouse in Moulton. After a short honeymoon in Russellville, they moved to the "Black House." The log cabin was located just up the Northwestern fork of Flanagin Creek about one-fourth of a mile from the Wilkerson house. Archie and Lucy (Wilkerson) Devaney had two sons who were born in the Black House. James Jerry Devaney and Kennard Craburn Devaney.

After Sanko Wilkerson died, Ms. Lucy and Archie moved down the creek to the Sally Ann House in the winter of 1938. After her two boys were good size, Lucy and Archie moved from the Sally Ann House in 1947 to the William Young place at Hickory Grove. They lived there one year and moved to the Reeves Place in the valley in the early 1950's.

Ms. Lucy said there used to be a lot of moon shiners in the mountains, but she smiled as if I wasn't supposed to ask that question. She did say that most are now dead and gone. Now, Ms. Lucy is deceased, but her stories will live on in the history of our forest.

I enjoyed writing about Ms. Lucy Devaney, but most of all I was honored to meet and talk to a grand lady of our beloved "Warrior Mountains.

# The Blankenship Family

Some family names of folks living in the Warrior Mountains have just faded away with time, but the Blankenship name has persisted from the earliest settlement days. The family originally settled near McDowell Cove and today Blankenship descendants are found throughout Lawrence County.

## Hezekiah Blankenship

One of the earliest families to live in the Warrior Mountains of Bankhead Forest were the descendants of Hezekiah Blankenship. Ms. Gladys Blankenship LuAllen was gracious enough to share this information on her family history. Ms. LuAllen is a descendant of many of the earliest pioneer families in the Warrior Mountains – Blankenships, Parkers, Hendersons, Pates, Wallis, Flanagins, Spillers, and Wilkersons. According to Ms. LuAllen as early as 1820, Hezekiah Blankenship was living in Morgan County, Alabama, with his seven sons. Hezekiah's family moved from Jasper County, Georgia to Morgan County, Alabama in the 1820's. Hezekiah had married the daughter of Augustine Potter from Georgia. The sons of Hezekiah Blankenship were Joshua, Sampson, Hudson, Cullen, Augustine, Joel, and Doctor.

Hezekiah was the son of Hudson and Edith Blankenship's family of eight sons and eight daughters. His parents lived and are buried near their Red House near Winfall, Virginia. Hudson was the son of John and Elizabeth Hudson Blankenship also of Virginia. John's father was Ralph, the son of a Ralph Blankenship from Northumberland County in England who landed at James City, Virginia on July 23, 1640.

## Hudson Blankenship

Hudson Blankenship moved from Morgan County to settle first in McDowell Cove and later on Blankenship Ridge, located in the northern portion of Bankhead Forest just a few miles southeast of Youngtown. McDowell Cove is in the valleys of Flanagin Creek and Dry Creek, while Blankenship Ridge runs south from Ridge Road between the two creeks.

Hudson Blankenship originally married Cherry Borden in Morgan County on February 10, 1825. According to two genealogists who have worked with both the Blankenship and Borden families, both Hudson and Cherry were of mixed ancestry of white and Cherokee Indian bloodlines. According to their family records, Hudson was 3/8 Cherokee and Cherry was ½ Cherokee. Today, some descendants, who are family members from both bloodlines, are registered as Indian.

*Hudson Blankenship's tombstone. Located in Blankenship Cemetery on Dry Creek in Bankhead Forest.*

According to the 1830 Census of Lawrence County, Hudson was living was living in the same area of the forest Joseph H. Wallis and Thomas Flanagin since they were listed on either side of his name in the census records. Several years after the building the Sally Ann House in the Cove area, Hudson officially entered the land on the ridge between Dry and Flanagin Creeks as a homestead.

Hudson and Cherry had one son who they named Hezekiah after his grandfather Hezekiah Blankenship. Cherry Borden, who was born in Tennessee about 1806, was the daughter of Christopher Borden, another early settler of the Warrior Mountains. Cherry's mother was a full-blooded Cherokee. Christopher Borden's children were: David; Zachariah; Christinna, who married Thomas Pate; Cherry, who married Hudson Blankenship; Jessie L., who married Senia Flannagin; Phillip Borden; and Malinda Borden, who married William Jeffreys. It is thought by some folks that Cherry Borden Blankenship was buried in the Bankhead Cemetery in Dry Creek Canyon. After Cherry died in 1831, Hudson married Martha Patsy Wallis (Wallace) Armstrong on January 23, 1832.

Martha Patsy Wallis had earlier married James Armstrong. Patsy and James had two boys, James and Jonathan, and one girl before she married Hudson Blankenship. After Patsy's husband, James, died and Hudson's first wife, Cherry, died, Hudson and Patsy were married on

January 26, 1832. Patsy and Hudson were married by Patsy's father, Jonathan Wallis, who was a Church of Christ preacher.

**Sally Ann House**

Since Patsy's daddy, Jonathan Wallis has owned the land in the cove. It is speculated that Patsy and Hudson first lived in the Sally Ann House near the forks of Flanagin and Dry Creeks, just south of the Blankenship Cemetery. According to Ms. Gladys LuAllen, Hudson Blankenship was the carpenter who built the Sally Ann House. The Sally Ann house was a log two-story building setting in an east-west direction. A large chimney was on the west side of the log house. Doors were located on the south and north side of the house that went straight through the building. Later a dogtrot hallway, a big room, and a kitchen were built on the south side of the house. The building was built about 1832. In 1992 the old Sally Ann House was bought by Mr. Norman Tidwell and moved from the cove to the Houston area of Winston County.

*The Sally Ann House that originally stood in McDowell Cove in Bankhead Forest.*

According to Mr. Rayford Hyatt, "The Sally Ann House is named for Sarah Ann Flanagin who lived in the house for many years. "Sally Ann" was a daughter of Thomas Flanagin and was born about 1825. According to Jack McDowell history notes, "she had two children by Francis "Frank" Henry, an early settler in the area, and was never married."

**Blankenship Ridge**

Hudson Blankenship entered land and built a five room log house on the top of the ridge that separates McDowell Cove into Dry Creek Canyon and Flanagin Creek Canyon. According to the Old Land Records of Lawrence County, Alabama by Margaret Cowart, Hudson

Blankenship entered 160 acres of land in Northwest ¼ of Section 4 in Township 8 South, Range 8 West on November 21, 1855. The land which Hudson claimed was located on the ridge just to the north of McDowell Cove. The land actually went to Flanagin Creek in the Cove and crossed the ridge to Dry Creek on the other side. In the Dry Creek Canyon, Hudson entered another 80 acres of land just northeast of the northeast corner of his original entry on April 2, 1857. This particular 80 acre block of land lay in the flat but beautiful valley of Dry Creek and was in the South ½ of the Southeast ¼ of Section 33 in Township 7 South and Range 8 West. The old Blankenship Cemetery is located on a beautiful knoll in Dry Creek Canyon located on the west side of Dry Creek. The cemetery still contains a small cedar pole shelter over the grave of Tobe Blankenship's wife, Frances.

**Census Information**

In 1830, Hudson is listed with one son under five years of age and a wife between 20 and 30 years of old. His wife, at the time of the 1830 Census, was Cherry Borden and their son Hezekiah. In the 1840 census, Hudson Blankenship is listed as having two males under five years of age, two males between five and ten years old, two males between ten and fifteen, one female between five and ten, and one female between ten and fifteen, in addition, to a wife who is listed between thirty and forty. His wife, at the time of the 1840 census, was Martha Patsy Wallis Armstrong Blankenship. It is obvious from the census records of 1830 and 1840, that some of

1910. Front L-R: *Vicy Tabitha Flanagin Borden (1/4 Cherokee and wife of William David), Luvina Borden Dutton (wife of William Dutton), Sarah Hannah Borden Blankenship (wife of Joshua), Lucinda Borden Parker (wife of William Parker). Back L-R: William David Borden and Joshua Blankenship (3/16 Cherokee). Luvina, Sarah Hannah, Lucinda and William David are 1/4 Cherokee and the children of Jesse L. and Senia Flanagin Borden.*

the children listed as Blankenship were those of his second wife, Patsy, and her first husband, James Armstrong.

Hudson and Patsy had nine children of their own who are: Sarah Jane who married James Dement; Joshua, born 10/17/1835 and died 2/22/1918, married Sarah Hannah Borden; William married Sarah Jane Chilcoat; Sampson, born 3/18/1838 and died 7/1913, married Caroline Patience Chilcoat on 8/10/1862; Dock married Nancy Flanagin; Elizabeth married John Flanagin; Martha married William McCullough; Jesse B. (Tobe) Blankenship, born 8/18/1849 married Frances McNorton on 8/16/1866, and later married Dolly Pate on 7/10/1884; and John married Martha Appleton.

According to the 1850 Census, Hudson (Hardin) Blankenship is listed as being a forty-eight year old native from Georgia and his wife Martha (Patsy) from Kentucky was listed as being forty-two years old. In 1850, Hudson and Martha's children were: Jane 17; Joshua, 15; William, 13; Sampson, 12; Dorton, 9; Martha, 7; Elizabeth, 4; and Jesse, 1.

In 1860, the Blankenships were living in three different households with the two youngest children being Calvin, five months, and Jonathan being eleven years old. Since a total of 15 Blankenships were living in the area in 1860, it appears that Blankenship relatives moved into the same area of the forest and lived with members of Hudson's family. The additional Blankenships in 1860, besides those already mentioned, could possibly be the wife of William also known as Jane, age 19, and another Blankenship known also as Jane at age 19. In all census records from 1830 through 1860, the family of Hudson Blankenship was living near the Flanagins, Pates, and later Wilkersons who settled the McDowell Cove. According to family legend, all Blankenships that lived in the Warrior Mountains of Bankhead Forest were related.

## Josh Blankenship and Sarah Hannah Borden

Hudson's oldest son from his marriage with Patsy Wallis Armstrong was Josh Blankenship. Josh Blankenship married Sarah Hannah Borden, the granddaughter of Christopher Borden. Hannah's parents were Jesse L. Borden who married Senia Flanagin. Josh and Hannah Borden Blankenship had Willis Blankenship. Willis Blankenship still has two grandsons that live in the mountains – Hoyt and Herman Whisenant. Willis Blankenship settled the land on Borden Creek. The cove he owned was originally settled by his great – grandfather Christopher Borden. Christopher Borden was thought to be buried in Dement Cemetery near Borden Creek. The creek also was named after Christopher Borden. Glenn Whisenant, who is the grandson of Willis still owns the old Borden or Blankenship Cove

*Jesse L. Borden, Sr. (1/2 Cherokee) & Senia Flanagin.*

## Civil War comes to the Warrior Mountains

Folks living in the Warrior Mountains were not exempt or isolated from the Civil War. Hudson and Patsy Armstrong Blankenship had eight boys in the service of the Civil War at one time. Jesse (Tobe) was the only son to fight for the Union Army of Northern Aggression. Hudson Blankenship tried to play a neutral role during the Civil War. It did not matter to him about the question of slavery or State's Rights. According to family legend, one day during the war, a Confederate general approached Hudson about being an informant for the South. The general wanted to prosecute the mountain people who were siding with the North or playing a neutral role. Hudson refused to tell on the activities of some of his mountain neighbors. The confrontation got heated in the presence of one of Hudson's younger sons, Tobe. The Confederate general threatened to hang Hudson in front of his son. Upon hearing the threat, Tobe became furious and went to Decatur where he joined the Union Army.

All of Hudson's and Patsy's sons served in the Civil War except John, their youngest son. All of the sons except Tobe served the South. According to Ms. Gladys LuAllen, in one battle during the war, Tobe was fighting against his brother Josh. It was said that the two brothers saw and recognized each other. Instead of shooting at each other, the brothers shot in other directions.

According to Spencer Waters' book <u>Confederate Soldiers of Lawrence County Alabama</u> is the following version of the Blankenship and Armstrong brothers and half-brothers serving in the Civil War: "But the unusual part is that Dock, Joshua, Samuel, and William Blankenship were all brothers, and Jonathan Armstrong was an older half-brother. They also had two other half-brothers who served the Confederate States, Hezekiah Blankenship and James W. Armstrong, and a full brother, Jesse (Tobe) in the Union Army for a total of eight sons in the Civil War. Hezekiah was the oldest son of Hudson and Cherry (Borden) Blankenship. His pension application reads: BLANKENSHIP, H., Orderly Sergeant in Company E, 5th Regiment of Alabama Calvary. Age is 76 in 1898.

Jonathan and James Armstrong were sons of Patsy (Wallis) Armstrong by a previous husband. She and Hudson Blankenship were married on January 26, 1832, by her father Jonathan Wallace, a Christian Minister. James Armstrong's pension gives this data: J.W. ARMSTRONG, Private in Company A, 4th Regiment of Alabama Calvary. 70 years old in 1898.

Joshua, William H., Samuel (sometimes Sampson), Dock and Jesse (Tobe), as well as a younger son, Jonathan (John) Blankenship (listed in order of birth) were sons of Hudson and Patsy (Wallis) Blankenship. The first four as shown above, served in the Confederate Army.

Jesse (Tobe) chose to serve the Union Army. His record reads: JESSE BLANKENSHIP, Private in Company G, 1st Regiment of Alabama Calvary (New).

The Jonathan (John) Blankenship is the great-grandfather of the wife of the Compiler. (He was born in 1850, therefore too young to serve in the Civil War.)"

Spencer Waters not only documents, but gives an excellent short narrative of the eight brothers or half-brothers in the Civil War. The remarkable thing is that all of the brothers returned home to the Warrior Mountains at the conclusion of the War. In no other account have I heard of eight brothers of the same family serving in the Civil War at the same time. The eight brothers also had a brother-in-law, James Dement, to serve in the Civil War, as well as several cousins and relatives.

After the ending of the Civil War, the Blankenship brothers split up. Three of the boys left the mountain and moved to Florence area because one of their brothers fought for the North. William and Samuel moved and talked their youngest brother, John, into going with them. Tobe, Dock, Josh, and their half-brothers Hezekiah Blankenship, James and Jonathan Armstrong stayed in the mountains and resolved their problems over the Civil War. None of the brothers were killed during the Civil War and Tobe was the only one to be wounded. While fighting for the North, Tobe got hurt when a team of mules pulling a wagon ran away with him.

**Tobe Blankenship**

After Jesse B. (Tobe) Blankenship returned from the Civil War, he lived in his parents old home place on Blankenship Ridge. After the war, Tobe married Frances McNorton in 1866. Tobe and his wife settled on Blankenship Ridge and lived in the home of his father and mother. In October 1881, Tobe was given the deed to the Hudson Blankenship Place and in return, he was required to take care of his parents until their death.

*The little cedar house built by Tobe Blankenship still covers the grave of his first wife, Frances McNorton. In addition, two of Tobe's and Frances' children are buried in the old Blankenship Cemetery on Dry Creek in Bankhead Forest.*

Tobe left home for three years to live with relatives near the Tennessee and Mississippi state lines, without knowledge of even his wife as to where he was going. The two stories say he went to the store to get a sack of flour and the other that he went to carry plow tools to a blacksmith. Anyway, he was gone three years and no one knew where he was until he returned home. Tobe never told anyone where he was going. It is thought by family members that Tobe went to stay with his younger brother John. Tobe's Civil War records show that he saw a doctor in Tennessee during his three year absence from the Warrior Mountains.

Tobe left home just before Pedro Blankenship was born. He left in 1875 and came back in 1878 for three years he lived in Mississippi with his brother John.

L-R: *Charlie Blankenship, Jessie Blankenship Hopkins, James Blankenship, Eula Blankenship Walker, Pedro Blankenship, Eunice Blankenship, Doll Flanagin Pate Blankenship, Tobe Blankenship and Henry Blankenship.* Note: *The old log house is presently owned and restored by William Dutton. Tobe's children were 3/16 Cherokee.*

One day without knowledge from anyone Tobe returned home. No one knows why he left or why he returned home three years later. Tobe was accepted back home with no questions asked. After Tobe returned, he met his three year old son, Pedro, for the first time.

The old Blankenship home on the ridge was a big log house with a porch all across the front. The old house was on sandstone rock pillars with wood shingles on the roof and poplar log floor joists. According to Ms. Gladys LuAllen, William Dutton got the old logs from the Blankenship home and re-built the little log cabin on highway 36. The log cabin is at the back of William Dutton's home near the junction of Pinhook Road and highway 36. Jim Hopkins help tear the old log house down and move it to Hickory Grove. William Dutton later moved the log cabin from Hickory Grove to its present location.

Tobe and Frances had James, Pedro, Jessie (female), Elizabeth (Eunice), and Sarah (Eula). They had two children to die one of which was a twin sister to Pedro. Tobe and Frances' second child was Pedro, who was born 3/8/1876 and died 10/19/1918. The two young children of Tobe and Frances are buried in the Blankenship Cemetery on Dry Creek. Frances McNorton Blankenship was also buried in the cemetery after her death. Frances' grave still has a little cedar house built over her grave by Tobe. Tobe's second wife was Aunt Doll Flanagin Pate.

Tobe and Doll had known each other all their lives. After both their spouses died, Tobe and Doll married. Doll was actually Tobe's niece. Doll was a sister to Martha Flanagin, Jim Spillers' wife. Jim Spillers mother-in-law, Elizabeth Blankenship who married John Flanagin, was Tobe's sister. Tobe and Dolly had two children, Charlie and Henry. Charlie lived in the Mount Hope area and Henry moved to the Hatton and Wolf Springs area.

Tobe Blankenship farmed the land on top of Blankenship Ridge. Doll died in the old Blankenship house on top of Blankenship Ridge. She was buried by her first husband William (Bill) Pate in the Wallis Cemetery. After the death of Tobe's second wife, Dolly, he moved to Landersville and lived with his daughter until his death. Tobe was buried in the Landersville Cemetery.

**Pedro Blankenship**

Pedro Blankenship grew up on Blankenship Ridge. Pedro became a carpenter who traveled around building houses. He married Mollie Hood, the daughter of Monty Hood, on November 1, 1896. Pedro and Mollie Hood, who was born 1/22/1880, had two sons: Jody B. Blankenship, born 8/3/1897 and died 11/4/1972, married Lucy Boger on 8/16/1914; and Ausie D. Blankenship, born 10/5/1905 and died 6/14/1993, married Susie K. Jarrett.

Pedro Blankenship eventually pulled the same caper as his father, Tobe; however, he was gone for seven years instead of three. Pedro was living at the Monty Hood Place west of Moulton near Penitentiary Mountain. One day Pedro left home heading toward Landersville and stayed gone for seven years. Two stories follow the disappearance of Pedro. One version says that Pedro went to look for a cow. The other version says that his wife Mollie sent him to the store to get some baking soda. Pedro did not

*Pedro Blankenship (3/16 Cherokee) and Mollie Hood (1/4 Cherokee).*

return home for seven years and no one knows why he left or why he returned. No one has ever found out where Pedro for was gone for seven years.

After seven years, Pedro showed up at his neighbor's house. Pedro asked the neighbor to go talk with his wife Mollie and to ask her some questions. The neighbor agreed to go talk to Pedro's wife. The first question asked by the neighbor was, "Have you heard from Pedro?" Mollie replied, "No." The neighbor asked Mollie, "Do you still love Pedro?" Mollie replied, "Yes, I still love Pedro." The neighbor then asked, "If Pedro came home would you take him back?" Mollie replied, "Yes, I would take him back, I'd take him back right now if he was to come up." At that time Pedro was hid on the road beside a fence row. The neighbor talked on with Mollie a while longer and asked the question again, "Are you sure you would take him back?" Mollie replied again, "Yes, I told you already I'd take him back."

Later in the afternoon, Pedro came across the pasture walking home. He was driving a cow and a young calf into the barn as though he had never left.

Pedro and Mollie went back together. After they went back together, the couple lived together just long enough to have a son. Shortly after the birth of her son, Mollie died on October 23, 1905. They had one son named Jody before Pedro left, and Aussie after he returned home. Mollie died from complications of childbirth about three weeks after Aussie was born. The baby woke Pedro up in the middle of the night. While checking on the baby, Pedro discovered his wife was dead in her bed.

After Mollie died, Pedro D. Blankenship married Thursday Parker on 7/19/1906. Thursday was born on 9/12/1880 and died in Tuscaloosa on 8/4/1911. Pedro and Thursday had a son named Elbert Lee Blankenship. Elbert married Ethel Wilkerson, the daughter of Sanko Wilkerson.

Pedro and Thursday lived at Landersville until she had a nervous breakdown and was sent to the asylum in Tuscaloosa. After Thursday was sent to Tuscaloosa, Pedro left his son Elbert Blankenship with Hathey Turner for about two months. After spending some time with the Turners, the little boy, Elbert was taken to live with his Aunt Zora Parker Spillers. Zora was the sister to Elbert's mother, Thursday. Elbert, who was three years old when his mother was sent off, was given to his Aunt Zora to raise.

Pedro traveled and did carpentry work for the rest of his life. He built the Young House at Landersville. The Young House was a blueprint house from Sears and Roebuck. Pedro was in charge of putting the house together. He also built the Armstrong House in Town Creek. He was one of the better carpenters and builders of his time.

**Cleve and Zora**

Thursday Parker Blankenship and Zora Parker Spillers were sisters and the daughters of Jeff Parker. Zora and Cleve Spillers lived just south of Mountain Springs Cemetery. Elbert Blankenship, who was born on January 19, 1907, was raised by Cleve and Zora. Elbert's mother Thursday died in 1911; therefore, Elbert was about three and half years old when his mother died. Cleve and Zora lived on the ridge next to the Mountain Springs Road. The Spillers home was about one half mile south from the Walter Perry home place. Elbert lived with Cleve and Zora the rest of his young life before marrying Ethel Wilkerson.

Prior to moving to the Mountain Springs Road, Cleve and Zora lived on the Oil Well Road. The junction of Oil Well Road and Ridge Road was located about one and half miles west of the Cheatham Road. The Oil Well Road ran south along the ridge between Montgomery and Borden Creeks. The name of the road was derived from an old oil well that was drilled on the ridge about one and a quarter miles south of Ridge Road. The old oil well was lined with steel and closed with concrete and is still visible today.

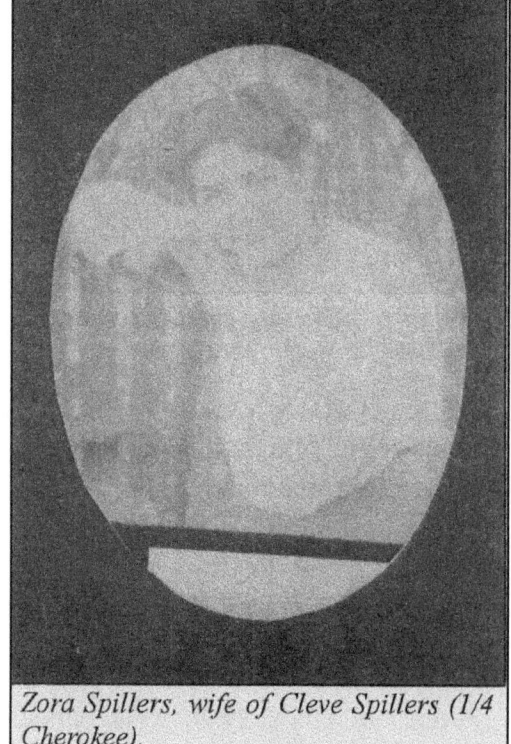

*Zora Spillers, wife of Cleve Spillers (1/4 Cherokee).*

Jeff Parker, Zora and Thursday's father, originally bought the land on the Mountain Springs Road from Mr. Dillashaw. When Jeff died, Zora Parker Spillers and her brother Hamby Parker divided the 160 acres. Cleve and Zora took the south 80 acres and Hamby took the north 80 acres where the Mountain Springs Cemetery is located. Originally, Jeff Parker owned the old place and later Hamby Parker sold his part to Walter Perry about 1920.

Cleve and Zora Parker Spillers had five children of their own; Malcom, Maxine, Norman, Henry, and Josephine. Cleve and Zora did not have any children when they took Elbert to raise, but later they had five children.

Cleve and Zora were small mountain farmers, but the old mountain distillery business was their livelihood. The old mountain trade in moonshine, wildcat, or corn whiskey was the most productive work for anyone surviving on the poor mountain soils. Cleve never allowed Elbert or his children to be involved in the distillery business. As far as anyone knows, Cleve Spillers never got caught making whiskey. He was one of the sharp mountain men to avoid the revenuers. After Cleve died in January 1930 of pneumonia, Zora sold the Mountain Springs home place to the government and moved to Wren where she died on February 19, 1932.

### Elbert and Ethel

Elbert and Ethel Wilkerson met while attending Mountain Springs School. Elbert Blankenship and Ethel Wilkerson got married on November 27, 1925, at the courthouse in Moulton. Elbert and Ethel lived in the house with Cleve and Zora for one year after they married. After moving out with Cleve and Zora, they moved over on the Ridge Road near the Hoyt Whisenant Place. Today, Starlin Blankenship still owns his father and mother's old home place which Pedro had originally bought. Elbert left the mountain in April of 1930 with his wife Ethel Wilkerson Blankenship and moved to the Harmony Community.

L-R: *Ethel Wilkerson Blankenship (1/8 Cherokee), Zora Parker Spillers (1/4 Cherokee), Elbert Blankenship (3/16 Cherokee) and Starlin Blankenship, son of Ethel and Elbert.*

After Elbert Blankenship and Ethel Wilkerson were married, they farmed and worked with Jack McDowell in the Forest Service. Elbert also worked some of the bottoms along Flanagin Creek. The road by the Perry Place on Mountain Springs Road traversed downhill to the creek bottom fields.

**Ethel**

Ethel, the youngest Wilkerson child, was the sister of Ms. Lucy Wilkerson Devaney and the daughter of Sanko and Mary Jane Pate Wilkerson. The Wilkerson family can trace their ancestry in the forest to the 1820's.

As was her daddy, Ethel was born in the McDowell Cove in the old Wilkerson log house on March 2, 1909. Later about 1919, Sanko built a new house close to the old Wilkerson home. The Cove was fairly heavily settled when Ethel was a small girl. Ethel lived in the old log Wilkerson house until she was about nine years old. In 1919 the new house was built with two log rooms and a dog trot through the middle. The chimney of their new house was built in 1920. Later boards were nailed over the logs and two side rooms were added. The family lived in their new house but maintained their kitchen and cooking chores in the old house. The Wilkersons farmed the bottoms along Flanagin Creek.

**Wilkerson Home**

Mary Jane Pate Wilkerson and family members. Elbert Blankenship, Christine Blankenship (Powers), Lee Blankenship (Jones), Ethel Wilkerson Blankenship, Starlin Blankenship, Agnes Blankenship Dutton, Clezille Wilkerson Oliver, Birtie Mae Spillers Wilkerson (wife of Jim Wilkerson), Mary Jane Pate Wilkerson, Floyd Wilkerson, Elree Wilkerson Parker, Jerry Wilkerson, Willie Belle Wilkerson Hand, Gladys Blankenship Lu Allen. All family members are of mixed Cherokee Indian ancestry.

The last people to live in the old Sanko Wilkerson home were Jim and Birtie Spillers Wilkerson and their children. Jim's mother, Mary Jane Pate Wilkerson, lived in the house with them. Jim died February 28, 1944. Birtie, her six children, and Ms. Wilkerson, her mother-in-law lived at the Wilkerson home until 1950. They moved out of the cove and settled at the bottom of Penitentiary Mountain. After returning from up north about 1951, Archie and Lucy

Wilkerson Devaney moved into the old Wilkerson home and were the last family to live in the house.

Jack McDowell tried to get Sanko Wilkerson to sell his land to the government. Jack was Sanko's nephew. Sanko told Jack, "If you want the government to have land, you sell yours." Jack refused to take his own advice and Sanko would never sell until Jack sold his; therefore, today, the land in the McDowell Cove is still private property.

**Nancy Henderson**

Before Elbert Blankenship married, he helped his grandmother Nancy Henderson Parker. Nancy Henderson was from the Henderson family on Borden Creek.

Nancy Henderson's folks farmed cotton land on Borden Creek and the lower end of Flanagin Creek. After the cotton was gathered and loaded in the wagon, the trip from the cotton patches at the forks of Flanagin and Borden Creeks to the Northwest Road would require crossing Narrows Ridge. Narrows Ridge is a high backbone ridge only some twelve feet wide at one point. Bluffs on either side of the road drop vertically some 30 to 40 feet. The family could not transport the loaded cotton wagon across the creek; therefore, Narrows Ridge was the best route to the Northwest Road where cotton could then be transported to Haleyville to be ginned.

Nancy Henderson was the grandmother to Ms. Gladys LuAllen. Nancy first married a Turner and had two children by him. While living near the Ridge Road, they went by wagon one day to see Nancy's brother that lived on the Bunyan Hill Road. It started to rain and later sleet before reaching the Henderson house. The next morning Mr. Turner got up with a cold that turned into pneumonia which caused his death. He is buried at the home place of Nancy's brother. Family members know he was buried at the Henderson home because the weather turned so bad they could not get him to the cemetery. Mr. Turner was buried at the back of the Henderson garden but no one knows for sure where his grave is located.

After the death of Mr. Turner, Nancy Henderson Turner married Jeff Parker. Nancy's people lived in the Henderson Cove area of Borden Creek. Nancy's brothers, including John C. Henderson, settled south of the area known as Narrows Ridge. During the Civil War, Nancy had one son out of wedlock before marrying Turner that she also named John C. Henderson. Nancy also had a sister named Margaret that married a Simmons. After Margaret's first husband died, she married an Austin.

## Jeff Parker

After Nancy married Jeff Parker, they lived on the Oil Well Road. According to <u>Old Land Records of Lawrence County</u> by Margaret Cowart, Jefferson C. Parker entered 160 acres of land in the northeast ¼ Section of 35 in Township 7 South and Range 8 West on July 16, 1901. The land is located on the Oil Well Road Ridge about one and a half miles south of Ridge Road. Later Jeff bought land on the Mountain Springs Road about 1905.

Jeff Parker was considered to be a half-blooded Cherokee Indian. His father William married Katherine Hardin who was known as Black Dutch. Katherine was short, dark haired and dark complected. Katherine was the second wife of William Parker. William and his first wife had John Campbell, Thursday, Martha, and Manerva. William and Katherine had Sally Parker, who married a Henderson; Elizabeth, who married a Dunlap; Samantha, who married William Straud Riddle; Docinda, who married a Walker; Jeff, who married Nancy Henderson; Joe, who married Scene Parker, and William who married Mary Beth Reynolds.

L-R: *Hamby Parker, Zora Parker Spillers, Jeff Parker (1/2 Cherokee), Thursday Parker Blankenship, Nancy Henderson, Katie Parker Richards and Jeffrey Parker. All of Jeff Parker's children are at least 1/4 Cherokee.*

Jeff Parker was a farmer and also peddled the old mountain brew. He farmed some of the Slayton Place southwest of Mountain Springs Church. Jeff Parker was involved in the old mountain trade. It was told that he was the only mountain dew peddler in the mountains. He made regular routes in his wagon delivering brew to the local residents for cough syrup or to sip for bad colds. Of course, some folks would make a hog of themselves and occasionally get drunk. Jeff would go from house to house in the mountains ever so often to replenish the family's supply.

Jefferson C. and Nancy Henderson Turner Parker had the following children: Hamby, Kate, Thursday, Jeff, and Zora. Thursday Parker was Ms. Gladys LuAllen's grandmother. Thursday married Pedro Blankenship and they had one son, Elbert. Jeff and Nancy lived at their old Mountain Springs home place, south of the Mountain Springs Church on the east side of the road, until their deaths.

## William Parker

Jeff Parker's father was William Parker. According to Coward, William entered 40 acres of land in the Henderson Cove area in Section 28 of Township 8 South and Range 8 West on January 28, 1859. The 40 acre tract of land was just north of the junction of Flanagin and Borden Creeks.

May 4, 1947. Seated L-R: *Christine (Powers), Ethel Wilkerson Blankenship (1/8 Cherokee), Elbert Blankenship (3/16 Cherokee), Starlin Blankenship. Standing: Clara Mae (Yarbrough), Agnes (Dutton), Gladys (Lu Allen), Lee (Jones). All the children of Elbert and Ethel are at least 5/32 Cherokee ancestry.*

William Parker is noted as being the man who got gored by a bull. William was trying to castrate the bull to make a steer for plowing and pulling wagons. After being gored and realizing he was dying, William told the family to "get the steer well and sell it to help raise the family." Shortly after he was gored by the bull, William died of the wound.

According to the Moulton paper account of July 11, 1878, "We have just learned the death of our old friend, William Parker who was killed by the gore of an ox, one day last week near Moulton."

**Blankenship Conclusion**

The families of Mountain Springs went to church every fourth Sunday to hear their preacher. Mountain Springs, which was a community church, would have the Methodist preach one Sunday, the Baptist one Sunday, the Presbyterian one Sunday, and the Christian Church (Church of Christ) one Sunday; therefore, the four denominations shared by the same building and alternated Sunday services. In later years, for the Church of Christ, Arch McCay started preaching at Mountain Springs School House north of the Mountain Springs Church; therefore, when the Church of Christ could not preach at the church, they would have service at the school house.

In 1919, Hamby Parker deeded the land to Mountain Springs for a cemetery when he sold the rest of his land to Walter Perry. A large number of the Parker family is buried at Mountain Springs Cemetery. All of the Jeff and Nancy Henderson Turner Parker children are buried at Mountain Springs except Nancy's oldest son, John C. Henderson, who is buried at Littleville in Winston County, and another son Hamby Parker, who is buried at Carbon Hill. Six generations of the Wilkerson family are buried in the nearby Wallis Cemetery. Both of the parents of Ms. Gladys Blankenship LuAllen are buried at Mountain Springs Cemetery, along with many relatives.

*Mountain Springs School and Church*

Now concludes another wonderful story that has followed one family from the early settlement days to modern day times. The Blankenship family history has added a long and colorful account of the lives of the early settlers of the "Warrior Mountains."

# Jack McDowell Family of the Cove

In 1967, I got a job at Piggly Wiggly in Moulton sacking groceries on weekends and during the summer when I was out of school. Prior to this, I had been told of a man who lived in Bankhead Forest where squirrels, deer, and wild turkeys were abundant. Not long after I started work, I had the pleasure of meeting the man who I knew was a legend of his own time – Henry Jack McDowell.

Every Saturday when Mr. Jack would come to the store, I made a special effort to be the one to sack and carry his groceries to his '52 Chevrolet. At that time, he had a black and white dog which would sometimes come to town with him. One Saturday, I noticed his dog was not in the car and I asked Mr. Jack about his faithful companion. Sadly, he told of the dog getting into a fight with a beaver. The dog was cut up so bad the he later died. Mr. Jack loved to tell stories of his forest domain, and I always took special advantage of the few minutes to listen and ask questions.

## Henry McDowell

Henry A. McDowell (father of Jack) originally moved to the "Cove" from the Blaylock Place near Mount Hope and rented a house from Andrew Jackson "Sanko" Wilkerson. Sanko swapped 40 acres of land to Henry for a milk cow. Henry McDowell farmed the open land with a big red mare.

L-R: *Jack McDowell, Henry Andrew McDowell, Toni McDowell Spillers (married Crave Spillers), Mary Ann Wilkerson McDowell (1/8 Cherokee).*

*Henry Andrew McDowell and Sarah Roach McDowell (Henry's second wife).*

Henry McDowell was married to Mary Ann (Sissy) Wilkerson, sister of Sanko and the daughter of Thomas Wilkerson and Sarah Jane (Mame) Pate. Henry and Sissy had one son, Henry Jack McDowell, born on November 4, 1884 and died on August 4, 1969.

## Jack and Sally Spillers McDowell

Jack McDowell married Sally Spillers, born in 1870 and died in 1961. Sally was the daughter of James (Jim) and Martha J. Flanagin. Jim Spillers was born in 1853 and died April 6, 1937. Martha was born June 2, 1845, and died April 24, 1915. At one time, Jim and Martha owned the Black House which they bought from John W. Riggs around 1905. In about 1908, they sold the Black House to Sanko Wilkerson. Jim and Martha Spillers are buried in Wallis Cemetery.

According to Ms. Birtie Spillers Wilkerson, Jim Spillers had two brothers and six sisters; William (Will), Robert (Bob), Martha Jane, Betty Ann, Kate, Georgia, Docia, and Caldonia (Donia). Their father and mother were Amos J. and Polly Armstrong Spillers. Amos was born January 12, 1836 and died September 28, 1902. Amos, a veteran of the Civil War, and Polly are buried in the Wallis Cemetery in the Cove. Including Amos Spillers, four Civil War veterans are buried at the Wallis Cemetery.

William Spillers married Mary Tennessee Garrison, a Cherokee Indian, and had a son who was also named Amos Spillers. The younger Amos Spillers was the first game warden in the forest and is buried at the Mt. Olive Cemetery. Amos was killed in a head-on wreck with a log truck in the forest.

Jack and Sally McDowell eventually bought his old home place from his father, Henry, about 1920. Jack and Sally had one child in January 1906 that was stillborn. Jack, Sally, and their infant daughter are buried in the Mountain Springs Cemetery which overlooks the Cove.

*Jack McDowell (1/16 Cherokee) and Sally Spillers.*

The first known account of Jack's career was as a school teacher at Mountain Springs School. Ambros Spillers, Jack's brother-in-law, was teaching at the Riggs School when it burned. The Riggs School children then began attending Mountain Springs School. Jack taught school for two terms or more at Mountain Springs.

The Mountain Springs School burned in the early 1940's and the school was moved to the Mountain Springs Church where it was continued for approximately two more years before being closed.

According to the Moulton Advertiser, Jack began helping with the preliminary survey in 1916 for the establishment of a national forest. In 1918, the forest was established and Jack was appointed the first forest ranger. Jack and Sally's home in the Cove served as the first headquarters for the forest. Jack served as ranger until 1934, because he would not accept a transfer. From 1935 to 1939, Jack served as state fire marshal under Governor Bibb Graves. After 1939, Jack returned to his mountain home where he farmed for the rest of his life.

**Short Stories of Jack**

Many stories could be told about the colorful life of Henry Jack McDowell. The following are a few I must share.

One day Jack rode up to his Aunt Doll's house to pay her a visit. Doll Flanagin Pate Blankenship was an aunt to both Jack and his wife, Sally. Jack, being a jolly man, got down off his horse and grabbed Aunt Doll and went to dancing with her around the old plank floor. Doll's great-granddaughter, Madgie Pate Campbell, was amazed at Mr. Jack and her great-grandmother dancing across the floor.

Jack and Sally were sitting by the fire one night when they were disturbed by something walking through the hallway and on the porch. Jack eased to the door and peeped out to see a large black bear helping himself to a churn full of milk. The bear had walked through the open hallway which separated the house into two large rooms. It made its way to the back porch where the churn full of milk was located. The bear drank the churn of milk by holding the container with his front paws and lapping up the milk with his long tongue. The bear also got into some of Jack's dog food. After drinking and eating his fill, the black bear carried the churn into the nearby woods.

Jack had a dog called Tad which was one of the best deer dogs in the forest. Tad got bit on the head by a large timber rattlesnake causing the dog's head to swell up real big. The dog eventually went blind but was still able to run deer and find his way home. He would get after a deer and come home all cut up from running through thickets of briars and bushes. One day the old dog never came home and Mr. Jack began looking for his dog. According to James Devaney, Mr. Jack searched two or three days before finding Tad floating in an old dug well.

Jack was fond of all animals, especially his big black horse named "Ramon." Jack rode his beautiful horse all over Bankhead Forest. Ms. Birtie Wilkerson, Jack's niece, recently showed me pictures of his dogs and horse, Ramon. Jack and Sally shared their home and horse with Ms. Vivian Moffitt, a teacher at Mountain Springs School. Ms. Moffitt would ride Ramon from the McDowell home to school each day.

Henry Jack McDowell was the last known permanent resident of the beautiful valley of McDowell Cove of the "Warrior Mountains."

L-R: *Audie Mae McDowell Garrison, Jack McDowell (1/16 Cherokee), Floyd Nenivah Garrison (3/16 Cherokee).*

## McDowell Cove Stories

Ms. Lucy Devaney related these stores before her death on May 28, 1993. Her grandmother, Sarah Jane "Mame" Pate Wilkerson, and her daddy, Andrew Jackson "Sanko" Wilkerson, both lived to be 88 years old. Mame was born in 1835 and died in 1923. Ms. Lucy's mother, Mary Jane Pate Wilkerson, lived until she was 96 years old.

Ms. Davaney got information first-hand from her grandmother, a survivor of some turbulent times in our nation's history. Indian removal was occurring when Mame Pate was a small child. Since many of the area's residents were Indian mixed-bloods, threats of removal sent a chilling fear through many residents of the isolated cove. Shortly after Indian removal, came the Civil War with many of the cove's young men going into battle for the South and at least one fighting for the North. Thomas Wilkerson, Ms. Lucy's grandfather, and William Pate, Ms. Lucy's great uncle, fought for the Confederate States of America and were casualties of the Civil War.

Ms. Lucy's folks left many wonderful stories which I must share with all those who love to read true adventures of Bankhead. Therefore, the following is a series of stories, some of which were told to Ms. Lucy by her grandmother Mame. The stories are considered to be true and factual.

**Mame and the Painter**

Wildlife stories always included close encounters with painters (cougars). Ms. Lucy's grandmother Mame told many times about a painter following her and her husband, Thomas Wilkerson, from Braziel Creek. The night was dark and the pine torch they were carrying was used to keep the painter from attacking. Every time the painter would get close and let out a big growl, they would wave the burning pine knot torch up and down. The painter followed the scared couple to their home located in the cove. They felt lucky and extremely happy to reach the safety of their home. On another occasion a painter regularly paid a visit to the Wilkerson home place; however, Ms. Lucy does not recall hearing about a painter being killed or of one killing somebody.

Mary Jane Pate Wilkerson (1/4 Cherokee) who married Thomas Wilkerson.

**Nancy and the Bear Cub**

Early one spring black bears were making raids on the freshly planted corn crop. Ms. Lucy's grandpa Wilkerson and other men who lived in the cove turned their dogs loose on fresh bear signs. Eventually, the dogs ran a sow bear up a large hollow tree. After unsuccessfully trying to get the bear out of the tree, the men got a crosscut saw and cut the tree down. When the tree fell, it killed the sow bear; however, they were still unable to get the baby bear cubs out of the hollow tree. The men again sawed the tree into pieces in order to get the baby cubs out. They made the mistake of sawing too close to the bottom of the hollow cavity and cut into one of the baby bears and killed it. The other bear cub survived unhurt and was carried back to the cove.

They were unable to get the cub to eat. Nancy Pate had a month old baby and was asked to breast feed the cub because it would not eat and would surely die. Nancy nursed the baby bear until it was a good size cub. As a baby, the cub would just grunt when it got hungry. The bear got big enough to tear Nancy's clothes when it wanted to nurse. The family finally had to carry the cub far from the cove and turn him loose. Ms. Lucy's grandmother Nancy was not about to let the bear be killed after raising it like one of her own children.

## Dave and the Yankees

Ms. Lucy's great-uncle Dave Pate, born in 1846, was involved in a memorable story involving the Yankees. This story is worthy of being passed along since all the relatives indicate the events truly happened.

When David was a young man, Yankee soldiers came to the forest to search for food stored in the caves and rock shelters. Once the Yankees found the grain, they would take the wheat or corn and scatter it to prevent confederate troops from using the grain. The Yankees arrested Dave who was accused of knowing the hiding place of ammunition and food for the confederates. They tied him to a mulberry tree and began shooting, asking questions and shooting some more. They were trying to scare Dave into telling where grain and ammunition was stored. After several hours of harassment, the Yankees left David tried to the tree. Other than being scared half to death and having shattered nerves, Dave wasn't hurt. His family found him the next day still tied to the tree which contained many bullet holes. Dave had scrapes and bruises but was basically in good physical health.

## Dave and the Bear

Dave was partially blind and could not judge distance very good. Dave always used a walking stick wherever he went. One day he took the dogs to the corn field to chase the bears off the ripening corn. The dogs caught a bear in the corn field and started fighting the animal. Dave got too close to the fight and became entangled in dogs and bear. Dave took out a big scabbard knife he carried and stabbed the bear, dogs, and anything else he could feel. After the mayhem ceased, Dave realized the bear had ripped open his abdominal cavity. Dave's guts were hanging out but were still intact.

After hearing the disturbance, family members went to look for Dave. When they reached the scene they found a dead bear, dead dogs, and Dave, holding his intestines in his hands. Dave had not only killed the bear, but had obviously stabbed some of the dogs to death in the melee. Some of the family members got a wide plank and placed his guts on the board. Dave held the board against his guts while family members helped him back to the house. After washing off his intestines with cold spring water, they sewed the abdominal cavity up with a beeswax thread. Dave eventually healed and lived for several years afterward.

**Timber Wolves**

Ms. Lucy's parents and grandparents used to have trouble with timber wolves. When she was born very few timber wolves were left, but when her folks were young people, wolves were very abundant. Timber wolves would kill a lot of chickens, hogs, and calves. Sometimes they would kill more than they could eat and leave animal carcasses everywhere. All the folks back then would kill wolves anyway they could. Wolf Pen located south of the cove got its name from a wolf trap where the wolves were baited and killed. Eventually through a bounty system and other means, the timber wolves were exterminated. Thus ended the beautiful timber wolves that one called home, the land known as the "Warrior Mountains.

# Families of the Black House

The McDowell Cove in Bankhead Forest was the home of many of Lawrence County's early settlers. These early forest dwellers built similar log houses which varied little in the style of construction. The Black House in the cove was no exception in style, but different in construction materials. The house was made of American Chestnut logs, taken from the surrounding area.

**Devaney Home**

I visited the old Black House home site with James Devaney and Dean Simms. James, the son of Archie

*The Black House. Lottie Wilkerson Bridges with James and Kennard Devaney.*

and Lucy Devaney, was born in the Black House and called the place home for several years. The only evidence of the house is the pile of chimney rocks and corner stones. The frame of Archie's old T-Model still sets beside the old house place. James said they did not have enough money to replace the worn out tires; therefore, the old truck was left to mother nature.

The Black House has a history all its own, beginning with its dark colored timber used in construction. Prior to destruction of the American chestnut due to a blight, huge chestnut logs were used to make the large house. Over the years the chestnut logs turned a very dark color; thus, it was called the Black House. The Black House had two large rooms and a kitchen with a dirt floor. The two rooms were some 20 feet square on either side of a 12 feet wide dogtrot hallway through the middle of the house. The only evidence which remains of the house is a large pile of sandstone rock from the crumbled chimney and foundation corner rocks. Two large black walnut trees and a large beech tree, which has a circular mark place there over 50 years ago by Archie Devaney, still stand in the back yard. The circle was cut into the tree by Archie as a target to see if his son James was a good shot. Scars of bullet holes in the old beech tree indicate James hit where he was aiming.

Several families lived in the house prior to Archie and Lucy Wilkerson Devaney. The earliest known family to live in the Black House was the Riggs.

**Riggs Home**

According to Ms. Nell Riggs Witt, David Riggs was living at Mt. Hope prior to the Civil War where he ran a woodworking shop. David had a son and daughter at the outbreak of the war. Members of the Confederate Home Guard visited David at his home to force his son John W. Riggs into service. David had an altercation with one of the Confederate soldiers and swung a long grass cutting blade at the man. He missed the soldier but hit his horse across the rump cutting a deep gash. Shortly after the incident, John W. Riggs joined the Federal troops and fought for the northern states. After the war, John returned to Lawrence County to find his entire family had died of a measles epidemic including his wife, child, sister, and parents. John moved to Bankhead and entered land near the cove. He married Rachel R. Lott and had two sons: William Tecumseh Riggs, born in 1867; and John W. Riggs, Jr., born in 1872. John, Jr. died at a young age and is buried at Mountain Springs Cemetery. The other son, William, and his father John, became noted chimney builders. They built many of the chimneys of the early families that lived in Bankhead. It is speculated by family members that John W. Riggs built the Black House. John sold his land in the cove in 1905 and moved to the valley with his son William. John W. Riggs is buried in the Aycock Cemetery in Colbert County.

William Tecumseh Riggs and his first wife, Sarah Janie Sutton from North Carolina, moved to the Black House after the Civil War. Will and Janie had three sons: Tillman, born July 8, 1889; George, born December 18, 1890; and John D. Riggs, born May 26, 1894. Will and Janie sold their land to Sanko Wilkerson and left the cove about 1901. They moved to North Carolina to work in the textile mills. After Janie died of typhoid, Will and his three sons moved back to Bankhead. Will's second marriage to Mattie Simmons produced ten children: Guy, David Washington (Wash), Eva, Ruth, Hollis (Jack), Dolphus (Doc), Euell, Farris, Forris, and Pauline. Will died around 1937 and is buried in Ferguson Cemetery near Hatton.

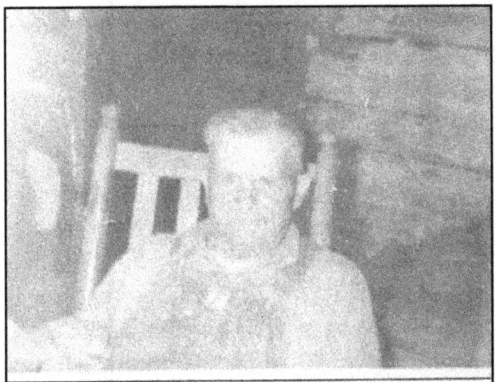

*Archie Devaney on the front porch of the Black House.*

## Spillers Home

The next family to live in the house was Jim and Martha Flanagin Spillers. Martha was a sister to Dolly Flanagin Pate Blankenship. The Spillers children included Johnson, Crave, Jim, Ambros, Cleve, Salley who married Jack McDowell, and Lucy Bell who married Jim Jenkins.

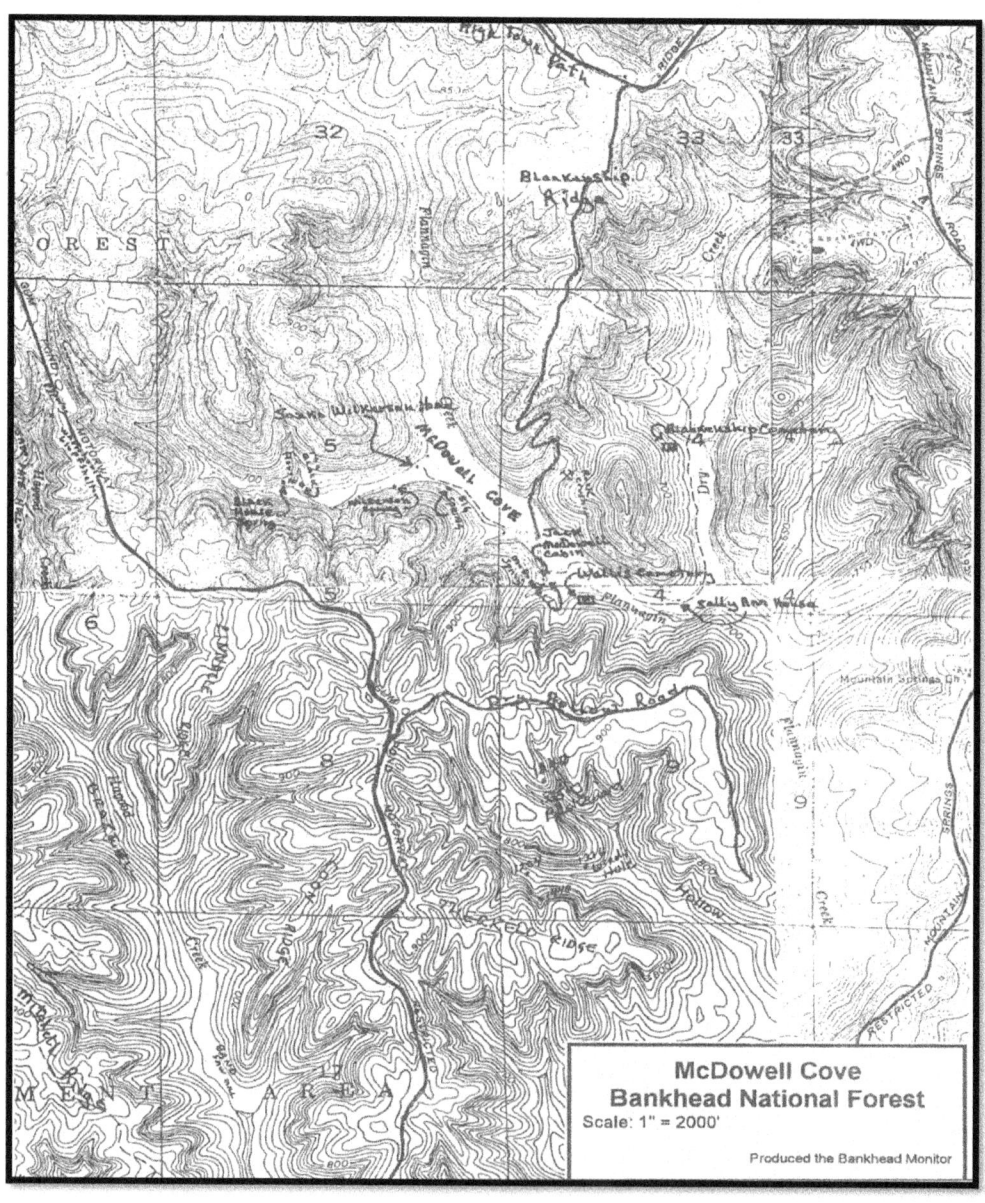

**Nelson and Scoggins Home**

Verge Nelson, married to Lillie Wilkerson, lived in the house before Henry Scoggins from Georgia began renting beds to workers at the stave mill. Archie Devaney boarded in the house while he worked at the stave mill. After Archie and Lucy Wilkerson got married, they set up housekeeping in the Black House which belonged to her daddy, Sanko Wilkerson. Archie and Lucy moved to the house in April 1928 and lived there until the winter of 1938. At that time, they moved down the creek into the Sally Ann House where they lived until 1947 when they moved from the cove to the Hickory Grove area.

Many families called the Black House home, but time has now reclaimed the home place in the land of the "Warrior Mountains."

# Chapter Five
# Families of Range 9 West

The families of Range 9 West lived in the western portion of the Warrior Mountains of Lawrence County. They lived in Township 7, 8, and 9 South which includes the area from Mt. Hope, Kinlock, and Wolf Pen on the Cranal Road. This particular range seemed to have the greatest concentration of Indian people who settled the poor mountainous soil. Today, this area presently has the largest portion of the Sipsey Wilderness Area.

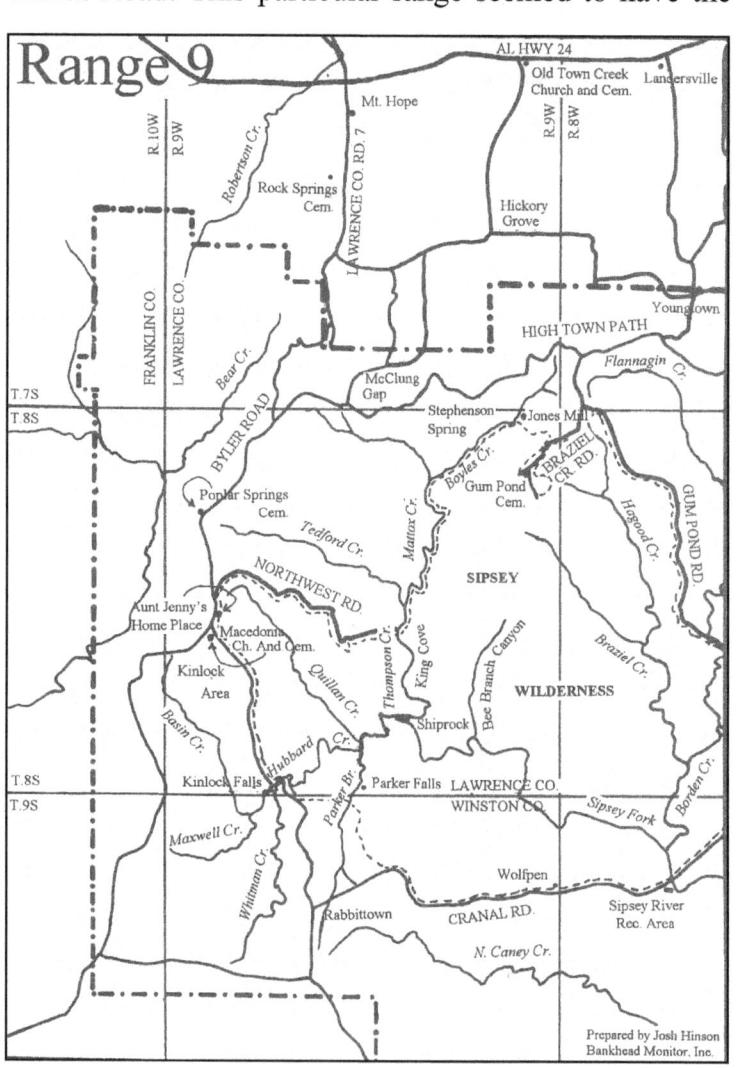

## The Stephenson Family of the Ridge Road

From the ridge top divide, a path turns into foggy history but the monument left behind clearly marks the historic site. The red men traveling on the High Town Path of years ago probably tasted of the spring's mysterious water which never fail to flow from the sandstone rocks. Many stories about the spring have died locked within the graves of those who have passed this way. Some say the water easing from the spring could cure the ills of those who sipped of the mountain's minerals captured by the thirst quenching flow.

**Stephenson Spring**

The spring is located some 100 yards south of Ridge Road, about three miles east from its junction with Byler Road, known as Stephenson Spring. According to family members, Stephenson Spring was named from the early Stephenson settlers of the mountain top area. Mr. Euell Stephenson said the spring has been known by his family name for well over 100 years. Euell's dad, Mr. Frank Stephenson, born on March 27, 1876, and died on August 26, 1968, was one of the elder Stephenson's who had a strong bond to the unusual spring site. Both families of Frank and his wife, Lela Elkins, had historic roots within the forest south of the Mt. Hope Community.

According to the Stephenson folks, the spring, located along a major forest route, was a place where people would come for the clean air and the strong mineral water, considered to be extremely healthy. It was thought a wayside inn or cottage near the spring provided weary travelers and health seekers short term lodging.

*Stephenson Spring*

Today, the trail leading from the Ridge Road has a wood handrail leading downhill approximately 25 yards where the trail levels. Continuing along the path, the downhill side of the trail has been lined with rocks and is relatively flat. The trail is approximately two feet wide and contains a slight depression in the middle worn by the feet of many spring visitors. Once reaching the spring, a large rock monument comes into view. The spring issues from the fireplace like cavity within the stone wall. In front of the spring are old wagon wheel rims which provide a patio-like area in front of the spring.

**Stephenson Family**

According to Old Land Records of Lawrence county, Alabama by Margaret M. Cowart, Hodge L. Stephenson entered about 40 acres in the area on February 20, 1856, and his son James M. Stephenson entered about 80 acres on August 3, 1860. Hodge L. Stephenson, born in Tennessee on June 30, 1803, was married to a North Carolina lady named Eliza P. Wasson, born on April 6, 1805, in Tennessee and died in April 1852, in Lawrence County, Alabama. She is buried in Rock Springs Cemetery at Mt. Hope.

Hodge L. Stephenson was the son of Hugh W. and Margaret Stephenson. Hugh W. Stephenson was born in Ireland on January 25, 1765, and came to America when he was seven years old. Margaret was also born in Ireland on November 28, 1770, and married Hugh in York County, South Carolina on October 16, 1787. According to the 1850 Lawrence County Census, Hodge L. Stephenson's children are listed as: Alfred W. (24), William (18), Hariet (15), James (10), and Eliza (8).

James Monroe Stephenson, the son of Hodge L. and Eliza P. Wasson Stephenson, was born on August 10, 1840, at Mount Hope. He served in the Civil War with the Confederate State of America. His father Hodge L. Stephenson was appointed as a special term commissioner in September 1861. Hodge served as the agent, reporting to Mt. Hope families about persons serving in the Civil War, according to Confederate Soldiers of Lawrence County, Alabama by Spencer A. Waters.

James Stephenson married Laura Dukeminer on January 3, 1871, and they had six children: Charles Mitchell, Russel E., Fredrick L., Frank David, Edward Alfred, and Deaton Monroe.

Carl and Monroe Stephenson were two of Frank Stephenson's sons who have labored in love to leave their family mark and history on the high ridge of Bankhead Forest. They have worked many hours on the trail and spring to insure their family's memory will live on even after they are gone in the land of the "Warrior Mountains."

# The Garrison Family of Sipsey River

In the Sipsey Wilderness is a beautiful glade located a short distance from Sipsey River. The peaceful glade near the Cullman Motorway has a spring which oozes up bringing minerals and salts from distant areas. The spring is known as Saltpeter Well. Deer and other animals are attracted to the area to get the minerals and salts. A rare ground cedar grows in this protected glade. Close by an early settler, Dennis Garrison, homesteaded the area of the Saltpeter Well. According to <u>Old Land Records of Lawrence County, Alabama</u> by Margaret Cowart, Dennis Garrison entered 40 acres of land in the Southwest ¼ of the Southeast ¼ of Section 31 of Township 8 South and Range 8 West on October 8, 1859.

**Dennis Garrison**

Recently, I talked with Mr. Cranal E. (Tom) Garrison and Mrs. Glen Hovater who are the great-grandchildren of Dennis and Sarah Garrison. Tom and Glen are the descendants of one of the early Garrison families who lived in the William B. Bankhead National Forest on the Sipsey River. The old Dennis Garrison home place is located on the east side of the old Cullman Motorway just north of Sipsey River about ¼ mile in the Sipsey Wilderness Area. The old home is now gone, but a single grave of one of the Garrison children still tie Garrison descendants to the old Sipsey River farm.

Dennis Garrison was the son of John L. Garrison and Mary Susan Trammell. John was the son of Stephen Garrison who was born in North Carolina in 1757. Stephen died on January 3, 1841 and is buried in the Payne/Garrison Cemetery ¼ mile south of the forks of North and South Caney Creeks. The children of John and Mary were considered to be ½ Cherokee Indian and were as follows: James G., 1816; Dennis, 1817; Malinda; David; William G. (Buck), 1832; Absalom, 1834; Mary, 1835; Sara Susan. 1844; Ellen, 1846; and Stephen, 1849. Buck was the father of Mary Tennessee Garrison Spillers.

The Dennis Garrison's home was north of the saltpeter well about 300 yards, on top of a knoll. The Garrison Spring which supplied the family water was behind the house. Remnants of the house still identify the location of the front porch, side room, and old main rooms. The house also had a small upstairs and a porch across the front. The house had two chimneys located about 10 feet apart on the same side of the house. One chimney was for the kitchen and the other chimney was for the main room. A barn stood just east of the house about 100 yards and the smokehouse was west of the house.

**Cullman Motorway**

The Cullman Motorway went to the left of the spring, by the site of Lawrence Garrison's cotton house. Lawrence was the son of William Riley Garrison and grandson of Dennis. The road forded the Sipsey River, but when the water was high the family crossed the river by boat or foot log.

The Cullman Motorway was originally a wagon road which most of the people used to travel to Haleyville to trade. The Cullman Motorway intersected the Cranal Road which was just an improved dirt road during the early 1900's. Later the Cranal Road was graveled then blacktopped. Most of the mountain children living along the Cranal Road and Cullman Motorway area of Sipsey River went to school at Wolf Pen. Cranal Road was named from Cranal Post Office and was intersected by the Cullman Motorway close to the Wolf Pen Cemetery.

Amos Spillers was one of the first persons in the Wolf Pen area to get an old T-model car. The car had a gravity feed gas tank and would not go up the hill in forward gear. So Amos would back his car up the steep hills. Amos was the son of Mary Tennessee Garrison Spillers who was a Cherokee Indian.

Straud Riddle, also a Cherokee Indian, lived west of Floyd and Audie Garrison at the forks of the road between the river and Wolf Pen. John Mize operated a store on the Cranal Road between Wolf Pen and Rabbit Town. Calvin Riddle lived south of the Cranal Road and east of Sipsey River. William Riley Garrison lived for a while at the old Riddle home place.

Henry McDowell lived on the Cullman Motorway between the Sipsey River and Bunyan Hill Road near the old game plot nine. Henry was a half-brother to Audie McDowell Garrison. In the early 1930's, Henry and Claude Boyles mined for gold on Mattox Creek. Several months ago, I visited the site where they were mining. Henry and Claude obviously spent many hours trying to extract the precious metal.

*Sarah Jane Blankenship Garrison (3/32 Cherokee) was the wife of William Wriley Garrison and daughter of Dock and Nancy Armstrong Blankenship.*

**Dennis and Sarah**

Dennis and Sarah Mary Dennis Garrison were married in Lawrence County on January 23, 1827. Part of their property was in Lawrence County and part was in Winston County. The Garrisons, who were from South Carolina, were farmers and raised a large crop of corn next to Sipsey River.

Dennis and Sarah's children and spouses were: James; Emily who married George Payne; Vie; Lynn who is buried at Gum Pond; and William Riley who is also buried in Gum Pond Cemetery. William Riley died when he was a young man and left his widow with five young children.

**William Riley Garrison**

William Riley Garrison was married to Sarah Jane Blankenship. Sara Jane was the daughter of Dock and Nancy Flanagin Blankenship. Dock's parents were Hudson and Patsy Wallis Armstrong Blankenship. William Riley and Sarah Jane's children and spouses were: Floyd Nenivah married Audie Mae McDowell; Clarence Milford married Sarah Roberson; Lawrence Trevis married Lillian Riddle; Synthia Alma married Amos Spillers; and Florence Ella married Johnny Mack White. All the children of Riley and Jane were mixed bloods of 3/16 Cherokee Indian ancestry.

William Wriley Garrison, (1/4 Cherokee)

The young Garrison boys would sometimes get into trouble by robbing wasp nests and slipping down to the river to go fishing. William would come in and whip the whole bunch for not doing their chores.

The Garrison family went to either Bunyan Hill or Gum Pond to church. Floyd Nenivah started to school at Bunyan Hill School before transferring to Wolf Pen School. After Bunyan Hill School closed, Wolf Pen School opened and children began attending Wolf Pen. Floyd joined the church at Wolf Pen which served the community as both a church and school.

William Riley Garrison lived near the Sipsey River and died before Floyd and Audie's children were old enough to remember him. William Riley and Sarah Jane Blankenship Garrison, along with Dennis and Sarah Dennis Garrison, are buried at Gum Pond Cemetery. Gum Pond, which is now within the boundary of the Sipsey Wilderness Area, was located at Gum Pond Church. The church was a one room log building with pole rafters and board roof with a large door facing east. All signs of the church are now gone but the cemetery is still cared for by the Garrison descendants.

## Audie's Family

James Jackson McDowell and Sally (Sara Ann) Harville were Audie's parents. Audie was a half-sister to Henry Andrew, Moses, and Ellen McDowell. Henry, Moses, and Ellen's mother was Peggy Garrison, the daughter of Silas Garrison.

Left: *James Jackson McDowell who is the father of Henry Andrew McDowell, Moses McDowell, Mary Elenor McDowell Cauthern, and Audie Mae McDowell Garrison. He was the husband of Margaret Garrison who was his first wife and Sarah Emaline Harville McDowell.*

Audie Mae was a half-sister to Appie and Hubert LouAllen. Wiley LouAllen married Audie's mother, Sally (Sara Ann) Harville McDowell. Wiley and Sally's two children were half-brothers to Audie McDowell Garrison. Audie Mae was also a half-sister to Arrie, Minnie, and Henry Pillow. Sally Harville was first married to Bob Pillow.

## Floyd and Audie

Right: *Sarah Emaline Harville McDowell, second wife of James Jackson McDowell and mother of Audie Mae McDowell.*

The day Floyd got married, he hooked up his buggy and drove from Sipsey River to McClung Gap where he picked up Audie Mae McDowell. They rode the horse drawn buggy to Moulton to be married. Floyd Nenivah Garrison and Audi

Mae McDowell got married December 19, 1915, by Judge Kumpe, at the Lawrence County Courthouse. The road around the courthouse was so muddy, the buggy sank nearly to the hubs and was extremely difficult for a horse to pull through the mud.

After Floyd Nenivah Garrison and Audie Mae McDowell married, they lived on the west side of the Sipsey River. Floyd Nenivah and Audie's oldest child, Drennon O.C., was born in 1918 in old Sipsey River home.

According to Tom, his mother, Audie Mae, was born on July 12, 1896. She still tells about crossing the river with her mother-in-law by boat. There were no bridges crossing the river; however, the river could still be forded today if traffic was allowed in the wilderness.

*Floyd Nenivah Garrison and Audie Mae McDowell.*

Floyd Nenivah and Audie lived for some two years on the Sipsey River before moving to McClung Gap. As a young mother, Audie use to take Drennon on her hip, with a load of clothes in the other arm, to the spring to wash the clothes. After moving from Sipsey River, all of Floyd and Audie's children, except Drennon, were born at the McClung Gap home. Floyd, who died on February 18, 1978, and Audie had six children: Drennon, Garvin, Clara, Elton Lincon, Glen, and Cranal (Tom). After moving from the Sipsey River-Wolf Pen area of the forest, Floyd Nenivah and Audie Mae McDowell Garrison began farming in the McClung Gap area of Lawrence County. McClung Gap was located at the northern edge of the forest a few miles from the Mt. Hope Community.

## McClung Gap School

Originally, all of Floyd and Audie's children attended school at McClung Gap. McClung School was about ½ mile north of the Garrison home. The road from Youngtown to McClung

Gap followed the edge of the mountain and crossed the ridges near the base of the forest. The old road was mail Route One from Mt. Hope.

The Garrison children lived so close to school they went home to eat dinner. When they carried their lunch to school, the old syrup bucket was utilized as a lunch pail. When McClung School closed, the Garrison children rode Rufus Flanagin's school bus to Mt. Hope School. The Garrison children would walk across the ridge to catch the school bus.

McClung Gap closed about 1937. Ms. Cleo Boyles passed Tom from the first to the third grade. Other teachers at McClung Gap were Ms. Christine Young, Rena Sue Sandy, Bessie Cowans, and Mr. Jim Counts. McClung Cap was a one room school house with six grades. Ms. Glen Hovater sat in Mr. Counts lap a whole lot during the first grade because he was afraid the larger children would hurt her.

**Making Molasses and meal**

Just to the north of McClung Gap was a community molasses mill owned by Floyd Smith and run by John White. Floyd got a toll for use of the mill. Sugar cane was made into syrup to feed the family through the winter. The mill was a mule drawn contraption with a long tree attached to cogs some 6 feet above the ground. As the mule pulled the pole in a large circle, the cogs turned three large metal rollers. Tom sat under the pole many hours feeding stalks of sugar cane into the rollers for the juice to be squeezed from the stalks.

*The family of Floyd Nenivah and Audie Mae McDowell Garrison includes, from left, (front) Glen, Clara, (back) Drennon, Garvin, Floyd Nenivah, Audie Mae, and Cranal (Tom).*

The mule continually circles the press while sugar cane stalks are continuously given to the man feeding stalks into the press. Another person constantly removes the crushed stalks. It took about three to four hours to get enough juice to fill the pan with 15 to 30 gallons. The juice is dipped out of the barrel in buckets near the press and placed in the pan for cooking. Initially the juice is real thin and must be boiled down to molasses.

The solid copper pan was about 10 feet long and 6 feet wide. The fire was made with pine wood which burned fast and hot. If the fire got too hot the molasses would become scorched. The mill was located near a big dug well which provided all those involved in syrup making a fresh supply of water.

Mr. John White knew exactly how hot to get the pan. When Mr. White saw the fire getting too hot, he would simply pull back the long sticks of wood and allow the fire to cool down. If White called for more fire, several people would add pine right then. The finished product was the finest molasses ever made and kept many people alive through the winter. Much of the syrup was also used in the old mountain trade for moonshining when sugar was scarce.

The Garrison family planted about an acre of cane which would supply a family of six. The acre of cane provided enough molasses to last until the next syrup season. Mr. Tom Roberson owned the general store which was about 350 yards from the syrup mill.

Mr. Roberson owned a grist mill and also took a toll for grinding corn. The grist mill had two large fly wheels on each side of the mill motor, about 6 feet in diameter, used to start the machine and keep it running. The flywheels were stepped upon and jerked down to start the mill engine. On the side of the motor was a large pulley with a belt running to the grist mill. The drive belt was approximately 8 inches wide and 12 to 15 feet long. The motor ran at a constant speed and the belt transferred the power to the crusher rollers which were standing vertical. The corn was fed in at the top of the rollers and came out at the bottom as meal. The meal was collected in a hopper and scooped up with a dipper to be placed in sacks.

**The Garrison Farm**

The Floyd Garrison family worked about 15 acres of cotton and corn per year with mules. The Garrison children grew up on a farm and helped raise the crops and earn family income. The family used mules to plow, plant, cultivate, and harvest crops of which some 15 acres was cotton. Cotton was carried to the cotton gin at Mt. Hope. The old motor that powered the gin would always scare the mules. The Garrison family could pick a bale of cotton (1500 pound) a day and go to the gin at night.

During the farming season, the mules were usually harnessed and geared up for the day by light of a lantern. After sundown the mules were brought back to the barn to be fed. The mules were fed corn in the morning, at 12 noon, and at night. In addition, they got hay each night.

The children also cut stove wood, firewood, split boards, and anything else to make a dollar. Boards were split from oak logs with a froe and stacked to dry and sell. The Garrison children helped cut and sell ricks of stove wood. A rick of wood was four feet high and eight feet long. The length of the stove wood did not make much difference. All stove and fire wood was cut with crosscut saws and chopping axes and hauled out with mules and wagons.

The old wagons had wooden wheel with steel rims. When the old rims would get loose, they would pull the wagon into a creek or pour water on the wheels so they would swell up and get tight again. The wagon had either cotton or corn sideboards. They planted 15 acres of corn and usually harvested about 500 bushels of corn per year.

The family usually kept two milk cows, several hogs, chickens, geese, and turkeys to keep the family a supply of meat. The goose down was used for feather beds and pillows. Nearly everyone in the community had chickens, hogs, and other farm animals.

*Floyd Nenivah Garrison (3/16 Cherokee)*

On Sundays the children spent a lot of time in the woods playing. One favorite game of the Garrison children was swinging from one small tree to the next. They would also climb to the top and ride small trees to the ground.

Another favorite game was playing marbles. Most people played four or five different games with marbles. During the late 1800's and early 1900's, marble games were very important, even to older men. The winner of a marble game would win the other player's marbles. During the peanut time, the children would dig a hole and build a fire. A piece of tin was placed over the fire with peanuts placed on top of the tin. The fresh roasted peanuts were always delicious.

## Hunting in the Early Days

During Tom's young days, a peddler would come by and trade store goods for eggs, chickens, and various farm goods. In addition to food items, farm goods were also traded for rifle shells for hunting.

When Tom was about 12 years old, the family would quit farming at dinner on Saturday and he would go to the woods to kill a mess of squirrels. Tom killed his first deer outside the management area in 1941. He got a brand new Stevens double-barrel shotgun in 1942 for $32.00. He could have sold it many times for more than double the price, but still has it today.

Floyd Nenivah ran the checking station during the deer hunting days and Drennon was assigned charge over hunters who were placed on stands. Drennon was the road patrol and kept watch for game violators. Both Drennon and his dad were paid by the game and fish division to work on the management area during the deer hunts. All hunters would arrive at checking stations before daylight to pick up their permits and warm by the fire while being assigned a particular stand. The hunters could only hunt within 100 yards or so of their stand. The road patrol would check each hunter sometime during the day. Drennon received about $3.00 per day and his dad made about $5.00 per day for their game warden duties. The game management area had a wire completely surrounding the area. In addition to the wire and signs, gates to the area were usually kept lock when hunting season was closed.

When the deer were first turned loose in the forest, they began eating the Garrisons' crops. The family depended on the crops and could not afford to have deer eat up their profit.

While eating up the crops, the first deer killed were dragged and left at a sinkhole. At first, the Garrison family did not realize the deer were good to eat. All the neighbors were protective of their crops. Finally some of the neighbors began eating the deer and everyone began to realize how good the meat was to eat.

When the deer began to attack the crops, Floyd would call the Forest Service office on an old Forest Service phone located nearby at John White's house. The call would go to either Kinlock or Central Tower. In turn, the Forest Service would call or contact Amos Spillers, the game warden of Bankhead Forest.

The Forest Service provided the phone and firefighting equipment along with "C" rations. Tom said he fought fires and if caught by dark, the firefighting crews went to sleep in the woods. The next morning, they would continue fighting the fire until it was extinguished.

Much of the old ways have changed over the years, but the Garrison children still fondly refer to the forest as the old home place. They continually return to the old Gum Pond Cemetery to pay their respects and to maintain the burial place of their ancestors in the "Warrior Mountains."

## Families of Gum Pond

On Monday, February 11, 1991, Mr. Rayford Hyatt and I hiked from Gum Pond Cemetery to Thompson Creek Bridge on the Northwest Road. It was an excellent day for hiking and talking about the life and times of Bankhead's early settlers. We began the day looking through the cemetery for folks who had settled near the area.

At one time, a thriving church was located at Gum Pond. Many settlers of the Warrior Mountains attended Gum Pond Church.

**Cole Family**

William Riley Cole, a Civil War veteran born in North Carolina, was the preacher at Gum Pond Church at the time of his death. Mr. Cole had lived most of his life in Winston County where he preached at several churches. His wife, Ellen Keith, left Bankhead with the family and is buried in Texas.

After walking about ¼ mile west along the Gum Pond Cemetery Road, we came to an old house place located on a high knoll. Just south of the road some 20 yards is an old dug huge well which is still some 30 feet deep. Mr. Hyatt thinks the well is the site of the old Bankhead home place of William R. Cole.

**Anderson Family**

We continued along the wilderness trail for a mile before arriving at the homestead of Alvin Anderson. The Anderson home is marked by two large chimneys which are seven feet apart. The sandstone rocks are still neatly stacked with the south chimney about eight feet high and the north chimney about seven feet high. The chimneys were much higher at one time, but the tops have fallen down. It appears that some 20 acres of land had been under cultivation at one time because field pines tend to indicate areas of cultivation.

Alvin Lyle Anderson was married to Rachel Emaline Cole, the sister of William Riley Cole. According to Mr. Hyatt, Rachel is buried next to her brother in an unmarked grave. The Cole family history states that Alvin and Rachel had five daughters and one son. After their daughter Mary Jane married Anderson N. Pruett, they lived in the old Anderson home on Gum Pond Cemetery Road. Two of Mary and Anderson's children were born in the house and one is buried in the nearby cemetery next to her grandmother, Rachel Emaline Cole Anderson.

*Double Chimneys at the old Anderson Homeplace on the Gum Pond Cemetery Ridge in The Sipsey Wilderness area.*

The double chimneys are located in a beautiful area of wide flat ridges. To the south of the home is a beautiful view of Mattox Creek Canyon which is visible because the house was located on the south edge of the ridge. West of the old home place is a natural gum pond which contained about ¼ acre of water. It was hard to leave such a beautiful site, but we knew several miles of hiking lay ahead.

## Thompson Creek

Shortly after leaving the Anderson place we entered the Mattox Creek Valley, now protected by the Wild and Scenic Rivers Designation and the Sipsey Wilderness Area. Presently, the Forest Service maps indicate Thompson Creek extending near the junction of Byler and Ridge Road to Hubbard Creek and Sipsey; however, many of the forest's early settlers and older people today refer to Thompson as the stream from the forks of Mattox and Tedford Creek to the forks of Hubbard Creek and the beginning of the Sipsey River. Thompson Creek, considered only two miles in length, was named after John Thompson who had a one room log cabin near its junction with Hubbard.

## Gold Mine

After continuing down Mattox some distance, we came to a sandstone rock shelter on the west side of the creek. The shelter had large sandstone rocks which had been drilled and broken. Mr. Hyatt speculated that early settlers used this particular sandstone for making grinding wheels to sharpen axes and other tools. Later it was revealed that Henry McDowell was searching for gold under the sandstone shelter.

**Early Timber Harvest**

After crossing Tedford Creek, we came to a large wide area which in the early days was used to cut rough white oak lumber. Mr. Hyatt was told of white oak logs over six feet in diameter being hauled to the site by teams of oxen. He said the big ends of the logs were pulled between two wheels supported by a heavy axle. The logs were then snaked through the forest to the steam operated sawmill. After the lumber was rough cut it was hauled out of the canyon by a wagon pulled by several oxen. Once the load reached the mountain top, some of the team was returned to the mill site. The wagon of lumber was carried to the Tennessee River and eventually hauled oversees to Germany.

The area of Gum Pond and east of Mattox Creek is now a part of the Sipsey Wilderness Area. Old dug wells and the remains of sandstone chimneys bespeak of a different day in the land of the "Warrior Mountains."

## Boyles Family of Mattox Creek

"History is a lie which two or more people agree upon and accept as the truth," jokingly stated Lawrence Warren Herron, a descendant of the Boyles family. After a little thought, I realized the amount of truth in such a profound statement. Writers control the course of recorded history; therefore, I make special effort to establish whether a spoken statement is an exaggeration or a fact.

**Boyles Cove**

Boyles Cove is located in the Northwestern portion of Bankhead Forest and is southwest of the junction of Ridge Road and the Braziel Creek Road. The valley has extremely steep to gentle sloping ridges with some flat bottoms located along the creek.

Downstream, approximately one mile from the Boyles Place on Mattox Creek (recorded as Thompson on Forest Service maps), is the "Narrows." The "Narrows" is a long stretch of the creek with steep bluffs on each side of the stream. A rock can be thrown from the east bluff to the west bluff with little effort. Just upstream from the Narrows is the baptizing hole, a clear deep pool of water. The hole of water lies between Buck Branch and Painter Branch and was used by early area settlers for baptizing people.

Near the upstream end of the valley is a small waterfall where Jones Mill was located. Evidence of the grist mill located at the falls is still visible. During the summer very little water goes over the falls; therefore, the mill was probably used on a seasonal basis during rainy weather. The mill was less than one mile from Ridge Road and about one mile from the Braziel Creek Road (which had access by way of Jones Mill Trail and Ridge).

**Boyles Homestead**

According to Mr. Herron, the Boyles Place was about one-half mile downstream from Jones Mill. The land was homesteaded by Phillip G. Boyles who migrated into the area from Georgia in 1875. Phillip G. Boyles had a house located next to the creek and, in addition, the family owned a house place east of Cole or Baker Cemetery. According to Rayford Hyatt, the only settlers living next to the cemetery was the Baker family. To the best of his knowledge, members of the Cole family are buried in Gum Pond Cemetery. Mr. Hyatt is uncertain how the graveyard, which he knows at the Baker Cemetery, became known as the Cole Cemetery. Several years ago I visited the old cemetery place which was grown up with large timber. It appeared that some 20 people had been buried in the graveyard. Presently, much of the Boyles Creek and Cove are protected by the Sipsey Wilderness Area.

Phillip Martin (Mart) Boyles and Hester Ann Borden (3/8 Cherokee).

**Phillip Boyles**

Phillip G. Boyles fought in the Civil War with the Confederate States of America. He had a brother who moved to Winston County that fought in the Civil War for the North.

Philip G. and Drucilla Nixon Boyles had several children: Harriett; Phillip Martin who was born in Georgia in 1863; James (Jim) who changed his name to John D., born in Georgia in 1865; Louisa (Pace) born in Alabama in 1872, and married Matt Moore who is buried in Cole Cemetery; George born in 1877; and Sarah who was born in 1880 and married Robert Mattox. The present name of the creek is probably from Robert Mattox's family.

Phillip G. Boyles began moving his family to Arkansas during which he made a total of seven trips. He was planning on moving his entire family west; however, his untimely death left Phillip Martin (Mart) Boyles in Bankhead. After crossing the Arkansas River by ferry, Phillip G. began riding his horse up a steep hill. The horse slipped and fell on him causing his death. Phillip G. was buried in Ozar, Arkansas and never completed moving all his family. Phillip Martin (Mart) Boyles lived on a ridge east of Cole Cemetery where most of his 14 children were born. Mart was married to Hester Ann Borden, born on February 1, 1864. Hester was the daughter of Phillip and Francis Wren Borden, the granddaughter of Reverend David Borden, and great-granddaughter of Christopher Borden, one of the first residents of Bankhead Forest. Both the wives of Christopher and his son, David Borden, where Cherokee Indians.

**Boyles Family**

According to Mr. Herron, his mother, Ms. Hester Boyles Herron, was born in Bankhead National Forest on Boyles Creek (now Mattox Creek). Ms. Hester Boyles married Eodies Warren. She had 13 brothers and sisters which are listed in order from the oldest: Emmy married Sterling Crittenden; Claude married Evie LouAllen; Clauson married Viola Borden; Maggie married Oscar Cothern; Minnie married

The Boyles Family. Top Row, L-R: *Luther, Claude, Magie Cothern, Minnie Hood, Clawson, Henry.* Middle Row, L-R: *Phillip Martin Boyles, Hester Ann Borden, Little girl — Lydia Porter, Johnnie Porter, Lellar Porter, Emma Crittenden, Baby girl — Dessar, Father — J. R. Sterling Crittenden, Sylvester Crittenden.* Bottom Row, L-R: *Next to dog (Bear Dog) — Phillip G. Boyles, Baby in arms — Hester (Odis Herron), Leonard Prince, Baby — Theodore (Bart) Crittenden.*

Cap Hood; Luther married Chelsea Blankenship; Henry married Mattie Mae Bynum; Johnnie married Oscar Porter; Prince married Nancy Blankenship; Lela married Roscoe Porter; Leonard (Lynn) married Martha _____; Lydia married John Porter; Phil married Cleo Reed and Hester born in 1906 was the youngest.

**Phil and Cleo**

Ms. Cleo Reed Boyles is the only surviving member of the 14 children and 14 in-laws of the Philip Martin and Hester Borden Boyles family. Years ago, Ms. Cleo and her husband, Phil, would go to the old Boyles home east of the cemetery in Bankhead and stay in the old log cabin on weekends. She said the Boyles cabin was made of oak logs. The house had one extremely large room with a lean-to kitchen. Both the large room and the kitchen served as bedrooms.

After Phillip Martin (Mart) Boyles sold his property to the Forest Service, he moved over the ridge to the Martin Place where he lived for approximately two years. Mart bought land from the McClung family and built a log house on the property near McClung Gap Road in about 1905. The house was two storied and contained poppa and momma's room which was the largest, the girls' room across the hallway, a large kitchen and dining room, and two upstairs rooms for the boys. Many of the Boyles children attended McClung Gap School which also served as a church. Mart and Hester are buried at Liberty Grove Cemetery located between Double Springs and Haleyville.

Phil and Cleo Boyles bought and remodeled his father's home place at McClung Gap. Ms. Cleo still lives in the last home built by Phillip Martin (Mart) Boyles. Ms. Cleo, who taught school in Lawrence County for 40 years stated, "If you don't know where you have been, you will never know where you are going."

The Boyles family lived and died in the area of Bankhead Forest where their ancestors struggled for survival. Phil and Cleo Boyles loved the land of the old Boyles home place in the heart of the "Warrior Mountains."

# The Feltman Family of King Cove

It is rare when one gets the opportunity to meet and talk to an individual who was a part of the last of a mountain civilization that is now extinct. Recently I had the opportunity to meet one of the last survivors who was born, grew up, and lived near the King Cove Area of Lawrence County. He stayed all night with Aunt Jenny Brooks many times and helped Jack McDowell survey a large portion of the original forest lands taken from early settlers such as his dad.

Even though I was a total stranger, Mr. Jake Feltman proudly shared part of his family history and life in the mountainous portion of Lawrence County that is now a part of the original Sipsey Wilderness Area. Each time people open up their heart and give me and others a rare chance to share in a life that will be no more, I feel extremely honored to record their personal history. Mr. Jake Feltman died within a year of my recording his memories in King Cove.

*The bow of Ship Rock.*

## King Cove

The King Cove Community was centered around the forks of Thompson and Hubbard Creeks at the beginning of the Sipsey River and the location of Ship Rock. King Cove extended as far north as the forks of Mattox and Tedford Creeks. The community was considered an area which covered some two to three miles north from the beginning of Sipsey River. According to Mr. Feltman, many people lived and farmed both the creek bottoms and ridges. The old mountain families remembered by Mr. Feltman included old Tom Bell, Hagoods, Gilbreaths, Webbs, Spillers, Rivers, Flanagins, Beavers, Lawrimores, Loverns, Riddles, Brooks/Johnstons, and Garrisons.

## Indian Country

Much of the creek bottom was utilized long ago by the American Indian people, who probably used the rich creek bottoms for farming and the adjacent bluff shelters for protection.

Descendants of the original Indian inhabitants, such as the Broosk, Spillers, Garrisons, and Riddles, continued to utilize the forest lands until the area was taken by the federal government as a part of the national forest system.

Mr. Feltman remembers being told of two of the original Indian people who were buried just on top of the hill above Mortar Rock. The Indian man and woman were buried in the land of their ancestors overlooking the great valley of Sipsey. After being reminded of the Indian family, I remembered being told by Spencer Waters of the old Indian man and woman riding their donkey. It was said the old Indian gentleman would face forward and his wife would face the rear. Setting back to back, the Indian couple would travel the areas that is now Sipsey Wilderness of the Warrior Mountains.

Today, five large grinding holes are still visible in the old Mortar Rock. Rayford Hyatt said he had discovered pieces of an old churn and other evidence of historic and early Indian occupation. Mr. Jake remembers going to Mortar Rock many times and seeing the old stone steps carved in the bluff. He said the steps have been there as long as he remembers and were there when he was a small boy. In addition, Mr. Feltman remembers finding flint arrowheads in the old corn fields he used to help work along Thompson Creek.

### Jake

Jake Feltman was the lone survivor of his family who worked, lived, and worshipped in the King Cove area of the Warrior Mountains. Jake did live alone in a house on the south side of the old Byler Road Fork from Moulton, about a mile before the old road turns up the mountains at McClung Gap to the Ridge Road, but recently died in December, 1993.

Jake was the eighth child of Andrew and Vina Sammons Feltman. According to their tombstones at Macedonia Cemetery, Andrew Feltman was born on September 20, 1868, and died February 23, 1939, and Vina Sammons, born on November 3, 1873, and died on August 27, 1950.

*Jake Feltman*

Jake Feltman was born some 87 or maybe 88 years ago but does not worry about the exact date. According to his tombstone located in the Heflin Cemetery, Jake was born on August 15, 1911. Since he is the only survivor of his mountain family it does not matter or seem important anymore. He was born in an area he calls "Hagood Ridge" just northwest above the junctions of Tedford, Mattox, and Thompson Creeks of Bankhead Forest. Later, his parent's house was not far from the beginning of the Sipsey River, referred by him as "the forks of the river" on a ridge near the King Cove Motorway and the Northwest Road.

**Andrew and Vina Sammons Feltman**

Not much is known of Andrew Feltman's family whom he left in South Carolina. As a young man, Andrew moved to the Warrior Mountains of Lawrence County and married Vina Sammons, the niece of Aunt Jenny's daughter, Dona Brooks Sammons.

Jake did not know or remember seeing any of his grandparents; however, according to Edward Herring, Frank Sammons was Jake's granddaddy and the daddy of Jake's mother, Vina Sammons. Frank was the brother to Neil Sammons who married Dona Brooks, the daughter of Aunt Jenny. When Aunt Jenny's son Henry Brooks was killed, Jake said his daddy, Andrew Feltman, was one of the men who helped tote Henry out of the woods. Jake said, they killed Henry just northeast of Macedonia School House. Both Henry and his horse were killed at a whiskey still northeast of the old field just across the road from Macedonia at a spring.

Jake recalls when the Indians (Brooks Family) and the Blacks (Hubbard Family) had a big fight at a place he referred to as "Battle Hill." He said the Indians were running the blacks out of the forest. The Lawson Hubbard family was the only black people to stay in the forest after the shooting. Jake said, "If people had to go through what we did back then, they would have to build a bigger penitentiary than they got."

Andrew and Vina had a total of eight boys and one girl: Robert T. (Bob) Feltman, born 8/29/1888 and died 12/1/1975, married Delia A. Spillers, born 9/27/1897 and died 8/12/1991; Tom Feltman married Rosie Garrison: Dick Feltman married a girl named Lela; Mattie Feltman, born 1897 and died 3/2/1925, married Emmitt Hagood; Lewis Feltman married Sherry Jane Frost; Kent married Florie Stanford; Bynum Feltman, born 3/18/1907 and died 5/19/1937, married Arizona Sanford; Jake married Viva Hood; and Oscar Feltman, born 9/13/1913 and died 11/8/1969, married Louis Riddle.

## Feltman Family

Later, Andrew and Vina Sammons Feltman built a typical dog trot log cabin on the ridge above the King Cove area in Bankhead National Forest. Also, Andrew Feltman helped build the local church on top of the mountain near the forks of Northwest Road and the King Cove Motorway. The church was located across the Northwest Road from the Feltman home. It was located west of Thompson Creek on top of the mountain. The church was at the curve before the road turned east, downhill toward Thompson Creek Bridge.

Jake went to church every Sunday. The preacher at King Cove Church was Jim Lovern. Andrew Feltman and his daughter, Mattie, joined the church and were baptized at a place Jake called the "Thompson Hole." The deep baptizing hole was just down the creek from the bridge.

After four years, the King Cove people decided to move their meetings and join the Macedonia Church congregation. Eventually the old King Cove Church made of logs just rotted down.

Over the years, people migrated into the area of the Warrior Mountains to find land and raise their families. Andrew Feltman was one of the earliest settlers of whom I have heard to arrive in the area by train. According to Mr. Jake Feltman, his dad came from South Carolina and traveled by train through Georgia to Hamilton, Alabama. After arriving by rail and living about one year at Hamilton, Andrew found and entered land near the Mattox Motorway in the area that would become Bankhead Forest.

L-R: *Willie Mae Feltman, daughter of Bynum and Arizona Sanford Feltman; Vina Sammons Feltman; Neal Hagood, son of Emmitt and Matt Feltman Hagood; Andrew Feltman; and William Feltman, another son of Bynum and Arizona Sanford Feltman. The young boys and girl are the grandchildren of Andrew and Vina Sammons Feltman.*

According to Mr. Jake Feltman, his dad Andrew owned land in three locations in Bankhead Forest. One block of land was located near Hagood Ridge on the Mattox Motorway, another block of his land lay on a ridge above the King Cove, and another place was near Macedonia Church. According to Margaret Cowart's <u>Old Land Records of Lawrence County, Alabama</u>, Andrew entered 200 acres of land in sections 8, 9, and 10 of Township 8 South and Range 9 West in the southwestern portion of the county.

Jake Feltman was born in a log cabin on Hagood Ridge, not far from the valley forks of Tedford and Mattox Creeks. The Feltman's closest neighbors were the Hagood family. The old cabin consisted of two log rooms separated by a hallway and had a porch all across the front. The back of the house had a lean-to-kitchen. Water was obtained from a small spring located at the head of a small hollow across the road from their house.

**Independent Mountain Life**

The Feltman family lived almost independent from the outside world. They had horses, mules, oxen, cattle, hogs, sheep, goats, and chickens. The family farmed and raised wheat, corn, and grew cotton. They also had an orchard with apples, peaches, and plums.

Andrew Feltman would shear his sheep and wash the wool until it was real white. Jake's mamma would then spin the wool to make thread. After she had enough thread, Vina would make her children knit their socks. Jake said it would take him about two days to knit one pair of socks. In addition, Jake said his mother would knit shawls and make quilts.

Andrew and other local farmers cultivated areas in the valleys and also on the ridges. Near his place in the Cove, Fatty Webb was one of the farmers who worked a corn crop next to Thompson Creek. The Webb Place was south of the bridge crossing Thompson Creek on the Northwest Road.

South of the Thompson Creek Bridge at the mouth of White Oak Hollow was the Beavers' old sawmill. The sawmill and several houses were located just on the west side of the creek across from the mouth of White Oak Hollow Branch.

In his younger days, Andrew Feltman was an expert at bottoming a chair. According to Jake, he could do a good job making chair bottoms. Andrew also made white oak baskets. Jake said, "Why he could make baskets that would hold a hundred pounds of cotton and feed baskets."

Jake also helped his daddy make boards. Jake said, "Back then that's all folks had to cover their buildings out of was boards." Jake helped saw logs for boards, helped split out boards about an inch thick, and helped tote them out of the woods to the wagon. In addition to boards,

Jake helped his dad split oak and make rails for pasture fences. Jake said he had toted many rails to make pastures. They used nails and wire to help hold the rails in place. According to Jake, "That's all the way we had, that's all the way it was."

**Mountain Folk Gatherings**

Life in the Warrior Mountains was not always boring. Quite often, Mr. Jake Feltman remembers his family having a big Sunday dinner and inviting other mountain folks from all around the King Cove area. Jake fondly remembers the good old mountain days when both his mother and daddy were in good health and in the prime of life. Jake said, "But now listen, folks is having a good time now and they better appreciate it. Daddy on Saturday, he would get up of a morning and he'd kill a goat, dress it really good, take it to the edge of the yard and he would bar-b-que that thing to. Boy you talk about something good. Now, Sunday, they would be more folks at our house on Sunday than they would be at these churches around here. Now, you think I am lying but that's the truth."

"Why my mammy on Friday and Saturday, she would get up of a morning, she would boil maybe two big chickens, have it all ready. Sunday morning, she would get up and make a pot of chicken and dumplings have a big pot of taters and boy, a big dinner. There was a big red oak tree that stood out front of the house, and my daddy made baskets and bottomed chairs out of oak, and he would take oak and make a big table. On Sunday morning about 9 o'clock, my mammy would get up, got out there, and she would fix that dinner on that table. Boy you would know by the dinner, directly you would hear wagons coming, folks riding horses, just get out there, set around and eat dinner. Some of them would sing a little and talk a whole lot."

*Andrew Feltman — Note the 1929 tag on his old car.*

Jake went on to tell about getting in trouble as a boy in the Warrior Mountains, "Back then gals wore their dresses plum down to the ground, you could not see their feet. So one Sunday, there was a bunch of them that come to our house. They was 10 or 12 pretty gals and they got out on the porch talking about the way they were going to fix their dresses. One of them got up and went in the house and got ma's needle and hemmed her dress up. You know like they said they was going to wear them. Come back out there in the yard, she was (unspeakable). I was setting on the door step, boy she had the prettiest legs you ever seen. I could not keep my eyes off of her. So after they left, ma got up and went in the kitchen and she called me. I got up and went in there to see what they wanted and she asked me, "What were you laughing about?" I laughed a little more and she said, "You ain't gonna laugh no more." She reach up over the door and got a great big ole, long hickory withe (stick) and she give me a good whupping. She told me, "Let me tell you if I catch you at that again you going to get another one." Now that, that was so! When my daddy and mammy told us what to do, we done it and we didn't jaw them."

*Kinlock Falls where Jake went swimming and the location of Stephenson's Water Mill.*

Jake went to school at Macedonia. According to Jake, "I'll tell you back then they just run school about two and a half months once a year and I went every time." Jake walked to Macedonia to school. Jake said, "I walked up there of a morning and toted my dinner in a little bucket under my arm and walked in at night. I walked about seven miles one way to school. My mammy would get us up of a morning, fix everything, and we would hit the road. If you come in of an evening and any of them said anything of what you said or done, they would get that hickory and tear you're a— up."

## Jack of All Trades

In the early pioneer days in the Warrior Mountains, people had to be a "Jack of all Trades" in order to survive. Andrew Feltman was one of the early settlers who knew the skills needed for survival in the mountainous area of Lawrence County.

Andrew did his own blacksmithing work. He had his own shop, where he would sharpen his plows, heel sweeps, bull's tongues, scratcher springs, and other farming implements. Originally Andrew Feltman farmed with steers. Jake Feltman said his dad would not let his sons work with the steers. After he got his horses, he would have a man to come fix shoes to go on the horses.

Andrew Feltman used to grow wheat, cradle the wheat, tie it in bundles, thrash it, sack it up, and carry it to Cullman Flour Mill to have ground into flour. Jake said his dad would come back from Cullman with a wagon load of flour. The family would use the flour to eat for the year. Andrew also shelled three to four bushels of corn to have ground into meal. He would place the corn in the wagon and carry it to Stephenson's Water Mill at Kinlock Falls. Jake said he remembered the mill at Kinlock Falls. The grist mill consisted of a big wheel with dippers. The water wheel would turn an axle which would turn the mill stones and grind the corn into meal. The mill house was on the bank on the side of the creek opposite the big rock. The Stephenson Mill was on the south bank next to the road.

**Mountain Store**

The closest store was at the Amos Spillers old place, near where the Flanagins lived and north of Macedonia. Joe Sandlin owned the store, then sold out and went to Haleyville. Mattie Feltman, Jake's sister, ran the store a long time. According to Jake, Amos Spillers owned the land where the store was located. Jake said, "They sold just anything you wanted to buy. They did not sell any gas because back then there wasn't any gas. It was a pretty big store. The store was located between Lawson Hubbard's place and Aunt Jenny's place."

**Uncle Sam Take His Land**

In the early days of 1900, the U.S. Government began taking land in Lawrence and Winston Counties for a national forest. Most of the people that lived in the mountainous portion were asked to leave and sell their land back to the government. Andrew Feltman's family was no different. Jake explains in his own words what happened. "Uncle Sam (government), he was taking up his land and he got all my daddy's land and when he got it all, why he come in there and told us we would have to move. They was going to grow timber. Pa got up and we went to Phil Campbell and stayed until we moved down here (McClung Gap)." Jake refers to the United States Government as "Uncle Sam".

Jake believed Uncle Sam just paid the taxes on the land they took from his daddy and did not pay for the place. "Hell, they run us off our own land. They come down there and told us we would have to leave. When we left from there I had a bunch of cows and had raised a bunch of yearlings and we moved and I went back to get them up and somebody had killed seven to eight of the animals."

After Mr. Feltman told me about his animals getting killed, he shook his head and let out a deep and painful sounding groan. I could tell it hurt him to remember the event of being removed from the land and animals he loved. Jake continued, "Pa had 30 sheep and they killed every sheep he had. The sheep were running on open range in the forest and we hunted them. We found them dead with a hold in them about the size of a shotgun blast. They (Uncle Sams' men) killed them and cleaned up the forest."

**Andrew Dies**

After Andrew Feltman left the McClung Gap area, Jake Feltman said his daddy moved to the Will Spillers Place where he lived until his death. In his later years while living at the Spillers old place, Andrew Feltman visited Jake and his wife. He told them, "If I call and send word, you come to see about me." A few days later, two boys came running up to Jake's house and said your daddy has called for you to come. Jake and his wife went to his daddy's home. He said "Pa laid there three days before he died."

**Jake and Viva Hood Feltman**

Jake married Viva Hood, the daughter of Willie Hood. Jake and Viva Hood were married by preacher Bill Bennett and lived on Willie's place some 60 years. Jake and Viva only had two little boys who died.

Jake said, "After I got married, I would plow a mule and make cotton for three cents a pound. I raised corn for three bushels for a dollar and did everything for a little money. I had to hunt and trap to survive. You had to get all you could get. Hell, I pulled a crosscut saw twelve hours a day for fifty cents. Picked cotton from sun up to sun down and would not get over 45 to 50 cents a day. Give 10 days a year on that road there."

*Jake and Viva Hood Feltman*

Jake still lives on the old Byler Road Fork from Moulton which runs on the north side of his old house. The old road use to go just south of the front yard of Willie Hood's house. Willie and his wife bought land on the old Byler Road near McClung Gap about the 1920's. The Hood family had moved from the Moulton area to settle at the foot of the mountains near McClung Gap.

The old road fork that is now closed is identifiable by a huge white oak tree that still stands in the front yard near Willie's home and old truck. Deep ruts mark where the Moulton Fork of the Byler Road ascends to the top of the mountain at McClung Gap just south of Jake's house. The more recent rock road runs adjacent to the old Byler Road which was worn deep into the mountain side. The original fork of the Byler Road from Moulton is closed toward the east at the Willie Hood old house place, just 200 yards north of where Jake did live; however, the old road bed is still very visible where it turns east toward Moulton. Jake said the road had been closed over twenty years.

Jake worked on the mountain roads for five dollars a month while he was in the CCC camp located at Kinlock Spring. Jake was assigned to the camp for six months. Jake said, "After I collected my five dollars and started home, everyone I would meet would want fifty cents to buy his coffee with."

Jake lived during the depression and sold cows and bulls that weighed 800 to 900 pounds for seven dollars. He sold pigs for 50 to 75 cents apiece. He cut logs in the mountains for $3.00 for twelve hours work; cut and sold stove wood for fifty cents per rick. He cut molasses pine, used for syrup making and sold it to Tom Roberson and Lawrence Garrison.

## Jack McDowell

Jake tells that Authur Pickens rode a horse to deliver the mail. Jake relates the following about disturbing mail. He said, "I'll tell you, they are a lot of folks now, they don't realize what I went through with, I had not been married about a week and went to bed one night, got up the next morning, mailman passed, I went to the box, and I got my call for the Army. I went up there to see about it. Hell, they wouldn't going to give me an examination. They was just going to send me on. Jack McDowell, you have of heard of him, Jack told me, he said, "You come on and go with me." I went on with Jack and when I come back home, I got my card that I was discounted. I did not have to go to the army." Jake also had two brothers who took the test for the military were turned down.

According to Jake Feltman, he and Jack McDowell measured many acres of land and run many land lines in Bankhead Forest while surveying the first land lines for the forest. When Jack McDowell was living and the boss of the forest, Jake worked for him many days helping him survey for the establishment of an Alabama National Forest. Jack McDowell was the first Forest Ranger in the Warrior Mountains and is fondly referred to as "The Boss" by Mr. Jake Feltman. Jake also helped Jack McDowell fight forest fires. Jake said he had fought fires all day and all night. For both day and night, each person would get about seventy five cents or a dollar. Jake whispered, "Now they won't fart for a dollar."

## Kinlock Experiences

Jake Feltman remembers helping tear down the covered bridge at Kinlock. He said the bridge was torn down the year he worked for six months for the CCC camps located at Kinlock. According to Jake, the old boards were rotten and were piled up and burned.

Jake related the following experience concerning his drinking, "Back then I was pretty bad to drink. A feller come and wanted to sell me a little. I got a pint for fifteen cents. Me and a lieutenant went down there (Kinlock Falls) to go in swimming. We were going on down there and I ask him, I said, did you ever drink any wildcat? He said, "No I don't drink wildcat." He would not drink none and I wouldn't either going on down there. Coming on back, I got it and walked from the Stephenson's Mill to right down yonder to that old house (McClung Gap) Saturday evening. When I got that pint and started home, I spilled a drink there was a white spot and I ain't never had another drop in my mouth." Jake did not know what was wrong with the whiskey except it just burned real bad. Jake knew he was lucky the whiskey did not kill him.

**Jake remembers wildlife**

Jake remembers seeing one of the bears that was turned loose in the fifties. Jake had been to Mt. Hope and was headed home when the black bear walked out in front of his vehicle. The bear turned from the road and ran down the creek just north of Jake's home. About a week later, Jake was in Moulton where he learned from a forest ranger that seven black bears had been turned loose in the forest.

In his younger days, Jake walked the area around Quillan and Hubbard Creeks quite often looking for roots, hunting, and trapping. Jake used to trap to make a little extra money. He caught polecats, possums, coons, foxes, wildcats, and many other animals to sell their hides. Sometimes trapping was the only way mountain people had of making a living. Jake also said he dug many pounds of ginseng, star root, golden seal, and other roots to sell. Jake said his daddy used to make medicine out of tree bark.

Jake said he loved to possum hunt. He said, "We had good dogs, we would not have nothing but a good one." He said they could not afford a bad dog. In addition to selling the possum hides, the family would eat the meat of the animals he caught. He said, "We would skin them bastards, eat the meat, and sell their hides for fifty cents.

*Jake Feltman stands by his daddy-in-law's (Willie Hood) old truck and home on the old Byler Road Fork from Moulton.*

**Early Farming**

I asked if he ever worked or farmed with mules. Jake said, "I farmed, God Almighty! I went up here to Moulton one day, after I got married and bought a pair of mules. I never did get them to where I could work them. I swapped the mules for another pair and kept them for three or four years. My brother, he got hold of a one row John Deere Tractor. He told me, he says, come get that tractor and use it I ain't going to fool with it, you can farm with it. I went out there and got it and sold my mules. You know what I got for them? I got fifty dollars for the mules and a walking cultivator, lines, gear, bridles, and all. I hooked them to it and took fifty dollars for it. Naw, now folks will, you know. I 'll tell you right now, I don't know what going to happen myself."

Jake raised about seven to eight acres of cotton and made four of five bales which sold for three or four cents per pound. Jake said his family had to live on the crop for the entire year. Jake farmed land which had been given to his wife by her daddy, Willie Hood. Jake said he did not own any land, but had a home here as long as he lived and that was all.

Shortly after writing this story, Jake Feltman passed away. Before he died, I had the opportunity to interview this rare mountain man. Jake said, "Folks are having a good time now. When you start home, just look on each side of the road and see what you see." Jake Feltman is now dead and gone, but the story he left behind will live forever in the land of the "Warrior Mountains."

## The Hubbard Family of Bear Creek

He stood 6 feet 6 inches tall and weighed over 350 pounds. He was a giant of a man whom the farmers knew well. He could face a bale of cotton, pick it up, and place it on a wagon. He worked from dark in the morning until after dark at night, earning from one to two dollars per day. From a Bankhead Forest slave and Indian family he came, and one morning with nothing but the clothes on his back he returned, determined to break the bonds of slavery that still plagued his every turn.

In one day, he walked the breadth of Bankhead Forest on the old worn trails he knew like the back of his hand and never looked back upon the Town of Landersville in the Moulton Valley. As he passed his old mountain home place where his early ancestors had lived, he thought back to his boyhood days which began in a log cabin located in the western portion of Bankhead. His mother was a beautiful lady of Indian ancestry, and his father a descendant of the black slaves of David Hubbard. His family lived in an old log house between Bear Creek and Byler Road in the Kinlock Community. He, as his sixteen brothers and sister, was delivered into the old mountain cabin by the matriarch of the forest, Aunt Jenny Brooks Johnston. His birthplace

*Robert Washington Hubbard (1/4 Creek) son of Odie (1/2 Creek and 1/2 Black) and Lawson Hubbard (black).*

was just east of Bear Creek, about ½ miles southwest of Poplar Springs Cemetery where Aunt Jenny is buried.

He continued past the old home with all of its memories, and with Kinlock at this back, he continued his walk toward Haleyville trying to find higher wages and better working conditions. He finally found what he was looking for in the Town of Haleyville where his dreams of owning his own home and land came true. His home is still the mountain top Town of Haleyville where he plans to live the rest of his life, and so begins the story of Robert Washington Hubbard.

**Robert Washington Hubbard**

Robert Washington Hubbard, born on March 3, 1910, to Lawson and Odie Hubbard, did not have the opportunity to receive any formal education and never attended a day of school in his life. He began work on his father's farm at a very young age and was taught how to cultivate the crops with a mule before he was strong enough to lift the plow. During the some 35 years he lived on the Hubbard farm, he learned all the secrets of being a successful farmer. Today, he produces enough vegetables to supply his entire family, to give to friends – both black and white, and to sell to those who need vegetables for canning or freezing.

Robert never went to a medical doctor or stayed in a hospital until about eight years ago when he was 74. The ball joint of his hip had completely worn out and he had gotten so lame he could barely walk in a stooped over posture. After successful hip replacement surgery, Robert is standing tall again, and one would never know he had an artificial hip joint unless they asked. According to his wife, the first day Robert was out of the hospital he was using his tiller as a walker while working in his vegetable garden. After hearing about the surgery, I was shocked to see the 82 year old gentlemen walk without the slightest limp.

Presently, Robert and his wife, Eva, live in a neat frame house, just west of the railroad tracks in the Town of Haleyville. His garden is still producing with neat rows of large leafy collard greens. I had been at his house for a short while and Robert was piling the trunk of my car full of freshly gathered collards. For the next couple of days, my family enjoyed the gift of greens, grown by the wise tiller of the mountain soils.

**Wash Hubbard's Family**

Robert Washington Hubbard's father was Lawson, a descendant of black slave ancestry. His mother, Odie Hubbard, thought to be the half-blood Creek daughter of William (Billy) Hubbard, was a beautiful Indian lady with long black flowing hair. Lawson was born to George Washington Hubbard and Nichola Freeman in 1875. Robert's mother died shortly after his birth, and he does not know many of his mother's people.

Since Robert Hubbard's mother was Indian, he was Indian as well as black. Even though he has lived his life as a black man, Robert still has those unique qualities that make him very much Indian, and the sacred fires of Kinlock still ride strongly in his veins.

Robert was the grandson of George Washington (Wash) Hubbard, a black man and slave of David Hubbard that at one time lived near Kinlock Springs. It is believed that Wash and his older brother, William Hubbard, worked on Major David Hubbard's forest plantation at Kinlock.

According to his tombstone at Rock Springs Cemetery at Mt. Hope, Wash was born in 1809 and died in 1919, living to the ripe old age of 110; however, the Lawrence County Census of 1880 indicates his year of birth as 1835 which would make his age 84. Wash's first wife and the mother of Lawson was thought to be Nichola Freeman, who died prior to the 1880 census.

Since Lawson was only five years old in 1880, he knew very little about his mother; therefore, Robert was familiar with his step-grandma, and knew little about his grandma Nichola. Robert's step grandmother, who was Wash's second wife, was a lady of Indian ancestry known only to Robert as Grandma Hubbard.

To the best of his knowledge, George Washington Hubbard was the first of his family to settle on the upper portion of Bear Creek in Lawrence County, Alabama. Robert's father, Lawson, inherited the land from his daddy. Lawson lived in one house and his dad, Wash lived not far behind in another log cabin.

Front Row, L-R: *Odie Hubbard (1/2 Creek), Ida Hubbard (1/4 Creek), Henry (Bud) Hubbard (1/4 Creek), George Washington Hubbard, Grandma Hubbard and Lee Hubbard.* Back Row, L-R: *Lawson Hubbard, Violet Hubbard, Lodie Hubbard, George Hubbard and Dee Pruiet.*

The 1880 Lawrence County Census probably lists all the names and ages of George Washington (Wash) Hubbard's children. According to the census of 1880, Lawson (5) had only one brother and five sisters: George (7), Jennie (8), July (16), Nodie (9), Emma (4), and Violet (3). Lawson was born and lived on the old Bear Creek home place all of his life. Lawson had a total of 16 boys and one girl, all of which were delivered by Aunt Jenny.

Some of the boys were: Henry (Bud), Nick, Luther, Clyde, James, Harvey, Abe, Lee, Robert, Wash, and sister Ida. Robert said he had so many step-brothers, he could not remember all their names, but Clyde was the only one still alive. Three of Robert's brothers served in the army and fought in World War II. Out of the seventeen Hubbard children, only three or four of the younger children had the opportunity to go to school.

Lawson is buried in the black section of the Rock Springs Cemetery at Mt. Hope along with his wife, Odie, his mother and daddy, and some of his brothers. Robert's mother died when he was real young, and he does not remember why or how she died. Shortly after Lawson's death, the Hubbard family left the forest and never returned to live on the old Hubbard home place.

According to Robert, Mr. Bob Almon, a lawyer from Moulton, eventually wound up with the land. After Lawson died, Robert's brother and sister could never work out a deal to sell the land. Because of the family differences in Lawson's estate settlement, Robert said the lawyers got the land.

Of the seventeen children, Robert had only one living brother, Clyde, who lives in Tharptown east of Russellville. Many of Lawson Hubbard's children and descendants settled, and still live in the Tharptown area of Franklin County.

**Fortune Teller**

A lot of people would come to mountain to visit the fortune teller, to hear about things yet to come in their lives, to have warts or goiters removed, and just to see the miracle man. The man, to which all the attention was directed, was Lawson Hubbard, a fortune teller, healer, finder of lost articles, and medicine man for his large extended family, neighbors, friends, and visitors. The Lawson Hubbard house, especially on weekends, was full of people and the yard full of vehicles. Lawson's son, Robert, said, "My house was like a big church house. All colors of people would come to daddy to solve problems, receive healing, find lost objects, reveal the unknown, and get their fortune told. He would charge nothing for his services, but accepted gifts if the people were satisfied, and people were always giving my daddy thirty or forty dollars for just telling them what they wanted to know. Most of the time before people left the house, they would count out the money to daddy because they were satisfied."

*Lawson Hubbard — The son of George Washington Hubbard, the former slave of Major David Hubbard.*

While telling people their fortune or things they wanted to know, Lawson would use his deck of cards. In the proper hands, the cards could reveal fortunes and Lawson depended heavily on his deck of cards. The cards shuffled, then the deck was cut, once the card was selected, Lawson would begin asking the person questions, and begin telling them their troubles and fortunes.

L-R: *Ottis Sanford, Lelton Sanford, Robert Hubbard, Max Sanford, Lawson Hubbard, and Henry Brooks Jr.*

My dad relates about my granddaddy, Dan Walker, getting some coon dogs stolen and going to Lawson to find the lost dogs. Lawson told my grandpa to look for the redbone hounds in Florence or the Tri-Cities. My dad went on two different trips to the towns to recover the hounds. The authorities showed them hundreds of stolen dogs which were kept in large kennels, but there were so many dogs they were unable to identify their lost hounds.

Lawson would carry people who wanted to be healed in a room by themselves. He would not allow anyone to see what he did when healing people or removing growths such as warts or goiters; however, Lawson passed on his abilities and taught his seventh son. Luther carried on his father's healing, finding things, and telling fortunes.

Robert said he never wanted to learn how to do those things, but he also has some abilities as unique as his father, Lawson. For example, a nest full of red wasps presents no problem to Robert. He just points his finger close to the nest and makes a circular motion. Instead of stinging, the wasps fly off and Robert pulls down the nest with his bare hand. Robert said he had never been stung while pulling down wasp nests.

It has been said, Lawson Hubbard could heal anything that a person was not born with. His seventh son, Luther, also received the healing and fortune telling powers. Lawson, and later Luther, healed a lot of people, goiters, warts, and numerous aliments. Lawson could tell people things that would come true, and because of his reliability, people flocked to his home. Robert has no idea how his father

*Lawson Hubbard in his garden.*

came about the miraculous powers, but I have heard many people testify to the healing powers of Lawson Hubbard and his son, Luther.

**Aunt Jenny**

One of the most important ladies of the Kinlock neighborhood was Aunt Jenny Brooks Johnston. Even the forest fortune teller, Lawson Hubbard, knew where to go when he needed help. Robert said his dad would hook-up the wagon, and go get Aunt Jenny to deliver the children. With sixteen boys and one girl, Lawson depended heavily on "Aunt Jenny" as the mid-wife who delivered all of his children into the world. Robert said, "Cold weather like this is, my daddy would get the ole buggy, hook-up the old hoss to the buggy, and go get her. She would hop in that buggy, and here she would come with a lantern set down in the floor between her feet to stay warm."

The Hubbard family also went to church with Aunt Jenny. Robert said, "We went to white church right down the road." The church was old Macedonia Church, built on land donated by Aunt Jenny. Robert's folks went to church at Macedonia Church with a bunch of different colored people – Indian, black, white, and mixed. The Lawson Hubbard family would sit where they wanted to because the church did not have special seating for blacks.

Some newspapers falsely claimed that Lawson Hubbard was killed during a shootout with Aunt Jenny Brook's boys. During the gun battle, Ganium Brooks was shot in the head by Henry Hubbard, the son of William Hubbard. In addition, a Deputy Phillips was killed, and Henry Brooks was wounded in the gunfight. However, the shootout was between William Hubbard's family and did not involve any of George Washington (Wash) Hubbard's folks.

According to the 1880 Lawrence County Census, it is thought that William, born in 1823, and Wash, born in 1835, were brothers. The two Hubbard brothers were bought to the Kinlock area as slaves for David Hubbard. Robert was sure he was kin to William's family, not sure how close kinship his daddy, Lawson, was to William Hubbard's children.

After the shootout that left Gains Brooks dead, most of the remaining Brooks children went to Indian Territory in Oklahoma. Years later, Henry Brooks returned to his old mountain home place near Kinlock.

Robert said that his dad, Lawson, was not involved in the gunfight that left Ganium Brooks dead. As a matter of fact, Henry Brooks, Ganium's brother, and Lawson Hubbard were best friends. Lawson would sometimes be the lookout for Henry at his whiskey stills, but Lawson always refused to go near the illegal operation.

When Henry returned to this country, he already had his peg leg. According to Robert, he stayed about six years, and had a brother get killed in Texas. Henry Brooks rode his big red horse back to Texas, and killed the man who shot his brother. After he took care of the man, Henry came home to Alabama.

Robert said that Henry Brooks was bushwhacked at this whiskey still, along with his beautiful horse. According to Robert, the horse, which was also named Henry, was dark red with a white blaze face. The horse "cut up so and had a wild fit," that the men ambushed Henry also had to kill the fine animal. The horse would not let anyone get close. Robert said, "if the horse could have gotten loose, the animal would have killed somebody.

After the last son of Aunt Jenny was ambushed, shot, and killed, Lawson went to the still to help carry his friend, Henry Brooks, out of the woods. According to Robert, the whiskey still, where Henry Brooks was killed, was located about ¼ miles south of Macedonia Church, to the west of Kinlock Road in a small hollow.

Robert said the entire Brooks family were good people and never gave them a minute of trouble. The Brooks were always coming to the Lawson Hubbard house and the families helped each other pick their cotton. Both families depended on the other and helped each other out during hard times. When Aunt Jenny died on March 29, 1924, the Hubbard family lost the last of their Brooks friends. Robert and his family attended her funeral at Poplar Springs Cemetery.

## Bear Creek Farm

Robert Washington Hubbard lived the good ole mountain life. His boyhood home was made of logs and consisted of five rooms. The old house had a typical hallway with the rooms located on each side. The large log house was covered with homemade wood shingles. The loft of the big house was sealed and used as two bedrooms. The kitchen and dining room were built as a lean-to shed all down one side the house. The kitchen contained a cast iron cook stove. In addition to the old wood stove, the log home had three fireplaces, used during the winter for added cooking space. Big ovens were placed in the fireplaces for baking bread and cooking other foods.

R-L: *Luther Hubbard, two of Luther's daughters, and Johnny Cartwell.*

The Hubbard family would go to Baker's store in Haleyville to get supplies. The family would get a barrel of flour, barrel of sugar, and box of soda or baking powder or other small items. Robert said, "That was about all we needed, we had everything else."

Robert said when he was young his family took their corn to the water mill called Stephenson Mill. Stephenson Mill was located at Kinlock Falls, and at one time belonged to David Hubbard. The water ran down a long trough and poured into the cups of the big wheel. He also remembers crossing the old covered bridge in a wagon with his family on the way to Haleyville. The covered bridge was located at Kinlock Falls on Hubbard Creek where U.S. Forest Service photographed it in 1927.

Another smaller log house set to the west of the larger log cabin, and was the home of Wash Hubbard. The houses had a glass window in each room. Beyond the two houses, a large log barn with eight stables was enclosed in a pasture with a high fence made by homemade rails.

The farm consisted of a total of 240 acres, with approximately 80 acres of cleared land that was under cultivation. Bear Creek split the land, with a small portion of the property lying in Franklin County. The Hubbard Family raised hay, corn, cotton, sugar cane, tobacco, and all varieties of vegetables. Sugar cane was an important crop and Lawson had his own syrup mill for making molasses. The syrup mill, which squeezed the juice, was mule operated and the sugar cane was manually fed through the press.

Robert's family farmed 15 to 20 acres of cotton, and made about seven bales of cotton each year. Robert said he remembered the old David Hubbard Cotton Gin on Bear Creek. At one time, a man got his arm tore off in the old gin and died, but Robert does not remember the man's name. According to early maps, the cotton gin was located directly west of Kinlock Spring and David Hubbard's old plantation home.

The Hubbard family farm included about ten cows, twelve sheep, some twenty head of hogs, two oxen, and eight mules. The farm animals provided the family with a supply of milk, butter, and meat, and other things necessary for independence from the outside world. The livestock was kept in the split rail fence pasture.

According to Robert, they made their own fence rails out of American chestnut or white oak. Some of the white oak trees, which grew on the Bear Creek portion of the Hubbard place, were ten or twelve feet in diameter, and over a hundred and fifty feet tall. Robert said, "We would take the old crosscut and saw awhile, then chop with an ax a while, and then saw more." On some of the forest's giant trees, Robert said it would take nearly all day to cut one down. Once the huge oak was on the ground, the tree was used for making boards, shingles, fence palings, and split rails. A steel froe used properly would split out some beautiful wood.

When I asked Robert about his favorite meal, he said, "Back then you just ate what you got and you could not pick out what you wanted to eat. You always went to the tables to eat what was cooked." Robert said they always had peas, beans, sweet potatoes, Irish potatoes, cornbread, molasses, milk, and meat. Every year, the Hubbard family would kill about eight hogs at different times to supply meat through the winter. Hog killing started when it got cold and stopped in the spring when the weather began getting warm.

Robert plowed and worked a yoke of oxen with a bull whip. Instead of using plow lines such as with the mules, the voice commands gee, haw, whoa, and get-up were used for plowing the oxen. If the oxen did not immediately respond to the voice commands, the bull whip got their attention quickly.

Robert said his family raised their own tobacco, and either sold or gave some twists of tobacco to their friends. His Aunt Lodie loved to smoke a pipe. Robert said in his boyhood days there was somebody at their house all the time and his dad always shared his tobacco. Today, people still come and are given things by Robert Hubbard.

## Hunting and Fishing

At a young age, the Hubbard brothers were taught by their father, Lawson, to properly use a gun. While living on Bear Creek, Robert and his brothers hunted all the time during the fall of the year. The Hubbard brothers hunted coon, possum, wild turkey, and deer. Robert said all the native deer were not completely wiped out, but were highly scattered and very few left.

The family ate nearly everything they killed, including coons and possums. The coons and possums were baked with sweet potatoes and were delicious. Robert said they had some good dogs, but his favorite was a squirrel dog named Minnie, a blue tick hound. Every time you went to the woods with Minnie, you knew you were going to bring some meat to the house. The Hubbards had some black and tan hounds they used for coon hunting.

Robert said nearly everyone in Haleyville, and all around, would come to their house to go coon hunting with them. During Robert's boyhood days, the forests were full of coons. They never had any problems treeing and bringing home coons and possums. During these early days, Robert said they could hunt anywhere they wanted to because the management area was not established.

When going on a coon hunt, they loaded the dogs in the wagon and drove either toward Mt. Hope, or in another direction, and hunt back toward home. When the dogs treed, they would go get the possum or coon, and bring the game back to the wagon, and wait for the dogs to tree again. Some nights they would catch five or six coons and several possums.

All the fur bearing animals were especially valuable because they could sell their hides and also the meat. Robert said they would swap the meat of squirrels, possums, and coons for more shells so they could go back hunting and kill more game.

Robert remembers when the deer were stocked in the forest in 1925 when he was 15 years old. After the deer were released, the land east of the Byler Road was closed and they did most of their hunting on Bear Creek and west of the Byler Road.

During the spring and summer, Robert and his brothers loved to fish. He got his fishing poles out of the bottom along Bear Creek. He could clean up some of the poles and carry the canes to sell.

Robert and his brothers fished mainly on Bear Creek, and the Blue Hole on Thompson Creek. He said, "Back then the creek's around here were full of fish." He caught mostly catfish and bream, and would not got back home until they had a mess of fish to eat. When the suckers ran in the spring, they would gig the fish, shoot them with rifles, or snare them with wire loops. To snare the sucker fish, the wire loop was easily lowered in front of the fish. As the fish swam into the loop or stood still while the loop was worked around the fish, Robert jerked the pole, and lassoed or snared the fish. He said they caught lots of suckers by the snare method.

On warm nights, lanterns were used to see the fish under water. After a fish was spotted in the shallow water, the .22 rifle was eased to the fish's head, and then, pull the trigger. After killing the fish, Robert would reach down and put the fish in their sack. By using the rifles, they could kill all kinds of fish in the mountain streams.

Robert said they hunted American chestnuts and chinquipins a lot of the time during the fall. They would take a sack full of chestnuts to Mt. Hope and Haleyville to sell. He said some of the chestnut trees were bigger around than his dinner table, which was some six feet across the stump.

At one time, Robert said there was a bunch of bobcats in the Bankhead Forest. When bobcats would sometimes kill their sheep, Robert said his brothers would stay up at night and wait for the cats to return. They killed several bobcats that were killing lambs and sheeps.

## Families of Kinlock

The Kinlock area of the William B. Bankhead National Forest appears to have been one of the most racially diverse communities in the whole forest. According to reliable family traditions, many of the people around the Kinlock area were of Indian ancestry. The family history of the Hubbard family indicates that William Hubbard, who was a black slave of David Hubbard, married a Creek Indian lady called Ginsey. In addition, Lawson Hubbard was married to Odie hubbard, daughter of Ginsey, a lady of Creek Indian ancestry, as was Lawson's stepmother; therefore, Indian and black mixed-bloods were common in the area according to oral family history.

Not only did black families claim to be of Indian ancestry, but so did some other families of the Kinlock area. Robert Hubbard's closest neighbors, the Will Spillers children were also Indian and white mixed-bloods. Will married and Indian lady by the name of Mary Tennessee Garrison. In addition to the Spillers family, the Brooks children were considered by many to be at least quarter-blood Cherokees.

Many families have lived in the Kinlock area, but during Robert Hubbard's time some families of Kinlock included the Flanagins, Hagoods, Peoples, Johnstons (Brooks), Spillers, and Whitmans.

The closest neighbors to the Hubbard farm was the Will Spillers family living about one mile north of Macedonia Church on the Byler Road. Amos Spillers' family was their closest neighbor. Robert grew up with Amos Spillers, whom he has known all of his life. One of Amos Spillers' sisters, Ruby Spillers, married Bill Johnson. Robert said Amos still has one sister living, Mattie Spillers Flanagin. Mattie now lives in Haleyville about three miles from where Robert now lives. Robert said he worked with, and for, the Spillers family many days.

Robert said the he remembered Mary Tennessee Garrison Spillers, who was Amos's mother. I asked Robert if she was an Indian and the reply was "yes sir." Robert said she was a dark Indian lady, and really showed her Indian blood.

Robert also remembers the first ranger in Bankhead National Forest, Mr. Jack McDowell. He remembers very well when his folks would visit Mr. McDowell's place in the cove to get some strong medicine. Robert said his family would go to the cove to get liquor to make cough syrup, bitters, or maybe for people to drink. He said, "The cove folks made some mighty fine whiskey."

When Robert was young, he and his brothers would get up early in the morning and walk to Mt. Hope to chop cotton all day long for Mr. Elmer Counts. Robert's brother, Harvey, lived with Mr. Counts until he died. All the Hubbard boys worked for Mr. Counts off and on, but Harvey Hubbard stayed with him.

**Robert Leaves the Family Farm**

After the family farm on Bear Creek was lost, Robert Hubbard moved to Landersville and worked for several years at the cotton gin and farm belonging to the Young family. Robert worked for Authur and Byron Young at Landersville, and lived on their place. He worked two years for one dollar per day and three years for two dollars per day. His wife was also working in the Young home. Robert's wife made one dollar per day doing the house cleaning, washing clothes, and cooking for both the Authur and Byron Young families. He worked from before daylight to sometimes midnight. Robert finally got up to three dollars per day; however, the other men were getting paid six dollars per day. The only difference was the Robert lived on the place.

Robert eventually left Landersville one day and walked to Haleyville, where his brother, Wash Hubbard, was living. When Robert Hubbard left Landersville, he walked off with only the clothes on his back, leaving his car behind. He did not want anything or any attachment to the people of town he was leaving. Robert rented a house from Wash, and went to work for a white fellow who owned a store. After working for a while at the store, Robert got a job working at a cotton gin for eight dollars per hour.

When Robert quit the store, he went by the cotton gin on his way home. As he passed the gin, the owner said, "Hey boy, you know how to work this gin." Robert replied, "I never worked in a gin in my life." Robert wanted to get hired, not by what he knew after working at a gin in Landersville for several years, but because he was needed. Before the owner offered Robert a job, he asked if he had a job and how much he was paid. Robert told him, "It doesn't make any difference what I make because you won't pay me anyway." The gin owner said, "I don't care who you are, if you work for me you will be paid." Robert agreed to go to work for $8.00/hour for regular time as well as $8.00/hour for overtime. Robert was tickled to death with his new job.

After Robert's house burned, he said all the white people brought him meat, lard, vegetables, and other necessary items. Mr. Ervin Batchelor, the gin owner, sold Robert a house and agreed to allow Robert to work out the payments. Mr. Batchelor had so much confidence in Robert, he told him to pay only if he was able to work. If he became unable to work, Robert would not be required to pay a dime for the house.

One day when Mr. Ervin was gone, Mrs. Batchelor asked Robert if he could operate the gin. Robert told her he would do his best, and had ten bales of cotton ginned before Mr. Ervin Batchelor returned. From then on, Mr. Batchelor took off whenever he wanted to, leaving Robert in charge of ginning. Mr. Batchelor became Robert's best friend, as well as his boss.

After working for Mr. Batchelor awhile, Robert said he needed a car; therefore, Mr. Batchelor gave Robert the company truck which he drove about two years. One day after being gone, Robert returned to find a car Mr. Batchelor left at this house. He told Robert to pay him for the car when he could. Ervin Batchelor, the cotton gin owner, was one of the finest men Robert ever knew.

**Robert Hubbard Story Concludes**

Robert attributes his good health to the fact that he never did set down, but just kept going. People would tell Robert hard work would kill you. His reply was work never killed my daddy, and he lived until he was 110 years old. Robert's aunt and his daddy Lawson's sister, Lodie, lived until she was 105 years old. Robert said his daddy made a crop the year he died. When the family took Lawson to the Russellville Hospital, it was the first time he went, and he died at the hospital.

Robert retired from Mr. Batchelor's cotton gin, and also from Fontain Trucking Company, about 1975. One day while Robert was working for Fontain Trucking Company, a white lady wrecked and was pinned under her car. People were hollering for a wrecker and an ambulance. When Robert saw what had happened, he ran over, stooped down, grabbed hold of the car, and with a mighty shove, rolled the vehicle off the lady. The woman lived and stops occasionally to talk to Robert.

*The remnants of Lawson Hubbard's old log cabin on Bear Creek (1957).*

Robert found he was a diabetic when he was about 72 years old and had his hip replacement at age 74. The doctor told him he might have a heart attacked and die because of his age. Robert asked the doctor if he knew what he was doing. After receiving a "yes" from the doctor, Robert told him not to worry about him dying, but give him the best hip he had. The doctor said, "I'm giving you the best hip joint we got." After the surgery, Robert never took anything for pain. With the new hip replacement, Robert would sneak up to use the bathroom. The doctor asked the nurse when his bowels had moved. The nurse said they had not since he had been in the room. Robert had to admit he had been getting out of bed and slipping into the bathroom since the first day in his room.

When Robert was young, he sold ginseng and some they used to make the "bitters tonic." He said they would take whiskey, yellow root, star root, and ginseng, and mix together to make the tonic. The bitters would turn slightly yellow and was taken for colds, headache, and other ailments. The children would drink a little cup of the concoction when they got sick.

Robert still makes cough syrup by using a gallon of whiskey mixed with rock candy, cod liver oil, hore-hound candy, and glycerin. After mixing in the proper portions, he says there is nothing better for coughs, colds, and flu. After telling all of the wonderful healing powers, I was convinced to take a big dose for a slight sinus drainage. I took a big gulp, and felt the liquid hit by stomach. The next day my nasal drip was gone.

Eva White, Robert's wife, and her father's family, Charlie White, were from Russellville. Eva's mother, Hattie Napier, had relatives in Moulton.

Today, all that remains of the Wash Hubbard farm and Robert's boyhood home are the fond memories of a past that seems so long ago. I hope you have enjoyed reading about the colorful life of this black and Indian mixed-blood family as much as I have enjoyed reliving the past with my newly found and old friend – Robert Washington Hubbard.

# The Will Spillers Family of King Cove

As you travel south on old Byler road through the western portion of the Warrior Mountains in William B. Bankhead National Forest, a quaint little log house with a tin roof sets on a rise to the west of the road. The little log cabin, about ¾ of a mile north of the Northwest Road junction, is the home of one of the last mountain ladies to be born near King Cove in the Sipsey Wilderness Area. The log house was built in 1940 and is the home of Ms. Mattie Spillers Flanagin.

**Will and Mary**

Recently, I stopped at the log house to talk with Ms. Mattie, born on November 1, 1907. Mattie was the daughter of Will and Mary Tennessee Garrison Spillers. She was born in an old log cabin on the ridge west of junction of Hubbard and Thompson Creeks, now within the Sipsey Wilderness Area.

*Mattie Spillers Flanagin (3/8 Cherokee) on the front porch of her log cabin which is on the old Byler Road in Bankhead Forest.*

Will and Mary had seven children: Millard married Dorothy Gilbreath; Amos married Synthia Garrison; Sary first married Prue Gilbreath and then Calvin Riddle; Delie married Bob Feltman; Willie married Grady Morgan; Ruby first married Luke Sammons and then Bill Johnson; and Mattie married Rufus Flanagin.

Mattie's folks lived on top of the hill west of the forks of Hubbard Creek and Thompson Creek. At one time, a road ran from the hill west of Thompson Creek Bridge to the southeast toward the head of Sipsey River, which begins at the junction of Hubbard and Thompson Creeks. The road was known as the King Cove Motorway. According to Ms. Mattie, several people had settled along the road during her younger days.

**Mary Tennessee's Family**

*Hook Rock House Shelter was thought to be named from Jessie D. (Hook) Riddle.*

Ms. Mattie's said her family "did not have nothing except bull yearlings to plow." Millard, Ms. Mattie's oldest brother, cut and snaked logs with his pair of old bulls to the top of the mountain and built the family a new log cabin farther up the ridge. The three room log cabin had a hallway between the two largest rooms. The loft was left open and used for storage. Mattie said, "We did not have stairs. When we wanted something from the loft, we would just climb up the wall."

Mattie said her mother had a lot of Cherokee Indian blood. Mattie's mother, Mary Tennessee Garrison, born January 26, 1865, was considered to be at least ¾ Cherokee Indian. William G. (Buck) and Manervie Vernon Garrison were the parents of Mary Tennessee. Mary Tennessee had the following brothers: David Sherman, born May 9, 1867; William C., born April 8, 1870; Lee, born July 27, 1891; and Jim M. Her half brothers and sisters from the second marriage of Buck to Caroline as follows: John, born 1862; Garrison, born in 1864; Sandra, born in 1866; and Elvira, born in 1868. Dicey was also a sister to Mary Tennessee but the date of her birth is uncertain (Will Buck was probably married to both women at the same time, which was a common practice in Indian Country). In addition, Mary Tennessee had a sister, Aunt Dicey, who married John Riddle. Uncle John's Cherokee Indian name was Devil John. Mattie said he got his name because he was just a mean man. John Riddle was 5/8 Cherokee Indian, and Dicey Garrison was at least ¼ Cherokee. Later, Mary Tennessee Garrison's mother married a man by the name of Whisenant. According to Mattie, Buck Garrison, Mary Tennessee's daddy, is buried in Caney Fork Creek south of Cranal Road, probably the Payne/Garrison Cemetery which is labeled on the forest service map as Robbins Cemetery.

The family had a picture made at the old log house down at the cove. Amos Spillers was 18 years old at the time the picture was made. Mattie said, "We did not even have any shoes when the picture was taken." Mattie Spillers Flanagin is the sole survivor of the folks in the family picture.

Back Row L-R: *Millard, William Amos, Sary, Delie and Willie. Front Row L-R: Ruby, Mattie, Mary Tennessee Garrison Spillers (3/4 Cherokee) and Will Spillers. All of Will and Mary's children are 3/8 Cherokee.*

In the early days of the 1900's, mountain folks had a rough independent life; however, some mothers were able to get a doctor to deliver their babies. Such was the case when Ms. Mattie Spillers Flanagin was born to Will and Mary Tennessee Garrison Spillers in the King Cove of the Warrior Mountains.

Mattie said, "When I was born, I was delivered by Doc Howell from Haleyville. Doc Howell has been dead for years and years. Doc rode all the way over to the cove to deliver me and just charged $25.00 and it's a hundred or two. He come in a buggy, he did not have no car."

**The Early Years**

Mattie was the youngest of seven children of Will and Mary Tennessee Garrison Spillers. Will Spillers moved his whole family into a new log house closer to the Northwest Road when Mattie was one month old. Mattie said, "That was the most beautiful country anywhere in the world. We would walk from the top of the mountain from our home and would tend the farm land along the creek bottom. Near the mouth of White Oak Hollow was a large flat rock. When we were not old enough to work, mother would put us on that rock while they would work the bottom land. We would stay right there all day while they worked."

Many times when it rained the family would go to the Hook Rock House. At one time old man Hook Riddle lived under the bluff in the old rock shelter. Hook Rock House was located about 1 ½ miles south of Thompson Creek Bridge on the east side of Thompson Creek. The family farmed a large patch between Hook Rock House and Herron Point (Ship Rock) called Bear Bottoms. The old folks said bears had a den nearby in Bear Hollow and would raid the cornfields along the creek bottoms.

Mattie said, "We had a spring near the house where we washed our clothes and got our drinking water. My mother would take three cedar pails to the spring and fill them with water. She would take one full pail of water and set it on top of her head and carry one of the other two pails in each hand. My mother could bring the pail on top of her head to the house without spilling any water."

Mattie and her sisters roamed all over the King Cove area. When she was young, the children would go to the waterfalls in Parker Branch, to the cascades up Quillan Creek, and to the Big Poplar in Bee Branch. Mattie played many days at the old mortar rock and well remembers the five big holes worn deep into the huge slab of sandstone rock. Mattie said she was told the holes were used to make hickory nut soup. The old mortar rock was not very far from her house. Mattie remembers the old steps that were carved into the sandstone bluff which lead to the top of the ridge. Mattie also remembers the Indian burials in the area being dug.

Mattie says, "I rode horses and buggies all over the forest. When I was growing up, I had a white horse called Old Gray. I would ride by myself when I could get no one to go with me, but I never did have to plow."

## Making Clothes and Shoes

While growing up and isolated in the Warrior Mountains, families not only raised their own food, but they also made their own clothes and shoes. Will and Mary Tennessee Garrison Spillers lived a very independent lifestyle. According to their youngest daughter Mattie Spillers Flanagin, "My momma would buy whole bolts of cloth and would also make her own cloth. Momma would spin thread on her wheel and use the homemade thread to weave cloth on her loom. She would card bats of cotton or wool and spin the material into thread for making cloth. Momma could get into that old loom and make us a dress in just a little while. She made most of the cloth she used. She also knitted wool socks and sold them for one dollar a pair."

Mary Tennessee Garrison Spillers raised sheep. According to Mattie, "Mother had a big bunch of sheep. The sheep run loose in the woods and did not bother the fields no which away, they would not even come in the field. She would catch and shear the sheep; wash and card the wool, then spin the wool into thread. She would weave the thread into cloth and make clothes."

Mattie let her sister's girl have her mother's old carding tools. Her mother's old spinning wheel and loom burned up in her son's house. Millard's wife also died in the house fire. Millard was gone fishing when his house and wife burned up. At the time of the fire, Millard and his wife lived in the Dime Community, and Millard is now buried at Dime Cemetery.

Besides making their own clothes, families got together to make shoes and moccasins. Mattie said, "There was a place where they tanned hides and made shoes. Folks would catch varmints, skin them, tan the hides, and make what we called old brogan shoes. Just the first one and the other would make the shoes. My daddy helped make shoes for our family."

The old furnace where they made the shoes was used for removing saltpeter from the soil. Saltpeter was the tanning agent obtained from the soil. The furnace was located downstream from the forks of Thompson Creek on the southwest side of the stream. Mattie said, "You would go down to the other fork and up under the bluff where they had their furnace and their vat. They tanned them hides in what they called saltpeter."

"They would boil the soil in order to dissolve the saltpeter in the water. The tan yard was in a place we called Tan Toffed Hollow. The tanning area was up under the bluff." Mattie said, "I have been to the tanning area many of a times. I had a lath that they used to make shoes in that hollow. My daddy would go with the men to make shoes. They would use coon hides and fox hides. I wore a pair of coon skin shoes, but we did not wear our shoes to school.

**School**

Every community in the Warrior Mountains had their local church that also served as a school. The King Cove Community, where Will and Mary Tennessee Garrison Spillers raised their family, had a one room plank building as the local school. Will and Mary's children started to school in a little school house on the King Cove Motorway. The little plank school also doubled as the local church. The school house and church were located on a ridge above King Cove known as the School House Ridge. The school building was south from the Northwest Road down King Cove Motorway.

Ms. Mattie said, "Mr. Odell's place was just uphill from the old school house. I went to the King Cove School until it went dead. The old school was just a plank building. After leaving the King Cove Schoolhouse, I went to school at Macedonia to the sixth grade. But today I cannot see to read and write."

After the King Cove School closed, Mattie went to school at Macedonia where many of Mattie's folks are buried. The Spillers children walked to school from the King Cove Community to Macedonia, a distance of some five miles.

*This Nutting stone at Mortor Rock is due North of Ship Rock on the west bluff line of Thompson Creek.*

Mattie joined the church at Macedonia and was baptized in the Elliott Pond. She said, "My sister and daddy was baptized in Thompson Creek in what we called the Man Hole." For a while, the Spillers family walked from the King Cove to church at Gum Pond. The old Gum Pond Church was a log building which eventually just fell down and was never built back. Mattie said Clarence, Sook, and Riley Garrison are some of the Spiller's distance relatives. The Garrison's were kin to Mattie's mother and some were buried at Gum Pond Cemetery.

**Amos and Synthia Garrison Spillers**

Mattie said she did not go to school very much because of the distance they had to walk. Later, Mattie stayed home with her older brother, Amos, and his wife Synthia Garrison Spillers, after they bought a home place on the Byler Road just ¼ mile north of the Northwest Road. While staying with Amos and Synthia, Mattie went to school because it was much closer.

Amos and Synthia had one child that died and is buried at the back of the old store house just a little southeast from where Ms. Mattie now lives. They did not carry the child to the cemetery but just buried it in an unmarked grave in the back yard. Mattie said, "Amos had flower bushes just set out around his child's grave but someone just cut them all down.

Mattie said, "After Amos got killed in his accident, they moved Synthia off. After they moved Synthia, Bill Johnson, Ruby's second husband, rented the place to an old drunk bunch and they burned the house down. Synthia's daddy was Riley Garrison and he is buried at Gum Pond Cemetery.

Amos, who was born on August 11, 1891, died on August 28, 1965, married Synthia Garrison on August 4, 1913. Synthia was born on September 6, 1889 and died on June 29, 1976. Both Amos and Synthia are buried in Mt. Olive Cemetery in Bankhead National Forest.

Mattie said, "My folks have lived in this area all their lives. When my mother got sick and unable to care for the family, Millard moved her and daddy in the little house up the road (Byler Road) near the Northwest Road. After being moved, mother fell and broke her hip and she never did get over it and she died." Mattie seemed to have a deeper sense of loss and sadness when she told of her mother dying, more so than the deaths of other members of her family.

Mary Tennessee Garrison Spillers was born on January 26, 1865, and died on October 20, 1941. She is buried at Mt. Olive Cemetery close to her son Amos. According to Mattie, Amos wanted her buried near him and Mary Tennessee wanted to go where no drunks would walk over her grave.

*Amos Spillers (3/8 Cherokee) and Synthia Garrison Spillers (3/16 Cherokee).*

Mattie said, "Both Amos and my mother are buried in Mt. Olive Cemetery near Grayson. I went to the all-day decorations at Mt. Olive Cemetery as long as I could. We would always carry a picnic dinner to eat."

**Farming in the Warrior Mountains**

Most families survived in the Warrior Mountains by farming. They made just enough to live through the winter and to start over again the next spring. Such were the lives of Will and Mary Tennessee Garrison Spillers who lived in the King Cove area of Bankhead Forest.

The family raised corn, beans, pumpkins, and just anything they wanted to plant. They raised a lot of sugarcane in Bear Bottoms and made syrup on the banks of Thompson Creek. Millard Spillers, the oldest child of Will and Mary, ran a syrup mill on Thompson Creek. Bear Bottoms near the mouth of Thompson Creek was rich farm land.

Both Will and Mary Tennessee plowed and did all the farm work. The children also helped with the farming chores. Mattie said, "They would put me down and get cotton seed and a pan of ashes. We would have to roll the cotton seed in the wet ashes. The seed would be placed in an old guano distributor which had a horn attached to it. Momma would take that distributor to sow the cotton seed in the row through a hole in the horn. Daddy made cotton baskets out of hickory splits, and momma would also take the splits and bottom chairs."

Ms. Mattie said, "Just look at my hands, I picked cotton and done any farm work necessary. We had several acres of cotton and carried the cotton to the gin over toward Haleyville. Charlie Hughes ginned our cotton. The gin was an old horse drawn gin. I sat there all day long with my family ginning their cotton."

Mattie told about making their own meal, "Daddy would take a lard bucket lid and punch holes in the lid with a nail. He would nail the lid on a board to make what we called a gridder. We would rub our corn on the gridder to make meal. We ate cornbread for breakfast and at all meals."

The family raised chickens, ducks, turkeys, and had a dozen geese. Mattie said, "Mother would drive those geese to the cotton patch to hoe the cotton. Why, those geese would pick all the grass out of the cotton field. We used the goose down to make our feather beds."

"My mother also had a bunch of sheep which she let run loose in the forest. We raised hogs and produced our own meat, made our own sausage. We would kill our hogs, grind the sausage, and get big wash pots to cook out the grease, making sausage into balls and place in the wash pot of hot grease and cook a wash pot of sausage at a time. We would take the cooked sausage out and place in what we called churn jars. Then we would cover the sausage balls by filling the jars with hot grease. Then when we wanted to eat the sausage, we would go to the churn jar and take a ball of sausage out of the lard to cook for breakfast. We had a big old smokehouse where we salted down all our meat and stored the churn jars full of sausage and grease."

"We raised what we had to eat, we did not do like they do now, run to the store to get every bite. We did not have to go to the store. We had cows which we milked every day. We always had fresh milk and would use the old churn to make our butter. We always had a big garden. Maw made a big garden. My daddy just worked in the fields and farmed. He farmed with old mules. We farmed the creek bottoms from the Blue Hole plum down to the Thompson Hole at the forks of the creek. Uncle Jim Garrison lived down near the Thompson Hole. We raised everything we eat."

*Sipsey River Rapids near Ship Rock.*

In addition to farming with mules, most families used horses as the major mode of travel in the Warrior Mountains. Mattie said, "Will had two horses, Amos had two and we had one horse. That is all there was back then, I never saw a car until I was a grown woman."

The Will Spillers family had 25 to 30 head of cows. The cattle had to be driven to the Government Pasture to be run through the dipping vat to kill ticks. The Government Dipping Vat was on top of the hill above the forks of the creeks. Ms. Shiverson's folks lived near the dipping vat.

**Living Off the Land**

Mary Tennessee Garrison was from an Indian family that had long ago settled in the Warrior Mountains of the William B. Bankhead National Forest. Mary was taught how to survive off the land, utilize the plants for medicine and food, and to cook and eat the animals provided by the creator. She had an undying devotion to the land of her ancestors which she loved. After marrying Will Spillers, the family settled in King Cove, now a part of the Sipsey Wilderness Area.

Mattie said, "I remember when the government started buying up the land in the forest. Maw would fight them to the very last! They wanted to buy her place but she would not let them have it. After my maw died, my daddy finally agreed to sell the land to the government but my mother would never let them have her land as long as she lived."

Mattie said, "My brother, Amos, would kill a deer every once in a while. There was not many deer when I was real young. I well remember when they restocked the deer in the forest. The government also restocked birds. They would bring big boxes of partridges (quail) and turn them loose. They would come up in our yard and we would feed them. There used to be a little deer that would come out in the pasture in front of our house. The young deer would come out and eat with our cows."

*Amos Spillers holding a bobcat.*

Ms. Mattie said, "We used to catch a lot of fish out of Thompson Creek and Sipsey River. The one I liked best was the big old eels. Back then there was a bunch of eels in all the mountain streams but the creeks are filled up now. My favorite fishing hole was just below the rapids south of the Windows (Needle's Eye) on the Sipsey River. We caught catfish and some real big eels. I loved to eat eels, because they did not have any bones. They looked like big old snakes but were good to eat. The river used to be full of eels."

Mattie's mother did not like to see trash in the creek and would tear out drifts in the stream. Mattie said all the old holes were named. One in particular was the hole just south of the Thompson Creek Bridge called the Plum Bush Hole. Mattie recalls, "We would go the creek and take our bread, grease, and skillet and cook fish right on the creek bank."

"Back when I was growing up there was not any game laws, you could go out and hunt anytime you wanted to and kill anything you wanted to. We ate rabbits, coons, ground hogs and most anything that come alone."

"We would go out in the woods and gather different types of plants for salads. We eat a lot of green salads from the woods."

Mattie remembers well about hunting ginseng and making ginseng tea. She said, "We went up what we call the Pump Hollow one time, it's down there near the forks of the creek. We used to go ginseng hunting in that hollow. We did not want to come back down the hollow. Bynum Feltman, he stacked rocks up beside the bluff and we climbed up those rocks he had stacked up to the top of the ridge. Oh, a long time ago we hunted a lot of ginseng."

**Medicine Woman**

During the early settlements of the Warrior Mountains, people depended on medicinal plants and home remedies. One of the best medicine women I have heard about is Mary Tennessee Garrison Spillers. According to her daughter Mattie, "We took ginseng for medicine. I got a box full in there now that my boy dug. It's a good nerve medicine. But you know now people won't use the old remedies. They just run to the doctor. Run to the doctor! If I could get out and get my own medicines, I believe I'd get better. You make a tea out of ginseng. You boil the roots, drink the tea, and it's good for your nerves. You don't boil the ginseng roots long. The ginseng tea does not have much taste at all."

The Will Spillers family also used ginger tea out of the ginger root and whiskey. Mattie said, "Mother used old timey remedies back then and they did not go to the doctor every time they got sick. We growed weeds and things that made medicine, we used that. Mother hunted and used Sampsons' snake root, star root, golden seal, pink root, ginseng, and many other plants. She would either place the roots in whiskey or make a tea from the roots for medicines. She made bear grass and potato poultices for making risens come to a head. The potatoes were scraped and placed in the poultice. The potato poultice was one of the best things I ever used for risens. She would roll onions in a wet rag and roast in the fireplace. The onions would be covered up with hot ashes until they were roasted. The roasted onions would be given to the babies to make them rest good at night."

"My mother, if she found a snake asked in the woods or anywhere she would gather it up and bring it to the house. It was good to draw a risen to a head. The snake skin was the best thing to draw a risen. She would wet the shed and place it on top of the sore. She kept her snake sheds. She would also bring hornets' nest to the house. Hornets nests were good for a sick stomach. She would put the nest in water and let it soak and we would drink the water off the nest. She kept all sich as that, her medicine. We didn't run to the doctor. We had all kinds of plants that growed to make medicine. Momma taught us all that, we didn't run to the doctor."

Mattie says, "I growed my garlic and all my medicine things along the edge of the yard but they let it grow up and died and I can't do much hoeing. My garlic was good for high blood pressure. Some folks drink garlic tea for their blood. If I was not afeered I'd turn over and could not get up, I would drag my chair out there and clean the weeds out of my plants. But my garlic is just about all gone and I can't help it. Jimson weed used to grow out there. When you had the piles, you could use the jimson weed for make a poultice. I don't know whether you know or not, hemorrhoids is what some people called it. I also had a mint that growed right out there. When you had a sick stomach, you could break off some of the mint, and put in a glass of water and let it set a little while. After you drank that mint water, it would just drop all the sick stomach.

Mary Tennessee. always raised her own tobacco and smoked her corncob pipe. The tobacco patch was near the house. Mattie said her mother would have her children catching worms off her tobacco. All of Mattie's sisters except one also dipped snuff. Mattie never did smoke a pipe. Mattie said, "My daddy did not use tobacco no which away. My daddy made some wildcat whiskey which got him sent off for having a still on his place. After he served his time, daddy never did make any more but would occasionally drink some. Maw would burn some whiskey and give to us children for bowel trouble and anything. She would set the whiskey on fire before giving it to us. Maw always kept her bottle full of whiskey. She would pour some whiskey in a saucer and strike a match to it until it had a pretty blaze.

**Mattie's Neighbors**

In the early days of the Warrior Mountains, the isolated families developed close friendships. Ms. Mattie Spillers Flanagin remembers some close neighbors of her family. Some of the close neighbors in the King Cove area were Andrew Feltman, Nathan Webb, Bill Garrison, and Tom Feltman who lived close to the Will Spillers place. Mattie said, "People in the surrounding area would come to our place and bring their guitars, banjos, and fiddles and make music. All the folks would have a big dance. "We would have a good time back then. Sometimes we would just get out in the yard and have a big gathering."

The Stephensons lived at Kinklock Springs when Mattie was a small girl. She could not remember their names. Mattie said, "I have been in the old Hubbard house many times. It was the prettiest old house you ever saw. Fireplaces were upstairs; it was a big old house. The house was painted white. The house was all together with bedrooms and the kitchen off to one side. The Bates, Maxwells, and other families lived near the old Hubbard house but they are all dead and gone now. The Mayhaws were also Cherokee Indian descendants and they lived over near Kinlock Springs."

Mattie knew Lawson Hubbard and his children, Luther, Robert, Ida and all of them. She said they used to come here and help kill, dress, and fix their hogs. Lawson Hubbard would not eat at your table. Mattie's folks would have to carry him some food out under the trees in the yard. He would not come in and eat at the table. Lawson lived about one mile north of where Mattie lives today.

According to Ms. Mattie, "Old man Bracken Gilbreath was Prue's daddy. His wife died in the asylum and he was crazy. Millard married Prue's sister Dorothy Gilbreath. Millard and Dorothy had Agnus, Hattie, William, and Mildred." Sary, Millards's sister, first married Prue Gilbreath and had three children, Carrie, Luke, and Authur.

Part of Mary Tennessee Garrison's folks lived close to the cove. According to Mattie, "Uncle Sherman Garrison lived pretty close, and uncle Bill Garrison left the forest and moved to Tennessee because he had children that moved out there. Martin Garrison's folks lived east of King Cove on top of the ridge. We would climb the bluff and go over to their house. They lived just north of Bee Branch."

*Mary Tennessee and Amos' daughter, Christine (not the child of Synthia).*

"I remember the Beaver's Sawmill in White Oak Hollow. Amos and Synthia lived in one of the old sawmill houses for a while. Millard also lived down there for a long time. Millard did not work long at the sawmill. There was colored folks that worked at the sawmill. There were a lot of houses scattered from way down the creek plum up to the bluff mostly on the west side of Thompson Creek. The sawmill was right at the bottom of the White Oak Hollow. Amos worked for the sawmill for a pretty good while. We had a ladder we went up and down from the houses on top of the ridge down to the sawmill. The old wooden ladder was laying against the bluff and was a quick route to the mill."

According to Mattie, "Mr. Beavers had a boy that married Millie Hagood. They moved off to Florida and he died. He wanted his body burned. Well her uncle went to Florida, burned the Beavers boy's body, and moved her back to the cove. She was buried at Macedonia Cemetery. Eventually the Beavers family moved off and I do not know where they moved."

**Memories of Aunt Jenny**

Ms. Mattie Spillers Flanagin recalls her memories of the family of Aunt Jenny Brooks. Mattie said, "Lord how mercy yes, I knew Aunt Jenny Brooks. I still got her picture in there under my bed. They said she was over a hundred years old when she died. I stayed all night with Aunt Jenny a many a night. My mother done her washing and things. We would go up there when Jesse had to go off. Jesse would come get momma to go up there and stay all night with Aunt Jenny. Aunt Jenny used to be at our house for a week at a time. Jesse was Aunt Jenny's daughter-in-law, Henry's wife."

Mattie relates the following, "When Henry got killed, I went up there to see him. One shot went through the front of his mouth knocking out his two front gold teeth. They shot his teeth plum out and his hat looked like a sifter. They was so many of them that shot and they all shot at once, they killed his horse. He was one legged, you know, he just had one leg. He was at the still but he would go around and hunt stills and report them to the sheriff and making whiskey his self."

"Price Peoples, the old boy did not ever hurt nobody, was just an orphan boy and was staying with Mr. Feltman's folks. He was out hunting their cows and Henry Brooks shot Price. The bullet went in the back of his shoulder and it did not kill him. They got the doctor there. Henry just shot him and I do not know why. Price never messed with the still, he was just a poor orphan boy and stayed with Mr. Feltman's folks. After the shooting, they went in on old Henry and killed him. Price had not got well but he had come to maws to stay all night. Price said he heard the guns when they killed Henry. Old man Will Sanford brought Henry out from the still in his wagon."

It has been said that Andrew Feltman and Lawson Hubbard helped load Henry Brooks in the wagon. Mattie did not get to go to Henry's funeral, but just went up to the house after they got him out of the woods. Lawrence Garrison came and carried Mattie and her mother to see Henry Brooks after he was killed. Lawrence carried Mattie and her mother to Aunt Jenny's house in a one horse buggy. When Mattie and her mother got to Aunt Jenny's house, there was hardly anyone at the home where Henry Brooks was laid out. According to Mattie, Henry Brooks was killed across the road from Macedonia Church, down in a little hollow at his whiskey still.

Will Sanford lived just south of Macedonia Church on the same side of the road as the church. Mattie said the old house place has grown up now and does not look like anyone had ever lived there. According to Ms. Mattie, it was thought that Will Sanford had something to do with the death of Henry Brooks because of his wife. Some have speculated that Will Sanford had reported Henry Brooks to the sheriff. Whoever setup Henry Brooks, well Will Sanford would up marrying Henry Brooks' widow, Jesse.

*Aunt Jenny (1/2 Cherokee)*

Mattie said, "I remembered when Aunt Jenny died but I had the measles and could not go to the funeral. Aunt Jenny would come stay with us a week at a time. She was the goodest old thing you ever saw." Mattie's husband, Rufus Flanagin, went to the funeral, but Mattie was too sick to attend. Aunt Jenny had served as a midwife for Mattie's sister, Delie Spillers Feltman, and delivered her children. Delie Spillers married Bob Feltman and they had a "bunch of children."

## Mattie and Rufus

Couples isolated in the Warrior Mountains usually married young and did not court for extended periods. Such was the case with Mattie Spillers and Rufus Flanagin, who met near the King Cove in the present day Sipsey Wilderness Area. Mattie said, "I met my husband at what they called the Government Pasture. Amos, Synthia, and I went to the area cow hunting. Everybody put their cows in the pasture to be run through the dipping vat to kill ticks. They would gather up all the cows in the area and dip them. I met Rufus over at the pasture that day."

*Rufus Flanagin*

After meeting Mattie, Rufus came into the area and lived with Mattie's sister, Ruby, and her "old man." After courting awhile, Rufus and Mattie slipped off to Cullman and got married. They were married at the Cullman County Courthouse on October 30, 1924. Ms. Mattie said, "I had to try to slip away from home to get married. So we caught the train to Cullman and got married."

After getting married, the couple lived near the Northwest Road west of Thompson Creek on top of the hill, just before you start down to the Thompson Creek Bridge. They rented an old house near the cove from the government. The old house was eventually torn down. Mattie said, "Three of my kids were born down there in the old house at the cove. The rent was not much but my husband got this place on the Byler Road from Mr. Hagood and he wanted to move up here."

Rufus (Roof) Flanagin's parents were Jim and Fannie Flanagin. They were buried at the Landersville Cemetery. Rufus Flanagin was born on October 6, 1888, and died September 6, 1943. He served his country as a private in the 334 Field Artillery of the 87 Division and is buried in Macedonia Cemetery.

Rufus and Mattie's family went to church at Macedonia. Mattie said, "My boy Bud and Ammon Whittiker would go all the way to Mountain Springs to church. Ammon was a good church man. Old man Blake was one of our preachers at Macedonia."

Mattie would take her family to the Ship Rock or Herron Point. Mattie said, "I have been up on top of the rock. Me and my kids would go to that rock to come through the windows where you could come from one side of the ridge to the other. One time we went up there and Ed Feltman was going to come down a tree from the top of the rock. He tore his breeches plum off sliding down that tree. There ain't many places down there but what I wouldn't."

"While we lived near the cove, we farmed a lot of corn down there next to the forks of the creek. The corn field was located right at the forks. We would pack our bucket of dinner and carry it with us. If it come up a rain, we had the old Hook Rock House to get under and there was a good spring at the bluff."

Mattie and Roof Flanagin built the house where Mattie still lives in during the 1940's. Roof had loaned Emmitt Hagood some money and he never was able to pay him back; therefore, Emmitt gave Rufus the place on the Byler Road to clear his debt. Roof then bought some more land from old man, Lou Magby.

When Rufus died in 1943, he just about had his log house completed. Rufus wanted to live in a log cabin. His wife and the kids helped him cut, peel, and lay the pine logs. Mattie said, "The house has just about fell down but it is still home."

Mattie helped her husband while they were building their house. Mattie said she would hold boards while Rood would nail on the ceiling boards. The house was built by her and her husband's own hands and she dearly loves the old place. Mattie wants to die at the home she loves so dearly because of all the good memories.

**Trips to Town and to Visit**

During the early settlement days of the Warrior Mountains, trips to town or to visit friends and relatives were at least a two day affair. Traveling by horse and buggy or in a wagon usually required people to stay overnight unless they were willing to travel after dark. Ms. Mattie Spillers Flanagin describes in her own words about a trip to town. Mattie said, "We did not go to town too often and usually stayed all night when we did. We would go in the wagon and come back the next day. You could get stuff cheap back then."

*Mattie Spillers Flanagin with her old hoe she uses as a walking stick.*

The local store was about ½ mile north of the Byler Road and Northwest Road junction. The store was owned by Mr. Joe Sandlin. Amos Spillers bought the place when Mr. Sandlin moved to Haleyville. The post office was close to the store at a small road which turns to the east. The post office was in Mr. Brock's house.

Mattie said, "It was a long, long time after we built our house before getting electricity in the mountains. We could just use old coal oil lamps and I still got them. I bought coal oil at Mr. Sandlin's store. Mr. Sandlin was a great big fleshy man. The store had one big room made out of planks. He sold about everything but gasoline, there was no such thing as a car when Mr. Sandlin owned the store."

After Joe Sandlin stopped running the store, Mattie said, "We would have to go farther down the road to Mr. Southern's store. We did not use much out of the store. We could buy salt and a barrel of flour."

*From the rocky glade on top of Ship Rock, visitors view the upper portion of Sipsey River Canyon.*

### Jack McDowell

Occasionally, Mattie and Roof would go to McDowell Cove to visit Jack and Sally. Most of the time, Mattie and Roof would stay all night. Sally was kin to Mattie since her daddy was a brother to Will Spillers. Sally Spillers McDowell was the daughter of Jim Spillers. According to Mattie, "Amos was fixing to carry the family over on Caney Fork to clean off our grandfather Garrison's grave just before he got killed in the wreck. I never did get to see my grandfather Garrison's grave. Steve Garrison was Buck's brother and both of them are buried side by side.

Jack McDowell carried tombstones over to the cemetery to place on their graves. Jack McDowell was just a good person who helped the family out. Jack worked for the Forest Service when Amos was the game warden."

William Spillers was Mattie's granddaddy and he is buried just above the Jack McDowell house in the Wallis Cemetery. Mattie does not remember her grandmother Spillers, but she is buried in the Rock Springs Cemetery at Mt. Hope.

**Mattie's Story Concludes**

Another chapter closes on the families of the Warrior Mountains. The following is the final segment as told by Ms. Mattie Spillers Flanagin.

Roof and Mattie had seven children: Mattie's first boy born, 1/13/1924, died 11/19/1924, was named Calvin Coolidge, after the president, by her brother Amos Spillers; James (Bud) Flanagin was born 8/16/1927 and died 1/12/1986; J.C. (Jay) Flanagin was born 6/23/1930 and died 1/10/1993; Frances Pauline Flanagin was born 12/25/1932 and drowned 6/6/1952; Burley Dennis Flanagin was born 10/30/1936 and died 5/31/1990; and two living daughters Gladys Flanagin Butler and Flourine Flanagin Black, Rufus Flanagin, daughter Pauline, and four boys are buried at Macedonia Cemetery.

Pauline drowned at Kinlock Falls when she was a beautiful 19 year old teenager. Pauline went to the falls to go in swimming with Mattie's sister and her children. Pauline went down and never came back up. She was just wading along holding to her cousin's shoulder and Gene Harris.

Roof worked here and there, including Florida, until he got one of his eyes put out in a factory. He helped put some of the first electrical lines in the forest and also drove a school bus for Mt. Hope School. All of the children that lived on the Byler Road portion of the mountain rode Roof's bus. The bus went as far as Mr. Sanford's place just past Macedonia Church. Mattie and Roof's children went to Mt. Hope. One of Mattie's girls and one of her boys finished at Mt. Hope.

Mattie Spillers Flanagin will be 86 on November 1, 1993, but says she will not have a birthday party because she has got "sugar and could not eat." Doc Kelly told Mattie to have a big birthday cake. Mattie said, "I told him I cannot eat cake. I will be at home when I have my birthday this year."

Mattie uses her hoe as a walking stick. Mattie proudly tells that Jay fixed her that hoe to help her get around. On Labor Day of September 6, 1993, I stopped by to talk with Ms. Mattie again. She pulled her chair out to the edge of her yard. She was setting in her chair hoeing her herbs that grew on the edge of her yard. As usual, Ms. Mattie was barefooted cause she does not like to wear shoes.

Mattie said she was not going back to Haleyville and she intends to remain at home for the rest of her days. Not long ago, Ms. Mattie fell and broke her arm and her youngest son moved her to Haleyville. Mattie said, "I do not like down there and I plan to come home this year."

When I talked with Ms. Mattie both times, she was always barefooted and had a dip of snuff in her mouth. She said snuff is a bad thing but growing up in the forest she never worried about having worms. Ms. Mattie said she started dipping snuff when she was seven years old and has been dipping ever since.

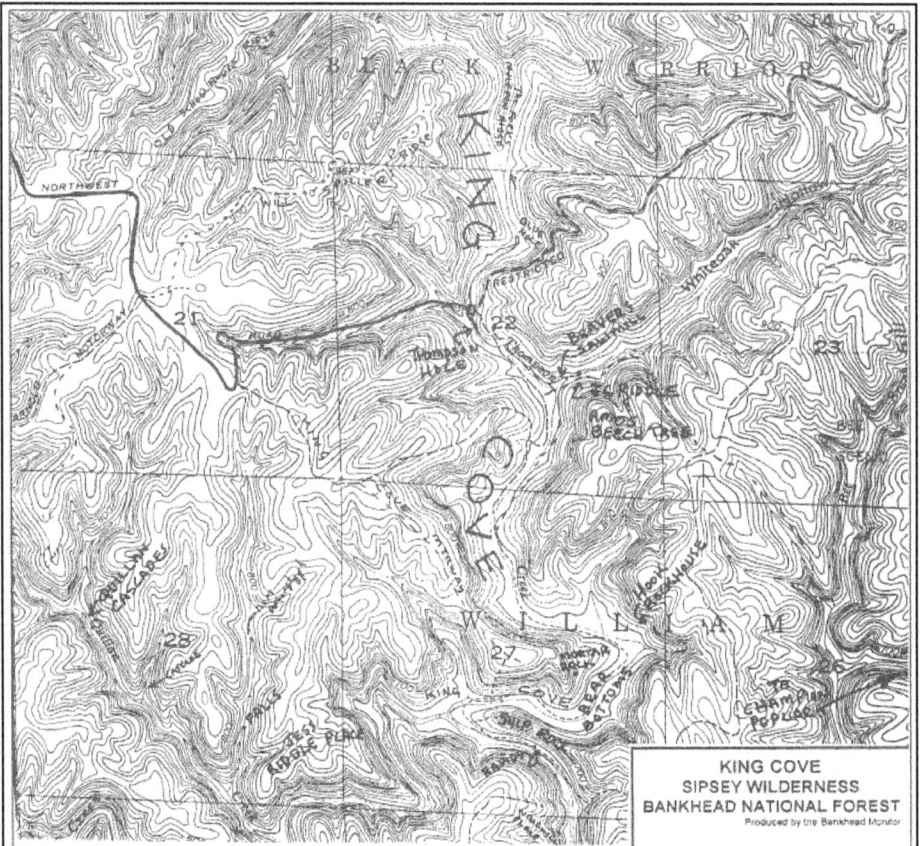

Mattie's mother also dipped snuff and smoked her pipe. Mattie still cherishes her mother's old pipe. Jay, Mattie's son, still has one of Mary Tennessee's old corn cob pipes. Mattie said, "I am old and not able to take good care of things, but I love to see my old things." Thus, the beautiful story ends about Ms. Mattie Spillers Flanagin, who lived and loved the "Warrior Mountains."

# Jane (Jenny) Brooks Johnston Family of Byler Road

On October 10, 1990, I stood in the front of the tombstone of Jane (Aunt Jenny) Brooks Johnston, located in Poplar Springs Cemetery in Bankhead National Forest. The cemetery is in southwest Lawrence County some four and one-half miles from the Winston County line to the south, and one-half miles from the Franklin County line to the west. As I stood there thinking about Aunt Jenny and my own daughters who were with me, I could not truly comprehend the pain and grief she must have felt by witnessing the death and burial of all nine of her children and her two husbands. Aunt Jenny was truly a lady who had to deal with heavy emotional burdens and the death of loved ones throughout her life. Aunt Jenny was finally released from her life of sorrows on March 29, 1924, at the age of ninety-eight.

*Aunt Jenny's grave at Poplar Springs Cemetery.*

The home place of Aunt Jenny, for some eighty-six years, is one of the most historical and beautiful places in Lawrence County's Bankhead National Forest. Her home was located on the east side of the forks of the Byler and Kinlock roads in the southwestern portion of Lawrence County. The area is noted for the magnificent Kinlock Falls, the tremendous narrow canyon of Hubbard Creek which runs for a few miles below the falls, the beautiful white sandstone outcroppings, the plunging rapids of Quillan Creek to the east, the falls of Parker Branch to the south, and Bear Creek to the west.

The area, which is along the Continental Divide in Lawrence County and separates the waters of the Sipsey and Tennessee River, was the route of two noted Indian trails – the High Town Path and the "Old Buffalo Trail." The particular portion of the Indian paths became the famous Byler Road, the connecting route of Nashville, Tennessee to Tuscaloosa, Alabama. The Byler Road, the first road approved by the State of Alabama on December 16, 1819, was built by John Byler who is buried at Mt. Hope. His son-in-law, William McCain, operated the toll gate and lived about one-half mile north of Aunt Jenny, just west of the forks of Byler and Northwest Roads.

One of the largest and most beautiful sandstone rock shelters, which provided the early Indian people a home and protection from the weather, is located just west of Kinlock Road. The Kinlock Rock Shelter is within some two miles of Aunt Jenny's home place. The rock shelter, existing as a memorial to prehistoric Indian life, contains some of the best known petroglyphs (Indian rock drawings) of the area.

To the west of the home place about a mile is Bear Creek, which eventually flows into the Tennessee River. Quillan Creek is a mile to the east of the Brooks home place and lies entirely within the Sipsey Wilderness Area. In my opinion, Quillan Creek is one of the most beautiful streams in Bankhead Forest. Hubbard Creek is south of Aunt Jenny's old home about two miles. Kinlock Falls is on Hubbard Creek. Hubbard Creek was named after the Hubbard family who settled the area prior to the 1820's. Green K. Hubbard, son of Thomas Hubbard, surveyed and originally purchased the area around Kinlock Falls. He later sold the falls area to his brother, David Hubbard who used Kinlock as his summer home and built a grist mill at Kinlock Falls.

On May 29, 1933, Company 1403 CCC (organized at Fort Benning, Georgia) arrived at their Kinlock Camp in Bankhead Forest. Kinlock CCC, one of the best known of the Bankhead Camps, had its headquarters in Major David Hubbard's home. Major Hubbard had been the Federal Commissioner of Indian Affairs for the Confederate States of America. His home was a large two storied house and was used by both the Army and Forest Service as headquarters. The beautiful home and headquarters was destroyed by fire in November, 1935. The military style work camp was maintained for several years before congress abolished all CCC camps in 1942.

**Aunt Jenny**

According to <u>The Legend of Aunt Jenny Brooks</u> by Thomas C. Pettus, Jane Bates, daughter of the prominent Bates family of Walker and Jefferson Counties was born on January 22, 1826. She was one-half Cherokee Indian. At the young age of fourteen she married Willis Brooks at Jasper, Alabama.

Jane (Aunt Jenny) Bates Brooks and her husband, Willis, first appear in the Lawrence County Census records in 1850. At that time they had three children – John, five years old; Angeline, three years old; and Mack, two years old. Aunt Jenny and Willis had six other children:

Amanda, 1850; Willis, Jr., 1853; Donna (Donie), 1855; Gainam, 1860; Henry, 1862; and Frances (Fannie), 1863.

According to Mr. Rayford Hyatt (noted historian of Bankhead Forest), about 1838, Willis and Jane Brooks bought 40 acres at the forks of Byler and Kinlock Roads from John W. Blackwell who had originally purchased the land in 1836. Mr. Blackwell eventually moved into Winston County and served two terms as probate judge from 1850-1856 and again in 1862.

According to <u>Old Land Records of Lawrence County</u> by Margaret Cowart, Willis Brooks entered 120 acres of land in Section 19 of Township 8 South and Range 9 West on October 22, 1855. Later, after marrying Jacob S. Johnston, Aunt Jenny entered an additional 80 acres of land in Sections 18 and 19.

*Aunt Jenny (1/2 Cherokee).*

Prior to the Civil War, the closest neighbors of Willis and Jane was the David Hubbard family who owned a summer home at Kinlock. The Hubbard family also had black slaves that used the Hubbard name. They were evidently caretakers of David Hubbard's home site and stayed in the forest at the conclusion of the Civil War. Many of the Hubbard blacks still call Lawrence County home. The William Hubbard home place was about one mile south of Aunt Jenny on Kinlock Road.

North of Aunt Jenny's home place, about one-half mile, was the home of William McCanin. He owned some forty acres of land between the Byler Road and Bear Creek. His land joined the Brooks place.

**Civil War Comes to Aunt Jenny**

Things with the Brooks family and the area appeared to move along quite smoothly until the Civil War broke out. Wilderness life in the mountains was tough enough raising nine children without complicating matters with war; however, the problems of war was brought to the home of Willis and Jane Brooks.

Willis and Jane Brooks were like other mountain families who had to work hard and struggle to provide for their family. Even though they lived in one of the most beautiful areas of Bankhead Forest, conflicts of the Civil War brought death and destruction to their front yard. During the war, from 1861 to 1865, at least three large groups of Federal troops (Yankees) passed along the Byler Road within a few feet of Aunt Jenny's front door; however, the precise events that claimed the lives of Willis and John Brooks will probably never be known. The deaths of the Brooks men in 1864 caused turmoil and grief in Aunt Jenny's home for many years to come. The deaths also caused a tremendous amount of speculation of several writers concerning the cause and effect on the remaining Brooks brothers.

Three versions of the fatal day in 1864 are told: In the first version, according to "Stars Fell on Alabama," Confederate soldiers, known as the home guard, were forcing men to join the army and take up arms against their northern brothers. Willis and his oldest son, John, resisted and fought to remain at home. Both Willis and John L. Brooks were probably shot and killed at home in front of their family.

The second version was printed in the April 3, 1924, issue of the Moulton Advertiser. Willis, who had been a soldier in the Mexican War, attempted to enlist with the South at the outbreak of the Civil War, but was refused because of his age. When the war came to North Alabama, he gained entrance and fought in numerous battles. Upon returning home, he learned his wife had been harassed by another man. Willis eventually killed the man, starting a feud with the dead man's family which lasted about sixty years. First, Willis Brooks was killed and later his son, John, was murdered and thrown into a sink hole.

The third version, according to family legend, relates that Willis and his son were killed by Yankees, probably those in route to take the grain and meal stored at Kinlock. The Yankees were probably planning to destroy the grist mill at Kinlock, or anything in their path; however, fighting broke out resulting in the deaths of several Yankee soldiers.

After the Battle of Shiloh on April 6-7, 1862, Union forces were occupying places in northwest Alabama, with guerrilla type warfare occurring along major routes such as the Byler Road through Bankhead Forest.

According to the "Annals of Northwest Alabama," in one such skirmish, a group of local citizens ambushed a foraging party detached by Colonel Abel Streight (Commanding Officer of the 51st Indiana Regiment) near old Granada – Aunt Jenny's home place. The ambushers poured a heavy volume of fire from both sides of the road into the ranks of the Federals, killing several men and driving the others off.

Aunt Jenny was said to have aided in the burial of the Federals. Some folks believe the Yankees were given descent burials in the black Hubbard cemetery at Kinlock.

It is very probable that Willis and John L. Brooks were killed while fighting the Yankees and trying to protect their loved ones, home, and property. In any event, all versions point to the fact that the result of the Civil War was either directly or indirectly responsible for the deaths of Aunt Jenny's husband and son. Therefore, I believe that Willis and John were killed by Yankees, exactly as Aunt Jenny had described to her remaining children and others.

**Death of the Brooks Boys**

Some previous writers have portrayed the whole Brooks family as an outlaw gang. These authors try to justify isolated, and apparently unrelated (to the deaths of Willis and John) acts of violence carried out by Aunt Jenny's sons and grandsons as a continuing feud or as a gang related event.

I believe the Brooks brothers were brought up in a time of war and had trouble accepting the violent deaths of their daddy and older brother. These early problems carried over to the post-war period where violence was their answer and in most cases the final solution.

Several events seemed to be connected with Bankhead's most famous tragedy that was responsible for the death of Willis and John Brooks. Each version seems to confirm the following: the deaths of Willis and John was directly or indirectly related to the Civil War; several of Aunt Jenny's outbuildings and probably her home were destroyed by fire; both men were shot to death; their death began a long period of violence and gun fighting for the younger Brooks boys and even some of the grandsons of Willis and Jane; and in the end, Aunt Jenny claimed "my sons died with their boots on."

Shortly after the death of Willis Brooks, Aunt Jenny married Jacob Stauder Johnston. Johnston who also had children, moved in and lived at Aunt Jenny's home. In addition to raising her own nine children, Aunt Jenny accepted the responsibility of helping raise step-children as well as many of her own grandchildren. The famous lady of Bankhead was always there when her family was in need, and did all she could to help her neighbors and friends. She served as a midwife to an herb doctor and was on call 24 hours a day. Folks learned quickly, if she liked you, she would do anything she could for you, but if she disliked you, be very careful.

Aunt Jenny's forest home in Bankhead became a place of sorrow, beginning as a result of the Civil War and continuing nearly sixty years. The following is a brief chronological description of the death and violence of Aunt Jenny's sons, son-in-law, and grandsons.

*Gainum Brooks (1/4 Cherokee).*

After the deaths of Willis and John Brooks, Mack was killed. Mack Brooks was born in 1843 and the events concerning his deaths are unknown. He is listed in the 1870 Census; therefore, he was killed after 1870.

Aunt Jenny's son, Gainam, was a noted crack shot and feared throughout the country. Gainam was shot and killed in a gunfight with the Hubbard blacks on April 12, 1884. The feeling among the black folks concerning the gunfight appeared to be "kill or get killed." At the young age of 24, Gainam was shot to death in the yard of William Hubbard, a black man. He was supposedly killed by Henry Hubbard, William's son, with a breech-loading shotgun. That night most of the Hubbard blacks moved from the mountains with all eventually leaving Bankhead. All of the William Hubbard's family moved to North Courtland area of the valley in Lawrence County. Wash Hubbard's family stayed on in the forest after the gunfight. All the black Hubbards have many descendants still living in the Courtland, Tharptown, and Haleyville areas of North Alabama.

After the gunfight with the Hubbards, Aunt Jenny's remaining sons, at least one daughter, and some grandsons moved to Indian Territory in the west where gunfights continued to take their toll on the Brooks family.

Aunt Jenny's son, Willis Jr., and her grandson, Clifton, were killed in September 1902, by the McFarlands at Spokogee, Indian Territory. Aunt Jenny's grandson, John, was also shot through and through but survived. This was the second major confrontation the Brooks boys had with the McFarlands.

Sam Baker, who was supposedly Frances Brooks' husband and Aunt Jenny's son-in-law, first rode with the Brooks boys and later served as a deputy. Eventually, Sam, killed several notorious gunmen. Sam Baker was killed in October 1911 over an account with a businessman in Muskogee, Oklahoma.

*Carl Sammans (left) and John Burl Sammans (right). The sons of Donie Brooks Sammans were 1/8 Cherokee.*

In 1920, Aunt Jenny's last remaining son, Henry, was killed at his moonshine still located not far from his old Bankhead home place. Henry had one leg due to a previous gunfight would which caused his leg to amputated.

As many of our ancestors struggling to survive on mountain land, moonshine whiskey was made and sold as a means of survival. Making moonshine whiskey usually brought trouble with the law; however, in the case of Henry Brooks, the law brought a quick end to the trade. Even today, there is still speculation as to the manner Henry Brooks was gunned down.

**Sammans**

Two other grandsons of Aunt Jenny, Carl and John Sammans, were charged with murder. Both Aunt Jenny and the heirs of her daughter, Donie Sammans, transferred some of their land in Bankhead to pay for Earl and John's lawyer. Attorney R.L. Almon of Moulton conveyed the Brooks' land to pay the attorney's fees of John A. Deweese in Denver, Colorado. Aunt Jenny's grandsons were eventually acquitted of murder on February 25, 1922.

*Donie Brooks Sammans (1/4 Cherokee).*

The Sammans brothers were the sons of Donie Brooks Sammans. Donis is listed on her tombstone at Poplar Springs as being born on October 18, 1848; however, census records show she was born in 1855. Donie died on January 1, 1905. Before her death, she was postmaster at Grenada from January 10, 1894 to March 25, 1903. The post office was in her home and was located across the road from her mother's place – Aunt Jenny.

At Donie's death her youngest daughter, Dora, was only eight years old. Dora moved in with her grandmother, Jenny, who was 80 years old at the time. Aunt Jenny was a truly remarkable woman who cared for her family through the years.

Old Macedonia Church and Cemetery — Aunt Jenny donated the land for the Macedonia Church and Cemetery. Before she died, Aunt Jenny became a christian and joined the old church.

According to Dora's son, Mr. Ottice Abbott, his mother lived with Aunt Jenny for some eight years. Ottice's mother told him of having to get up at all hours of the night to milk the old cow. Aunt Jenny or Dora heard the bell ringing; they would get up and milk before the cow wandered off. The cows roamed an open range and usually wore a neck collar and bell to aid in locating the animal. Dora Sammans married Ben Abbott when she was 16 years old and moved from Aunt Jenny's home. Most of the Abbott family eventually moved to the Mt. Hope area.

During my visit to Mr. Abbott's home, he and his cousin said, "People use to go to the mountains and have their fortune told by an old black man – Lawson Hubbard." Many of the Hubbard and Brooks descendants still call Lawrence County home. In her later years, Aunt Jenny donated two acres of land for a church, became a Christian, and joined a Missionary Baptist Church at Macedonia. When once questioned by a storekeeper about a large sum of money she carried she replied, "I pay myself twenty dollars a week just to tend to my own business." Aunt Jenny's remarkable and colorful life continues to be a vital part of our beloved history of the "Warrior Mountains."

# The Riddle Family of Sipsey

In this riddle of the Riddle Family, the following is an explanation of the story of this mysterious Indian family's beginning in the Warrior Mountains of Bankhead National Forest. Early in the 1800's with the threat of removal to the west affecting many Indian people, the Warrior Mountains provided protective refuge in the vast expanse of hills, hollows, canyons, bluffs, and coves scattered across the Sipsey portion of the eastern wilderness.

## Sipsey Indian Land

Indian claims to the land were acquired from 1814 through 1816 by numerous treaties made and broken by the U.S. Government. During this time of turmoil, Rake Riddle's, a full-blood Cherokee Indian, made his home near the rough country of Sipsey River. His folks settled near the present day Lawrence – Winston County lines on the upper portion of Sipsey River. It is not real clear if other family members also

*Tombstone of Rake Riddle located in McLemore Cemetery. The stone has a sunflower carved in the top.*

settled the Sipsey country with Rake Riddle, but it is certain that a number of Indian and mixed-blood Indian families settled in the same area. It appears that Rake probably married a mixed-blood Indian woman because all of their children were considered to be Cherokee Indians.

## Pigeon Roost Cove to King Cove

From a couple miles south of the present day Lawrence County line where Davis Creek flows into Sipsey River at a cove known as Pigeon Roost, to the upper portion of Sipsey River at King Cove, the Riddle family made their land claims to the Warrior Mountains. The Riddle Cherokees hid out in the coves deep in the upper Sipsey River portion of the Warrior Mountains to avoid removal to the West. Most of the Riddles and their descendants that inhabit Lawrence and Winston Counties are direct descendants of Cherokee Indians. Old timers say that some members of the Riddle Family were actually removed to the West on the Trail of Tears in 1838.

According to one family legend, soldiers came to remove the Riddle Cherokees from their eastern homelands. A fight ensued with the killing of some soldiers and the capture of at least one Riddle who was the brother of Rake. He eventually escaped the forced removal group and made his way back to the protective coves along the Sipsey River.

Since, Rake Riddle was already in Sipsey country by 1835, it is highly possible that some of his Indian family and friends could have sought refuge in the Warrior Mountains with him during the 1838 removal known at the Trail of Tears. During the Spring of 1838, soldiers under the command of General Winfield Scott began the forced removal of Cherokees east of the Mississippi River. While forcing Indian people against their will into stockades, conflict occurred between soldiers and Indians. One such incident could have easily occurred between the soldiers and members of the Riddle family.

*Ronal Boyles, Adell Riddle, John White, Lawrence Garrison, Edsel Riddle, John Little, Johnny Warren, Garvin Garrison, Drenon Garrison, Trannie Little (Riddle), Lillian Garrison (Riddle), Therron Garrison, Ella White (Garrison), Sarrah Jane Garrison (Blankenship) (Sook), Synathia Spillars (Garrison), Trannie Warren, Fennell Warren, Lellar Spillars (Riddle), Erie Boyles (LouAllen), Mae Garrison (McDowell), Nenivar Garrison.*

## Rake's Family

According to the 1850 Winston County Census, Rake and his wife, Martha, probably had seven children and a daughter-in-law. The Winston County Census of 1850 includes the following members of the Rake Riddle Family: Jonson (Rake), age 45, born in Virginia;

Martha, age 34, born in North Carolina; Jackson, age 25, from Tennessee; was not the child of Martha because she would have been only nine (9) years old when he was born; James C., age 19, from Tennessee, probably married to Eliza and not the child of Martha; Eliza, age 18, from Missouri, probably the wife of James C.; Joseph T., age 15, was probably the first child of Martha listed born in Alabama; William St. (probably Stroud or Straud), age 10 and born in Alabama; Jessie D. (Hook), age 7 and born in Alabama; Thomas S., age 6, Alabama; Elizabeth, age 4, Alabama; and John, age 3, Alabama.

## Devil John I

The Riddles have lived in what is today the Warrior Mountains of Bankhead National Forest since the early 1800s and probably longer. The earliest Riddle with a bad reputation that we have records of in this area was John, the son of Jonson (Rake) Riddle who was a full-blood Cherokee. John, Rake's youngest son, was known as Devil John because he was a mean man. The history of John is not real clear. It is thought that his name was John Manuel Riddle. If this true, John's wife was Cathlene James. John Manuel Riddle also names his son John and he became Devil John II.

Devil John was a legend among the modern-day people of Bankhead. One story has it that a man named George Townsend came to kill Devil John, but John shot him off his mule. Devil John was arrested and placed in the old jail in Double Springs. His wife came to the jail and asked, "When are they going to hang you, John?" "I guess when they get a scaffold and a rope," Devil John answered.

Before the scaffold and rope were ready, John's older brother, Jessie, and two other boys slipped dynamite into this cell and blew out the jail house wall. After hiding out in Tennessee for a long time, John came back for a hearing which was held to determine if he acted in self-defense. Some people believe John was freed because bricks and mortar were too expensive to risk incarcerating him a second time.

## Devil John II

Another notorious grandson of Rake Riddle, and son of John Manuel Riddle, was John Riddle who married Dicey Garrison. John was also known as Devil John because of his character. This John was born about 1878 and married Dicey on the 30th day of April, 1895.

L-R: *John Riddle (5/16 Cherokee), husband of Dicey Garrison and Lillie Hamby, and Russell McClellan (John's son-in-law).*

Dicey, who was at least ¼ Cherokee, was the half sister of Mary Tennessee Garrison Spillers. According to Mattie Spillers Flanagin, Devil John would shoot at her father's feet just to make him dance. Mattie said John would tell Will Spillers to dance or he would shoot his feet off. John would have shot off her daddy's feet if he had not danced for him.

John and Dicey lived near the forks of the river (the junction of Thompson and Hubbard Creeks). Dicey and John's six children were: James Julius Claude Edgar Riddle; Rhodae Victoria Rosanna Elizabeth Riddle; Artie Georgianna Lovestar Riddle; Luther John Henry Riddle; and Fred Jack (Babe) Riddle. John left Dicey and her six children. Mattie said, "Momma and us went down there and got the poor old thing (Dicey and children). They were about to starve to death. We brought their stuff out in an old two-wheeled ox cart." After moving to Spruce Pine, some people believe that John killed Dicey by putting poison in her food. John was never convicted or questioned about the possible murder of his wife. However, John served several years in prison for killing two revenuers.

After Dicey's death, Devil John married Lillie Hamby on October 22, 1927. Lillie and John had four children: Christine; Obie; Tally; and Herman. Lillie poisoned his wildcat whiskey, thereby ending the life of Devil John. Claude, John's oldest son, had the body of John exhumed. According to the autopsy, John had enough arsenic in his body to kill 18 men. Lillie was tried for murder and eventually sent to prison. In 1968, Lillie Hamby Riddle was given a full pardon by Governor George C. Wallace. Lillie died about 1984.

According to several older women interviewed, some of the mean and cruel men who lived in the Warrior Mountains could get away with abuse and even murder, while their wives were held accountable for their misdeeds. One lady related that the men would always dominate the household by being the first at the table. During the early days women in the Warrior Mountains were somewhat in servitude to the men.

**Hook Riddle**

Jessie Duraney (Hook) Riddle, son of Rake and Martha Riddle, was born in 1843. The following is a listing of the 1870 Census of Winston County, concerning Jessie (Hook) Riddle: Jessie, age 27, born in Alabama; Francis (Fanny) Cornelius, age 26, Alabama; Sarah, age 12, Alabama (Sarah married Jim Bogles); and Jess age five (Jess eventually married Ellen Anderson). In addition to Sara and Jess, Jessie and Fanny also had the following children: Martha Jane (Sis) Riddle, married Issac Buckner Walker; Angeline Riddle, married Hugh Simmons; Naoma Riddle, married Luther Sanders, and Manson (Bud) Alexander Riddle, married Louella Walker.

*Samantha Parker Riddle, wife of William Straud Riddle (1/2 Cherokee).*

Hook's son, Jess, entered land not far from King Cove. According to Old Land Records of Lawrence County, Alabama by Margaret Cowart, Jess R. Riddle entered 120 acres of land just west of Ship Rock on Hubbard Creek. Jess entered the land in King Cove on July 14, 1884.

Within King Cove, a bluff overhand has been named the Hook Rock House Shelter. At one time, Hook lived under the rock shelter, just about ¼ miles from the north end of Bear Bottoms and less than a mile from the mouth of Thompson Creek. The area is presently part of the Sipsey Wilderness Area.

## William Straud Riddle

Rake and Martha had another son named William Straud Riddle, born on December 12, 1841. William Straud Riddle married Samantha Parker who was also ½ Cherokee. They settled on the southwest bluff overlooking Pigeon Roost Cove. Straud and Samantha Parker had the following children: William Riddle, married Amelia Curtis; John T. Riddle, married Winnie Calvert and later Delie Gray; Walter Riddle, married Rosa Riddle and Lydia Clark Thomas; James Calvin Riddle, married three times, (1) Roxana West; (2) Sarah Spillers; and (3) Willie Mae Strawn; Alventine married Monroe Sparks; and Sarah married Jim Mize.

*James Calvin Riddle's home in Pigeon Roost Cove.*

Straud's wife, Samantha Parker, was the daughter of William Parker. She was born on April 30, 1851. Straud and Samantha had eight children, three of whom died young. One of those poor unfortunate who did not survive childhood was called Okla, and he was rumored to be buried in the Parker Cemetery near Borden Creek and the Northwest Road. Samantha died on June 6, 1929, and Straud died shortly after on July 30 of the same year.

Straud lived across Sipsey River from the mouth of Davis Creek where his son, James Calvin's cabin was located. Straud built a road up the bluff and called it Sweaden Gap or Sweeten Gap, and he then built his house on top of the hill. According to Mr. Rayford Hyatt, it was at Sweeten Gap where the first Cheatham Road was to cross the Sipsey River. Matthew Payne lived on the northeast side of the river where the road was to cross; however, Wyatt Cheatham got the road job because of his friendship with Joseph Coe, a State Legislator from Lawrence County.

One story has it that Rake was living with Straud and Samantha when Will was a baby, and then one day the baby was lying on a pallet in the hallway porch when he began to cry. Rake kicked little Will out into the yard, angering Samantha so that she ran Rake off and would not let him live with them anymore.

## James Calvin Riddle

Of all the children of Straud and Samantha, it is James Calvin about whom we know the most. James Calvin Riddle first married Roxanna West, the daughter of Peter M. West and Sara J. Curtis, on April 20, 1902. When James Calvin Riddle and Roxanna West first married, they lived in a log cabin

*Roxanna West (1/4 Cherokee) and James Calvin Riddle (5/8 Cherokee).*

off Cranal Road on top of the hill before going down the ridge into the Sipsey River valley near Davis Creek. Since James Calvin was farming the rich bottoms, he decided to move his family's cabin into Pigeon Roost Cove.

The Cove is located in the Bankhead National Forest where Davis Creek runs into Sipsey River, between Cranal Road and the Wilderness Parkway. According to Judge John B. Weaver, this was the first place where white people lived in what is now Winston County. When Calvin and Roxanna moved their cabin to its new location in the cove, they added another log room, a breezeway, a cook room, and two chimneys. The cabin was built on bench land overlooking the cove, and stood there until it burned in December of 1990.

Calvin was a good rock mason, and he built many chimneys that remain today. Among his surviving structures are the pillars for the mill on Collier Creek, which were built for Sam Ellenburg and later became the Will Riddle Mill.

*James Calvin Riddle (5/8 Cherokee), Sarah Lillian Riddle (Garrison), Roxanna West Riddle and Lelar Riddle.*

Calvin and Anna had six children named Sarah

Lillian, Leonard Fay, Lelar, Trannie, Etsel, and Milton Adell. While they lived in Pigeon Roost, Calvin and Anna's children had to walk about four miles to attend Spiegel School. However, Calvin moved away when Roxanna died on September 30, 1919, and Looney Riddle moved into the Pigeon Roost house. Looney would be the last permanent resident of the cove.

Calvin's second wife, Sarah Spillers, was the daughter of Will Spillers and Mary Tennessee Garrison. Calvin and Sarah moved to the Ben Morgan place. They had a son named Earnest, and Sarah died along with their second baby during childbirth. Ms. Mattie Spillers claimed it was Doctor Blake's fault that her sister died. She said that Amos Spillers agreed to go get Sarah what she wanted from the store. According to Mattie, Sarah was dead by the time Amos returned. Amos and James Calvin were eventually brother-in-laws and probably close friends before Roxanna died. In the mouth of White Oak Hollow about ¼ mile southeast of Thompson Creek Bridge is an American beech tree with the following carvings: J.C. Riddle 1918 Amos.

Calvin's third wife was a widow named Willie Mae Horton. Calvin and Willie had four children named Raymond, Ray, Bob, and Billy. After Calvin died, Willie stayed on the farm that they had owned north of Moreland. As of 1995, when she was 97, she was still active, tending her house and riding the bus to Double Springs to trade. Bob lived with her, and the three other boys lived nearby. Calvin is buried with his first wife, Roxanna, in the Mount Olive Cemetery in Bankhead National Forest.

## Doc Riddle

John Thomas (Doc) Riddle, born on October 3, 1883, was another son of William Straud and Samantha Parker Riddle. Doc first married Winnie Telitha Calvert in Winston County on July 19, 1902. Doc and Winnie had the following children: Issac, Arzula, and Ida, who married Henry Frost. According to family members, Doc was so mean to Winnie and the children that she left him. It was reported that Doc would made Ike chew of the hog weeds if he could not pull them out of the corn patch. Doc would also sometimes chain his children if they did not mind. Doc said if his children acted like dogs, he would treat them like dogs.

*John (Doc) Riddle (5/8 Cherokee), son of William Straud and Samantha Parker Riddle.*

After his first marriage failed, Doc married Cordelia (Delie) Gray, who was full blood Cherokee Indian. Doc and Delie had the following children: Fletcher, Authur, Dollie, Odis, Pearly, and Pinkney.

While living near Wolf Pen on the Cranal Road, Doc went into a rage. Supposedly he took a 12 gauge shotgun and blew off the top of Delie's head while she was holding Pinkney. Delie had started out the backdoor, probably to escape the wrath of Doc. After realizing the tragedy of his horrible actions, Doc went outside and blew off the top of his head. It is said that some family members wanted to leave Doc to rot. It is said that neighbors came by to observe Doc's body as it lay in the yard. In the later afternoon, he had laid in the yard all day, his body was removed. Doc was buried in Mt. Olive, and Delie was buried in Moreland Cemetery. According to the tombstone, Doc died on November 16, 1924.

*Cordelia (Delie) Gray, wife of John (Doc) Riddle (full Cherokee).*

Doc's sister, Alvetine, would not let both Doc and Delie be buried in the same cemetery. She said that Doc was so mean to Delie while she was alive, he would not be near her in death. Alvetine never put flowers on her brother's grave and warned everyone else to keep flowers off Doc's grave. Now in the heart of the Warrior Mountains, Doc's remains are put to rest but most believe his spirit is in torment.

**Will Riddle**

Will Riddle, the oldest son of William Straud and Samantha Parker Riddle, was 5/8 Cherokee Indian. He was born on June 13, 1869, and died on February 4, 1933. Will Riddle married Emma Armelia Curtis, who was born on September 12, 1868. She was the daughter of William V. (Bill) and Martha Jane Lyle Curtis. Bill and Jane had twelve children and lived near the Lawrence – Winston County line on the Cheatham Road. Both Will and Armelia Riddle and her parents Bill and Martha Curtis are buried in Mount Olive Cemetery. Will and Armelia had seven children: Roy Haynes; Lonnie; Lannie; Effie; Evie Riddle (Ellenberg); Mattie Riddle (Gray); and Odis who died.

As mentioned earlier, Rake Riddle kicked Straud and Samantha's baby, Will Riddle, off the porch for crying. Straud was eventually accused of doing the same thing to Will and Amelia's son. According to family history, Will and Amelia really jumped on Straud because of his actions. Some say that Straud never visited Will's home again.

William Straud Riddle (3/4 Cherokee) and Will Riddle, son of Straud (5/8 Cherokee).

Will was also of very strong character. Because of his lifestyle, it is said that he would sleep with a loaded shotgun beside his bed. Will was seldom without a gun. He ate with his shotgun beside his chair with the barrel resting against the table. According to family members, Will never sat with his back to a door or window. For fear of being killed or to kill someone that might attack him during the night, Will would sometimes sleep with the shotgun in his bed.

Will's children told family members how he would whip or beat them with plow lines and sometimes trace chains. Usually, Will would not eat at the same table with his children or grandchildren. Instead he would have his meals brought to him at a small table in the corner of the kitchen. After being served, Will never allowed anyone to take anything from his table.

The following stories and information was provided by Ms. Reba Riddle:

"Odis was playing in an old truck with a pistol, while playing he accidentally shot himself. Will told Lonnie that if anything happened to the kids he (Will) would kill him. When Will got back home and found out that Odis was dead, he went after Lonnie. In the meantime, Lonnie, fearing for his life, went to the neighbor's for help. Bob Povey, Sr. and Will Scogins took Lonnie to Haleyville to catch a train for Tennessee. When Will heard about this, he got his gun and headed for Haleyville. Mr. Bob Povey had got the men in the neighborhood, they took their shotguns and stood shoulder to shoulder while Lonnie got on the train. When Will saw them, he turned around and went home. Lonnie never returned home until after Will's death.

Then he returned quietly to the home of Wash Ellenberg, where Will lay a corpse. It was said that instead of coming directly to the house he crept through the woods until he saw Mr. Povey standing at the back door, Lonnie was white with fear as he touched Bob Povey on the shoulder and asked if Pa was really dead. He didn't believe Bob, he thought they had just told him Will was dead to get him (Lonnie) back down here for Will to kill him. Will had told Lonnie that if he ever laid eyes on him again, he would kill him where he stood. Lonnie's family lives in Lawrenceburg, Tennessee. It was said that Will's face was still bleeding from the cuts from where he was shaven."

*Ray Riddle, son of James Calvin (5/16 Cherokee) and Willie Mae Strawn Riddle, wife of James Calvin, age 97.*

"Another story about Will Riddle was when Will caught a Mexican fellow washing his hands in his pond and shot him. The man is buried in an unmarked grave by Amon Armstrong at Moreland Cemetery. The man was just passing through, working his way home, when Will caught him and shot him. After he was shot, the Mexican lived until the next day and made it to Willie Riddle's house. He died on her front porch."

"As related by Fannie Riddle, Will died of heart dropsy. She would tell of how his feet and legs would swell up, he would have her to break a limb of a holly bush and hit him on the legs and ankles to make the water drain off his legs. At the time, she was pregnant with Cloie. She said that afterwards she would go to the woods and vomit."

## Walter Riddle

Walter Riddle was the son of Straud and Samantha. Walter was said to be difficult to wean, and he would pitch fits if not allowed to nurse, even up to the ages of five and six. His father, Straud, made a trade with him. If he would stop nursing, Straud, would give Walter a fifty gallon barrel of syrup. "Walter," historian John West says, "swapping his tittie for syrup." He would later have his syrup and his tittie, too, when he married his first cousin, Rosa, and again when he married Lydia Clark Thomas. Walter lived with Straud and Samantha until they died.

After the death of Doc and Delie, Dollie Riddle was given to Walter Riddle, who was a brother to her father, John. Walter legally adopted Dollie on April 25, 1925. According to the adoption papers, Dollie was six years old on April 30, 1925.

Dollie's children indicate that Walter and Jim England worked up a deal. Jim owned a lot of land and was considered by many to be well off. According to the family many young men wanted to court Dollie; however, her hand was given in marriage to Jim England who was many years older. Jim and Dollie had one child before his death. Dollie's second marriage was to Travis Armstrong. Travis and Dollie had the following children: Margaret Treavor, Eddie Max, Jerry, Hollis, Doris, Flim, and Jack. Travis Armstrongs's parents were Flim and Dora Pear Armstrong.

*Walter Riddle with two bobcats standing by his old car!*

L-R: *James Louis (Jim) England (3/8 Cherokee), son of Joshua and Susan Hooper England (3/4 Cherokee); Dollie Riddle England Armstrong (3/4 Cherokee), daughter of John (Doc) and Delie Gray Riddle; Sarah Tankersley.*

*Flim and Dora Pear Armstrong (with their two daughters: Vivan and Eva) wee the parents of Travis Armstrong. Flim and Dora were at least 3/8 Cherokee Indian.*

# BIBLIOGRAPHY

Atkins, Leah Rawls. Manual For Writing Alabama State History. Alabama Historical Commission, 1976.

Borden, Lester and Myra. 1860 Lawrence County Alabama Census. Borden's Genealogical Books. Mt. Hope, Alabama, 1992.

Cambron, James W. and David C. Hulse. Handbook of Alabama Archaeology. David L. Dejarnette, ed. Alabama Archaeological Society, Huntsville, Alabama. 1986.

Carter, Clarence Edwin, ed. The Territorial Papers of the United States: Alabama 1817-1819. United States Government Publishing Company: Washington. 1952.

Cowart, Margaret Matthews. Old Land Records of Lawrence County Alabama. Huntsville, Alabama. 1991.

Elliott, Carl, ed. Winston: An Antebellum and Civil War History of a Hill Country of North Alabama. Alabama: Oxmoor Presee, 1972.

Fowke, Gerard. Forty-Fourth Annual Report of the Bureau of American Ethanology. United States Government Printing Office. Washington, D.C. 1928.

Gentry, Dorothy. Life and Legend of Lawrence County, Alabama. Tuscaloosa: Nottingham-SWS, Inc., 1962.

Hunter, Jonathan. Alabama Geological Survey. Oil and Gas in Alabama – The Watson Wells. Tuscaloosa, Alabama. Date unknown.

Kappler, Charles J. Indian Affairs – Law and Treaties. Volume II Treaties. Government Printing Office. Washington, D.C. 1904.

McDonald, William Lindsey. The Lore of Chief Doublehead and His Home at Muscle Shoals. Journal of Muscle Shoals History. Tennessee Valley Historical Society. Muscle Shoals, Alabama. 1981-83.

-----, Melton's Bluff. Journal of Muscle Shoals History. Tennessee Valley Historical Society. Muscle Shoals, Alabama. 1993.

Moore, Albert Burton. History of Alabama. New York: Lewis Historical Publishing Company, Inc., 1951.

Owens, Marie Bankhead. The Story of Alabama. New York: Lewis Historical Publishing Company, Inc., 1949.

Ponder, Odalene. Lawrence County Census 1820, 1830, 1840, and 1850. Gregarth Company, Cullman, Alabama, 1983.

Prucha, Francis Paul. Documents of United States Indian Policy. University of Nebraska Press. Lincoln, Nebraska, 1975.

Royall, Anne. Letters from Alabama 1817-1822. University of Alabama Press, 1969.

Saunders, Colonel Saunders. Early Settlers of Alabama. Easley, S.C.: Southern Historical Press, 1977. Reprint of the 1899 ed published at New Orleans by L. Graham and son.

Summersell, Charles Grayson. Alabama History for Schools. Montgomery, Alabama: Viewpoint Publications, 1981.

Walker, Rickey Butch. A Cultural Hertiage Outline of Indian History in Lawrence County and North Alabama. Lawrence County Schools' Indian Education Program. Lawrence County, Alabama, 1988.

-----. High Town Path. Lawrence County Schools' Indian Education Program. Lawrence County Alabama. 1992.

Waters, Spencer A. Confederate Soldiers from Lawrence County, Alabama. Thomason Printing Company. Carrollton, GA. 1992.

W.H.G. and Spencer Waters. Ittaloknah of the Battle of Indian Tomb Hollow – A Story of North Alabama. The Moulton Democrat. Moulton, Alabama, 1856 and researched by Waters in 1967.

Webb, William S. An Archaeological Survey of Wheeler Basin on the Tennessee River in Northern Alabama. Smithsonian Institute Bureau of American Ethnology Bulletin No. 122, 1939.

# Index

## A

Abbott, Ben, 314
Abbott, Ottice, 314
Adair, Hoyt, 128
Adair, Levi, 121
Adair, Martha, 132
Aldridge, Guy, 64
Aldridge, Mary, 109, 115
Alexander Mound, 7
Alexander, Artimsey (Ms.Timm), 116
Alexander, Dave, 134
Alexander, David Walker, 110
Alexander, Don, 1, 111
Alexander, Eliz Louisa, 109
Alexander, Eliza Bell, 116
Alexander, Henry, 62, 63, 110, 111, 146
Alexander, Henry Johnson, 120
Alexander, Ider Mae, 116
Alexander, Jake, 46, 110, 111, 112, 115, 117, 135
Alexander, James, 109, 110, 116
Alexander, James (Jim Monk), 115, 116, 117, 122
Alexander, James W., 116
Alexander, Jane Caroline, 109
Alexander, John, 115, 116, 120, 160
Alexander, John L., 116
Alexander, John Tyler, 110
Alexander, Julie, 134
Alexander, Kitty Eleanor, 109
Alexander, Kitty Walker, 110
Alexander, Mary, 110
Alexander, Mary Belinda, 109
Alexander, Mattie, 116
Alexander, Nettie, 116
Alexander, Pullar, 64
Alexander, Sarah Ann, 110, 116, 122
Alexander, Thomas (Tom) Jefferson, 109, 110
Alexander, Tim, 116
Alexander, Tom, 112, 122
Alexander, William, 109, 110, 115, 117, 122
Allen, John A., 36
Allen, Lydia J., 178
Allred, Charlie, 164, 172
Allred, Ella, 121
Allred, Martha, 62
Almon, Bob, 274
Almon, R. L., 313
Anderson, Alvin, 253
Anderson, Alvin Lyle, 254
Anderson, Ellen, 319
Anderson, Mary Jane, 254
Anderson, Rachel Emaline Cole, 254
Appleton, Martha, 216
Arbor Cemetery, 81
Armstrong Cave, 40
Armstrong, Amon, 325
Armstrong, Dora Pear, 326
Armstrong, Doris, 326
Armstrong, Eddie Max, 326
Armstrong, Flim, 326
Armstrong, Freeman, 172
Armstrong, Hollis, 326
Armstrong, Jack, 326
Armstrong, James, 214, 216, 218
Armstrong, Jerry, 326
Armstrong, Jonathan, 214, 218
Armstrong, Margaret Treavor, 326
Armstrong, Martha Patsy Wallis (Wallace), 213
Armstrong, Mary Ann, 188, 192
Armstrong, Patsy (Wallis), 218
Armstrong, Travis, 326
Asherbraner Cemetery, 79
Asherbraner, Bessie, 82
Asherbraner, David, 85
Asherbraner, Emaline, 89
Asherbraner, Henry, 85
Asherbraner, Imogen, 82
Asherbraner, Jim, 84, 89
Asherbraner, John L., 85
Asherbraner, Mary E., 85
Asherbraner, Miriam C., 85
Asherbraner, Noah, 85
Asherbraner, Sarah, 85
Asherbraner, Staymee, 85
Asherbraners, Jim, 89
Asherbranner, Cathrine, 140
Asherbranner, James, 160
Asherbranner, Johnny, 140
Aunt Jenny Brooks, 1, 34, 35, 259, 300, 308
Austin, John Harvey, 208, 209
Aycock Cemetery, 238
Ayers, Compy, 146

## B

Baggett, Pearl, 140
Bainbridge Ferry, 34
Baker, Sam, 313
Bankhead Forest, 1, 8, 9, 13, 18, 23, 32, 35, 37, 38, 39, 40, 43, 44, 45, 46, 48, 49, 52, 54, 55, 56, 59, 62, 66, 67, 75, 77, 79, 92, 93, 94, 96, 106, 108, 113, 116, 119, 125, 127, 138, 139, 152, 166, 167, 168, 176, 181, 187, 191, 212, 216, 230, 233, 237, 243, 252, 255, 257, 258, 261, 263, 269, 271, 282, 294, 308, 309, 310

Bankhead Forest's Sipsey
   Wilderness Area, 26
Bankhead National Forest, 38
Bankhead, Wm. B., 11
Barbee, Levi, 69
Barkley, Arie, 203
Barkley, Cathlene, 203
Baron De Crenay, 3
Basham's Gap, 23, 138
Batchelor, Ervin, 284, 285
Bates, Jane, 308
Battle of Horseshoe Bend, 18
Bear Creek Ridge, 22, 25
Beaty Hollow, 23, 66, 67
Beaty School, 71, 72, 80
Beaty, Adrian, 73
Beaty, Angeline, 68
Beaty, Benjamin, 67
Beaty, Carlie, 73
Beaty, Charlie, 71
Beaty, Clara, 71
Beaty, Edward, 71
Beaty, Faye, 1
Beaty, Faye Cash, 69, 70, 73, 77
Beaty, Frances Cornelia, 67
Beaty, George, 67
Beaty, James K., 69
Beaty, Janee, 71
Beaty, John Jackson, 67, 68, 69,
   70, 71, 72
Beaty, John Tolbert, 71, 72, 73
Beaty, Johnny, 72
Beaty, Lamender Doss, 72
Beaty, Lucille, 72
Beaty, Lucy, 71
Beaty, Martha, 67
Beaty, Nancy, 67
Beaty, Nancy C., 67, 68
Beaty, Ottice, 71
Beaty, Ottis Verbon, 71
Beaty, Thomas Alexander, 67, 68,
   69, 71, 77, 78, 79, 80
Beaty, Thomas Alexander, 67
Beaty, Thomas Alexander, 67
Beaty, Thomas Alexander, 68
Beaty, Tommie, 73
Bee Branch Canyon, 50
Bee Branch Falls, 50
Bennett, Bill, 267
Beulah Church, 65, 119, 125
Bird, Elizabeth, 178
Black Dutch, 15, 19, 227
Black House, 204, 211, 231, 237,
   238, 240
Black Irish, 15, 19
Black Warrior Forest, 10
Black Warrior River Valley, 23
Black Warrior Town, 24, 25
Black Warrior Town Trail, 23, 67
Black Warrior Wildlife
   Management Area, 25, 43
Black Warriors' Path, 20, 23, 24,
   25, 51, 52, 67, 115
Black, Flourine Flanagin, 305
Black, Silas, 144
Blackwell, John W., 309
Blankenship Cemetery, 200, 214,
   215, 220
Blankenship Cove, 56, 168, 217
Blankenship Ridge, 212, 215, 219,
   221
Blankenship, Augustine, 212
Blankenship, Ausie D., 221
Blankenship, Aussie, 222
Blankenship, Calvin, 216
Blankenship, Charlie, 198, 203,
   220
Blankenship, Chelsea, 258
Blankenship, Cherry Borden, 213,
   218
Blankenship, Cullen, 212
Blankenship, Dock, 216, 217, 218,
   246
Blankenship, Doctor, 212
Blankenship, Dolly Flanagin Pate,
   232, 239
Blankenship, Dorton, 216
Blankenship, Edith, 212
Blankenship, Elbert, 202, 222, 223,
   224, 226, 228
Blankenship, Elizabeth, 216, 220
Blankenship, Elizabeth (Eunice),
   220
Blankenship, Elizabeth Hudson,
   212
Blankenship, Ethel Wilkerson, 224
Blankenship, Frances, 215
Blankenship, Frances McNorton,
   220
Blankenship, Hannah Borden, 216
Blankenship, Henry, 198, 203, 220
Blankenship, Hezekiah, 212, 213,
   215, 218
Blankenship, Hudson, 212, 213,
   214, 215, 216, 217, 218, 219,
   246
Blankenship, Hudson (Hardin), 216
Blankenship, James, 220
Blankenship, Jane, 216
Blankenship, Jesse B. (Tobe), 216,
   217, 218, 219
Blankenship, Jessie, 220
Blankenship, Jody B., 221, 222
Blankenship, Joel, 212
Blankenship, John, 212, 216, 217,
   218
Blankenship, Jonathan, 216, 218
Blankenship, Josh, 203, 216, 217,
   218
Blankenship, Joshua, 212, 216,
   217, 218
Blankenship, Martha, 216
Blankenship, Martha (Patsy), 216
Blankenship, Nancy, 258
Blankenship, Nancy Flanagin, 246
Blankenship, Patsy Wallis, 218
Blankenship, Patsy Wallis
   Armstrong, 192, 216, 217, 246

Blankenship, Pedro, 219, 220, 221, 222, 228
Blankenship, Ralph, 212
Blankenship, Sally, 190
Blankenship, Sampson, 212, 216
Blankenship, Samuel, 217, 218
Blankenship, Sarah (Eula), 220
Blankenship, Sarah Jane, 216, 246
Blankenship, Starlin, 224
Blankenship, Thursday Parker, 223
Blankenship, Tobe, 197, 198, 203, 215, 218, 221
Blankenship, Tom, 203
Blankenship, William, 216, 217, 218
Blankenship, Willis, 56, 190, 203, 216, 217
Blount, William, 30
Blowing Spring Mountain, 96
Boat Rock, 56
Bogar Cemetery, 183, 187
Bogar, Maranda, 183
Boger, Lucy, 221
Bogles, Jim, 319
Booth, Vaughn, 91
Borden Creek Canyon, 54
Borden, Anna, 149
Borden, Charles, 38, 59, 145, 149, 153, 154, 159, 163, 164
Borden, Cherry, 213, 215
Borden, Christiana, 197, 202
Borden, Christinna, 213
Borden, Christopher, 56, 163, 213, 216, 217, 257
Borden, David, 213, 257
Borden, Dock Adley, 162
Borden, Edley, 153, 162
Borden, Elizabeth Hooper, 155, 162
Borden, Evaline (MeHerg), 162
Borden, Francis Wren, 257
Borden, Hester Ann, 257
Borden, Jesse, 203

Borden, Jessie L., 213, 216
Borden, Lester, 85
Borden, Lou Annie, 162, 163
Borden, Malinda, 213
Borden, Mannie, 163
Borden, Mildred, 153
Borden, Myra, 69, 85
Borden, Phillip, 213, 257
Borden, Robert Lewis, 165
Borden, Roscoe, 163
Borden, Rosie, 203
Borden, Sarah Hannah, 216
Borden, Thomas, 146
Borden, Thomas Phillip, 163
Borden, Thurlow, 163
Borden, Tom, 163
Borden, Viola, 258
Borden, Walter, 163
Borden, Zachariah, 213
Bordon, Lester, 69
Boren, Jacob, 128
Boyles, Claude, 245, 258
Boyles, Clauson, 258
Boyles, Cleo, 249, 258
Boyles, Drucilla Nixon, 257
Boyles, Emmy, 258
Boyles, George, 257
Boyles, Harriett, 257
Boyles, Henry, 245, 258
Boyles, Hester, 258
Boyles, James (Jim), 257
Boyles, John D., 257
Boyles, Johnnie, 258
Boyles, Lela, 258
Boyles, Leonard (Lynn), 258
Boyles, Louisa (Pace), 257
Boyles, Luther, 258
Boyles, Lydia, 258
Boyles, Maggie, 258
Boyles, Martha, 258
Boyles, Minnie, 258
Boyles, Philip Martin, 258
Boyles, Phillip G., 256, 257

Boyles, Phillip Martin, 257, 258
Boyles, Phillip Martin), 257
Boyles, Prince, 258
Boyles, Sarah, 257
Brannon, John M., 140
Braziel Creek Trail, 26
Bridges, Clifford, 202, 203
Bridges, Lottie Wilkerson, 203
Brindley Mountain, 75
Brooks, Amanda, 309
Brooks, Angeline, 308
Brooks, Clifton, 312
Brooks, Dona, 261
Brooks, Donna (Donie), 309
Brooks, Frances, 309, 313
Brooks, Gainam, 309, 312
Brooks, Gains, 278
Brooks, Ganium, 277, 278
Brooks, Henry, 261, 277, 278, 301, 309, 313
Brooks, Jane, 309
Brooks, Jane (Aunt Jenny) Bates, 308, 310, 311
Brooks, John, 308, 310, 311, 312
Brooks, Lula V., 131
Brooks, Mack, 308, 312
Brooks, Myrtie, 131
Brooks, Sam, 139, 140
Brooks, Willis, 308, 309, 310, 311, 312
Brooks, Willis, Jr., 309, 312
Brown Cemetery, 79
Brown's Ferry, 12, 32, 33
Brush Arbor Cemetery, 68, 69, 71, 77, 78, 79, 80, 81
Brush Lake, 107
Bull, John, 4
Bunyan Hill School, 246
Bunyon Hill Cave, 40
Burnett, Bill, 85
Burnett, Henry, 85
Burnett, Johnny, 85
Burnett, Lester, 146

Burnett, Wesley, 141
Burrus, Mourning, 128
Butler, Gladys Flanagin, 305
Buzzard Roost Mountain, 61, 65, 75, 79, 80, 84
Byler Road, 283, 310
Byler, John, 33, 34, 307
Bynum, Mattie Mae, 258

## C

Cadzy Cadiza Coluda Caco, 121
Calvert, Winnie, 320
Calvert, Winnie Telitha, 322
Camp, Bill, 203, 207
Camp's Church, 207
Campbell, Madgie Pate, 232
Caney Falls, 40
Captain Jack's Cave, 40
Captain's Room, 40
Carter, Clarence E., 22
Carter, Matt, 89
Cash, Faye, 71, 72
Cave Springs Cemetery, 51, 79, 124, 138, 156
Cave Springs School, 94
CCC Camp School, 96
Cemetery, Friendship, 80
Center Cemetery, 51, 52, 79, 87, 139, 156
Center Church, 51, 61, 85, 93
Chaney, Enzie, 66
Cheatham, Elizabeth, 36
Cheatham, Francis, 36
Cheatham, George, 36
Cheatham, Lavina, 36
Cheatham, Thomas, 36
Cheatham, Wyatt, 35, 36, 37, 320
Cheatham, Wyatt D., 36
Cheatham's Turn-Pike, 35, 36
Chenault, Callie Johnson, 87
Chenault, Carol, 92
Chenault, Christine, 92

Chenault, Eva, 1
Chenault, Eva Poole, 82
Chenault, Icy Mae, 88
Chenault, Ike, 84, 86
Chenault, Issac, 87, 88, 89, 91
Chenault, Jewel, 88
Chenault, John, 92
Chenault, Louise, 88
Chenault, Mary, 88
Chenault, Paralee, 88
Chenault, Pleas, 88, 92
Chenault, Price, 88, 91
Chenault, Prince, 86, 87, 88, 90, 91, 92, 93, 94
Chenault, Rick, 92
Chenault, William, 89
Cherokee, 10, 12, 13, 14, 15, 16, 17, 18, 19, 20, 21, 22, 23, 26, 27, 28, 29, 30, 31, 33, 34, 35, 44, 51, 65, 66, 78, 97, 102, 104, 108, 109, 111, 112, 113, 119, 120, 121, 139, 148, 155, 162, 163, 176, 178, 182, 194, 197, 202, 203, 213, 227, 231, 244, 245, 246, 257, 283, 288, 299, 308, 315, 316, 317, 318, 320, 323
Chickasaw, 11, 12, 14, 17, 18, 19, 22, 23, 28, 29, 30, 31, 34, 35, 53, 194
Chickasaw Bluffs, 11, 28
Chickasaw Boundary Treaty, 17
Chickasaw Island, 31
Chickasaw Old Fields, 12, 17, 18
Chief Doublehead, 12
Chief George Colbert, 12
Chief Tuscaloosa, 3, 11
Chilcoat, Caroline Patience, 216
Chilcoat, Sarah Jane, 216
Chocktaw, 26, 34
Choctaw, 3, 27, 105
Cline, Elender, 139
Cline, Soloman, 139

Coe, Joseph, 36, 320
Coffee, John, 24
Colbert, George, 18
Cole, Ellen Keith, 253
Cole, Rachel Emaline, 254
Cole, William Riley, 253, 254
Collier Falls, 41
Continental Divide, 3, 11, 17, 18, 19, 22, 28, 30, 31, 37, 307
Cooper, Monroe, 156
Cornelius, Francis (Fanny), 319
Corum, Frances, 195
Cothern, Oscar, 258
Cotton Gin Port, 21, 22, 25
Cotton Gin Treaty, 17, 18
Counts, Elmer, 283
Counts, Jim, 190, 249
Cowan, John, 24, 120
Cowan, Margaret, 36
Cowans, Bessie, 249
Coward, Margaret, 4
Cowart, Margaret, 124, 128, 150, 178, 196, 215, 227, 243, 244, 263, 309, 319
Craig, Lucy, 164
Creek, 3, 10, 11, 12, 13, 14, 15, 17, 18, 23, 24, 25, 26, 27, 28, 29, 30, 34, 35, 51, 53, 62, 66, 104, 194, 273, 282
Crittenden, Sterling, 258
Crockett, David, 24, 25, 120
Culver, Will, 146
Curtis, Amelia, 320
Curtis, Bessie, 179
Curtis, Emma Armelia, 323
Curtis, George, 183
Curtis, George B., 178
Curtis, Ila, 179
Curtis, J.A., 178
Curtis, Johnny, 179
Curtis, Jonathan Bird, 178
Curtis, Martha Jane Lyle, 323

Curtis, Mary Elean Sparks, 179, 192
Curtis, Mary Ellen Parker, 183
Curtis, Minnie, 126, 179
Curtis, Sara J., 321
Curtis, William V. (Bill), 323

# D

Davidson, Mary, 102
Day, John, 186
Delshaw, Willie, 137
Demasters, Jetson, 180
Demasters, Leona, 168
Demastes, A.M., 69
Demastus, A.J. (Bud), 132
Dement Cemetery, 217
Dement, James, 216, 218
DeSoto, 3, 9, 10, 11, 27
Devaney, Archie, 202, 210, 211, 237, 240
Devaney, James, 233, 237
Devaney, James Jerry, 211
Devaney, Kennard Craburn, 211
Devaney, Lucy Wilkerson, 201, 202, 203, 204, 205, 208, 210, 211, 212, 224, 225, 233, 234, 235, 236, 237
Devil John, 288
Devil's Well, 40
Deweese, John A., 313
Dillashaw Mountain, 65, 122
Dillashaw, Beckie, 123
Dillashaw, Joseph, 123
Dillashaw, N.G., 110
Dillashaw, Nobe, 115, 122
Dime Cemetery, 291
Ditto Landing, 17
Dobbs, Mary, 140
Dodd, Donald, 35
Dodd, Wynelle, 35
Dodge, G.M., 35
Doss Cemetery, 77, 79

Doss, Ezekiel, 69, 78, 79
Doss, Ezibell, 84
Doss, J. M., 124
Doss, James, 70
Doss, John David, 69
Doss, Lamender Sue, 69, 71
Doss, Lucinda, 78
Doss, Mattie, 82
Doss, Walter, 84
Double Springs, 28, 317, 322
Doublehead, 12, 17, 18, 33
Doublehead Springs, 12
Doublehead's Reserve, 17
Dover, Mattie Lou, 65
Dragging Canoe, 12
Dry Creek Canyon, 213, 215
Dukeminer, Laura, 243
Durrette, Mildred, 128
Dutton, Alma, 146
Dutton, Mary Plant, 183
Dutton, Minnie, 183
Dutton, Wes, 94

# E

Eddy, Marvin, 160
Eddy, Nick, 139
Eddy, Roof, 120
Edmundson, Jim, 91
Elkins, Anth, 204
Elkins, Lela, 242
Elkins, Martha, 204
Ellenberg, Evie Riddle, 323
Ellenberg, Wash, 325
Ellenburg, Mattie, 126
Ellenburg, Sam, 321
Elliott, Samuel, 128
Elmore, Grady, 91
England, Claud, 146
England, Claude Dean, 162
England, Dellie, 146
England, Doris, 1
England, Eva, 148

England, Jim, 326
England, Johnny, 162
England, Josh, 162
England, Joshua, 163
England, Lessie, 146
England, Louis, 146
England, Mallie, 146
England, Mary Lou (Dusky) Pearson, 146
England, Mildred, 146
England, Minnie, 163
England, Neil, 146
England, Pearl, 146
England, Susan Hooper, 163
England, Uranis (Tirey), 146
England, Walter, 146

# F

Fairfield Church, 23, 135
Fairfield School, 135
Fairview Methodist Church, 179
Feltman, Andrew, 261, 262, 263, 264, 266, 267, 299, 301
Feltman, Bob, 287, 302
Feltman, Bynum, 262, 297
Feltman, Delie Spillers, 302
Feltman, Dick, 262
Feltman, Ed, 303
Feltman, Jake, 259, 260, 261, 262, 263, 264, 265, 266, 267, 268, 269, 270, 271
Feltman, Kent, 262
Feltman, Lela, 262
Feltman, Lewis, 262
Feltman, Mattie, 262, 266
Feltman, Oscar, 262
Feltman, Robert T. (Bob), 261
Feltman, Tom, 262, 299
Feltman, Vina Sammons, 261, 262
Ferguson Cemetery, 238
Ferguson, J. D., 122
Ferguson, John T., 122

Fish Dam Ford, 23
Fitzgerald, Sallie, 110
Fitzgerald, Sallie A., 110
Fitzgerald, Sally, 110
Flanagin Creek Canyon, 54, 215
Flanagin, Burley Dennis, 305
Flanagin, Calvin Coolidge, 305
Flanagin, Dolly, 197
Flanagin, Fannie, 302
Flanagin, Frances Pauline, 305
Flanagin, Hose, 202
Flanagin, J. C. (Jay), 306
Flanagin, J.C. (Jay), 305
Flanagin, James, 196
Flanagin, James (Bud), 303, 305
Flanagin, James (Jim), 231
Flanagin, James M., 44
Flanagin, Jane, 196
Flanagin, Jess, 202
Flanagin, Jim, 302
Flanagin, John, 216, 220
Flanagin, Joseph, 196
Flanagin, Martha, 187, 220
Flanagin, Martha J., 231
Flanagin, Mattie Spillers, 283, 287, 288, 289, 290, 291, 292, 293, 294, 295, 296, 297, 298, 299, 300, 303, 304, 305, 306, 318
Flanagin, Nancy, 216
Flanagin, Nelson, 196
Flanagin, Parthena, 196
Flanagin, Pauline, 305
Flanagin, Rufus (Roof), 249, 287, 301, 302, 303, 304, 305
Flanagin, Sarah, 196
Flanagin, Sarah Ann, 214
Flanagin, Senia, 216
Flanagin, Thomas, 196, 213, 214
Flanagin, Tom, 190, 202
Flanagin, William, 196
Flannagin, Senia, 213
Flat Mountain, 75, 79, 83
Flat Rock, 11, 18, 19, 29

Fort Hampton, 23
Fort Mitchell, 23
Fowke, Gerald, 6
Freedom Trail, 26
Freeman, Nichola, 273
French Lick, 26, 27, 34
Friendship Cemetery, 69, 71, 72, 79, 83, 106, 162
Friendship Church, 156
Frost, Henry, 322
Frost, Sherry Jane, 262
Ft. Hampton, 18
Ft. Mitchell, 25
Fuller, John, 160
Fulmer, Mel, 157

# G

Gailey, Tom, 133
Gaines Trace, 20, 21, 22, 23
Gaines, Edmund Pendleton, 21, 22, 25, 34
Gaines, George Strothers, 21
Garnett, Annie, 82
Garrison Cemetery, 79
Garrison, Absalom, 244
Garrison, Audie Mae McDowell, 245, 247, 248
Garrison, Bill, 299, 300
Garrison, Clara, 248
Garrison, Clarence, 292
Garrison, Clarence Milford, 246
Garrison, Cranal E. (Tom), 244, 248
Garrison, David, 244
Garrison, David Sherman, 288
Garrison, Dennis, 244, 245, 247
Garrison, Dicey, 288, 317
Garrison, Drennon, 248, 252
Garrison, Ellen, 244
Garrison, Elton Lincon, 248
Garrison, Elvira, 288
Garrison, Emily, 246

Garrison, Florence Ella, 246
Garrison, Floyd, 245, 250
Garrison, Floyd Nenivah, 246, 247, 248, 252
Garrison, Garrison, 288
Garrison, Garvin, 65, 248
Garrison, Glen, 248
Garrison, James, 246
Garrison, James G., 244
Garrison, Jim, 295
Garrison, Jim M., 288
Garrison, John, 288
Garrison, John L., 244
Garrison, Lawrence, 244, 268, 301
Garrison, Lawrence Trevis, 246
Garrison, Lee, 288
Garrison, Lynn, 246
Garrison, Malinda, 244
Garrison, Manervie Vernon, 288
Garrison, Martin, 300
Garrison, Mary Tennessee, 231, 244, 283, 288, 296, 300, 322
Garrison, Peggy, 247
Garrison, Pink, 190
Garrison, Riley, 292, 293
Garrison, Rosie, 262
Garrison, Sandra, 288
Garrison, Sara Susan, 244
Garrison, Sarah, 244
Garrison, Sarah Jane Blankenship, 246
Garrison, Sarah Mary Dennis, 245
Garrison, Sherman, 300
Garrison, Silas, 247
Garrison, Sook, 292
Garrison, Stephen, 244
Garrison, Sudearia, 1
Garrison, Synthia, 287, 293
Garrison, Synthia Alma, 246
Garrison, Vie, 246
Garrison, William C., 288
Garrison, William G. (Buck), 244, 288

Garrison, William Riley, 244, 245, 246
George Hampton, 101, 102, 155
Gibson, Silvanus, 111
Gilbreath, Bracken, 299
Gilbreath, Dorothy, 287, 299
Gilbreath, Prue, 287, 299
Gillespie Cemetery, 53
Gillespie, Bobbie R., 119
Gillespie, James Richard, 25, 53, 119, 120
Gillespie, Lucy Johnson, 119
Gillespie, Mary, 120
Graves, Bibb, 232
Graves, Francis, 128
Graves, Thomas, 128
Gray, Cordelia (Delie), 323
Gray, Delie, 320
Gray, Mattie Riddle, 323
Great War Path, 11
Griffin, Mary A., 67
Gum Pond, 186, 187, 188, 200, 203, 246, 253, 255, 292
Gum Pond Cemetery, 207, 246, 247, 253, 256, 292, 293
Gum Pond Church, 207, 247, 253, 292

# H

Hagood, Buddy, 203
Hagood, Emmitt, 262, 303
Hagood, Millie, 300
Hall, Arie, 180
Hall, Tom, 153
Hamby, Lillie, 318
Hamby, Mance, 170
Hamilton, G. T., 128
Hamilton, Mary, 81
Hampton, Ephram, 148
Hampton, Ephriam, 69, 78, 79
Hampton, Eunice, 82
Hampton, George, 100

Hampton, Haley, 82
Hampton, Jimmy, 82, 84
Hampton, Lamenda, 69
Hampton, Lamender, 78
Hampton, Lizzie Poole, 84
Hampton, Lucinda Doss, 148
Hampton, Olga, 97, 102
Hampton, Wesley, 86, 101, 147
Hardin, Katherine, 227
Hardrick, Charlie, 90
Harmony Church, 189
Harmony School, 189
Harville, Roger, 93
Harville, Sally (Sara Ann), 247
Havens, Charlotte Ann, 4
Havens, James, 4
Heflin Cemetery, 261
Henderson, Billy, 74, 75
Henderson, John C., 226, 229
Henderson, Nancy, 226, 227
Henry, Francis "Frank", 214
Herd, Bart, 144
Herring, Norris, 148
Herring. Edward, 1, 137, 138, 261
Herron Point, 56, 289, 303
Herron, Hester Boyles, 258
Herron, Lawrence Warren, 255, 256, 257
Hickory Grove Cemetery, 139, 156
Hickory Grove Church, 101, 102
Hickory Grove Road CCC Camp, 94, 95
Hicks, Charles, 17
Higgins, Bertha, 146
Higgins, Bud, 154
Higgins, Robert Carl, 146
High House Hill, 53, 108, 115, 116, 118, 119, 132
High House Hill Ridge, 108
High House Plantation Home, 108
High Town Path, 3, 11, 12, 13, 18, 19, 21, 22, 25, 27, 28, 29, 30, 31, 32, 34, 35, 51, 67, 105, 118,

119, 150, 166, 167, 194, 241, 307
Hightower, Leon, 51
Hightower, Syble, 102
Hill, Angeline Elizabeth (Betty), 62
Hill, Bob, 62
Hill, Dallas, 62
Hill, Dora, 66
Hill, Eloise, 65
Hill, Ernest, 121
Hill, Essie, 66
Hill, Felton, 65
Hill, George, 146
Hill, Grady Alton, 65, 66
Hill, Hazel, 65
Hill, John, III, 62, 63
Hill, John, Jr, 62
Hill, John, Sr., 61, 62
Hill, Johnny, 65
Hill, Julie, 62
Hill, Lois Essie, 65
Hill, Manervia C., 62
Hill, Martha, 62
Hill, Mary E., 61
Hill, Miladean, 146
Hill, Nancy, 61
Hill, Newt, 61, 62, 63, 65, 66
Hill, Rayburn (R.B.), 65
Hill, Robert A., 61
Hill, Samuel, 61
Hill, Tollise, 65, 66
Hill, William S., 62
Hitt, Marion, 152
Hobb's Island, 17
Hodges, Martha, 128
Hoffman's Horrible Hole, 40
Hogan, Ed, 67
Hogan, John, 67, 68
Hogan, Lena, 72
Hogan, Louenda, 72
Hogan, Moody, 73
Hogan, Tommie, 73

Hollaway School, 157
Hollaway, Will, 157
Holley, Les, 162
Holmes Chapel Falls, 41
Holmes Chapel School, 155
Hood, Cap, 258
Hood, Mollie, 221
Hood, Monty, 221
Hood, Viva, 262, 267
Hood, Willie, 267, 268, 271
Hook Rock House Shelter, 319
Hooper, Darthula (Dotson), 163
Hooper, Elizabeth (Borden), 163
Hooper, Grover, 163
Hooper, Hattie, 163
Hooper, Hattie (Yeates), 163
Hooper, John, 163
Hooper, Mary (Dobbs), 163
Hooper, Melvina McVay, 163
Hooper, Onner (Hill), 163
Hooper, Roof, 163
Hooper, William, 163
Hooper, Winnie (England), 163
Horton, Willie Mae, 322
Hovater, Glen, 244, 249
Hovator, Glen, 1
Hubbad, Lawson, 273, 276
Hubbad, Robert, 280, 281
Hubbard Creek Canyon, 57
Hubbard, Abe, 274
Hubbard, Clyde, 274
Hubbard, David, 35, 271, 273, 278, 279, 280, 282, 308, 309
Hubbard, Emma, 274
Hubbard, Eva, 272
Hubbard, George, 274
Hubbard, George Washington (Wash), 273, 274, 277
Hubbard, Ginsey, 282
Hubbard, Green K., 308
Hubbard, Harvey, 274, 283
Hubbard, Henry, 277, 312
Hubbard, Henry (Bud), 274

Hubbard, Ida, 274, 299
Hubbard, James, 274
Hubbard, Jennie, 274
Hubbard, July, 274
Hubbard, Lawson, 261, 266, 272, 274, 275, 276, 277, 278, 281, 282, 285, 299, 301, 314
Hubbard, Lee, 274
Hubbard, Lodie, 285
Hubbard, Luther, 274, 276, 299
Hubbard, Nick, 274
Hubbard, Nodie, 274
Hubbard, Odie, 272, 273, 274
Hubbard, Robert, 272, 273, 274, 275, 276, 279, 281, 282, 283, 284, 286, 299
Hubbard, Thomas, 308
Hubbard, Violet, 274
Hubbard, Wash, 274, 279, 284, 286, 312
Hubbard, William, 273, 277, 278, 282, 309, 312
Hughes, Charlie, 294
Hunter, Addie, 82
Hunter, Allred, 164, 172
Hunter, Claude, 82
Hunter, Ellis, 82
Hunter, Harrison, 82
Hunter, Herschel, 82
Hunter, John T., 82
Hunter, Jonathan, 51
Hunter, Lizzie, 82
Hunter, Mamie, 82
Hunter, Tom, 82
Hunter, Wiley, 82
Hunter, William, 82
Hyatt, Rayford, 2, 44, 51, 181, 186, 214, 253, 254, 255, 256, 260, 309, 320

# I

Indian Marker Tree, 53

Indian Tomb Hollow, 4, 7, 25, 41, 52, 53, 107, 114, 120, 123, 125
Indian Tomb Hollow Cemetery, 120
Indian Tomb Hollow Falls, 41
Irish/Cherokee, 15, 19, 20
Irwin, Price, 148, 185

# J

Jackson, Andrew, 13, 14, 15, 18, 19, 24, 36, 115
Jackson, Holbert, 148
Jackson, Quill, 148
James, Cathlene, 317
Jarrett, Susie K., 221
Jeffreys, William, 213
Jenkins, Allie, 150
Jenkins, George, 151
Jenkins, James, 150
Jenkins, Jeff, 151
Jenkins, Jim, 151, 239
Jenkins, John, 151
Jenkins, Lillie M., 152
Jenkins, Mary, 150
Johnson Bill, 87, 181, 183, 283, 287, 293
Johnson Callie, 87, 88
Johnson Marge, 87
Johnson, Alice, 73
Johnson, Dick, 86
Johnson, Dora, 126
Johnson, Fannie, 110
Johnson, Fanny, 126
Johnson, Frank, 126
Johnson, Harvey, 87
Johnson, Henry, 119
Johnson, Issac, Sr., 88
Johnson, Janice T., 176
Johnson, Jim, 62
Johnson, Manley, 87
Johnson, Margie, 89
Johnson, Mary Jane, 87

Johnson, Nobe, 64
Johnson, William Franklin "Buttermilk Bill", 86, 87
Johnson. Lizzy, 72
Johnston, Jacob Stauder, 309, 311
Johnston, Jane (Aunt Jenny) Brooks, 307, 309, 311, 312, 313, 314
Johnston, Jenny Brooks, 271, 277
Johson, Arrie, 72
Jones, Earl, 146
Jones, Eugene, 146

## K

Kelly, Brian, 109
Kelso, Bill, 89
Kelso, William Todd "Boss", 112
Kelsoe, Austin, 161
Kelsoe, Ava, 66
Kelsoe, Bill, 72, 91, 161
Kelsoe, Celia Mae, 66
Kelsoe, Claude, 66
Kelsoe, Clyde, 66
Kelsoe, David Crockett, 66
Kelsoe, Edward, 65
Kelsoe, Eric, 66
Kelsoe, Eric Bradley, 65
Kelsoe, Eric Junior, 65
Kelsoe, Grace, 66
Kelsoe, John, 66
Kelsoe, Lawrence, 66
Kelsoe, Leldon, 96
Kelsoe, Marlin, 65
Kelsoe, Mary, 66
Kelsoe, Paralee, 66
Kelsoe, William Riley (Will), 66
Kelsoe, William Todd (Boss), 65
Killian, Mary Jane, 195
King Cove, 55, 57, 259, 261, 262, 263, 264, 287, 289, 290, 292, 294, 296, 299, 300, 302, 315, 319

King Cove Church, 262
Kinlock Falls, 40, 266, 269, 279, 305, 307, 308
Kinlock Rock Shelter, 38, 58, 308
Knox, Ralph, 172

## L

Lackey, Columbus, 102
Lamb's Ferry, 28, 33
Lamon, Sovola, 190
Lawrence County, 139, 177, 182, 195
Lebanon Cemetery, 72, 137
Lebanon Methodist Church, 94
Ledlow, George, 73
Ledlow, Nellie, 132
Ledlow, Terrance, 126
Ledlow, Vinie, 73
Ledlow, Wilburn, 73
Lee Creek Canyon, 118
Legg, Addison, 106
Legg, Ben, 180
Legg, Elizabeth Speakman, 106
Legg, Good, 180
Legg, Maudy Nevady (Vady), 105
Leigh, Hershel, 164
Leola Road, 141
Lester, Mary Frances, 150
Letson, Jack, 159
Lindsey Cemetery, 23
Lindsey Hall, 89, 137, 141, 143, 144, 145, 148, 154, 155, 157, 162, 163, 164
Lindsey Hall Church, 124, 153
Lindsey Hall School, 80, 146, 157, 158, 159
Lindsey, Jim, 110
Lindsey, Sally, 110
Little, Maggie, 140
Lock, Bettye, 190
Logan, Delphia, 115
Long, Shorty, 89

Lookout Mountain, 32, 167
Looney, Dyke, 162
Looney, Floyd, 144, 162
Looney, James, 73
Looney, Monroe, 73
Looney, Walter, 73
Lott, Rachel R., 238
LouAllen, Appie, 247
LouAllen, Ed, 202
LouAllen, Evie, 258
LouAllen, Hubert, 247
LouAllen, Wiley, 247
Lovern, Jim, 262
LuAllen, Gladys, 1, 188, 192, 214, 217, 220, 226, 228
LuAllen, Gladys Blankenship, 212, 229
Lyge Wiley Ridge, 79
Lynch, Darius, 70, 81
Lyndon, L.B., 192

## M

Macedonia Cemetery, 261, 300, 302, 305
Macedonia Church, 262, 263, 277, 278, 283, 301, 305
Macedonia School House, 261
Magby, Lou, 303
Manasco, Jim, 26, 27
Marshall, Lamar, 1, 67
Massey, Mag, 186
Mattox Creek Canyon, 254
Mattox, Gordon, 88
Mattox, Robert, 257
Mays, Irene, 121
Mc Dougal Hunter's Camp, 49
McCaghren, Lillian, 78
McCain, William, 34, 307
McCanin, William, 309
McCarty, Bill, 173, 203
McCarty, Jess, 190
McCay, Arch, 190, 229

McClung Gap, 34, 247, 248, 249, 258, 260, 267, 268, 269
McClung Gap School, 248, 258
McCrary, Cassandra Adair, 195
McCrary, Irwin P., 195, 196
McCrary, Irwin Paul, 195
McCrary, Joseph, 195
McCrary, Mary O. Holland, 195
McCrary, Matthew, 195
McCrary, Thomas, 195
McCullough, William, 216
McDaneil, Lula, 72
McDaniel, Phil, 73
McDaniel, Rube, 73
McDaniel, Willie, 72
McDonald, William Lindsey, 24
McDonald, WilliamLindsey, 33
McDougal Shelter, 27
McDowell Cove, 8, 49, 166, 188, 191, 193, 198, 199, 201, 212, 215, 216, 225, 226, 233, 237, 304
McDowell, Audie Mae, 246, 247, 248
McDowell, Ellen, 247
McDowell, Henry, 230, 231, 245, 255
McDowell, Henry A., 230
McDowell, Henry Andrew, 247
McDowell, Henry Jack, 199, 230, 233
McDowell, Henry M., 197
McDowell, Jack, 49, 122, 155, 190, 197, 198, 202, 204, 214, 224, 226, 231, 232, 233, 239, 259, 269, 283, 305
McDowell, James Jackson, 247
McDowell, Moses, 247
McDowell, Sally, 204, 207, 231
McDowell, Sally (Sara Ann) Harville, 247
McDowell, Sally Spillers, 304
McKay, Arch, 203

McKelvey, Fletcher, 109
McLemore Cemetery, 179, 191
McLemore, Marie White, 103
McMahan, Richard, 13
McMillan, Bessie, 122
McMillan, Emmett, 122
McNair, David, 69
McNorton, Frances, 216, 219
McVay Cementary, 79
McVay, Dock, 163
McVay, Henry, 160
McVay, K., 122
McVay, Nancy, 113
McVay, Tom, 122, 140, 154
McWhorter, Alton, 69
Melborn, Howard, 126
Melish, John, 23
Melson, G. H., 53, 112, 113, 114, 115, 117, 122
Melson, George, 113
Melson, George Harvey, 113
Melson, Louie, 160
Melton, John, 17, 20, 21, 24
Melton, Moses, 17
Melton's Bluff, 12, 15, 17, 20, 21, 22, 23, 24, 25, 51, 116
Mill, Jones, 209, 256
Miller, Daniel, 65
Miller, Glenna, 146
Miller, Ida, 65
Miller, Lee, 86
Milligan, Mary E., 138
Milligan, William Houston, 138
Millwood, Roy, 121
Minor, Dola, 121
Minor, Dona, 121
Minor, Eunice, 121
Minor, Henry Butler, 121
Minor, John Norman, 120, 121
Minor, Lena, 121
Minor, Lewis, 121
Minor, Nola, 121
Minor, Rena, 121

Minor, Will, 97
Minor, Worda, 121
Mitchell Trace, 20, 21, 22, 23, 24, 25, 51, 67, 115
Mitchell, David Brady, 23
Mize, Jim, 320
Mize, John, 245
Moffitt, Vivian, 190, 233
Montgomery, Ellis, 187
Montgomery, Fannie Parker, 181
Montgomery, George, 180, 187
Montgomery, Hal, 66
Montgomery, Sam, 66
Moody, Leon, 88, 91, 190
Moore, Matt, 257
Moreland Church, 96
Morgan, Grady, 287
Morgan, Janie, 132
Morgan, Minnie, 132
Morgan, Tranny, 126
Morris, Luther, 82
Mortar Rock, 55, 260
Mount Olive Cemetery, 323
Mountain Springs Cemetery, 189, 190, 200, 223, 229, 231, 238
Mountain Springs Church, 190, 200, 207, 227, 228, 229, 232
Mountain Springs School, 189, 190, 200, 204, 224, 229, 232, 233
Mountain View School, 172, 186, 187
Mt. Hope School, 249
Mt. Olive Cemetery, 231, 293
Muscogee, 3

# N

Napier, Hattie, 286
Narrows Ridge, 54, 55, 226
Natchez Trace, 12, 18
Naylor, Bular, 130, 132
Naylor, Buster, 135

Naylor, George W., 125, 130, 131, 132, 134, 135
Naylor, Jeremiah, 125, 131
Naylor, Jim Mat, 132, 135
Naylor, Kir Benjamin, 127, 132
Naylor, Lillian, 132
Naylor, Lousia, 131, 133, 134
Naylor, Lousia Simmons, 130
Naylor, Mary E. Welborn (Segars), 125, 130, 131
Naylor, Mile Jack, 127, 131
Naylor, Pearl Lee, 131
Naylor, Ruthie, 132, 136
Naylor, T. Wash, 132
Naylor, Theral, 132
Naylor, Thomas, 127, 131, 132, 135
Naylor, Tilda, 132
Naylor, Tilda Demastus, 132
Naylor, W.C. (Buster), 132
Neal, Frances J., 69
Needle's Eye, 56, 57, 58, 296
Nelson, Lillie Wilkerson, 203
Nelson, Nellie, 204
Nelson, Verge, 202, 203, 240
NeSmith, Carl, 113
Newman, Stanley, 69
Nichols, William, 123
Norwood, Arrie, 72
Norwood, G. W., 73
Norwood, Johnny, 73

# O

Oak Ridge Church, 82, 84
Oak Ridge School, 80, 82, 84
Oakville Indian Mounds, 8
Oden, "Hughs", 138
Oden, Ada, 137, 141, 143, 144, 146
Oden, Andrew J., 138
Oden, Charlie, 153, 154, 155, 156
Oden, Charlie Monroe, 140
Oden, Curtis, 153, 157

Oden, Herman, 153, 157
Oden, Hughes, 155, 162
Oden, Hughs, 140
Oden, Isabell Roberts, 138, 140, 155, 156
Oden, Lewis, 138, 152, 153, 155, 156, 157, 158, 159, 160, 161, 164
Oden, Lewis S., 138
Oden, Lou Annie Borden, 153, 155, 165
Oden, Lucy, 157
Oden, Lucy Fulmer, 153
Oden, Lucy Irene, 137, 141
Oden, Luther, 137, 141
Oden, Mary E. Milligan, 138
Oden, Mary Isabell Roberts, 138
Oden, Monroe, 148, 155
Oden, Renee, 140
Oden, Robert Lewis, 152, 153
Oden, Rosannah Jenkins, 138
Oden, Sarah Osborn, 137, 140, 141, 142, 143
Oden, Steve, 1
Oden, Versie, 153, 157
Oden, Will, 137, 138, 140, 141, 142, 143, 145, 155
Oden, William D., 138
Oden, William Houston, 138, 140
Old Buffalo Trail, 25, 26, 34, 35, 307
Old Bulah Church, 130, 131
Old Emus Cemetery, 105
Old Friendship Cemetery, 79
Old Looney's Tavern, 43
Oliver, Roy, 191
Oliver, William, 202
Ortmann, A.E., 7
Osbon, John Ed, 140
Osbon, Ziller, 140
Osborn, Alexander, 139
Osborn, Ammon, 161
Osborn, Anzy, 140

Osborn, Frank, 140, 148
Osborn, George Washington (Wash), 140
Osborn, James (Jim), 139, 140
Osborn, James Ingram, 139
Osborn, Jasper E. (Jake), 140
Osborn, Jim, 140, 141, 142, 154, 156
Osborn, Lena (Lenny), 140
Osborn, Louisa A. Roberson, 140
Osborn, Orlena Eddy, 139
Osborn, Sarah, 140, 141
Osborn, Wash, 154
Osborn, William R., 140
Owen Chapel, 207
Owen Chapel Church, 208
Owl Creek Horse Camp, 49

# P

Parker Cemetery, 182
Parker Cove, 56, 175, 181, 182, 183, 186
Parker Falls, 41
Parker, Addie (Dutton), 183
Parker, Alice, 180
Parker, Bessie, 183
Parker, Charlie, 183
Parker, Dee, 180, 181
Parker, Docinda, 227
Parker, Dora (Willis), 183
Parker, Edna, 183
Parker, Elijah, 182
Parker, Elise, 183
Parker, Eliza, 183
Parker, Elizabeth, 182
Parker, Ellie Vera (Robinson), 183
Parker, Emmitt, 183
Parker, Ester, 180
Parker, Fannie, 183, 185, 186, 187
Parker, Frances, 180
Parker, Frank, 183
Parker, Hamby, 190, 223, 228, 229

Parker, Henry, 180, 182, 183, 184
Parker, Henry Washington, 183
Parker, Horace, 183
Parker, James B., 183
Parker, James D., 182
Parker, Jane, 182
Parker, Jeff, 223, 226, 227, 228, 229
Parker, Jefferson C., 227, 228
Parker, Joe, 227
Parker, John Campbell, 227
Parker, John T., 181, 182
Parker, Kate, 228
Parker, Letha (Simms), 183
Parker, Lewis, 181
Parker, Lewis C., 182
Parker, Lona (Zeeny), 182
Parker, Lucy, 183
Parker, Luther, 180
Parker, Maggie, 183
Parker, Manerva, 227
Parker, Maranda Bogar, 183
Parker, Martha, 182, 227
Parker, Mary (Polly) Neely, 182
Parker, Mary Ellen, 180, 183
Parker, Mat A., 141
Parker, Mattie (Simms), 183
Parker, Minnie Dutton, 183
Parker, Minnie Mae, 183
Parker, Nancy Henderson Turner, 228, 229
Parker, Nellie (Ellis), 183
Parker, Sally, 227
Parker, Sally (Dutton), 183
Parker, Samantha, 93, 320
Parker, Sarah Ann, 182
Parker, Scene, 227
Parker, Sid, 180
Parker, Thursday, 222, 227, 228
Parker, Walter, 183
Parker, Washington Wilshire, 182
Parker, William, 93, 227, 228, 229, 320

Parker, William Carroll, 182
Parker, William D., 181
Parker, Willie, 183
Parker, Zora, 228
Partridge, Charlie, 88
Partridge, Eula, 140
Pate, Bill, 199, 204
Pate, Christiana Borden, 196, 197, 203
Pate, Dave, 235, 236
Pate, David, 197
Pate, Dolly Flanagin, 197, 198, 220
Pate, Dolly Flangin, 199, 204, 216
Pate, DollyFlanagin, 197
Pate, Douglas, 192
Pate, Jeremiah, 196
Pate, Johnny, 197
Pate, Junior, 197
Pate, Lucinda, 196
Pate, Madgie Campbell, 197
Pate, Mary, 197
Pate, Mary Jane, 197, 202
Pate, Mathew, 196
Pate, Nancy, 197, 202, 235
Pate, Roddy, 199
Pate, Sara Dale, 197
Pate, Sarah, 196
Pate, Sarah Jane, 197, 231
Pate, Stephen, 196
Pate, Thomas, 196, 197, 202, 213
Pate, William, 197, 198, 234
Pate, William (Bill), 197, 221
Pate, William Dale (Roddy), 197, 198
Pate, William F., 197
Pate, William F. (Bill), 197
Patsy, Wallis Armstrong, 216
Payne, George, 246
Payne, Matthew, 320
Payne, W. Winter, 78
Pearson, Emaline, 85
Pearson, Mary, 87
Pearson, Matt, 63, 65, 86, 87, 154

Penitentiary Mountain, 169, 170, 171, 173, 185, 221, 225
Penn School, 82
Peoples, Price, 301
Perry, Walter, 190, 203, 223, 229
Pettus, Thomas C., 308
Pickens, Authur, 269
Pigeon Roost, 46, 315, 322
Pigeon Roost Cove, 166, 315, 320, 321
Pike, Gus, 82, 157
Pillow, Arrie, 247
Pillow, Bob, 247
Pillow, Henry, 247
Pillow, Minnie, 247
Pine Torch Church, 59, 72, 133, 159, 164
Piney Grove, 23
Pinhook, 220
Pinhook Church, 127, 133, 135
Pinhook School, 64, 127
Pinnacle Ridge, 211
Ponder, Odalene, 79
Poole, Floyd, 159
Poole, Harrison, 83
Poole, Herschel (Hutch, 84
Poole, Johnny Burgess, 80, 84, 85
Poole, Lorenzo, 81
Poole, Mary, 82
Poole, Mattie Doss, 84
Poole, Tom, 66, 82, 83, 159, 160
Poole, Walter, 159
Poplar Log Cove, 8, 23, 51, 52, 61, 66, 67, 68, 69, 74, 75, 77, 78, 79, 80, 81, 82, 83, 84, 85, 86, 87, 88, 89
Poplar Springs Cemetery, 34, 272, 278, 307
Poplar Springs School, 65, 132
Porter, John, 258
Porter, Oscar, 258
Porter, Roscoe, 258
Potter, Augustine, 212

Povey, Bob, Sr., 324
Preuit Cemetery, 136
Preuit, Allen,, 136
Preuit, Barbara Ann, 137
Preuit, Billy, 137
Preuit, Carolyn, 137
Preuit, Carrie Hampton, 136
Preuit, Essie, 136
Preuit, Forrest Rose, 129
Preuit, Frances, 129
Preuit, Jackie, 137
Preuit, Jerry, 137
Preuit, Mabel, 136
Preuit, Robert, 136
Preuit, Ruthie Naylor, 137
Preuit, Sadie, 136
Preuit, Tolbert, 136
Proctor, Ira, 126
Proctor, W.D., 126
Prucha, Francis P., 14
Prueit, Ruthie Naylor, 131
Pruett, Anderson N., 254
Pruitt, Alba L., 92

## Q

Quill, Almond, 148
Quill, Dennis, 148
Quill, Hodge, 148
Quill, Martha, 148
Quillan Creek Cascades, 42

## R

Rainey, George, 145
Red Hill Cemetery, 69
Red Stick Creeks, 18
Reed School, 82
Reed, Cleo, 258
Revis, Lee, 126, 133, 144
Reynolds, Mary Beth, 227
Richards, Elmira, 188
Riddle, Alventine, 320

Riddle, Alvetine, 323
Riddle, Angeline, 319
Riddle, Anna, 321
Riddle, Artie Georgianna Lovestar, 318
Riddle, Arzula, 322
Riddle, Authur, 323
Riddle, Billy, 322
Riddle, Bob, 322
Riddle, Calvin, 93, 245, 287, 320, 321
Riddle, Christine, 318
Riddle, Claude, 318
Riddle, Cloie, 325
Riddle, Devil John, 317
Riddle, Devil John II, 317
Riddle, Dollie, 323, 326
Riddle, Earnest, 322
Riddle, Effie, 323
Riddle, Eliza, 317
Riddle, Elizabeth, 317
Riddle, Etsel, 322
Riddle, Fannie, 325
Riddle, Fletcher, 323
Riddle, Fred Jack (Babe), 318
Riddle, Herman, 318
Riddle, Ida, 322
Riddle, Issac, 322
Riddle, Jackson, 317
Riddle, James C., 317
Riddle, James Calvin, 93, 321, 322
Riddle, James Julius Claude Edgar, 318
Riddle, Jess, 319
Riddle, Jessie, 317
Riddle, Jessie Duraney (Hook), 317, 319
Riddle, John, 288, 317
Riddle, John Manuel, 317
Riddle, John T., 320
Riddle, John Thomas (Doc), 322
Riddle, Jonson (Rake), 44, 316, 317

Riddle, Joseph T., 317
Riddle, Lannie, 323
Riddle, Lelar, 322
Riddle, Leonard Fay, 322
Riddle, Lillian, 246, 322
Riddle, Lillie Hamby, 318
Riddle, Lonnie, 323, 324
Riddle, Looney, 322
Riddle, Louis, 262
Riddle, Luther John Henry, 318
Riddle, Manson (Bud) Alexander, 319
Riddle, Martha, 44, 316, 319
Riddle, Martha Jane (Sis), 319
Riddle, Milton Adell, 322
Riddle, Naoma, 319
Riddle, Obie, 318
Riddle, Odis, 323, 324
Riddle, Okla, 320
Riddle, Pearly, 323
Riddle, Pinkney, 323
Riddle, Rake, 315, 316, 317, 319, 320, 324
Riddle, Ray, 322
Riddle, Raymond, 322
Riddle, Reba, 1, 324
Riddle, Rhodae Victoria Rosanna Elizabeth, 318
Riddle, Rosa, 320
Riddle, Roy Haynes, 323
Riddle, Samantha, 320
Riddle, Samantha Parker, 322, 323
Riddle, Sarah, 319, 321, 322
Riddle, Straud, 245, 320
Riddle, Tally, 318
Riddle, Thomas S., 317
Riddle, Trannie, 322
Riddle, Walter, 320, 325, 326
Riddle, Will, 320, 323, 324, 325
Riddle, William Straud, 44, 227, 317, 320, 322, 323
Ridge Path, 3, 17, 19, 27, 28, 194
Ridge Road School, 204

Ridge, John, 13
Riggs School, 187, 188, 200, 204, 232
Riggs School House, 187
Riggs, David, 238
Riggs, David Washington (Wash), 238
Riggs, Dolphus (Doc), 238
Riggs, Euell, 238
Riggs, Eva, 132, 238
Riggs, Farris, 238
Riggs, Forris, 238
Riggs, George, 238
Riggs, Guy, 238
Riggs, Hollis (Jack), 238
Riggs, John, 203
Riggs, John D., 238
Riggs, John W., 231, 238
Riggs, John W., Jr., 238
Riggs, Pauline, 238
Riggs, Ruth, 238
Riggs, Tillman, 238
Riggs, William Tecumseh, 238
Roberson, Sarah, 246
Roberson, Tom, 250, 252, 268
Roberson, Zeila or Zillar G., 140
Roberts, Dyann T., 176
Roberts, Isabell, 155
Roberts, J. T., 72
Roberts, Joseph P., 138
Roberts, Margaret, 111
Roberts, Mary E. Milligan Oden, 139
Roberts, Mary Isabell, 138, 139, 140
Robertson, John J., 140
Rock Springs Cemetery, 33, 243, 273, 274, 305
Rocky Plains, 27, 28
Roden, Archie, 71
Roden, Martin, 71
Roden, Victoria, 71
Rodgers, J.T., 133

Rodgers, Jones, 131, 133
Rose, John T., 157
Royall, Ann, 20
Royalle, Ann, 12, 46

## S

Sally Ann Cemetery, 198
Sally Ann House, 50, 211, 213, 214, 240
Sally, Elizabeth, 227
Sally, Samantha, 227
Saltpeter Cave, 40
Saltpeter Well, 243
Sammans, Carl, 313
Sammans, Donie Brooks, 313, 314
Sammans, Dora, 314
Sammans, John, 313
Sammons, Dona Brooks, 261
Sammons, Frank, 261
Sammons, Luke, 287
Sammons, Neil, 261
Sammons, Vina, 261
Sand Mountain, 8, 28, 30, 32, 125, 131, 150, 167, 197
Sanders, Luther, 319
Sanderson, Robert, 164
Sandlin, Claude, 164
Sandlin, Joe, 266, 304
Sandy, Rena Sue, 249
Sanford, Arizona, 262
Sanford, Will, 301
Sapp, Allen, 96
Sapp, Blaxton, 96
Sapp, Charles, 96
Sapp, Frank, 121
Sapp, Howard, 96
Sapp, Tommy, 96
Sapp, Wallace, 121
Sapp, Willis, 96
Sauder, James Edmonds, 78
Saunders, Edmonds, 4
Scoggins, Henry, 211, 240

Scogins, Will, 324
Scott, Winfield, 316
Segars, Pascal Sandy, 130
Segars, Sarah Mandy, 125
Segars, Thomas, 125
Sequoyah, 17
Shaddix, Jim, 121
Sheets Cemetery, 79
Sheets, Archibald, 79
Sheridan, Richard C., 24
Sherron, Sally, 110
Shiloh Cemetery, 150, 164
Shiloh Church, 118, 133, 140, 146, 148, 150, 153, 154
Ship Rock, 55, 56, 57, 58, 259, 289, 303, 319
Simmons, Hugh, 319
Simmons, Mattie, 238
Simms Cementary, 79
Simms, Annar Rose, 129
Simms, Bluit, 129
Simms, Dean, 198, 237
Simms, Edgar, 128
Simms, Edgar T., 129
Simms, Evie, 97
Simms, Frances, 129
Simms, Frances Panola, 129
Simms, Frank, 129
Simms, J.O., 194
Simms, James, 128
Simms, Minnie, 129
Simms, Panola Eugenia, 129
Simms, Preuit, 129
Simms, Ruben C., 128
Simms, Sarah Hamilton, 128
Simms, Thomas, 129
Simms, Thomas D., 127, 128, 129
Simms, Willia, 129
Simms, William Lawrence, 129
Simpson, Edgar Murphey, 129
Simpson, Frances Mildred Ann, 129
Simpson, John Preuit, 129

Simpson, Pandora, 124
Simpson, Panola Simms, 129
Simpson, R. M., 124
Simpson, Robert Emmett, 129
Simpson, Robert Murphey, 129
Simpson, William Lawrence, 129
Sims, Dan, 72
Sims, Donnie, 73
Sims, Evie, 102
Sims, Harvey, 164
Sims, Johnny, 73
Sims, Martha E, 128
Sims, Nay, 73
Sims, William, 102
Singleton, Blue Will, 180
Sipsey Wilderness Area, 37, 48, 49, 50, 56, 241, 244, 247, 254, 255, 256, 259, 287, 296, 302, 308, 319
Sipsie Trail, 27, 33, 35
Slayton, Bill, 202
Slayton, Donnie, 202
Sloan, Cathy, 1
Sloan, Cathy B., 146
Smith Cemetery, 79
Smith, Ada Oden (England), 139
Smith, Dave, 148
Smith, David, 4
Smith, Dyke, 148
Smith, Floyd, 249
Smith, Huey, 148
Smith, Lamender Penolia (Sis) Hampton, 148
Smith, Lillian Naylor, 132
Smith, Liz, 131
Smith, Lorene, 176
Smith, Lucy Ordean, 148
Smith, Mable, 148
Smith, Peggy, 77
Smith, Ray, 77
Smith, Shirley, 131, 132, 136, 159
Smith, Tressie, 148
Smith, Will, 132

Smith, Willard, 148
Smith, William, 148
Smith, Willie, 159
Southern, Lou, 73
Southern, Maggie, 72
Sow Creek Falls, 41
Sparks, Asa, 121
Sparks, BD, 152
Sparks, Britt, 152
Sparks, Delomer, 152
Sparks, Dempsey, 152
Sparks, Guy, 152
Sparks, Leo, 152
Sparks, Lillie M. Jenkins, 149, 151, 152
Sparks, Lillie Roden, 152
Sparks, Lola Terry, 152
Sparks, Mary, 179
Sparks, Monroe, 320
Sparks, Mullican, 180
Sparks, Parker, 152
Speake School, 8, 66, 72, 77, 89, 91, 94, 95, 96, 103, 137, 152
Spears, Gid, 75
Spears, L.R., 74
Spears, Ted O. (T.O.), 74, 75
Spiller, Bessie See, 190
Spillers, A.J., 192
Spillers, Ambros Milton, 187, 188, 189, 190, 203, 232, 239
Spillers, Amos, 44, 198, 231, 245, 246, 252, 266, 283, 287, 288, 292, 293, 296, 302, 304, 305, 322
Spillers, Amos J., 188, 231
Spillers, Bessie See, 188
Spillers, Betty Ann, 188, 231
Spillers, Birdie Mae, 202
Spillers, Birtie Mae, 187, 188, 190
Spillers, Caldonia, 188
Spillers, Caldonia (Donia), 231
Spillers, Cleve, 190, 203, 223, 224, 239

Spillers, Cliaronee O'neal, 188
Spillers, Crave, 190, 203, 239
Spillers, Craven, 192
Spillers, Delia A., 261
Spillers, Delie, 287
Spillers, Docia, 231
Spillers, Dolia, 188
Spillers, Elmira, 188
Spillers, Georgia, 188, 231
Spillers, Henry, 223
Spillers, James (Jim), 188
Spillers, James Curtis, 188
Spillers, Jim, 187, 188, 203, 220, 231, 239, 304
Spillers, Johnson, 239
Spillers, Josephine, 223
Spillers, Junior Lee, 188
Spillers, Kate, 188, 231
Spillers, Lucy Bell, 239
Spillers, Malcom, 223
Spillers, Martha Flanagin, 239
Spillers, Martha Jane, 231
Spillers, Martha Jane (Made), 188
Spillers, Mary Ann Armstrong, 188
Spillers, Mary Tennessee Garrison, 244, 245, 283, 287, 289, 290, 292, 293, 294, 318
Spillers, Mattie, 287, 302
Spillers, Maxine, 223
Spillers, Millard, 287, 288, 293
Spillers, Norman, 223
Spillers, Percy Clark, 188
Spillers, Polly Armstrong, 231
Spillers, Robert (Bob), 188, 231
Spillers, Ruby, 283, 287
Spillers, Salley, 239
Spillers, Sally, 231
Spillers, Sarah, 320, 322
Spillers, Sary, 287
Spillers, Silas, 192
Spillers, Synthia, 302
Spillers, Synthia Garrison, 292
Spillers, Toni, 190

Spillers, Will, 267, 283, 287, 289, 290, 292, 294, 295, 296, 297, 299, 304, 318, 322
Spillers, William, 231, 305
Spillers, William (Bill), 192
Spillers, William (Will), 188, 231
Spillers, Willie, 287
Spillers, Zora, 190, 203, 209
Spillers, Zora Parker, 222, 223
Spillers., Mary Tennessee Garrison, 297, 298
Spivey Gap, 36
St. Stephens, 25
St. Stephens Trading Post, 21
Stanford, Florie, 262
Steele, Jack, 103
Stephenson, Alfred W., 243
Stephenson, Carl, 243
Stephenson, Charles Mitchell, 243
Stephenson, Deaton Monroe, 243
Stephenson, Edward Alfred, 243
Stephenson, Eliza, 243
Stephenson, Eliza P. Wasson, 243
Stephenson, Euell, 242
Stephenson, Frank, 242, 243
Stephenson, Frank David, 243
Stephenson, Fredrick L., 243
Stephenson, Hariet, 243
Stephenson, Hodge L., 243
Stephenson, Hugh W., 243
Stephenson, James, 243
Stephenson, James M., 243
Stephenson, James Monroe, 243
Stephenson, Margaret, 243
Stephenson, Monroe, 243
Stephenson, Russel E., 243
Stephenson, William, 243
Stevens, Vicey, 104
Stewart, Charlie, 153
Stover, D.T., 70
Stover, Elijah, 115
Stover, Louisa, 109
Stover, Louisa M., 115, 116

Stover, Malinda, 70
Stover, Nancy, 70
Strawn, Willie Mae, 320
Streight, Abel, 35, 311
Strickland, Charlene, 148
Strickland, Mary, 121
Suggs, Sedenina Gillespie, 94
Sutton, Sarah Janie, 238

# T

Tahlonteeskee, 17
Tankersley, Ed, 168, 175
Tankersley, Maggie, 168, 169, 172
Tankersley, Steve, 168, 184
Tanksley, Abe Paul, 154
Tanksley, Ed, 180
Tanksley, Leona, 180
Tanksley, Steve, 180
Tapsville Cemetery, 172
Tar Springs Hollow, 50, 51, 106, 156, 157
Teague, Mary, 65, 112
Templeton School, 80, 85, 86, 91
Templeton, David, 79
Templeton, Earnest, 72
Templeton, Jackson, 85, 89
Ten Islands, 19, 30
Thomas, Ester, 91
Thomas, Lydia Clark, 320, 326
Thompson Creek Canyon, 58
Thompson, Eunice, 144
Thompson, Inez, 144
Threlkeld Ridge, 187, 188
Threlkeld, Phillip, 188, 198
Thurman, Frances, 78
Tidwell, Norman, 50, 214
Tingling Hole, 39
Towers, Green, 132
Townsend, George, 317
Trail of Tears, 19, 28, 315, 316
Trammell, Mary Susan, 244
Treadway, Betty Ruth, 169

Treadway, Cleo, 169
Treadway, Dan, 167, 168, 180
Treadway, Evelyn, 169
Treadway, Finnis, 1, 167, 168, 169, 172, 173, 174, 175, 176
Treadway, Finnis D., 168, 176
Treadway, Finnis O., 176
Treadway, Hazel, 169
Treadway, Henry, 168, 169, 170, 173, 174, 175
Treadway, Irene, 169
Treadway, Janie White, 168
Treadway, Lennon B., 169
Treadway, Levona, 169
Treadway, Maggie Tankersley, 168
Treadway, Mitchell, 169, 175
Treadway, Odis, 169, 175
Treadway, Ozell, 169
Treadway, Quincy Ray, 169
Treadway, Randy D., 176
Treadway, Ricky F., 176
Treadway, Willard, 169
Treaty of Fort Jackson, 13, 15, 18
Treaty of New Echota, 19
Tugboat Rock, 56, 58
Turkey Foot Creek Falls, 40
Turkey Town Treaty, 12, 17, 18, 19, 22, 31
Turner, Harly, 189
Turner, Hathey, 203, 222
Turner, Hechahans, 190
Turner, Mandy, 190
Turner, Mchathey, 190
Turner, Nancy Henderson, 226
Turrentine, Frank, 102
Twin Springs Cave, 40

# U

University of Alabama, 91

## V

Vest, Dick, 96
Vester, Annar Rose Simms, 129
Vines, Missouri Jane, 197

## W

Wadkins (Watkins), Willis, 69
Wafford Settlement, 21
Waits, Dot Dutton, 94
Walker John, Jr., 104
Walker, Bell, 104
Walker, Brady, 105, 106
Walker, Celeste, 191, 193
Walker, Cindy, 104
Walker, Clara, 71, 73
Walker, Dan, 104, 105, 106, 275
Walker, Dolly, 72
Walker, Gooder, 55
Walker, Issac Buckner, 319
Walker, James, 104, 106
Walker, James W. (Jim), 71
Walker, Jim, 71, 104
Walker, John, Sr., 104
Walker, Kitty, 109
Walker, Lilly, 73
Walker, Lou, 104
Walker, Louella, 319
Walker, Robert, 73
Walker, Sidney, 43, 104
Walker, Vicey, 105
Walker, Will, 104, 105
Wallace, Dan, 4
Wallace, George C., 318
Wallace, Jonathan, 218
Wallace, Willie, 95
Wallis Cemetery, 49, 191, 192, 195, 196, 197, 198, 199, 204, 211, 221, 229, 231, 305
Wallis Cove, 49
Wallis, Jonathan, 195, 214
Wallis, Joseph, 195, 196
Wallis, Joseph H., 195, 213
Wallis, Joseph Hall, 195, 196
Wallis, Sally Ann, 202
Wallis' Cemetery, 188
Warren, Eodies, 258
Warren, Pope, 110, 111
Warren, Sarah, 110
Warren, Sarah C., 110
Warren, Sarah Caroline, 110
Warrior, Black, 3, 4, 10, 11, 12, 13, 30, 56, 176
Washspring Mountain, 69, 79, 136
Wasson, Eliza P., 243
Waters, Spencer, 4, 139, 217, 218, 260
Waters, Spencer A., 243
Watkins Cemetery, 79
Watkins, Lewis, 93
Watkins, Willis, 68, 69
Watson, Jonathan, 51
Way, Dorothy, 148
Weaver, John B., 321
Webb, Fatty, 263
Webb, Nathan, 299
Webb, William, 7
Welborn, Authur, 126
Welborn, Celie, 126
Welborn, Dora Johnson, 126
Welborn, Francis, 124
Welborn, Gus, 124, 126
Welborn, Josh, 126
Welborn, Lockey B., 124
Welborn, Luther, 126
Welborn, Lynch, 126
Welborn, Mamie (Harden), 126
Welborn, Mandy, 125, 126
Welborn, Martha, 124
Welborn, Martie, 126
Welborn, Monroe, 126
Welborn, Nathie (Proctor), 126
Welborn, Nellie, 126
Welborn, Nelly, 126
Welborn, Nola, 126
Welborn, Sandy, 126
Welborn, Thomas, 124
Welborn, Willard, 126
Welborn, Willie Myrl (Proctor), 126
Welborn, Wood P., 124
Welborn-Alexander Cemetery, 109, 127
Welburn, Martha Segars, 124
West, John, 325
West, Peter M., 321
West, Roxana, 320
West, Roxanna, 321
Wheeler Dam, 26, 33
Whisenant, Florence, 190
Whisenant, Glen, 190
Whisenant, Glenn, 56, 217
Whisenant, Herman, 200, 217
Whisenant, Hoyt, 224
Whisenant, Will, 190
White, Bob, 97, 99
White, Calvin, 103
White, Charlie, 286
White, Eva, 286
White, Ida, 97
White, James, 103
White, Janie, 167
White, John, 249, 250, 252
White, John Quincy, 168
White, Johnny Mack, 246
White, Manco, 96, 97, 99, 102, 103, 104
White, Olga Hampton, 97, 102
White, Seborn, 103
White, Warren, 102
Whittiker, Ammon, 303
Wilburn, Arthur, 53, 63
Wilburn, Authur, 126
Wilburn, Authur Pascal, 124
Wilburn, Curtis, 111
Wilburn, Ila, 1, 181, 192
Wilburn, Ila Curtis, 179
Wilburn, Sandy, 63

Wilburn, Sandy Pascal, 124
Wilburn-Alexander Cemetery, 110
Wilderness Parkway, 35, 37, 56
Wilhoite, Bill, 170
Wilhoite, Hayes, 121
Wilhoite, Jack, 170
Wilkerson Cove, 49
Wilkerson, Andrew Jackson, 206
Wilkerson, Andrew Jackson (Sanko), 197
Wilkerson, Andrew Jackson "Sanko", 230, 233
Wilkerson, Archie, 240
Wilkerson, Birtie, 192, 233
Wilkerson, Birtie Mae Spillers, 187, 192
Wilkerson, Birtie Spillers, 189, 190, 191, 225, 231
Wilkerson, Clarinell LouAllen, 192
Wilkerson, Clezell Oliver, 192
Wilkerson, Cora Blankenship, 202
Wilkerson, Elbert, 224
Wilkerson, Ethel, 202, 222, 223, 224
Wilkerson, James Jackson (Jim), 202
Wilkerson, Jerry Maury Andrew Jackson Sanko, 201
Wilkerson, Jim, 190
Wilkerson, John Jackson, 202
Wilkerson, Julie, 202
Wilkerson, Lillie, 202, 203, 240
Wilkerson, Lottie, 202
Wilkerson, Lucy, 205, 224, 225, 237, 240
Wilkerson, Lucy Irene, 202
Wilkerson, Mary, 205
Wilkerson, Mary Ann (Sissy), 197, 231
Wilkerson, Mary Jane Pate, 201, 202, 206, 224, 225, 233
Wilkerson, Sanko, 190, 202, 204, 205, 209, 211, 222, 224, 225, 226, 231, 238, 240
Wilkerson, Sarah Jane "Mame" Pate, 233
Wilkerson, Savannah, 202
Wilkerson, Thomas, 197, 198, 202, 231, 234
William B. Bankhead National Forest, 10, 11, 28, 39, 50, 74, 75, 97, 108, 137, 244, 282, 287, 296
Williams, Buster, 64
Williams, Florence, 133
Williams, Leamon, 86, 146
Williams, Mary Jane, 65
Willis, Laura, 111
Willis, Lucy, 111
Willis, Will, 111, 135
Wilson Dam, 7
Wilson, J. H., 35
Wilson, Jim, 63, 65
Wilson, Tom, 161
Wise, William, 128
Witt, Nell Riggs, 238
Wm. B. Bankhead National Forest, 3
Wolf Pen School, 246
Woods, Rhoda White, 1, 97
Wren Mountain, 27, 35, 37, 56, 167, 168, 169, 170, 171, 172, 174, 176

# Y

Yeager, Dallas, 46, 111, 123
Yeates, Joe, 163
Young, Arthur, 207
Young, Authur, 284
Young, Byron, 91, 284
Young, Christine, 249
Young, Joe, 207
Young, William, 211

I am extremely honored and humbled by the many people who read my books. I greatly appreciate the readers that enjoy truthful historical stories of the Warrior Mountains and the great Tennessee River Valley. I send all the followers of my books a heartfelt thank you; without people who love local history about North Alabama, all my research and work would be in vain.

I graciously request that each of you who acquire one of my books from Amazon to please post an honest review. A short two to three line evaluation of my books would be greatly appreciated. Again, thank you to all who take the time to read a book by Rickey Butch Walker.

www.ingramcontent.com/pod-product-compliance
Lightning Source LLC
Chambersburg PA
CBHW081846170426
43199CB00018B/2826